History of Ancient Odia Literature

History of Ancient Odia Literature

Ramesh Prasad Panigrahi

BLACK EAGLE BOOKS
Dublin, USA | Bhubaneswar, India

 BLACK EAGLE BOOKS

USA address:
7464 Wisdom Lane
Dublin, OH 43016

India address:
E/312, Trident Galaxy, Kalinga Nagar,
Bhubaneswar-751003, Odisha, India

E-mail: info@blackeaglebooks.org
Website: www.blackeaglebooks.org

First International Edition Published by
BLACK EAGLE BOOKS, 2024

HISTORY OF ANCIENT ODIA LITERATURE
by
Ramesh Prasad Panigrahi

Copyright © **BLACK EAGLE BOOKS**

[All rights reserved. No part of this publication may be reproduced, copied, stored in a retrieval system, transmitted or used in any form or by any means, whether electronic, mechanical, photocopying, recording or otherwise, without the prior permission from the author or publishers, except for a brief quotations in critical articles or reviews.]

Cover & Interior Design: S.S. Printers, Cuttack

ISBN-978-1-64560-580-5 (Paperback)

Printed in the United States of America

Dedication
Dedicated to my daughter -Rupsa-

PREFACE

The moment I chose to write this book to outsource Odia literature, a part of my commitment as a historian impels me to seek and serve truth. The writing of history demanded a special kind of observation because all events, having slipped into the past, become hazy and indistinct except the documented traces. The undocumented events turn into memories. I learned to interpret the clues, signs and tracks through cultural memories of the past. But there is no reliable witness in the absolute sense. There is only more or less, reliable testimony.

The book, in the process, turned out to be a means of clarifying my own ideas on the subject. I discovered the humanist dimensions of historical consciousness, although my western contemporaries seem to deny-or at least, put in doubt-the principles of humanism. I have also been guided by the practice of historical reconstruction in literary studies forced by the need to understand historical materials in their own context.

I construct my propositions in two ways-by culling the signifying actions, characters, habits, aims and circumstances of writers and literary terms signifying attributes of literary works. I have followed R.S. Crane's Critical and Historical Principles of literary History to organize my materials in succession of time, distribution in space and likeness and difference in character. I have undertaken to survey systematically the literary productions of my race through time. In all these primary units of interpretation are either works or, more commonly, authors viewed as the most immediate cause of the characteristics exhibited by their works; but the individual histories differ widely according to the fashion in which the basic principles of succession and of likeness and difference are construed.

Mu, Ambhe-O-Ambhemane   **Ramesh Prasad Panigrahi**
105, Rasulgarh,
Bhubaneswar-751010 India

CONTENTS

CHAPTER-I
FROM ORATION TO LITERATURE:
THE GLOSSOPOEIC TRANSITIONS IN CHARYA SONGS   9

CHAPTER - II
FROM ORALITY TO TEXTUALITY:
MEDIAEVAL ODIA LITERATURE   51

CHAPTER-III
LITERATURE AS SUBSTITUTE RELIGION:
THEOSOPHICAL POETRY OF THE PANCHASAKHAS   122

CHAPTER-IV
TRAFFICKING IN SOUL: COLLUSION BETWEEN THE
COSMIC SOUL AND THE SOUL OF POETRY   216

CHAPTER-I

FROM ORATION TO LITERATURE: THE GLOSSOPOEIC TRANSITIONS IN CHARYA SONGS

PRIMORDIAL ODISHA: MEN AMID ANIMALS AND TREES

I will take you back to an epoch when "time" was about to begin. It was in the dawn of the world when the "black cow of cosmic night did lie with the ruddy cows of morning" (Rg. Veda, 10.61.4) The Nature was the master.

Lord Shiva was there, but he did not create mortals. He stood by the Great Goddess, his Shakti, who stemmed from him, gave Brahma the power to create women. She gave to him of herself, of her own power (Shakti), When a Shakti issued from the point between her eyebrows Brahma gave her to Daksha, his son, the progenitor, to be his daughter. Brahma's many experiments with and modes of creation led in the end to this dividing himself into a progenitive couple: Manu and Satarupa. Their progenies invented language around 150. 000 years ago, which is around the time when modern homosapiens evolved. People communicated with each other with gestures and later, gestural language generated a space for vocal language, Western historians calculate that language started around 150,000 years ago. One theory argues that the origin of all language was the same, but they slowly evolved and made thoroughly different entities, just like the animals did.

Perhaps the Odias of this primordial epoch communicated with each other with howls and hoots, and much later, around 8th century they spoke our language, a primitive Odia.

Panini talks about four kinds of speech: para, pashyanti, Madhyama and Barikhari: In Vakya Padhiyam Of Bhratruhari (570 AD, Ujjain)these stages are described as four stages (teerthas). Para-Vak is anirvachaniya Pashyanti Vak is that which witnesses (Where there is no distinction between Vak (word) and artha(meaning) Pashyanti is the sound vibration heard in the causal worlds, Madhyama emerges into the world through the nose, via the breath. Pashyanti is spoken with the eyes, Paraa is telepathic, materialising directly from the faculty of awareness. That which gets pronounced and is ready for others' listening is Vaikhari... According to Hindu and yogic philosophy the Vaikhari sabdas go through a stage as they come to be perceptible and audible. It is considered the gross level articulated sound of living beings and physical objects.

By the first part of 8th Century solitary primitive Odias individuals acted according to their basic urges (for instance hunger) as well as their natural desire for self preservation. This later is instinct, however, tempered by an equally natural sense of compassion.

They never felt the need of one more symbolic system called writing. It was considered rather as a "dangerous supplement" (Rousseau's term) which opens the way to manifold abuses of nature. Writing is par excellence the instrument of social control; since those who possess it are the law-givers, priests and the wielders of ultimate Power.

Our ancient literature began with out scripts. The first creative poets were Buddhist Mahayana monks who called their poems charya-Gitika and Doha. They were composed as songs to be recited on the streets of tribal villages. They could communicate between themselves through gestures as well as through oral language.

The language was a random mix of Aryan, non-Aryan, Dravid and Tribal (Munda) languages. The Charyapadas, now generally accepted as being present in old Bengali, Magadhi, and Kamarupi (Assamese) had been preserved in manuscripts form in Nepal since they had developed their own scripts. There were about 47 songs and we find them in a language which has been claimed to be the old Oriya, as well as old Assamese, Old Maithili. as much as old Bengali.

Late Prof. Khageswar Mahapatra (1933-2017) writes in his book Charya Gitika (Eighth Edition, 1999): "It was awesome to study Charya poems in Bengali scripts and claim them to have been written in Oriya, " (Bhoomika, P-I)". He studied Tibettan language, went to Nepal Several times and published the Charya Poems in Odia in 1965.

History of Ancient Odia Literature | 11

Articulation of the Origin: The Discovery of Charya Texts
The Apabhramsa texts discovered by Prof. Haraprasad Sastri from the Durbar Library of Nepal in 1907 and published in 1916 contained the following three books of Charya poems:
(a) The Dohakosha of Sarahapada
(b) The Dohakosha of Kanha pada
(c) Dakarnava (The Ocean of wisdom)
The Dohakosha of Tillopada and another text captioned Sankinna Doha songs are edited by prof, N.C Choudhury. (Tripathy, 55).The scripts are deciphered as "Eastern Aryan" prevalent in Bengal, Bihar, Assam, Odissa, Awadh and Mithila around 7th-8th centuries when they were composed.

Sastri's discovery has aroused a huge interest among the scholars from all over the country. They endeavoured mostly to trace the philological antiquities of their own languages through these Buddhist Dohas called Charya songs. These Arias and lengthy choral recitatives were composed for oratorical congregations and for preaching Vajra yana metaphysics to the people of a preliterate culture. The troubadour poets travelled far and wide singing the songs on the streets to a preliterate society of 7th century AD.

In the absence of scripts and alphabets the songs might have been lost after the death of the composers who were mostly siddhacharyas and monks. Finally they were re-performed in Nepal through memory and were recorded in the Buddhist monasteries of Nepal around 11th-12th centuries.

Reputed scholars like Rahul Sankrityayana, Dharamvir Bharati, Kasi Prasad Jaiswal, Jayakanta Mishra, Dr. Sahidulla (from Bangla Desh), Suniti kumar Chatterjee and Dr Dimbeawar Neog (Assam) have worked on the charya poems in addition to the foreign Scholars (Like Prof. Bendell and Sylvan Levy). The corpus of criticism, to our disappointment, turns out to be a monolithic discursive formation with views that the poems belonged to the above linguistic communities and the authors belonged to them. (i.e. Bengali, Magadh, Awadhi, Assamese, Maithili and Odia). The Odias have failed to prove on the national platforms that the charya songs belonged exclusively to Odisha, except Late Gopal Chandra Praharaj,(1874-1945) who in his research paper read in the Oriental conference held at Patna (1930) strongly advanced his argument in favour of Odissa. Praharaj wrote, "Before we can claim the fruits of the Mahamahopadhaya's labour to be ours, we must devote much more research endeavour to the subject that we have done yet and unearthed some material from which we can independently establish that the language and script used in the manuscripts are Odia and not Bengalee."2 However, all the ten historians of Odiya literature have claimed that the charya songs evidenced the earliest specimen of spoken Odiya.

Mr. Praharaj could not comprehend the critical strategy of the other linguistic communities. It was an epoch of historical linguistics. The critics of linguists searched for genealogical 'family' relationships and they were identified through comparative studies of the basic vocabulary of languages and language groups that otherwise appeared to be disparate and discontinuous. Following William Jones and other European scholars they intended to establish linguistic contiguities and on the basis of feeble evidence and a week methodology spoke of an Eastern Indian culture as opposed to Northern or Southern Indian culture.

It is important to note that historical linguistics, by and large, was only concerned with the relationships among the sound form of limited vocabulary of the Charyapadas, and was utterly devoid of an analysis of their semantic structure which in later periods become one of the sites for studying culture.

This author, on the other hand, relies on Ferdinand de Saussure's proposal for semiological studies that concentrate more on the life of signs in society. The language of charyapada is one among the various systems of signs and being undeniably the most important one, as the semiotic model for studying other social and cultural experiences of the time. I do also believe in Noam Chomsky's "cognitivism" of formal mental operations essentially syntactic and hence universal-with semantic representations.

We can also include Julien Greimas who wanted large areas of the study of culture, such as literature, myth, folk tale etc. to be based on the "science of signification", or semiotics, the culture of the 7th – 8th century Odissa can also be viewed as an assemblage of texts- linguistic, phonetic oral, perceptual, cognitive etc. But before lunching this broad based structuralist study, let us introduce our language called Odia, its identity under the lens of historical linguistics.

Dr.Kunjabihari Tripathy in his Origin and Development of Oriya Language places the Oriya language under the Eastern Branch of the Indo-

Aryan Languages, (the other members of the branch are Bengali, Assamese, Maithili and the other two Bihari languages – Bhojpuri and Maghi.) The Old Indo-Aryan (The 0.1.A.) between C 2800 B.C. to C.500 B.C. was Vedic and Sanskrit. The Middle Indo Aryan (M.I.A.) is periodized between C.500 B.C. to C.1000 A.D. and this period is dominated by Pali and Prakrit languages. The New Indo-Aryan period (N.I.A.) that began around C.1000 onwards dominated the language of the charya songs. (3)

The charya poets were the siddhacharyas of the Vajra Yana and the Sahaja yana cults of Buddhism. Although the records trace a long list of 84 such Siddhacharyas, only 23 of them have tried to compose Bauddhagana (Song). The following table would show the names of these poets and the numbers of the dohas composed by them.

TABLE – 1

No.	Name of the Charya Poets	No of the Dohas composed.
1.	Sahara Pada.	22, 32, 38, 39.
2.	Sabari Pada.	28, 50.
3.	Lui Pada.	1, 29.
4.	Kanha (u) Pada	7, 9, 10, 11, 12, 13, 1836, 40, 42, & 45, 19, 24
5.	Bhusukupada.	6, 21, 23, 27, 30, 41, 44, 49
6.	Santi pada.	15, 36
7.	Kukkuripada.	2, 20, 48
8.	Gunduripada.	4
9.	Arya pada	31
10.	Veena pada.	17
11.	Darika pada.	34
12	Dombi pada	14
13.	Mahidhara pada	16
14	Kankana pada	44
15.	Kambala pada.	08
16.	Jayantandi pada.	46
17.	Tadaka pada.	37
18.	Tanti pada.	25
19.	Bhade pada.	35
20.	Dhamma pada	47
21.	Viruba pada.	03
22.	Chatilla pada.	05
23.	Dendana pada.	33

N.B. The numbers of the dohas assigned here are given according to Pt. Haraprasad Sastri's collection.

It should be remembered that the Odia script was not invented by 7th century and these songs were orally composed. Buhler has noticed that Brahmi script was shaped by the influence of cunei form or Egyptian scripts and around the 8th century B.C. and was used in India. Probably the Arayans imported this Cunei form (Talukdar, 1979), (4) Panini and Yaska, ancient Indian philologists and grammarians have scientifically regularized the Brahmi scripts in ancient India.

The shape of Brahmi scripts varied because of the geographical reasons in India. The scripts of Sanskrit, Hindi, Marathi and Odia have been shaped by Northern Brahmi and the South Indian scripts have evolved out of the southern Brahmi.

The Brahmi scripts used in the rock inscriptions of Ashoka and the scripts of Kharavela's inscriptions are found to have changed slightly A comparative paleographical chart used between Ashokan (3rd century B.C.) and Kharavela's (C150 BC - 100 B.0) Brahmi would show the difference in the Odissan context.

What this historiographer intends to reiterate is that the Odia scripts were not invented by the time the Charya songs were composed. In other words, the Charya songs were neither written nor scripted. The songs were orally composed, tuned, performed and were transmitted to Nepal through memory work and oral performances. This oral tradition of the distant past could not be recorded and everything which we learn of it in the sources, the texts of the literary traditions is only an indirect reflection. What is more, this reflection of the oral through the written, which is always and inevitably transformed and distorted, has been filtered to us through Buddhist ecclesiastical ideology and phonetic principles.

These works, mostly of a didactic nature, had probably been orally authored as a means of influencing the religious life of the highlanders who were totally dominated by the Brahminical institutions. But to achieve these aims the author had to enter into a dialogue with his audience who must have exerted certain pressure as a kind of feed back or reciprocation. One finds therefore, fragments of the popular cultural tradition in the charya texts. Sometimes, the sophisticated critics viewed them as low genres.

The final version was lost with the death of the prophet-composer- singers and the palm leaf textification was done around 11th - 12th centuries, after a lapse of 400 years.

The primitive signs of cultural Emergence: pictography & oral poetry

These four hundred years embody a period of transition and it is crucial in relation to the study of the textification of the oral songs since the various stages of historical and technical evolution of writing are hidden within these long years of repression. All civilized cultures assume that the sophistication of form is achieved only when the writing presents a faithful transcription of self present speech.

People all around the world trace this evolution from the primitive pictographic script of the stage in which man learns to articulate the sound structures of natural language. Different theories have been evolved with regard to the invention of the phonetic alphabetical scripts. Rousseau, Hegel and Jacques Derrida have discussed on this issue extensively But 'writing' for Rousseau is a "dangerous supplement"[5], writing is perceived as a positive threat, as parasitical order of signs that can work to destroy the natural relation between sound meaning and truth. It belonged to that stage of cultural development where the living community of face-to-face contact had given way to a vast, impersonal network of social relations, a degenerate state of existence which Rousseau never ceased to lament (Norris-97) 6

With scripted writing began the entire discourse of the logo centric metaphysical thought of the west. Despite its innumerable advantages, "writing" is that which invades the happy sphere of one to one familiar address setting individuals at a distance from each other and in posing an alien order of social existence" (1bid) 7 The preliterate highlanders of Odissa had switched over from pictographic stage of the middle Pleistocene era to the phonetic era. They were happy to communicate among themselves in spoken language. Singing is older to speech and the primitive Odias expressed their relatedness of things and men through their songs. Even in the pictographic stage of their culture they believed in the primeval communion of all their song poems (pre Charya period) were/are associated with fertility rituals as well as with the situations related to the crises of life, birth, with puberty rituals and death etc. The worship of the Kondhs, the recitation of sacrifice the bakhens of the Santals were recited like the Aryan mantras. The Buddhist and the Jain gurus who came from Magadh talked in Pali, Prakrit and Sanskrit. Thus there was no necessary for them to go for some written script, the sign of a sign. The spoken words were thought of as symbolizing ideas directly, without the further passage through a supplementary medium of written signs. Writing to them was an inferior term which was marked by its exclusion from the intimate circuit of exchange set up between ideas and speech.

The migration of the Brahmins from Sakadvipa and Kannauj etc.and the Buddhist Jain mendicants had taught them that nature and human nature have the power to reduce man to a fearful sense of his own smallness, his own aloneness in a seemingly indifferent or even malicious universe. They a suggest a way to confront such fear is to imagine life stripped down to a minimum, to decide whether enough is left to go on with them to consider the question whether the possible gains of inventing a sign system called script are worth the required strain.

The notion of an author did never come into being to constitute the privileged moment of individualization by building up the author's persona. Our Mundari tribal man never desired to disclose who exactly wrote the following love song:-

The glistening white jasmines
blossomed in your garden
invite the mad dark bees.
When the flowers fade
And the aroma is no more
the bees will vanish;
If they are caught, send them
to the Keonjhar cutchery. (8)

This author does not consider this Mundari song any way inferior to the ones written by our modern enigmatic poets remythicizing the dynasties of Mahabharata in defective Odia. The typographic culture has invested them with the ego to stamp only a name and an 'award' nothing more than the display of an authorial ego. Scripting does, in no way, excel the persuasive power of the primordial intuition and presents to us a 'defacto' truth in our experience of language that appears so massively self evident as almost to brook no question. The sixty two tribes who lived in this land were satisfied with their phonocentric expression. They lived in Rousseau's state of nature and on the borderline of civilization. The power of speech granted them a presence which scripting takes away. Inscribed graphic literature only teases interpretations out of thought. Hegel believed that hearing is the ideal form of sensory perception since it produces the effect of proximity of absolute properness.

The organic community of Rousseau's imagination is simply the equivalent in socio- political terms, of that pervasive 'metaphysics of presence' which requires the absolute subordination of writing to authentic (spoken) language. Our modern, complicated order of social existence is a bad necessity that somehow supervenes upon nature and forces us into all manner of violent, corrupt or inhuman relations. Writing is likewise the 'dangerous supplement' which opens the way to manifold abuses of nature. Certainly it has allowed man to extend the communicative reach of language far beyond the limits of face-to-face contact. But it also brings with it a whole neglected range of harmful distorting effects. Writing is par excellence the instrument of social control, since those who possess it are law-givers, priests and wielders of ultimate power. Without writing, so Rousseau believes we might yet exist is a state of communal grace, untouched by the evils of social inequality and class division. Rousseau's ideal is, thus based on the model of a small community with a "crystalline" structure, completely self present, assembled in its own neighborhood (9) (Derrida: 137). It is only when language breaks with this original ethos of speech and self-presence that it needs to fall back on the "dangerous supplement" of writing.

According to Derrida writing is the supplement 'par excellence' since it marks the point where the supplement proposes itself as a supplement of supplements, sign of sign, taking the place of speech already significant (10) (Derrida,281)

In the classical works of Aristotle spoken words are the signs we adopt to communicate thought or ideas. Written words are the secondary symbols that stand in for speech and so, at a further remove, assist in the process of communication. Already there is the outline of a hierarchy here, a descending order of priority in which writing ranks a very poor third position on account of its irrevocable distance from origins, truth and self present meaning. For ideas, says Aristotle, are common to all men and can have the subject of a genuinely universal knowledge.

The charya poets understood perfectly that the spoken words were capable of symbolizing ideas "directly", without a supplementary symbol system like the written words. Thus they considered writing as an inferior term in this series, the term that is marked by its exclusion from the intimate circuit of exchange set up between ideas and speech.

We do not know evidences which eastern Indian language community invented its script exactly in which time. Hence, it would be logical to treat Charya songs as components of oratorical literature. But what was there prior to that? L.K. Mahapatra, professor of Anthropology believed that the Odia primitive man used to "have some form of culture" Since he used symbolic forms of expression" of which the language is the most advanced form."(11) The statement prompts us to trace the roots of this Odia symbolic system of communication. (pre) Historical configurations about prehistoric Odissa stay limited to the discovery of stone implements belonging to the early, middle and late stone age cultures G.C.Mahapatra in his The Stone Age culture of Orissa (1962) observes that "The tools of this culture, taking shape in the secondary laterite pits and cemented coarse gravels of the river sections are generally made out of coarse grain quartzite pebbles." (12)

Dr.Rekha Devi's study on primitive geography of Odissa, on the other hand, subdivides this Northern mountain region into four sub-units: a) common interfluves of the river Suvarnarekha. b) Nilagiri hills c) Baitarani-Brahmani interfluves and the d) Bramhani-Mahanadi interfluves.(13) The possibility of a civilization in the mountain zone is erased after the 325 punch–marked silver coins were discovered from the valley of Suktel, around contempory Suvarnapur. The archaeologists identified the coins as one of the sets of the oldest coins of the world. Used around 10th century B.C. Panini and Kautilya have referred to these coins.

These silver coins now available in the state museum bear the mark of sun, trees, river and the six nerve plexus of the body (chakras). Over the six chakras there is a deer and in some other coins dogs, ammunitions of those days, bulls, elephants & snakes etc. are embossed. The lexicon embossed on the silver coins also substantiates the language of the Suktimati myths, legends and the dominant systems of belief of 10 century B.C. The deer in the rock art of those days symbolized the hunting culture of the lower Paleolithic man (Middle Pleistocene) (14) An essay on paleontological Odissa published in the Exploring Orissan History deals extensively about the memories of middle Pleistocene Odissa (15)

The spoken language during this Pleistocene age belonged to the Mundari family of the Dravidian origin and it had multiple dialects: Santali, Kolha, Kui and Gond etc spoken in different geographical zones. Those languages had not developed phonetic signs for each word. The conversationalists deployed a relatively limited vocabulary, and were inclined to hedge their lexical choices and thus, were referentially inexplicit. They made considerable use of colloquial words. They created relatively brief intonation units, which they chained together, stopping every so often to make a sentence boundary which was not always well justified in terms of topical coherence.

However, in M.A.K. Halliday's opinion, the spoken languages were grammatically intricate, but lexically sparse. They inter-mingled phonetic signs with gestures. The languages of the Savaras, Bhuyans, Juangas, Gadabas and Parajas (these are different tribal linguistic communities) used such lexically sparse dialects.

Subsequent evidence of Odissi civilization dates back to the reign of king Karakandu (a contemporary of king Nemi of Visaka) during whose reign the Jainist saint and warrior Parswanatha preached his religion in this vratya country. Ashok K.Rath, in his Odisare Jaina Dharma determines his period between 877 B.C.to 777 B.C.(16) (P.66). Herman Jacobi's Sacred Books of the East, XIV informs that Karakandu became a disciple of Parswanatha during 9th century B.C.(P.87).(17)

Parswanatha preached his religion in Munda group of languages and the earliest lights of civilization were beamed into this half-semiotic-half-articulated group of languages of the Munda origin. Scripts had already developed in Bikramkhole area and the Jainist preaching of Parswanath and Mahavira necessitated grammatical codification for meaningful communication.

The earliest language spoken in this land belonged to the Munda group which had 15 dialects: Didayi, Gadaba, Jwang, Koda, Birhar (Mankadia), Mundari, Santali, Saura, Parenga, Remo, Kharia, Koru, Bhumij, Ho (Kolha) and Mahali. However, during these days of spoken language, a rich linguistic system had developed in Tamilnadu and because of their inter connection, hundreds of Dravidian words got intermingled with the Odissan tribal languages. Parjji, Kui, Konda, Kuvi, Lari (Gadabha), Kurukh, Gondi, Madia, Pengu Kissan languages have been classified as language of Dravidian (Tamili) origin. Photocopies of Saura, Kui, Ho and Santali (Alchiki) alphabets would show the affinities with the Dravidian scripts.

These scripts have been retrieved from their primal usage by Raghunath Murmu (1905-1982), Loko Bodra (Jhinkapani, Singhbhum) and Mangei Gomango (1916-1980), who have also codified tribal grammar, books following the rules of Odia grammar. But mostly, these primitive languages of Odisa have come down to us in the forms of spoken Odia: their proverbs and ritual songs. For example, the Bhatri language, which does not have a script, has lots of proverbs that provide an insight into their culture:

(a) "Grare randa nain duare khali/ Aburu jaisi boli"

[There are people in whose home fire does not burn in the hearth, yet they brag of having elephants and horses]

(b) Musha Podai lenj khaibara

[To roast a mouse and eat the tail only, which means acute poverty]

(c) Khairi meshia manush/ Pandiri meghar pani/ Emanar manke keve nai jani

History of Ancient Odia Literature | 21

[It is futile to expect rain from brown coluds, so is futile to expect honesty from a man with brown mustaches]

Dr. Sitakant Mahapatra has collected and translated many such unscripted song poems of the Kondh, Santal and Juang communities,that bear evidence of their rich imaginative ability. Bondas, who do not have a script used to sing great love songs that can be compared with any rich poem of our times:

The night seeks farewell
Field, trees, hills
Are now being disgorged
From its dark womb.
the time for parting has come,
I am so angry at this dawn,
why could not it wait, sleep on a little more ?
Without you the home
Will not be a home;
Without you the village
Will not be a village
Will not be a village
Our enemy, the dawn has come.(18) [Mahapatra, 117]

This unscripted Bonda song of the hoary past shows how language connects the micro -cosmos with the macro and immediately transports us to the unchartered symbolic frontier of the primitives. The language belongs to the Dravidian family and later, it has been accepted as a dialect of Odissa.

Kharavela who studied Udra-gandharva Veda (C.200-150 B.C) knew Sanskrit, Pali and Brahmi languages. His tribal subjects, however, could comprehend Pali, Brahmi and Sanskrit to grasp the intricacies of Buddhist metaphysics.

During Ashoka's time Pali was used as the spoken language since Kalinga was the mother of Pali. But Brahmi alphabets were used for the rock edicts.The present Samblpuri dialect, which was created / spoken in those days retains some of those antique qualities. The language was used for official purposes. Hence, it comes down to us in an uncorrupted form. Prof. N.K Sahu in his famous book, Odia Jatira Itihasa has written a chapter captioned Kalinga-ra bhasa (The language of Kalinga) and has proved that Pali was spoken during the 3rd century B.C. (19)Prof. Suniti Kumar Chatterjee, National professor of India in

Humanities corroborates, "The Aryan language, in the third century B.C was perhaps confined to the Magadhan garrison and officialdom in Odissa, and also among the merchants and Brahmins, Jain and Buddhist priests and scholars who came from Magadha. Kosala and Madhyadesa and lower officials, state employees, business men and such other people of the locality who had dealing with the Maurya Government from Magadha had to pick up the language of the rulers as it was the language of the administration and of a higher and better organized culture." (20)

The palm and the bhoorja leaf writings began around 2300 B.C, but no historical dating is available with regard to Brahmi. Tripathy quotes Jaiswal in his essay: "The characters of Vikramkhole inscription belongs to a period intermediary between the scripts of Mahenjodaro and Brahmi. Some letters still retain their original or secondary Mahenjodaro form and some have assumed the Brahmi or proto Brahmi form. This throws a flood of light on the history of writings as from Brahmi, the Phonecian and European scripts are derived." (Jaiswal 58) (21)

The archaeological remains of a Neolithic fort at Ullapgarh, twenty Kilometers away from Bikram Khole, and the pictographs discovered on the caves of Ushakothi are dated around 5000 B.C. Rock inscriptions of undecipherable characters at Manikmuda, Lekhamunda, Chichirakhol, Sargikhol, Kendukhol, Sukhamakar and Phuldunguri caves in Sundarharh district provide evidences about some extant primitive civilization of the same period (5000B.C).The rock arts signify that these primitive people of Odissa were adept in martial arts, stone carving, the craft of building forts and digging tanks. (Pradhan, 35-45, Chatterji, P.19) (22)

The preliterate tribal people of Odissa were used to listen to these traveling Jain gurus.Hieuen T' Sang's accounts reveal that the Buddhist pundit Dhamma Kirti had his Ashram on the Jagamanda hills of Koraput. (23) He attempted to convert the Jain saints of Odissa after defeating Kumaril Bhatta (a Brahmin from Kanchi), but he could not be successful. (24)

Kharavela who studied Udra-gandharva Veda (around 200-150 B.C) knew Sanskrit and a typical variety of Brahmi that was used in his time. Probably this Chedi king communicated in Brahmi, Pali and Sanskrit languages. But the preliterate Odias were used to understand the metaphysical language of the Jain and Buddhist siddhas (Scholar saints)

K.P. Jaiswal's discovery of the Bikram Khol caves near Jharsuguda in 1933 reveals a wealth of rock arts and Pre-Brahmi script that are deciphered to be the oldest alphabetical models of the world. In a recent essay captioned, "Odisare Prak-Brahmi Lipi Khodita girigumpha-Bikramkhole" (Pre-Brahmi alphabets engraved in the caves of Bikramkhol) Sri Gobinda Chandra Tripathy gives an opinion that these pre-Brahmi alphabets inscribed on the rocks constituted the oldest alphabet type of the world. Tripathy dates them around 5000 B.C (Tripathy, 40). Mr. Tripathy argues that the evidence of the alphabets found in Harappa cunei forms are older than the Sumerian hieroglyphic writing and the Cunei forms, periodized around 3500 B.C. If the pre-Brahmi alphabets of Bikramkhole caves are older than those found in Harappa and Mahenjo Daro, Tripathy's dating may not be an exaggeration. (25)

Orality in Odissi Music

The oral culture of the preliterate Odissa was suitable for the Jain preachers and the Buddhist Siddhacharyas to propagate their new philosophy that was grafted into the grass root level of the preliterate Odias. Music was deployed as the most popular and entertaining medium for teaching Buddhist metaphysics. The siddhacharyas had chosen the popular ragas of the Odissan soil so that the songs would appeal to the popular taste. Let us glance at the following table of the ragas deployed in charya songs.

Lines of the songs Ragas   Lines of the songs Ragas

1.	Kaa Taruvara Pata manjari	7.	Samarasa charya Bankala
2.	Bhaba Nahoi Patamanjari	8.	Charya No.42.Kamoda
3.	Uncha Uncha Baladi	9.	Charya No. 45Majasi
4.	Gaanata Gaanata Ramakree	10.	Charya No.40 Malasi abuda
5.	Nagara bahire DombiDesakh	11.	No 22Gunjari
6.	Aruna pihade Vairabi	12.	No 39Malasree

Dr. Pranati Mund, in her research paper captioned "Odissi Music", writes "The Buddhaganas and Dohas, which claim a common Udra-Magadhi tradition, had their share of songs composed by Odia mendicants, The 37th Charyagiti, according to scholars, is an example of the ancient form of Odissi music. As these compositions were meant for singing, Dohas like the 37th one, may be taken as the earlier examples of Odissi Music". (26)

This Author has checked up the efficacy of Mrs. Mund's statement at the Odissi Research Centre in the course of shooting a docu mentary film on Odissi dance for Mrs Lina Mohanty and Mrs Lisa Mohanty (Famous Odissi dancers operating from Bombay and Malayasia). Dr. Ramahari Das, the Dean of Odissi Music was interviewed and he sang the above charyas effortlessly explaining to me that the charya songs belonged to the Udra-Magadhi tradition of music, Dr. Bijay K. Rath and Paul Yule have researched about the origins of Odissi music and have published an essay demonstrating how rock lithophones have been discovered in a village called Sana Kerajang. There stone lithophones, according to them belonged to 150 B.C. (27) It is the time around when Emperor Kharavela of Odissa studied Udra-Gandharva Veda, a pre Natya Sastra text written in Brahmi alphabets in sanskritzed Pali. The text is destroyed during Aurengzeb's invasions, but its remnants are available in Maheswar Mahapatra's (1670) Abhinaya Chandrika. (28)

However, despite these evidences of Odissi ragas having been incorporated into the charya songs this author feels reluctant to accept the charya poetry as evidences of pure literature. Since no Odia script was invented by 7th century A.D. Odissan land, whatever might be its territory and geographical stretch was preliterate by that time and hence the charya poetry should be classified under the oral poetry. A small conceptual preamble would be necessary here to trace the features and a poetics of oral poetry.

Nelson Goodman in Languages of Art (29) uses the word 'script' for a (compound) character in a linguistic symbol system, for a written text- rather than for a system of writing. Scripts are composed of alphabets and words, and later were used like patterns in the concrete poetry (see chitra-kavya bandhodaya) of Upendra Bhanja (c.1675-1753). A text is constituted of a sequence of words in a certain order.

Further, a script is connected by the rules of pronunciation with a prefixed sequence of verbal sounds. Each time it is correctly read aloud or recited, we have an utterance; the class of all such utterances builds up the oral composition, the dicts that corresponds to the script. Perhaps, that is why our literary anthropologists have accepted dicts as texts.

However, it may ever be that in the preliterate Odissan oral culture, complex dicts tended not to secure exactly by each successive speaker of the Tibettan linguistic community. In the absence of a fixed text, the Tibettan scribbler might have learnt the sounds imperfectly, or, was unconcerned about the minutiae, and had passed a slightly different version of what he or she had received from the original charya composer. Under those conditions, there might not be so much use for the rigorous concept of dicts, as we have in the chirographed texts. Oral sounds might have been further distorted when the songs were re-performed in Tibbetan monasteries and were textified in Nepalese. Verbalization which had no direct connection with writing must have led to mispronunciation and textual manipulation by the Tibbetan monks.

This gap between the original language and its loose pronunciation might have created a space to claims by other linguists of Bengali, Assamese, Maithili and Marathi to Magadhi languages to argue that the Siddhacharayas belonged to their linguistic communities. It was an oral life style and the oral-chirographic contrast or similarity might have been accepted as the product of a cultural interface. No one can lay an authentic claim in view of the fleetingness of the spoken word. Further, the phonetic symbols do posses a binary character of the symbolic system (the strong sounds and the weak sounds, the pronunciational difference in uttering the complex and compound sounds). Such binary opposition might have been reconciled by noetic function of the script writers of Tibbet, but the ultimate interpretation might not be unambiguous since the inroad to meaning was not noetic, but semantic, Guru Deba Prasad Das(1932-1986) of Odissi dance added "Sabda-svara-patha" (readings of the sounds of percussion during performances), so that the dancer's steps would move according to the production of percussion sound by mouth) and moved them in the direction of chirographic culture so that his disciples like Gajendra Kumar Panda and Durga Charan Ranbir would continue the tradition of the percussion beats. But it would not be considered proper to study the flux of the lyrical pronunciation of Lui Pa or Kanha Pa and conclude that the Tibbetan Buddhists pronounced and rendered the charya songs exactly. A drummer of the Sambalpuri dance or the Tiger dance of Ganjam communicates with the dancer through his drum sounds, but the oral/aural exactitudes cannot be produced by a Tibbetan monk while singing the charya songs in patamanjari, baladi (baradi), ramakri, Desakha, gauda, mallari, kamoda, malasree, malasi gabuda or kamodi ragas. (This author has tested the performative exactitude of these Odissi ragas with Dr. Ramahari Das, Dean of music at Odissi Research Centre the charya songs had been written in the raga and meters laid in, Table-II)

It becomes evident that musicality at this point of origin dominated the charya songs. Since the milieu allowed a cultural interface, many languages coexisted simultaneously and there was no reason for the preliterate man of 7th century to feel animosity between languages.

Dr. Satyanarayan Rajguru has published two essays in Satchi Routray's Diganta (Aug' 1977) captioned The "Udrabhasa of Ceylone" collecting data from the inscriptions.

Dr. Suniti Kumar chatterjee is of the opinion that "the presence of the vowels in the middle and end of words (which are generally dropped by Bengali and the rest) gives the Oriya a musical quality or character, which is no doubt archaic, but it is quite characteristic of the Odia speech. The extraordinary development of "Sabdalankar" or the rhetorical flourishes and figures of speech based on sound, i.e. on assonance and jingle which characterized Odia poetry from the 7th century onwards, became very easy for Odia because of the language having retained a good deal on the phonetic atmosphere of Sanskrit and Prakrit and because of the habit it developed like Malayalam and Telugu of borrowing Sanskrit words to saturation'. (p.45) (30)

The most astonishing point of our language is that it has developed the musicality only through phonetics and without a written script to calculate the metrical compositions. These days, however, literary critics and poets, be they from any part of India, are so severely bonded to the prejudice of modern typographic culture against illiteracy that they cannot comprehend the primitive impulses and the language of passion, one that had not yet evolved the complex rhetorical structures required to articulate abstract thoughts. Rousseau's theory of the origins of language could, however, be able to state "It is only when language breaks with this original ethos of speech and self-presence that it needs to fall back on the dangerous supplement" of writing. And the same applies to music, where Rousseau detects the gradual weakening of the expressive impulse of melody- the pure, spontaneous element of song- gives way to harmony, or the skilful arrangement of multiple voices in consort. The more sophisticated harmony becomes, the more completely it depends on graphic notation, on the existence of scores which make it possible to read and perform such difficult music. Rousseau thinks of this as an absolute loss, as a falling-away from that happy condition when music and speech were perfectly united in the natural medium of song'. (Norris, 104)(31)

The twenty first century scholars, however, nurture a belief that great works of literary art cannot survive without chirographical aids. Greek literary culture was in fact, an oral culture until the last third of the fifth century and writing was used only to transcribe texts that had been composed and transmitted through the rules of oral art and memorization.

The phonocentric charya songs were musical and therefore structurally rhythmic. The body language and the performative voice of the Siddhacharya singers had also contributed to the sensuous experience of the songs. It was a great aesthetic experience which, in turn, created significant relationships among the poets and the listeners of the oral society.

In other words, the musical nature of orality offered a fertile ground for phenomenological enquiry. This enquiry uncovers elements and principles generally neglected by other, more 'objectivising' theoretical approaches. The performing with the help of a primitive musical instrument, field of the wondering mendicants of Buddhism put into plays variables and issues that have comprised the special province of phenomenological enquiry. It began from the day the first siddhacharya adopted the technique of per- formative poetry sessions on the streets of preliterate settlements of Bhaumakara countryside. Perceptual and aural experience was related here to the construction of meaning: the mendicant's dress, appearance, the voice and the instrument he played, subjectivity and otherness, presence and absence, body and world—all put together helped the listeners to construct the meaning of the playful Buddhist metaphysics imbedded in the Charya songs. Let us imagine and configure the perceptual environment.

It was the pristine, bucolic space of the 7th century tribal Odissa. They had to withdraw their attention from the moving, passing visuals and focus on the bald, wandering minstrel who sang the charya poem with an underdeveloped percussion. On the one hand the bucolic perceptual field constituted of the object and it was a consumer's item for the listener's perceiving eye. On the other hand, the composer-singer-poet metaphorized the environment as the subject. The metaphorized subject was also the object. Thus, in the process of communication and construction of meaning there was interplay of both: the subject becoming the inter-subjective, and the object turning inter-objective. Then one remembers Merleau- Ponty's statement," experience discloses within objective space, in which experience is merely the outer covering and which merges with the body's being.(Merleau -Ponty,148)(31-a)

What for the literary scholar is more important in the charya song's orality is its immediate relationship to the culture it was performed to. The more we can learn, for example, from the studies about the role of the performer in relation to his or her tradition, the better idea we will have of how to talk about the nature and function of these songs of Buddhist metaphysics. Oral performances in the charya era generate a participatory situation. The Janughanta, the Chakulia Panda and the Nathist Yogins are compulsive performers begging on the Odissan countryside even today. But in the Charya period the world was recent, so recent that many things lacked names, an in order to indicate them it was necessary to point.

The settlements were mobile. Every year, during the month of March a family of leaf and bark clad gypsies would set up their tents or mud-and-wattle huts. Tradition played a vastly more important role for these preliterate listeners of the charya songs. Earlier, they had listened to the Jain mendicants. Parswanatha and Mahavir visited them in 9th century B.C. But they were not as lovable as the bald headed singer siddhacharyas. The woman too, understood them, their metaphysics. The mind was one with the mooladhara, the sky could unite with the dirty soil, a Siddha with a Dombi. They were all omega men and women, with no goals for themselves, no qualms about cooking and life advanced from one disaster to the other, with no leader to politicize disasters to his advantage. They were anti-theses to the Alpha male/the Siddhacharyas. Most probably, their song poems were never planned.

On a multitude of levels the charya performance engaged the operations of preaching Buddhist metaphysics. On the one hand, the field of performance was the scenic, bucolic space of the Bhaumakara preliterate settlement given as spectacles to be processed and consumed by the perceiving, eye, objectified as field of vision for a spectator who aspires to the detachment inherent in the perceptual act. On the other hand, this field was environmental space "subject-ified" (and inter -subjectified) by the composer-singer-preachers who bodied forth the space they inhabited. From this perspective, the performative space of the oral Charya songs, governed by the body and its spatial concerns, a non-carte sign field of habitation which undermines the stance of objectivity and which the categories of subject and object give way to a relationship of mutual implication.

From Talking beasts to the tribal songs: The Geography of Oral Literature

Some of this Oral literature escaped into folk tradition as bits and pieces of literature do. We do not know who exactly wrote the tales told by Grand Ma and what sources the Abolakara Kahani had emanated from. The stories of the origin of autochthonous deities are not authored evidence of folk belief system. The tales of the talking beasts, the stories like those of the dog in the manger, the dinner served by the crane to the jackal, the conference of the rats to tie a bell on the neck of the prying cat, the shrewd jackal dying its body to frighten the fellow beasts or declaring the grapes as sour etc. also belong to the Odia oral cultures.

The Santals of Mayurbhanj lived in preliterate culture till 1930, when Raghunath Murmu (1906) invented their alphabets called Ol-chiki..Prior to that the women tattooed their bodies, put burnt marks on their breasts for identification and used symbolic marks on stones and on the barks of the trees to convey special meanings. The symbolic pictographs were hidden codes of informing about danger or safety in the deep forest. The symbols also communicated announcement about a communal gathering. In addition to such pictographic language the Santals used an oral language that embodied lots of Sanskrit words. The Santal invocation song (bakhen), on the occasion of sowing seeds (Ero sim Bonga) runs like this.

Our obeisance to you, Mother Jaher Era
On the occasion of the Erok festival we offer to you
Young fowls and freshly husked rice;
Accept it in pleasure
We pray to you;
For every seed we sow, let there be twelve
And lit not disease attack them
Bring in the rain bearing clouds in plenty, Bring them in time. Let the earth be green with our crop'. This Santal "bakhen" is passed from generation to generation like the "lagnes" (Songs of rejoicing and entertainment). It is not a sample memory work. A metrical frame work fitted out with matching formulas might also have facilitated the work of memorization. The charya lyrics were, thus, transmitted because of their metrical order.

This author has witnessed one more prayer song in Kui language in a play called Meria, presented by Eski, a cultural organization in which a Kandh girl named 'Rajme' (Raj-Jema, or a princess, she reported) acted in Lakshmipur tribal settlement in, Koraput. The prayer song of Meria had a stunning effect of hypnosis. It was evoked by the particular meter and the throw of the voice, though a single word from this Dravidian group of tribal language was intelligible to the Odia audience. There was absolutely no intonational variation in repeated performances of the same prayer song. The study of the relationship between the structure of the Kui language and its usage in the context and along with semantics forms some meaning, which is implicit and it includes much of the unsaid utterances too. The cognitive effects of Charya songs in the pre-linguistic period also need a consideration, from the listener's perspective.

The grammatology of Utterance

We have already discussed how the Charya poetry was composed and transmitted verbally without any text. The siddhacharya singers underwent a complicated process of conceptualization and transmission of ideas since there was no written alphabet and people understood only through phonetic utterances; without a clear operative division between the signifier and the signified. Besides, the poets deployed the language metaphorically, densely coded and alluding to different icons. Such codes and iconicity generated another typical discourse situation between the speakers/ singers and the listeners in a pre-linguistic stage. This reminds one about the "speech-act" situation of the Kui drama, Meria, and to some extent Yokoyama's 'transactional discourse model'(TDM) (1986). The singer-speakers sang/spoke with an expectation of a response, agreement, sympathy, objection, execution and so forth (Kindly refer to Mikhail Bakhtin's Speech genres and other late Essays, 1986, P 69 for explanations). Without a proper consideration of this aspect, the utterance-interpretation process in verbal communication stage would not be clear. In postmodern linguistics, such grammatical analysis is called the Study of Pragmatics. This includes both the propositional and non-propositional effects (the emotional effects generated by the performance of the charya songs like pleasure, joy, anguish etc) in the process of studying the theories of utterance.

A single performance is, in this respect, analogous to a single reading of a literary text, fleeting, partial and imperfect. Lui Pa or Saraha Pa's oral performances were not versions and variations of a "work", but were, in stead, the actualization of complex philosophical religious structures stored in a highly abstract form by their cultures.

My point is focused to state that the presentational structures and the competence of the siddhas in propagating Buddhist philosophy were the cultural features existing prior to their acquisition by individual poet-performers. The individual levels of competence were never rewarded either by the head of the monasteries or by the audiences. The transactional discourse model (TDM) was different. The performer-audience relationship cannot be treated as equivalent to the author-reader relationship. The audience of the oral performances of the Bauddhagana and Doha were fully dependent on those charismatic performer-poets for understanding, enjoying, accepting, and remembering the song events in their exact verbal form. Thus, the importance of the utterances could not be ignored. The lyrical utterances were composed in accordance with the rhythmic conventions. These were remembered as much as those non-lyrical utterances that distinguished literature from non-literature.

As we are widely distantiated from that primitive period of verbal culture, we are not sure whether the advent of chirography that lent durability to the written texts sapped the power of memory from the listeners. We are also not sure whether writing took away our power of attentive hearing which is the ideal form of sensory perception, known as shruti in later Vedic period. The aural form of perception (as in Charya), comes closest to transcending the hateful antinomies of subject and object, mind and nature, and reason and experience.

The Bhaumakara period of 7th -8th century Odissa was most conducive for the effective transmission of the Buddhist metaphysics. The Siddhacharyas were appointed by the kings as court pundits. Lui Pa, for example, was the court pundit of Sivankara Deva-I (c736- 780). The Sanskrit pundits were replaced by the charya poet Lui Pa' since Sivankara Deva-I was an audacious Buddhist who rejected the decadent Brahminical tradition.

The charya songs can also be analyzed as "processual" poems that synchronized the processing of language through the linguistic consciousness of the poets. The poets had to process their words since they had to interact with their audiences which needed impromptu improvisation. The poets might have mastered improvisatory techniques to build on the rhythmic effects on the spot. The sensuous verbal rhythmic effects produced an immediate aesthetic and linguistic experience that was fuller and richer than that can be accomplished by the reader-writer interactions, if any.

Thus, the type of discourse the charya lyrics generated was different from what a contemporary recital session of poetry would generate. The metric, musical utterances of the siddhacharya poets are different from the recital of the modern poets. Linguistic matter constitutes only a part of the utterance. There exists another part that is nonverbal, which corresponds to the context of the enunciation. Although some of the charya poems would appear commonplace, their utterance is endowed with some yogic signification. The Buddhist mendicants sought to transcend the operating on a semiotic level during the performance of the song. Pragmatics is applicable here since within the theory of meaning the study incorporates and negotiates with inference and the unsaid, and with the way in which language structures trade on the back ground of the presumed and the inferred. Thus, future scholars may investigate into the play of pragmatics as an important part of the general linguistic study of charya songs.

The utterance-expression situation in oral cultures needs the poems to be produced/ rendered in a particular social context. All utterances are addressed to someone (which means that we have, at the very least, the micro society formed by two persons, the speaker and the reciter). Secondly, the speaker/singer is always already a social being. The poet-performer decides and orients his discourse toward the person(s) addressed, oriented toward what that those personnel is/are.

The extra verbal context of the performer poet is absent in the verbalized texts. But in the case of the recitals of charya songs the voice/sound of production and its acoustic perception would generate emotional social responses. The individual perception or the "I-experience" would be transformed into "we-experience" erasing the boundary lines between the interior and exterior speech forms. This sociality of the utterances obviously fitted well with the explicit Vajra and Sahaja yana intentions of the poets.

These socio-religious intentions determined the themes and Musical-structure of the songs. As it has been suggested earlier, the rhythmic element of the songs (i.e. their phonic, metrical, grammatical, metaphoric, imagistic and thematic) seem to set certain utterances aside to be remembered and repeated and to provide a noetic for doing so. Utterances, not characterized by these features are assigned a more ephemeral and work-a-day status in oral cultures.

One of the intentions of these Vajrayana Sahajayana poems was to cultivate the memory of the listeners so that they would hold in the words in their memory. Taking all thre three features into consideration, the Siddhacharyas did not take interest to create a supplementary written symbol which would create a division in the society-between those who were literate and those who were not.

The Charya poets, therefore, believed in their utterance, and endowed it with values in the broad sense of the term. Only the utterance could be beautiful, just an only the utterance can be sincere or false, courageous or timid etc. All there determinations bear only upon the organization of the utterances, in conjunction with the function they assume in the unity of social life, and especially in the concrete unity of the ideological horizon.

This absolute fusion of discourse and concrete ideological meaning (Buddhist reflections, though) is, doubtlessly, one of the constitutive features of myth, determining, on the one hand, the development of mythological representations, and on the other, determining the specific apprehension of linguistic forms, signification and stylistic combinations. At this point, the textified oral literature tangentially touches the margins of literature. Thus, the verbal signs (phonetic though) cannot be separated from the social situation without relinquishing its nature as sign.

The verbal communication of the 7th century Odissa could have never been understood and explained outside of this connection with a concrete situation. The language of charya songs is not therefore a neutral medium which would be the private property of Odissa, Bengal, Assam or Bihar. It is over populated with intentions and interpretations. Hence, the old concept of claiming charya belonging to any particular linguistic community is erased.

The written version of charya songs constitutes a single textuality. It is a social space, and it leaves no language safe outside or any subject of the enunciation in position (whether one is a philologist, national professor, philosopher, Buddhist, analyst or decoder). The idea of "text", in this sense, as one that stresses the process of their signification, the context and the enunciative situation around the 1930s is important to us in this time of postmodern discourses. It is better, no longer to believe in the "author" as a person belonging to any particular geographical and ethnic terrain (whether Bhusuku pa is Santi Deva and he belonged to Keonjhar or to Saurashtra).) (34) He may not be the only terminus to restore the wholeness of the act of enunciation. He is, to restore the wholeness of the act of enunciation. He is, to use a term from Terry Eagleton, to be considered from "subject positions," that are not extra textual, but are, instead, essential constitutive factors of the text.

By calling attention to the authority structures of these positions within the charya texts, we would attempt either to subvert or even to reinstall the idea of originality which subtends them. Edward said, talking about the writer's thought process, comments, that the writer "thinks less of writing originally, and more of rewriting originally, and more of rewriting. The image for writing changes from original inscription to parallel script". (1983, 135), a change attested to by the proliferation of forms of postmodern parody" (35)

Charyasongs as Literature: Text and Axiology

The detailed study of the 50 charya songs discovered by Hara Prasad Sastri would make a volume. Our project does not accommodate space for a detailed annotative study of all the songs. Hence we would aim at a sample study of few poems.

We should remember, at the outset, that the songs are vajra-yana-sahaja-yana tantric enunciations were written in secret codes called 'twilight language.' The Buddhist Tantras, on the basis of Mahayana principles dictate practical methods for the realization of the supreme goal. The Siddhacharyas stressed on different method of religious perseverance (sadhana), but not with any system of abstract philosophy. Tantricism, both Hindu and Buddhist, lays stress upon a theological principle of 'duality' in 'non-duality'. The ultimate non-dual reality possesses two aspects in its fundamental nature, the negative (Nivritti) and positive (pravritti), the static and the dynamic. These two are represented in Buddhism by Prajna (the female) and Upaya (male) or a soonyata (the female) and karuna (male). The ultimate goal of both the schools (male and female) is the perfect state of union – the union between the two bipolar aspects of reality and the realization of the non dual nature of the self. The Bauddha ganas and the Dohas explain these methods to the common preliterate people through different symbols and metaphors.

We have traced the worship of female energy called Sakti in Suktimati civilization around 10th cectury B.C (C 1000 B.C) basing on the discovery of 325 embossed silver coins on the bank of river Suktel (district Suvarnapur)in 2002. It was the pictographic culture that had commercial links with the Tamil countries where the Naga kings ruled having Tantricism as their state religion. The numismatic studies reveal the details.

The pictographic culture continued in the Santal and kuvi tribal cultures till 1930s when Raghunath Murmu of Dandbose (4 km. from

Rairangpur) invented a chirographic system of writing for the Santals. A Santali play captioned Kherwal Bir depicts the Santal mythology of the early Pleistocene Age which has come down to Baripada stage as a lively episode from the oral culture. As such, by the time the Bhaumakaras ruled Orissa during the 7th century A.D. the Buddhist siddhacharyas were appointed as court poets. Lui Pada was a court recordist (kayastha) in Subhankar Dev-1's court (c736-780). Subhankar Dev did not subvert the shibboleth of appointing the Brahmins as court pundits. A tradition had already started from king TivaraDeva of the Somavamsi dynasty (c. 695-725). The Vajrayana sect of Buddhism was introduced by Indrabhuti (c 707. A.D) - the king of Sambala (Sambalpur). His sister Laxminkara began a new branch called Sahaja-yana and her first monastery was founded in 747 AD. Padma Sambhava, the foster son of Indrabhuti (c721-22 A.D.) fled to Tibbet to preach Mantrayana and settled there. What we would discuss as charya literature, therefore, belongs to the 8th century. By this time, Tantric Buddhism had already spread in Odissa, Tibbet and Nepal.

Lui Pa (c. 736-c780)

In the absence of an exact date we place him in Subhankar Dev-1's reigning period (c 736-780) since Lui was his court kayastha (a record keeper). Prof N.K. Sahu, in his Buddhism in Orissa mentions that his guru Sabari Pa was a famous Siddhacharya of Odissan region. After the discovery of an old manuscript captioned Lohi Gita, (36) Prof. Khageswar Mahapatra states that Lui Pa' is also known as Lohi and Lohita. The phonetic utterance of 'O' sound becomes 'U' in certain areas of Odissa.

Pt. Binayak Mishra in his Odia Sahityara Itihasa (Odia) (37) mentioned that king Darika and his minister Dengipa became Lui's first disciples and then king Bajraghanta accepted him as his teacher. He was honoured as a divine figure in Mayurbhanja and people, even today, observe a day called "Lui pooja" (Day of Lui's worship). Hara Prasad Sastri mentions him as a guru belonging to Radha country (Mayurbhanja was a part of ancient Radha desa).

Lui's Kaya-Taru-Charya dealing with human body as a Taru, (i.e. tree) is charya No 1 and it is sung in Raga Patamanjari:

Ka-aa Taruvara pancha vi dala
Chanchala chi-e paitha Kara
Didha Kara mahasuha parimana
Lui bhanai guru puchhina Jana.
(Translation/Paraphrase)

The human body is like a tree. It has five branches (the five sensory organs). If you want to strengthen the quantity of your Mahasuha (mahasukha, Supreme bliss, nirvana) consult with your guru and learn how to control the fleeting constituents of the mana (mind). The way to Maha-sukha is easy and accessible, not a difficult one. You need not have to pass through the inaccessible terrains of austere practices of disciplined Yoga...

The charya song preaches the concept of the Sahajiya School which is an off shoot of vajrayana. Lui Pa, the author of four vajrayana treatises including Abhirama Bibhanga and a compendium captioned Lui pada Gitika uses the metaphor of a tree as an eco-feminist image that conveys to the preliterate tribal people that truth cannot be realized through fasting, bathing and other paraphernalia of rites and rituals prescribed in Jain texts and also in Vajrayana. Lui Pa, probably switches over from Vajrayana to Sahajayana to convince the naïve tribal people.

In the Mahasukha Prakasa (collected in the Advaya Vajra-Sangraha) Mahasukha is described as the Lord Vajra -sattva (male principle in creation) of the nature of unity of Prajna (female principle) and Upaya (male principle). Sukha is not possible without the body and it cannot weather the rough seasons of life like a tree if it pulls itself away from the experiences of the trunk/ body. Sukha is 'Vyapaka' (pervading the whole world)) as well as vyapya (that which can pervade). As the smell of a flower cannot be experienced without the flower, so also sukha as the quintessence of all that is originated can never be realized without the world of originated objects. The Kaya (body) as the taruvara (reverend tree) embodies the different tattvas (essences) with in this corporeal structure.

Lui pa as a strong advocate of Vajra yana and Sahaja yana holds that "the pleasure that is realized through the discharge of matter is much lower in respect of degree as well as in quality, than the bliss that can he realized through the control of this matter, i.e. by checking its downward flow of semen through subtle yogic processes and by giving it an upward flow so as to make it reach the lotus situated in the cerebrum region (Usnisa- kamala corresponding to the Sahasrara padma of the Hindu Tantras) and to make it steady there: the bliss resulting from the steadiness of the matter is the mahasukha (either/pronounced by Lui or transcribed by the Tibbetans as mahasuha. But in a popular way, we often find semen-virile as mahasukha and it is the lord Buddha himself." (38)

Saraha Pa (c. 736-780)

He was a senior contemporary and the Guru of Lui Pa and was born during this period. Saraha Pa was also known as Sabari Pa'. Pagsam-jon-Zung records that Saraha was born in a Brahmin family, married to a girl from a black-smith's family and had been to Maharashtra on his preaching tour. He converted king Ratnapala and his minister into Buddhist Vajrayana pantheon and came back to Odissa. The Tanngyur monastery records register that Saraha Pa had written around 25 Buddhist treatises, Saraha Pada also advocated the practical side of vajra yana:

Saasamvitti ma karahu re dhandha
Bhava-bhava sugati re bandha
Nia mana munahure niune joi
Jima jala jalahi milante soi

In this Doha No32 Saraha Pa warns not to confuse the truth. That is only to be realized within. Both positive and negative thought constructions bind the man. In the final stage the individual consciousness or ego hood should merge in the all-pervading universal consciousness like water merging into water.

Some of the commentators explain that to identify the final state with sukha is a mere confusion. No positive conception of this final stage or any negative conception or any construction of this type can conduce to perfect enlightenment. There is no difference between a golden chain and an iron chain, for both will bind a man and therefore both are to be avoided.

Sarah Pa proceeds a step higher and contemplates about the material world and the thoughts of nirvana in Achintya Dharma charya. 22):

Amhe na janahu Achinta joi
Kama marana bhava kaisana hoi.

The commoners think about the possession in this material world and still think of nirvana. This duality binds them in the enclosure called this world. I never think about such things. I am a thought- free, (tension-free) yogi. I do not contemplate on topics like birth, death and existence. What I understand by birth is also what I understand by death. I never feel a chasm between birth and death. (In Charya No.49 he says "jivante maile nahin visesha). Those who are afraid of births and deaths they should go for a sadhana (yogic perseverance) to attain a long life through Rasa-Rasayana siddhi (Attainment by Rasa-Rasayana yoga). But why then the men who are able to traverse the land or divinity fail to live forever? Do they take birth because of their karma or do they perform karma because they have taken birth? "Why?" asks Saraha and concludes that thoughts are irreducible.

Bhusuku Pa (809-849)

Dr. Karunakar Kar (1895-1967), in his thesis on Ascharya Charyachaya (1949) locates zahor the birth place of Bhusuku to be jhar or Kendujhar. A mountain named Zahorai still exists there. Dr. Kar was of the opinion that Santi Deva, Bhusuku and Rout are not three different persons, but one. He quotes from some palace records that the kings of Keonjhar were designated as "Ayoni sambhuta.... Chauda sahasra Routala Kendujhara sthanadhipati". Dr. Kar quotes two lines from Bhusuku pada.

"Aji Bhusuku Bangali Bhaili
Nia gharani chandali leli"

(From today onwards I became a Bangali by accepting a wife from a Chandal's family. Bengal was a Vratya country and there was no caste division in matters of marriage in Bengal by the time Bhusuku wrote these lines)

Dr. Kar also interprets that Banga Desh, in those days was a vratya desha, and casteism did not prevail there. Santi Deva did break away with the shibboleths by accepting a girl from the downtrodden class. (39)

Prof. Nabin Kumar Sahu, in his Buddhism in Orissa corroborates Santi Deva to be a prince from Kendujhar who studied at Nalanda under Acharya Jayadeva and came back to his native place as an advocate of Tantric Buddhism to concentrate on the concept of Sahajiya Sexo-yogic esoterics. (40)

The Tibetan legends report about many siddhacharyas bearing names like Santi Pa, Santa Rakshita and a Santi Deva from the royal family from Saurashtra whose father was Kalyana Burma. The latest book of micro-history written by Niranjan Barik mentions Bhusuku to be from Kendujhar in his Kendujhar Itihasa (1998) (41)

The folk legends of Keonjhar narrate Prince Santi Deva (Bhusuku Pa') as a king's eccentric son who used to move with a sword made of pine wood. The pelf and power of his father's kingdom frightened him. He apprehended danger from every side and decided to renounce the illusive material pursuits of the worldly life. He narrates his psychic plight in his Deer Song (Harini charya). Bhusuku metaphorizes his speeding mind with a deer:

The hunters have rummaged the forest
And closed in with snares on you
Don't put your head in the noose, Deer!

Your own flesh has turned against you.
Where to flee? Whom to espouse?
You've forgotten her address.
The deer is in danger, mawkish
Frightened to graze and drink.
The she-deer warns him, 'Flee this forest immediately'
And run as fast as you can'
The deer leaped fast,
So fast that his hooves were not visible.

The further developments of Santi Deva, transformed as Bhusuku can be discerned from the following poem. .We would discuss Bhusuku's Samarasa Charya written in Raga Bangala (Charya No. 43)

Sahaja Mahataru faria ae teloe
Khasama savabe re ba na muka koe (1
(Second stanza not available)
Jima jale pania Talia reva na jao
Tima mana ra-anare samarasa ga-una samao (31)
(Translation and paraphrase :)

Sahaja is like a 'Tree Supreme' that spreads over the three spheres (bhubanas). An awareness of the void (feeling of sunyata) has to be evoked to internalize the Tree supreme, i.e. the concepts of sahaja. The ampleness of the mind would emancipate one from the bondage of the worthy feelings and emotions (ragas).Once you enter into this feeling of the void within, you would attain "Samarasa". He who drowns him/her self within "Samarasa" the feeling of the self and the other would vanish. The Charya songs and the Dohas of Saraha and Kanhapada also embody this Buddhist jargon in the sense of non-duality (Advaya) in the Sexo-Yogic practices of Sahaja yana-Vajrayana. Bhusuku illustrates 'Samarasa' as a Sexo-Yogic moment in which the feeling of 'I-Thou' or the 'self' and 'Other' are washed off as water (rasa) mixed with water (rasa) leaves no difference to be discerned. So also the 'jewel' of mind enters the 'sky' of samarasa. In samarasa both the positive and negative aspects of the mind vanish, it is pure and free from all existence as well as non existence.

Samarasa is the induction of a feeling of vacuity, a liberated state in which the idea of raga or transcendental emotions is the idea of Samarasa. It is the sameness or oneness of emotion. In a deeper sense samarasa is the realization of the oneness of the universe amidst all its diversities it is the realization of one truth as the one emotion or the all pervading bliss. The meaning of samarasa is well explained in Hevajra-Tantra, where it is said that, in the sahaja or the ultimate stage, there is the cognition of neither the prajna nor the Upaya, there is no sense of difference anywhere... (42)

Kanhu Pa (exact date not available)

There are several Kanha/u Pa's in Tibbetan records known as Kanhu (Author of charya Nos. 7, 9, 40, 42, 45), Krishnacharya pada (Nos 11, 37), Krishna pada (Nos 12, 13, 29), and Krishna Vajra (No.18). There is one more Kanhu Pa in Charya No.6 in which he declares himself to be a disciple of Jalandhari Pa and himself as Panditacharya. Dr. Dharmavir Bharati in his Siddha Sahitya (Hindi) introduces him as one with long ears and as a Saivite and also known as Karina Pa.

We would browse through the works of Krishnacharya, the disciple of Indrabhuti (707 A.D.), the king of Oddiyana. He was a prominent scholar of Vajrayana during the reign of the Somavamsi king Tivar Deva (C. 695 – C725). Prof. Khageswar Mahapatra places him between 687 and 717 AD. This study prioritizes literature and the contents of the Dohas, not on the dates/places of birth of the authors. It would be fruitful at least to consider the texts written by him. Kanhu Pa was a brahmin, but a great propounder of Vajrayana as the disciple of the originator of Vajrayana (Indrabhuti). He was also an adherent of Sahaja yana since Laxminkara, the first propounder of Sahaja yana was his Guru Indrabhuti's sister. Kanhu Pa was, thus an ardent believer of the Sahajayana concepts laid down in Lakshminkara's Advaya siddhi

In the fifth doha of the Dohakosha of Kanhu Pada, the word sura-vira has been explained in the following manner: "The union of Prajna and Upaya is the union (surata), there, he (the yogin) is the hero, because he controls all discharge by the strength of his incessant and intense emotion (Maharaga). Sura-vira iti/prajnopayardvandva-yogah suratan /tatranava-chhinna-Maharaga- rupina viraga - dalanad virati definition/explanation in Sanskrit).

Again the Sanskrit scholars explain, "Surata-virutaya' chuta-Maharaga-sukham anubhuti' by arthah" which means that (The yogin) experiences undischarged bliss of the nature of intense emotion (Maharaga) through his strength in union. Kanha pada explains in another Doha,"He who has made his mind steady in Samarasa which is the sahaja, becomes at once perfect, no more will he suffer from disease and death".

These examples prove that like Saraha and Bhusuku, Kanhu pada, too, felt liberated in using the concept of Samarasa as propounded by

Laxminkara boldly. Charyapada song No. 43 (H.P.Sastri), Doha No. 11 of Tillopada, Doha No. 46 of Saraha pada, Doha No. 74, 19 and 32 provide us with illustrations of the of Samarasa (The union of the Prajna and lthe Upaya). A text called Subhasita-Samgraha also defines" Prajnopaya-maha-guhyam Samarasamuchyate (P.69) (43).

The average reader, who is new to such initiatory literature of Odia country, would discern effortlessly that prophets of Vajrayana-Sahajayane undergo and state metaphysical experiences in a playful, witty language, spoken in the preliterate tribal land. However Kanhu Pa is famous for his Dombi charya:

> Your hut stands outside the city
> O, untouchable maid
> The bald Brahmin passes sneaking close by
> O, my maid! I'd make you my companion. See,
> Kanha is a Yogi and a Kapali
> He's naked, yet nourishes no disgust.
> There's a lotus with sixty four petals in you,
> Come, Maid! I'd climb on you
> and we'd dance there!

(Paraphrase and Translation):

The untouchable Dombi is the female power (Shakti) lying hidden within her body. She lives outside the city of ordinary consciousness. Since he is a Kapalika, (a tantric, initiated in Vajrayana), he dared to negotiate her to make her his companion. The bald Brahmin (all wise men including Krishnacarya) hunkers to climb on this lonely maid. He is naked and the dombi is an outcaste. Both of them would climb upon the 64- petalled lotus or the Sahasrara chakra and dance to attain maha-sukha and the Sahaja.

The prophets intended to communicate their metaphysical experience to two sets of people: to the qualified people who had been initiated into these esoteric cults and to the innocent high landers who were discarded by the Northern Indian people (Aryans) as the despicable vratyas. Anga (Assam), Banga (Bengal) and Kalinga (Odissan tracts) were unholy and untouchable lands for the Indus valley Aryans. Buddhism, in its radical effort for dislodging the so called "purity" of the Hindu religious texts, attempted its alternate teaching throughout the country. The Vratya lands like Kalinga, Kangoda, Utkala, Mosala and Kosala were treated as ideal places by the Jain and Buddhist prophets for propagating Vajrayana-Sahaja Yana religion.

The Sexo-yogic Sahaja yana was a style of life practiced by the preliterate pagans of this country and prophets like Indrabhuti and his sister Lakshminkara from Sambala (Sambalpur) and Lanka (Sonepur) picked up these charya writers as able lyricists and performers to spread the knowledge of Buddhist practices of yoga as an alternative religion. In a country that did not educate the commoners about the alphabetical script, these orally composed/ rendered songs were of great significance to the preliterate milieu. The language was more important since its poetic deployment provoked and titillated the minds of the hill tribes to decide whether to enter into the civilization brought by the alien Aryans to their Vratya country.

When the experiencing psyche and (things it perceives), subject and object melt and are observed into one another, what takes place may be called a metaphysical experience. Lakshminakara's Sahaja yana led the tribal people toward new endeavours like "gathering in" of the frivolous mind, sometimes metaphorized by the poets as a 'running deer' (Harini charya) and sometimes as a 'mouse' that digs in holes into the deeper terrains (Mushika charya) tucking in of the mind, detachment in the highest moment of attachment (Maharaga and Samarsa) absorption etc. The prophets, at a later stage, realized that the naïve forest dwellers might go astray and their lives may fall into eternal darkness if they misinterpret their language. There was also a belief that if the Sexo-yogic secrets would be divulged in public, the yoginis and the terrible sprits would devour up the prophets. So they used a type of language that was recognized as sandhya bhasa, in which the meaning blinks between light and darkness. Jacques Derrida coined a French word called 'glossopoeia',- a state of prewriting stage in which meaning / concepts start exploring for the right word, and at times, the mind plays hide and seek with the right word. The writer needs a greater degree of meditative concentration to enter into the esoteric terrains where the duality of the subject and object melts down (like the conditions of sexual 'Yuganddha' advaya propounded by Lakshminkara).

Indrabhuti, The Vajrlayanist king of Sambalaka "organized Mantrayana into Vajrayana and wrote Jnanasiddhi, in consecration of this school, to an increasing popularity"44). Padmavajra wrote Guhyasiddhi and Anangavajra, who also belonged that part of Oddiyana wrote Prajnopaya vinischaya siddhi".

Since the texts of these metaphysical works needed secret and coded language, one notices far-fetched images and heavy use of con-

History of Ancient Odia Literature | 43

ceits in Charya poetry. Charya No.2. of Kukkuripada would provide an apt illustration of its coded language. This allegorical song (Milked a tortoise, my pot overfilled) challenges its listeners to detect the secondary, partially hidden level of significance. Frequent allusion to beasts evokes an Aesopian milieu or an environment generally discovered in the Jataka Tales with allegorical meaning. The producer of the charya song has to depend on the listener's awareness of the conversions of the form, and he, then flouts them by defeating their expectations in a bizarre manner. This is game of enigma initiated by the Buddhist mendicant with his preliterate listeners.

Taking into consideration the mindset of the primordial listeners of the Bhaumakar Odisa (7th-8th century), one may assume that the singer - composer of the Charya song initiates a game of playfulness. The narration of the improbable is a strategy of inducing an enigma. Playing games is a primitive instinct and literary art adapts them to activate the lazy, dysfunctional minds and to make it ready for receiving the ensuing puzzle. Mendicants intended to titillate the preliterate so that they can master over the biological realities controlling their baser instincts. We may examine the poem, and its dialogic narration:

"Milked a tortoise, my pot
was filled. Crocodiles eat
tamarind from the height
of the tree. Things like this seem inappropriate."
The waking father-in-law addresses
The sleeping daughter-in-law
"Listen to me you bitch, you rot
You've turned this courtyard
Into a room, yet
A thief sneaked in and cut
One of my ears, at
Midnight."
The dad-in-law had to keep
Awake. Poor Lady, timid.
The daughter-in-law
alarmed at the crow's kaw
Makes a tryst with Kamarupa (a place in Anga desha famous
for sexual practices)
To traverse such distance in the night.
Kukkuripada has wrought

this song difficult
One out of twenty may get
its meaning, secret.
(Paraphrase /translation).

'Bodhichitta is the milk one should extract, but it comes to you and hides itself like the head of the tortoise. The tamarind stands for semen. It has to be raised up to the top of the tree (body: sahasrara). The semen has to be lifted up to the sahasrara by Kumbhaka pranayama (allegorized here as crocodile).

The sneaking thief is the bliss one gets in Sahaja-ananda (ecstasy attained easily) during sex practice. The daughter-in-law (biatee) is the Vajrakanya (The sex partner of sahaja Yana practice). The ear that the thief cut/stole away denotes the baser feelings and the sinful thoughts of dual feeling. The midnight stands for deep-core 'Samadhi' of the old father-in -law while the poor Vajrakanya (daughter in law) sets out toward Kamarupa (site for sexual practice), where Upaya and Prajna would get united in an advaya (non dual) Yuganaddha (union) state.

The narration is fabular and dense metaphorization and the speaker's view of the discourse situation is based on pronunciational punning: kumbhaka and kumbhira Bodhichitta is like the milk of spiritual attainment alluding to milk-like semen. The tamarind also stands for semen, but it is on the top chakra (sahasrara)of the human body (raised up to the top of the tree). The sahaja yana mendicant advised the folks also to raise their semen upward and to check its downward flow. The 'Crocodile' (Kumbhira in Odia) stands as a phonic code for 'Khumbhaka' a process of yogic pranayam(breathing exercise) or the controlling of the breath for double the time of intake through the left nostril and exhaling it through the right nostril slowly extending the process for double the time of retention). The sneaking thief is the bliss of Sahaja-ananda. The biatee or the daughter-in-law is the Vajrakanya (The sexo-yogic partner of sahaja Yana); and the ear that the thief (ananda or ecstasy) stole away denotes the evil feelings and the sinful thoughts. Interlaced between the vajrayana metaphysics and the performative lyricism are metaphors that generate surplus meaning characteristic of literary works. The charyapada performers consider metaphor as the touch stone of the cognitive value of the literary arts. If we can incorporate the surplus meaning of metaphors into the domain of semantics, the interpretative enterprises would be given its greatest possible extension.

The surplus/meaning goes beyond the oral linguistic signs. But in this poem the metaphors turn into symbols, which by their semantic structure exude double meanings. Even with the deployment of metaphors as symbols, occasionally there remains some of the semantic, as well as something non-semantic. The sleeping father-in-law establishes a relation between the literal meaning and the figurative meaning that makes the complex interplay of significations. Besides, metaphors incorporated here into the language game lend an axiological praxis to the performative poem.

The metaphorical conceits deployed in the poem are capable of encompassing all fields of knowledge-commonplace or esoteric, practical, theological or philosophical, true or fabulous for the allegorical comparisons, succinct or expanded, the conceits (tortoise, tamarind, milk, midnight and daughter-in-law etc) unfold novelty. The playful mindset full of wit aimed to produce a startling affect on the preliterate listeners. The Bengali critics termed the device as sandha (sandhya) bhasa (twilight language, a language of borderlines).

Our sample study of charya poetry, small though, establishes that the prophet writers of the Buddhist school were familiar with the axiological concerns of literature since its aim was to propagate religion and their aim was to educate the ordinary men, marginalized by religious pantheons. They intended to uplift the spiritual status of the people by training them about the yogic practices to attain 'sahaja ananda' (transcendental supreme bliss in the easiest way). Sarahpada in a doha warns not to confuse the truth that is only to be realized within. Both negative and positive thought constructions bind the man. Man has to keep up a balance between them.

Most of the Siddhacharyas have tried to convince through their songs that the universe can be identified with the body, even the seas, rivers, mountains etc can be located in different parts of the body. The mode of depiction invited a playful, witty and performative lyricism and the historians have appropriated this mode into the fold of literature. The deployment of dreams, imagination and jokes are always in relation to the unconscious of the collective audience and as a whole, the communication was allegorical. The origin of allegory is philosophic and theological rather than literary. Since the charya metaphysics is narrated through songs, the prophet composers have attempted narrative modes, small though, through their songs. Kukkurupada's allusions to the sleeping father-in-law in the night, and the seemingly coward daughter-in-law going to Kamarupa in the dark midnight embody elements of an allegorical narrative. Myths, too, are transmitted orally at first and they are revered only by priesthood. Later, it appealed to a larger body of initiated people who could be able to comprehend the dual meaning of fantasy.

Dante, in La Divinia Commedia, refers to such creative devices as 'imaginative' and 'fantasia.' Such writings appear to be closely linked with men, their rational being and perception of the natural world. It is a paradox that the prophets of charya, while creating such imaginary worlds considered it necessary to observe faithfully the rules of logic and inner consistency. Although they may differ from those operating in our own world, they must, never the less, be as true to themselves as their parallel operations are in the normal preliterate world of the tribal people.

These prophet poets broke out often into speech in a language that was inadequate. Yet they surround with the vivid atmosphere of life the directness of their message; they have followed up a single injunction which Sri Aurobindo pronounced later: "Take no thought for the morrow". They deployed revealing images of beauty of the truth they enounced, in life of Nature, in the figures of the lotus and mouse, in deer and in the crocodiles and related to human life by apologue and parable. The Kavi in the Aryan Rigveda meant a seer, one who has seen, and not merely seen but shows, a darsanika - one who shows the way.

One of the major foci of Charya poets is the fear of death, a hazy, densely coded mystery that shrouded their forest life. These poets in action were born and unborn continually and alternately. Their 'here-and-now' reality also imbedded the 'before-and-after', the linear and the lateral, the vertical and the horizontal realities. Bhusuku and Kanha are our contemporaries. The time they conceived is not the same as experienced by the flat headed men. The stanzas they wrote thirteen hundred years ago have been written continually in instalments, by all those poets till today in their idiosyncratic splendour. Their poet craft is not generally clung to any fixed form of presentation. It becomes difficult for us to describe the way in which poems can be grouped together in terms of their attitudes and social functions. Thus the implicit irony noticed in the Charya poems may be called a genre by itself. However, one notices certainly the numerous meanings readers draw: homilies for the religious reader, images like a snare discerned in the call of the hunters, the Sahaja Yana metaphysics in imagining a lotus unfolded in dark nights and the melting of the she-lotus in the water (the concept of samarasa in sex-yoga). They have attempted to guide a tribal generation on the modes of achieving a state of renunciation through sumptuous enjoyment of life.

NOTES
Chapter - 1

1. Kunja bihary Tripathy — The origin and Development of Oriya language, Orissa Sahitya Akademi, Bhubaneswar, 2001, p.1
2. Gopal Chandra Praharaj. — Proceeding of the Oriental conference, Patna Vol- VI, 1930 P.381.
3. Kunja B.Tripathy. — The Origin and development of Oriya 3. Language P.1.
4. J.N.Talukdar. — "The Non Aryans of Rig Vedic Society", The Journal of Asiatic society, Vol- III, No.5 Calcutta, 1979.
5. Jean-Jacques Rousseau. — See Essay on Origin of Language. Trans, John H.Moran, Newyork, F:Urger, 1967.
6. Christopher Norris.Derrida, — Fontana, London, 1987.
7. I bid.
8. Sitakant Mohapatra. — The Tangled web. Tribal life and culture of Orissa, Orissa Sahitya Akademi, Bhubaneswar, 1993, P.121
9. Jaclqus Derrida. — Of Grammatology trans. Gayatri Chakravarty Spivak.Baltimore, John Hopkins Univs. Press 1976. P. 281.
10. I bid.
11. L.k.Mohapatra. — 'Tribal Art, Primitivism and Modern Relevance 'in Tribal Art, Ed. Dinanath Pathy, working Artists Alssociation of Orissa, Bhubaneswar, 1991. P.5.
12. G.C.Mohapatra. — "The stone Age Culture of Orissa, 1962" quoted in K.C...Panigrahi, History of Orissa, Cuttack, 1981, P.1

13. Rekha Devi.

14. Giacomo Chamuni,

15. Ramesh Panigrahi

16. Ashok K Rath

17. Ibid.
18. Sitakanta Mohapatra.

19. N.K.Sahu.

20. Suniti Kumar Chattrjee.

21. Sadasiva Pradhan.

22.

Locational study of Tribal settlements in Orissa Bhubaneswar, 1993, P.19 and P.33.
Angleo Fossati and/Yasodhar Mahipal Ed .Deer in Rock Arts of Indlia and Europe, Indiragandhi National Centre for the arts, New Delhi 993. P.113
"Pale-Ontological Orissa: Configurations from Suktimati Civilization" Exploring Orissan History Ed. Nihar Ranjan Pttnayak, Kitab Mahal, Cuttack, 2005. Pp.I-14
"Odisare Jaina dharma -O-Samskriti (Oriya) (Jainisim and culture in Orissa) Taratarini. Pustakalaya, Beherampur. 1991

The Tangled web, Tribal life and culture of Orissa Sahitya Akademi, Bhubaneswar, 1993.
"Kalingara Bhasa" qtd. in Odia Sahityara Itihasa, Pathani Pattnayak, Nalanda, Cuttack ,1978, 8th Edn. 1997, P-19
The People Language and Culture of Orissa, Orissa Sahitya. Akademi, Bhubaneswar, 1996, Pp.27-28. K.P. Jaiswal. "The Vikramakhol Inscription, Sambalpur District" The Indian.
21. Antiquary, Vol.62, 1993 Pp 58 - 90.
Painted Rock Shelters of Orissa. A casestudy of Manikmoda
TheOrissa Historical Research Journal Vol.XXXIX No.1-4. Pp.35-45. Journal of Orissan History, Vol. No.1. Pp. 26-28.

23. P.S.Sastri.	Some Budhist thinkers of Andhra, H.Q. Vol XXXII, No.2 and 3, June Sept1956. (Gautam Buddha 25 th centenary special Issue)
24. Gobinda Chandra Tripathy.	"Odisare Prak-Brahmi-Lipi khodita Giri-Gumpha" (A cave with pre-Brahmi inscriptions inm Orissa-Bikramkhol) Dharitri xxx, 25. November, 2003, Pp 40-42.
25. Pranati Mund "Odissi Music"	The continuity in the Flux"Ed. Dinanath Pathy and Ramesh P.Panigrahi, Herman Publishing House, New D e l h i, 1999. P-140.
26. B. K.Rath and Paul Yul e	Journal of Orissan Research Society, No 4, 1991, Quoted in "Odissi Music", by Pranati Mund, in The continuity in the Flux Ed. Dinanatha Pathy and Ramesh P.Panigrahi, Harman Publishing House, New Delhi, 1999 P.140.
27. Nelson Goodman	Languages of Art, Indianapolis, 1968 Pp. 199-201.
28. Suniti K.Chattrjee	The People, Language and Culture
29. Christopher NorrisDerrida,	Fontana Modern Masters, Hammer Smith, London, 1987.
30. (a) Maurice Merleau-Ponty	Phenomenology of perceptions, trans Colin Smith, Routledge and Kegan-Paul, London, 1962, P.148.
31. S.K.Mahaptra	The Tangled web, Orissa Sahitya Akademi, Bhubaneswar, 1993, P.105.
32. Niranjan Barik	Kendujhar Itihasa, Tangara Palasa, Naranapur, 1998, P.12.
33. Khageswar Mahapatra	Charya gitika, Friends Publishers, Cuttack 1999 (8th Ed.) P.139.

34. Linda Hutcheon — A Poetics of Postmodernism, History, Theory, Fiction, New york and London, Rout ledge, 1988 P.81.
35. Khageswar Mahapatra — Charya Gitika, Friends Publishers, Cuttack, 1965. rpt. VIIIth Ed.1999. P.55
36. Binayaka Mishra — Odia Sahityara Itihasa, Cuttack 1928 qtd In Odia Sahityara Itihasa Dr. Bansidhar Mahanty, Friends Publishers, Cuttack, 1970, Rpt.1978, 1984, P.48.
39. S.B.Dasgupta — An introduction to Tantric Buddhism, Calcutta, Univ- of Calcutta, 1950, Pp. 156 - 157
40. Kurnakar Kar — Ascharya Charyachaya Pp46-47 qtd in Odia Sahityara Itihasa Dr.Bansidhar Mohanty, Friends Publishers, Cuttack, 1970, Rpt. 1978, 1984, P.48.
41. N.K.Sahu — Budhisim in Orissa, Utkal University, Bhubaneswar, 1958, P.150-152. Kendujhar Itihasa.Op.Cit. P.12
42. Niranjan Barik — (Details given in item No33)
43. S.B.Dasgupta — An Introduction to Tantric Buddhism, Culcutta, University of Calcutta, 1950. P.138
44. I bid, P.141.
46. B.Bhatacharya, Ed. — "Introduction" Two Vajrayana works qtd in Surendra. Moharana's "Vajrayana in Orissa" Ed.Nihar Ranjan Pattnayak, Religions of Orissa Indian Publishers' Distributors, Delhi, 2004. P. 79

■■■

CHAPTER-II

FROM ORALITY TO TEXTUALITY: MEDIAEVAL ODIA LITERATURE

A language called Oida was growing, growing from 'madhyama' to vaikhari stage unfolding its power, and yet faltering through distorted utterances and textification in Tibbet The Sanskrit scholars working in the courts and in urban areas and the kings of different Mandalas of Kangoda, Koshala and Toshali were inspired to invent their own 'supplementary signs', the sign of the sign, the alphabet. Orality, in the rural and the forest areas had already admitted fusion of multiple artistic genres into its fold, sometimes including antonymic genres, too and produced semantic paradoxes, Language mixed with music was aimed at some kind of axiological performance. Buddhist metaphysics got buried under pornographic representation and was wrapped in fabular enigma. They called it twilight language, a kind of coded pop language.

The study of orality had grown into a massive discursive terrain of amalgamations calling for discussions on the totality of art rather basing on a unitary cultural manifestation called literature. By the time Kukkuripada verbalized his "tortoise milk" song, a dense metaphoric symbolic game had already started in oratorical compositions of charyapada. This oral composition had all the effects of aphasia owing to its wrong combination and defective contexture of words that were deployed with the aim of lending a ludic element to the recital. But it was grammatically risky. The objective correlative was lost; and the 'relation of similarity' (Eg. Crocodile eating tamarind from the top of the tree) was also distorted. That was the main cause for this aphasia. The scholarly people in the courts must have detected this 'similarity disorder' in Odia language and would have assigned reasons for this defect to the absence of alphabets in our language, that left no chance for the Buddhist mendicant to revise his selection of words for improving the communicability of the song. In other words, the "prakrit" oral language necessitated an inversion of the priorities: inscribing the words first, and then make a move toward hermeneutics for an effective critique.

This means, language was no longer linked now to the knowing of things, but to men's freedom". (1) As this statement from Foucault's The order of things speaks about our linguistic movement of 19th century, we do compare the language of the Odias with that. The language was entering for the first time a new boundary of freedom, where it started operating with its own laws. Once it becomes a transparent medium, the meta linguistic usages would be deduced and understood as a social-collective medium of relationships.

And it happened with Odia scripts, too. The kings availed of the first opportunity and began inscribing their orders and proclamations for the knowledge of the public on the rocks so that their names and historical events could be chronologized as it was done at Dhauli (Bhubaneswar) and Jaugarh (Ganjam) inscriptions of Ashoka in which he records his aversion to war and indoctrination into Buddhist principle of non violence and non-injury.

The initial shape of Odia alphabets and language was deciphered in Urjam and the date of inscription, converted into contemporary standards, comes to 12th October, 1051 A.D. The inscription was engraved by Vajrahasta Deva of Ganga Dynasty. The inscriptions engraved prior to that contained one or two Odia words only. A 7th century rock edict of Madhava Burman includes 'Pandara' an Odia word for fifteen and the Manjusha copper plate of the 10th century AD includes a typical Odia word 'Bhitaru' (from within) (2). The Khambeswari Temple inscription of Suvarnapur was engraved in 1268 AD (03.03.1268) by Bira Bhanu Deva-1 in Odia.

It is interesting to note that the scripts available in Suvarnapur (Kosala), Urjam (Kalinga, now in Andhra Pradesh) and Toshali inscriptions were not one. Those three regions were independent Odia speaking countries with different sovereign kings very often engaged either in war or tied up in marital relationships. The inter-Vishaya Odia relationship was as complex as their scripts and cultures. The pictures of the Odia alpahabets would drive the point a focus.

(A)

SOMAVAMSI SCRIPT

a a ā ă i ī i u u e ai o au
ka kha kha ga gha ca ca cha ṭa ṭo ṭo
ṭa ṭha ḍa ḍa ḍha ṇa ta ta tha tha tha
da dha na na na pa pa pha ba bha bha ma
ya ra ra ra la va va śa ṣa sa
sa ha ha kṣa kṣā ṭuva ṭca ṭca ṇī
si si di su pu ṭu bhū pe le ṭui pu
bhaṁ ṭhya ṅgā ndrca ku trī sui

Dr.Sudhakar Das, in his Odia Language, Literature and Culture (2005) has shown the evolution of Odia scripts. The alphabet types may be classified into four groups:

54 | History of Ancient Odia Literature

(a) Old Brahmi (5th C.B.C.-1st Cent.B.C) Dhauli and Jaugada.
(b) Later Brahmi.
(c) Gupta scripts, and
(d) Kalingan scripts (3).

It would not be fatuitous, therefore, to provide the specimen of the Gupta scripts (3rdcent.A.D) and a script used by Maharaja Tustikara Deva of Kalahandi during 4th century A.D.

GUPTA SCRIPT (PRAYAG PILLAR)

[script specimen]

Sudhakar Das, in his book, concludes at one point, "So, in conclusion, we ascertain that the Odia language is the standard language of a vast area of Kosala region from the 2nd half of the 1st century B.0 till date in spite of the existence of so many local dialects.(P.19) (4) The Terasinga plate of Maharaja Tushtikara Deva of Kalahandi proves that by the 4th century A.D some kind of Oriya script was in use in the courts and in the urban areas along with Sanskrit and Pali. The Mathara kings also ruled over Orissa(Koraput and Ganjam etc) during 4th cent. A.D and some of their copper plates are dated between 4 and-7th A. D. Similarly, the Sumandala copper script of Dharma Raj ath(Ganj am, 570 A.D), Sambhu Yasa's Soro copper plate (Blalasore, 6th cent.A.D) and the Kanasa copper plate of Lokabigraha (Kanasa/Puri, 7th cent.A.D) give evidence of scripts existing in different parts of the Odia speaking regions. The language existed only for use in copper plates and stone engravings, while the Charya songs were composed, sung and performed in Oral form in the countryside, where preliterate Odias lived their secluded life untouched by the elite Brahmins, and Royal agents and the touring merchants who used different kinds of Odia alphabetical signs.

Since the transition from orality to textually is the main focus of this chapter, we would accept "text" not only as books written in palm-leaf or as a paper bound material or as "commodity" purchased by Raja Rammhan Ray library and destroyed at the Block level before they are distributed to the libraries in the Grama Panchayat level. The department handling Raja Rammohan Library materials are unaware of what happens to the Odias of Jharkhand, Medinapur and Manjusha, now under the political control of Bengal, Bihar, Chhatisgarh and Andhara Pradesh. Their Odia children do not know what happens in Odia literature.

Research reports circulated by Dr. Manindra Mohanty and an extensive field study account published by poet Akshaya Behera, Editor, Katha-katha-kavita-kavita informs that the Odias in Bihar, West Bengal, Chhatisgarh and Andhra are eager to see how an Odia Magazine looks. Dr.Mohanty appealed the Odias to donate their surplus magazines to the half-dead libraries, built once upon a time, for the Odias, politically deported to other linguistic states forcibly by the government of India.

It should be noted that acquisition of language, whether oral or textual, may begin with production of sounds or perception of alphabets at the individual level. The act of learning, here, as in the oral period of literature, should, however, not be considered only as a physiological process. If we take into account the process of reception of meaning, the sociality of the language has to be presupposed.

Similarly, when we transit to the level of textuality the same level of social reception cannot be ignored. Thus, we have to accept the copper plates and the rock edicts as texts in a broader postmodern sense. We have to accept this expanded use of the term "text" which includes artefacts ranging from architecture to events. A minute facial reaction, a tree or a flower or the nature outside, historical facts and the implicit power struggles inscribed therein should also be included within the parameters of the "text".

If so, the coded pictographs of the Santals in the pre Ol-chiki era carved on the trees as messages were also texts and they generated an interpretative situation. This leads to the logical conclusion that while a variety of expressions can be put under the rubric of "text", no text can remain single without reference or allusion to another text. This leads us again to the philosophy of language. Language is something internally coherent and not merely a natural collection of travelling points with which we indicate "real things." Elizabeth Deeds Ermarth, in her Sequel to History provides an interesting postmodern definition of language: "Language is the constant by which we compare forms of "Writing" in the expanded sense that postmodernism gives to that word: writing, that is, conceived as unique, finite and local specification of a particular sign system. Considered as discursive "Writing", activities are not instruments of production but the activation of different opportunities of residence and of engagement. A "text", further more, is no longer a singular "thing", it becomes constituted by the process of enactment that engages this or that particular personnel or material" (Ermarth, 1992, P.4) (5).

Ermarth's postmodern definition of a "text" supplants the discourse of representation characteristic of the long and productive era that produced historical thinking, or what Meyer Schapiro calls "the immense, historically developed capacity to keep the world in mind" (6).

With these expanded premises, let as examine the transition of Odia language from oral phase of our literature to the textual phase that would follow. The oral composition of the Charya songs was "writing in the soul". With alphabetical writing we created a phonetic presence on the palm-leaf or on printed pages. This inevitable and gradual "fall back into a system" (This is Derrida's phrase. He always despised writing as "poison and cure" that caused some sort of displacement) has certain perceptible effects on Odia literature.

i. Nathist literature is available to us also in palm-leaf manuscripts and Sri Sribatsa prasad Nath (1934) has translated them into Oriya in two volumes. Although the Nathists are ignored in History, We would accept them in the following pages because scripts had been invented by this time (11th-14/15th century).

ii. A major change that comes to literary studies is that the highly imagist Charya poetic imagination stoops down to matter of fact prose writing. The Nathist poems are statements with limping, multi-cultural pronunciations.

iii. The major prose works of this period are Sisu Veda and Rudra Sudhanidhi.

iv. While Odia language was struggling to transcend the maverick stage to adapt the discursive mode, with poetic prose and prosaic poems, Sarala Das (Siddheswar Parida, 15th. century) makes a remarkable enterprise, at once ingenious and audacious, to write an epic in the running and flowing meter called 'Dandi Vritta.' The language was lapsing into prose and the phonetic vocabulary of Mahaveena Vrata Katha (Natha literature) gets reflected in Rudrasudhanidhi The epic surpasses the events and the structural details of the original Sanskrit work and finally comes down to us as a chronicle, a book of the tribe, a vital record of Odia customs and tradition and at the same time as a story book loaded with pop-vision for general entertainment through performance of recitals at Bhagabata Tungis (the club houses for reading Bhagavata) of the rural Odia, a country of the Odras unified for the first time.

v. Textified Odia acquires the status of pure literature during this period that begins with copper plate and embraces all the epigraphical studies and then moves toward an epical entrepreneurship.

Let us delight, then, in a beginning that opens in 'free play' and stumbles on paradoxes out of aphasia and receives intimations of the folly committed through the epical adventures of Sarala Das. With textification and "writing," the Odias have taken up and improved the forms of discourse we inhabited in our post literate days in sloppier, less visible versions; they make the premises of discourse evident. And there is another, less obvious reason to include the transcriptions from the palm-leaf text of Nathist literature. The Nathist mendicants intended to engage their pulse and intellect simultaneously and consequently permitted no easy escape from practical chores of civilized living. With the advent of the discursive prosaic texts, the Nathists focused on practices and refused in so many ways to accept the distinction between practice and thought, poetry and prose, and between material and transcendental reality.

The literature of the Natha Prophets
(i) The background.

In most of the modern versions of Odia history of literature, the works of the Natha poets/writers are either precluded or ignored. The period between the 11thcentury and 15thcentury is treated as a 'dark age' in Orissa in terms of administration, culture and religions movements. The rise of the Natha prophetic literature developed simultaneously with the invasion of the Afgans throughout India when they demolished Hindu temples and the idol worshippers. We would discuss here its impact on Oriya literature, after the scripts were invented. The reign of Bhaumakara dynasty was stooping down to decadence after Subhakar Dev (V) breathed his last and his last three queens ruled Toshali successively. Dandi Mahadevi, the last queen sovereign of Toshali was extremely beautiful, but she could not marry because of political reasons.

There was no political homogeneity. Harshawardhan's friend Hiuen T' Sang's records divulge that the Odra Vishaya (Ucha) (Kangoda, Odra, and Utkal combined together) was divided into small "Mandalas" with different kings. Thus, the period between the 8th and 10th century was politically unstable and culturally decadent. Lady Bhumakaras ruled in Toshali, Somavamsi Kings in Kosala and the kings of Ganga dynasty ruled over Kalinga.

As Mr.L.A.Waddell reports, "About the end of the 6th century AD Tantricism or Saivic mysticism with its worship of female energies and the spouse of the Hindu god Siva began to tinge both Buddhism and Hinduism. Consorts were allotted to the several celestial Bodhisattvas and most other gods and demons and most of them were given forms wild, terrible and often monstrous. By the middle of the 7th century AD India contained many images of Divine Buddhas and Bodhisattvas with their female energies. Such was the distorted form of Buddhism introduced into Tibet about 640 AD and during the three or four succeeding centuries, Indian Buddhism became still more debased. Its mysticism became silly mummery of unmeaning jargon and magic circles dignified by the title Mantrayana (Waddell, 1972, 14-15) (7)

S.B.Dasgupta, in his Tantric Bhuddhism (1950) has equated Nathism with Kalachakrayana (P.72). Dasgupta has observed:

"The Bhuddhist Tantras are generally divided into three schools, viz, Vajra yana, Klalachakra yana and Sahaja yana. We do not know on the authority of what texts this division of schools has been made. Of course, these names are often met with in the Tantric texts, but the characteristics of the schools have never been sufficiently explained. Mahamohapadhyaya Hara Prasada Sastri in his introduction to Modern Buddhism and its Followers in Orissa of N.N.Basu speaks of Nathism as another school of Tantric Buddhism in addition to the three already mentioned above. M.M Sastri seems to have viewed this on the basis of some popular misconception" (Dasgupta, 72) (8).

The name of Kala-Chakra-Yana also appears to be perplexing. About it Waddell says in his Lamaism, "In the tenth century A.D., The Tantric phase developed in Northern India, Kashmir and Nepal, into the monstrous and poly-demonist doctrine, the Kala Chakra, with its demonical Buddhas, which incorporated the Mantrayana practices, and called itself the Vajrayana or the Thunder bolt vehicle, and its followers were named Vajra-Charya or followers of the Thunder bolt...In another place he says, "The extreme development of the Tantric phase was reached with Kalachakra, which although unworthy of being considered as a philosophy, must be referred to have as a doctrinal basis. It is merely a coarse Tantric development of the Adi-Buddha theory combined with puerile mysticism of the mantra –yana, and it attempts to explain creation and the Secret powers of nature, by the union of the terrible Kali, not only with the Dhyani Buddhas, But even with Adi-Buddha himself". (Dasgupta, 72-73). (9)

Dr. Smt.Kalyani Mallik, in her essay the "Philosophy of the Nath cult" informs, "The names of some of the important Natha Siddhas are found in the list of these eighty-four Siddhacharyas, but no historical authenticity can be given to this list of Siddhas numbering eighty four, the number might be having rather a mystical significance than historical. Yet the general religious outlook of the Natha Siddhas and the Buddhist Sahjia Siddhacharyas has led earlier scholars to believe that the Nath Siddhas were crypto-Buddhists. This conception, is, however, not correct, as has been proved by further researches on the subject of the philosophy of the Natha cult". (Mallik,101) (10). This author attempts to make a study of the literature of the Nath prophets basing on Sribatsa Prasad Naths' "Natha Dharma-O -Natha Sahitya" (11). Mr. S.P.Natha (1934) has collected the ancient palm-leaf scripts from different Natha Monasteries and gadis of Orissa and has published them in two volumes: Natha Literature, Part-I is published by Orissa Sahitya Akademi in 1971 and the second volume is published by Kasturee Nath Sharma in 2004. The collection includes the following extant scripts:

1. Hatha pradeepika and Hathapradeepika Tika (Commentary on Hatha pradeepika collected from the palm-leaf scripts (Prescriptions related to the practice of Hatha Yoga).
2. Sri Guru Pranam Mantra (Mantras related to the Gurus of Natha Sect).
3. Ekadasa Rudra-O-Natha-nka Anga Sajja. (The dress code and the symbolic marks of the Nathists).

4. Mantravali (Different Mantras related to the work-a-day chores in the life of the Nathists).
5. Saptanga Yoga (and Astanga yoga discovered by Dr.Bansidhar Mohanty).
6. Panchanga yoga.
7. Gorekha Gita (Containing the history of Natha religion).
8. Mahabeena Vrata Katha.

These texts can be classified as spiritual literature. Most of the books depict the details of yogic practice. The Nathists have followed Maharshi Patanjali's yoga sutras and have delivered them in a language that appears to be a mélange of poetry, prose, Pali, Apabhramsa Sanskrit and Odia that appears little developed from that of the charya prophets. Alphabets in Oriya had developed in the meanwhile and the inscriptions of the Somavmsi kings show a different kind of alphabet in Kosala. The kings of Ganga dynasty in Kalinga used another variety of alphabets (pease refer to the charts).

Yuan Chwang's report informs that the people of the Odra country "spoke a language different from the language of central India. The Chinese pilgrim further informs that the people of the Kangoda country (Ganjam and Puri) spoke a language which was similar to that of Central India." 11 The observations are confusing. Kangoda being the neighbor of Andhra Country was influenced by Telugu and the language incorporates lots of Telugu/Tamil words.

Yajati -I. (Somavansi King) united Kosala, Kangoda and Utkala under one rule in 931 A.D and during Yajati-II's rule the capital was shifted from Suvarnapur to the coastal region. This political change brought in a kind of linguistic amalgamation. The people of Kosala speak a language which is akin to the Bhojpuri Prakrit while the language of the coastal region had an affinity with Magadhi. Both the languages were cocktailed now to generate a Prachya Prakrit Odia.

The next political period was dominated by the Ganga dynasty that brings us lots of specimens of the Oriya language that we evidence in stone and capper plate inscription.

The first full-fledged Odia inscription was inscribed in 1051 by Vajrahasta Deva at Urjam of Srikakulam district. Thus, by the time the Nathist literature was written in palm-leaf scripts, the Oriya scripts began to develop.

The script in which Indrabhuti wrote his Jannasiddhi before 717 A.D was different from the script/language of Nathist Yogasutra and Hatha Pradeepika Teeka. The Somavamsi scripts discovered after some years proves that those were different from the Kalingan scripts. However, both the scripts were angular in shape. Let us examine the language:

Sri Hatha yoga vidya prathamam. (Let us begin the Hatha Yoga Vidya first)Sri Raghunathanku namaskara kari.(Ovation to Sri Raghunatha) Sri Adinathanku namaskara kari,(Ovation to Adinatha) Hathyoga vidya karibi boli swamy Ramayog bicharila....etc. (Swamy Ramayog proposed to narrate the subject called hathayoga) (Nath-85) (12).

The Hatha Pradeepika Tika and this entire corpus of Nathist literature substantiate Shreemati Kalyani Mallik's statement that Nathist literature does not belong to a part of "sahajiya" seat of Buddhism. On the contrary, it is a revolt against the sexo-yogic practices of 7th- 8th centuries Maha Yana.

The Siddhacharyas of the Sahajayana stooped down to the Vamachara practice of Panchamakar (taking liquor and meat and indulging in libertarian sexual practices.) The requirements of the common people were different from the desires of the sexo-yogic practitioners. It is inconceivable for a twenty first century reader to believe in an association of prophet-scholar-poets whose philosophy was based on principles of pure pleasure, the unfettered expression of sexual impulse. Before a streak of reality entered into the organization of their psyche the Bhaumakar social life was reduced to group sex and communal sex.

If their apprenticeship and 'guru hood' resulted in a mastery of altered states of consciousness involving voluntary entry into and exit from those states, that might have generated cognitive distortion and mal-adaptive behaviour on the societal level. These Buddhist Sliddhacharyas lived perhaps in an idiosyncratic universe suffering from an impairment of reality testing. The way they contaminated the society by organizing an annual festival of Madana puja was considered despicable. During this ritual worship of Cupid every one, from the king to the untouchable woman, gathered and enjoyed communal sex under an Ashoka tree. The saner few of the society must have predicted a culturally constituted delusion and pathological symptom that would have ruined the Odra society, if the Nathists would not have started a counter radical movement through yoga.

The serious thinkers, who did hardly differentiated between the Saivite kapalikas and the Buddhist worshipper's terrible "Kali" united with some Adi-Buddha, must have come forward under the umbrella of reformative yoga sutra. The main object and goal of their yoga was to endeavour to discover the absence of what the people have misunderstood to be the individual personality. The Nathists embraced the Hindus and the Buddhists and finally the Muslims did also join them to get enlightened. If the inner intelligence is wide awake, life flows smoothly, without problem. They intended that this "awakened intelligence" would fill and penetrate every aspect of their lives.

The yogies of Nathism were spiritually elevated people; they were levitating yogis and preached the gospel of enlightened living as contrast to the Sahajia principles that were deployed to provoke and attract Hindus into their religious fold.

There are about 50,000 Nathists in Orissa who belong to Brahmin, Kshatriya, Vaisya, Sudra and Muslim castes. The Nathist Gadi (seats) or monasteries at Ali, Manitri, Simulia, Chha'pada (Tirtol), Jagatsinghpur (Gorekh gadi, Harinath Gadi), Kulanagari, Birswati (Kendrapara), Kapali Nath of Bhubaneswar, Kala bhairab Matha of Padmapur and many other seats that exist beyond our knowledge.

The Oriya rendering of Nathist literature published by Sri Sribatsa Prasad Nath proves that the Nath Siddhas acknowledge Matsyendranath (of the Charya School) as one of their Adi (primal) gurus. Matsyendranath finally had settled down in Nepal and become a devotee of Avalokiteswara. There is also a belief that Matsyendra was himself Avalokiteswara. A car festival takes place in Nepal every year in the name of Matsyendra.

A comparative study of the Buddhists and the Nathists can be made since both have shared similar yogic processes along with Tamang Shamanistic practices of Tibet. The Buddhists basically believe in non-violence (ahimsa) whereas Matsyendra, a fisherman by caste caught fish for a living.

The Nath Yogis use 'cannabis indicia' (ganja) as Siddhi, since it was a favorite intoxication of Lord Siva. Our field research studies inform that the sky-gazer elders in the aboriginal society also took the help of intoxicants and said after that the mind is no longer in the body but is reflected out into the cosmos'. Although they gazed at the sky (some concentrated on the sun and practiced the act of internalization of the sun), it was infact, a

Tamang Shamanistic practice and an invitation/invocation within to the spiritual cosmic force to engulf the focus of his mind. It can, therefore, be called a form of "Yoga"- of the mind with the infinite. The Bengalies believe that Matsyendra received his instructions from Addinath Lord Siva trusting on the Nepalese tradition. But Gorekhnath's teachings are found also in Hindi and Sanskrit. Gorekhanath is defined as Siva in Nepal and Matsyendra is honored as Avalokiteswara.

It is not also true that the Nathists seceded from Buddhism and embraced Saivism. There were common elements of Yoga and Tantra, and were practiced by both the sects during the 8th and 10th centuries, which led to such confusion. Lots of "fallen brahmins", people believe, had succumbed to the Vajrayani practices and they partly appropriated the Jain disciples also. There had been a fusion between different religious practices. Probably the methods of meditation had something in common.

But while the Buddhist monks were clean shaven, the Natha Yogies used the "tripundra" sect mark on their forehead and a mark of 'Yoni-linga' on their right arm. Some of them put on a 'Kundala' or large ear rings as a symbol of their boasting of immortality. Sribatsa Nath's Oriya book captioned Natha Dharma-O-Natha sahitya Part-II (2004) prescribes a dress code for them.

In contrast to the Sahaja Yana, and the Kalachakrayana precepts, the Natha Yogies were strict celibates and Hatha Yoga helped them to discipline themselves and keep their bodies cleansed of sex. The Nathas considered sexual libertarianism as anti-social since seeking pleasure for the individual in a blind and mechanistic way contained within itself the elements for rampant destruction.

To a large extent, the Nathist yoga had (13) somaticized the symbolism and rites of shamanism. The concept of the "axis mundi" so common to the Shamans, the ladder reaching through the numerous levels of heaven, corresponds in Tantric Yoga to the spinal column and the chakras that are likewise traversed in order to attain the final initiatory experience. In all the Tantric practices the yogi identifies himself as god's representative of universal forces to the extent of becoming one with them and thereby coming to utilize those forces.

This takes place in Patanjali's Yogasutra by awakening and raising the kundalini up (the power coiled below the bottom of the spinal chord like a serpent)

This digression into the cultist practices for secluding Nathism from other contemporaneous systems of belief gets reflected in the Nathist books available to us. The language of Saptanga yoga and Panchanga yoga are yogic treatises written as replicas of Sanskrit Bhagabata and Gita. It seems books like Mahaveena vrata Katha (Observed on the day of Makar Sankranti in the month of Magha/January) of Nathist Literature were written in later 14th century or little before Panchasakha literature. A Specimen may be taken from Mahaveena Vrata Katha's beginning.

Sri Ganesaya Namah.(Ovation to Lord Ganesa) Abighna mastu,(Let all evils be dispelled) Katha suniyate.(we would narrate the story) Prathame Magha masa hoila(The month of Magha had set in), Makara sankaranti hoila.(the day of Makara Samkranti had come) Isvara Parvati Sarga teji Mahiku aile.(Iswara and Parvati left their heavenly abode and descended down to the earth) Ratna kathau pade madile. (Put their feet into the bejewelled wooden sandals) Ganga ku sire bahile.(put river Ganges on the head as an ornament) Aasi mancha mandale bije kale(They emerged on the mundane earth). (Sribatsa Nath, Natha Sahitya. P.241) (14).

Natha literature records its origin and history in Gorekha Samhita which bring allusions to Sisu Veda. Prof. Bansidhar Mohanty in his "Odia Sahityara Itihasa' judges that Gorekha Samhita belongs to 16th century. Archaic usages like 'Sunimaka,' Karibaka', Prathamahum, Achambuta, Upurana, Drasana, Kevana, Jevana and Sasradala etc. compel us to compare the language with that of Rudrasudhanidhi and the Mahabharata of Sarala Das.

It is therefore not safe historically to place the Nathist writings in this time span between 10th and 11th centuries. What has been retrieved from the palm-leaf scripts by Sribatsa Prasad Nath might have been written in post Sarala and Panchasakha era, also. Natha literary writings continued along three/four hundred years and set a trend. Since the Natha gurus came from Gujarat and Jalandhar, some of the works are discovered in a mixed language. The literature is important to us since the Odias got assimilated with the National stream of literature for the first time after the scripts were invented.

The disciplined yogic section of Nathism protested against all kinds of casteist and sectarian narrowness and they gradually urbanized scripted literature of Odisa; they paved the way toward a distinct kind of mediaeval literature that hardly believed in the generic divisions between prose and poetry. Scripting, on the other hand, allowed a polymorphous production of literature which is never recoverable in its entirety.

The History of Mediaeval Literature 68

A review of Odia literature written between Natha literature and the literature of the Bhakti movement (The Panchasakha Period) seems to me as a constant cultural state and not specific in terms of literary genres: Madala Panji, Rudrasudhanidhi, the literature of the rural vows that begins either with Mahaveena Vrata Katha of the Nathists or the Somanath Vrata Katha of the, Odias, Sisu Veda, Chacherilila, running parallel at later point with Tulabhina and Gopalanka Ogala and Kataka Raja Vamsavali, Chronicles of the Bhanja dyanasty ending with Brajanath Badjena's Rasavinoda appear linguistically belonging to one expressive mode and idiom.

The historical endeavors of Artabalava Mohanty, Bansidhar Mohanty, Kedarnath Mohapatra and K.C.Panigrahi seem so confirming that a new comer like this author gets confused to fix their chronology. The polemics starts since none of these investigators assign reasons as to why Rudrasudhasnidhi would be periodized either as a post-12th century writing (Kedarnath Mahapatro) or as a work that appeared to have been written around 15th century (K.C.Sahoo) (15). This discovery 'of lack of reality' (A phrase borrowed from Jean-Francoise Lyotard) together with the invention of other realities saps my confidence to stick either to strict historical dating or to generic nomenclatures. Probably Odia prose did not proceed through an evolution between Mahaveena Vratakatha and Chatura Vinoda. (12th and 18th centuries).

To my naïve understanding the language and small sentence narrative style of Mahaveea Vrata Katha and Somanatha Vrata Katha is found in Sarala Dasa's Mahabharata. This apparently similar discourse of representation is characteristic of a long and productive era that optically/linguistically appears flat to me. The immense, historically developed capacity to keep the National Cultural ambience in mind inspires this author to sabotage the imaginative constructs imported to the margins of our cultural discourse so that this would act as the repressed foundation for a rationalist order. Since the space of our literary memory shifts, we should, probably, realign a sense of continuity by inter mixing the genres.

To begin with, this mediaeval literary landscape is overgrown with pornographic entertainers and diplomats. More that half of them were kings. Perhaps a literary poetic cocoon provided them with the right kind of covering to exploit successfully as it does help the contemporary bureaucrats. Even Rousseau, if alive by that time, would have banned all kinds of poetry from Odissa branding the genre as "Necessary Evil". Rousseau, however, was a politician and thought that with poetic opacity an evil civilization slouches with all its armour of complications. Prose, on the contrary, was just used for discourses. It is a fortune for the Odias that in the mediaeval age, in which poetry flourished in all possible directions, the practitioners applied themselves to the writing of prose, which had, to a large extent, become a pliant and serviceable medium. Prose writing in Orissa has always been connected with rock inscriptions.

In Tractatus Logico Phiosophicus Wittgenstein proposes that language is a picture of reality and the earliest evidences of language are therefore, found in pictographs. The pictographic symbols represent some sense. They are media for any theory of "proposition" or that of "sense". The Pre-Brahmi scripts/symbols discovered by K.P.Jaiswal at Bikramkhol are dated around c.5000 B.C. But the first evidence of Odia script was found in the Urjam inscription of South Kalinga written around 1051 A.D by one.mahapatra (full name not mentioned), a resident of Srikakulam district, who modelled the Odia scripts following the round-headed Telugu alphabets to suit the stylus, has been forgotten now. The cultural politics of regionalism has raised its ugly head and made blasphemous attempts to suppress this fact and the Department of Culture has neither made attempts to treat Urjam as a heritage site, nor has it ever conducted a meeting at Urjam to celebrate the birth date of Odia alphabets.

In the absence of any other evidence, we take up the beginning of prose writing only through rock inscriptions. Histories, in different literatures of the world, prove that prose writings develop in times of speculation or fierce questioning; in times when powerful minds did begin to think about human experience and the nature of man.

Sanskrit writings from Odissa Vishnu Sharma (5th century):

The evidence of the first prose writing in Odissa is in Sanskrit: Vishnu Sarma's Panchatantra written in 5th century A.D. As the title indicates, the book has five sections (tantras) (i) Mitrabheda (the separation of friends), (ii) Mitrasamprapti (Acquisition of friends), (iii) Sandhi Vigraha (Peace and War), (iv) Labdha Pranasa (Loss of one's possessions and (v) Aparikshita Karaka (unjudicous action). Whether any one knows that the place of origin of this notable book is Odissa or not, it has been circulated all over the world through translation. Macdonell periodizes the time as 5th century (Panda and Nanda, Pp 4-6) basing on the translation of the work into Persian by king Khosru Anushirvan (531-539 A.D.) under the title Karataka Wa Damanaka in Pehlevi (Mc Donell : 307-329). (16)

The narrative of Pancha tantra does not follow the "once-upon-a-time"structure of the occident. On the other hand, when we read "Asti Godavari teere vishala salmali taru" kind of beginning, we tend to put it under the category of realism: "There is a huge salmali tree on the banks of river Godavari" cannot be anything else other than the first sentence of a story. Thus, Panchatantra has as great amount of influence on the Odia prose writing, the influence of the realistic narrative.

Sri Jayadeva (12th century)

The translation of a famous inscription written in Ganga alphabets in Lingaraja temple, Bhubaneswara is read by Satyanarayana Rajguru as follows:

"Medama Devi, her father Komi Nayaka and each of Medama's mothers hereby have donated unextinguishable flames in the service of Lord Kirtivaseswara (Lingaraja). The expenses would be met by our entire landed property at Bahedakhanda, bought from the Sadhupravara Sri Jayadeva of Kurma pataka."

This inscription is identified in Orissa by its first few words, eg. Swasti Raghava devasya...etc" still existing at the frontal adjunct (jagamohana) of the Lingaraja temple at Bhubaneswara. Medama Devi's father, Komi Nayaka and his wife Nangma have also donated two unextinguishable flames (akhanda dipam) to Madhukeswara temple of Mukhalingam in 1113 A.D. and 1128 A.D.

These inscriptions are important from various angles, but it reveals some vital information with regard to Sri Jayadeva of Kurma pataka. He was a student of religion, philosophy and histrionic arts in the Sanskrit college functioning within the precincts of Sri Kurmeswara temple of Kurma pataka and was already indoctrinated by the cults od Madhwacharya and Nimbarka. He was a famous Siddhapravara by the time he was the principal of that Sanskrit college.

Jayadeva's college admitted lots of 'apoorva nata' girls in the faculty of histrionic arts and Nangma, Komi Nayaka's wife, was one of Jayadeva's dance students. Medama Devi, Nangma and Komi's daughter was also a student of dance department. This account proves that Sri Jayadeva stayed there as a Principal for a very long time. He composed songs, taught Kalingan classical music and choreography to the students along with teaching religion and philosophy.

Chodaganga Deva had invited Jayadeva on the occasion of his son Kamarnava Deva's coronation ceremony held in 1147 A.D. at Puri. It was also the day on which the renovated temple of Lord Jagannatha was inaugurated. Sri Jayadeva, the Sadhupravara was invited from Srikurma pataka to perform Hari Lila on the nata- mandapa of Sri Jagannatha Temple. Most of the apoorva nata girls enthralled the scholastic audience of Puri by the performance of Hari Lila that embodied the songs of Gita govinda. Choda Ganga Deva, on the recommendation of the pundits of Puri, granted a large piece of landed property to Sri Jayadeva at Kendu Vilwa village and the apoorva nata girls were settled on the north side of the Jagannatha temple. The street in which these natis (dancers) settled was called Chudanga Sahi, named after Chodaganga Deva. R.D.Banerjee's History of Odissa, Vol-1 "records an order for the performance of dances at the time of bhoga (the time for offering the cooked food to the Lords) from the end of the evening Dhupa up to the time of Badasingara (the jargon of the temple is used to denote the Lord's bed time). It refers to a number of dances from the Telugu country and that besides dancing four Vaishnava singers would sing Jayadeva's Gita Govinda" Sri Jayadeva had written two Odia songs at his Kenduvilwa monastery, but he would be remembered only for his Gita Govinda, a Sanskrit poetic work (hymns, narratives, and songs combined), unique and incomparable. Composed in 12 sargas (cantos) and twentyfour songs in different classical ragas, the Gita Govinda exercises tremendous influence on Kavisurya, Gopalakrishna and lots of poets who composed champu and chautisa poems in 18th and 19th centuries. Prior to that when Sri Chaitanya visited Puri in 1510 A.D. and indoctrinated the Pancha sakhas, Odia poetic milieu invested all the qualities of Srikrishna on Jagannatha and turned the temple into a hub of Vaishnavite culture. Lord Jagannatha was also envisioned as Srikrishna, as one clad in yellow silk and decked in a garland of wild flowers with a bluish dark skin anointed in sandal paste and sandal oil and jeweled ear-rings playing on his cheeks.

Gita Govinda begins with a narrative that is nonlinear the description of an environment that induces suspense: meghei meduram ambaram vanabhuvah:

The sky is overcast, the woodland's dark
With the boughs of tamala creepers
Dark nights frighten Kanha
O, Radha! Take him back home, back!
Take him quick!"
-thus said Nanda,
The cowherd's chief, and at his behest
They all had left.
But Radha took him for a sport
Under the bower's rest
By the bank of Yamuna.

The tryst between Radha and Krishna depicted in this long Sanskrit poem in 12 cantos and the couple of Odia poems were very often inspiring to the Panchasakhas and king Purushottama Deva wrote Abhinava Gitagivinda.. With the help of the apoorva natis, the king had introduced mahari rituals in the temple.

Jayadeva's Vaishnavite philosophy imbedded a streak of eroticism and the interpreters who attempt to repress it raise ridiculous doubts. What generates controversies today is the contention of the Vaishnava devotees. They interpret the emerging darkness in the woodlands as a metaphysical code, as the "clouds" of nescience overcasting the the world. Odissan transcendentalists would interpret reading something beyond the physical sex, that takes place 'under the bower's rest', "by the bank of Yamuna." The act of crossing the boundary of sexuality and idealizing the action of Radha and Krishna under the darkening bowers as 'divinity' appears untenable to the western readers of Gita govinda. Does philosophy equate carnality with divinity? Can the nature of spirituality be different from ordinary experience? By what measures does one distinguish divine ecstasy from physical frisson? If so, why don't the Vaishnavites elaborate on the topic? And how do they differentiate Sahaja Yana from the Raganuga bhakti of Vaishnavism?

All these questions gain extra significance in the context of Vaishnavism that still overpowered the Odia society of 12th century. The crux of Odia poetry is a growing polemics between sex and morality, and this sense of tension keeps the Charya -Natha divisions alive after the alphabets in Odia were invented. The libertine sex of charya poems contrasting with the urgency of a yogic discipline of the Nathas has somewhere given a philosophic synthsis, a resolution in Jaya Deva's Gita Govinda. The conflicting time of the 12th century needed a Jaya Deva in Kalingan milieu infested with Pali, different scripts and a different mindset.

Different scripts were in use in different mandalas where kings from different dynasties ruled. The scripts engraved on rocks symbolized knowledge as power. Authority flowed from the power of knowledge to matured recipients. Inscribed in the epigraphic records from Ashoka onwards was a politics of learning and of politico-cultural transmission. The power of learning and textification is manifested most authoritatively in Madala Panji. M.M.Chakravarty, in an essay captioned, "Geography of Orissa in 16th century records", writes, "Madala Panji would thus, mean a chronicle of the Royal orders". (17)

Thus, after the inscriptions, we get the subsequent traces from Madala Panji, or, the temple chronicles, that began to be scribed under the initiation of king Chodaganga Deva toward the last part of the 11th century or the first part of 12th century A.D. This proves that some kind of hybrid prose was in vogue between 5th to 11th century and the records were destroyed during the Mughal Afgan atrocities in Odissa.

With the invasions and atrocities changed the mindsets of people. They no longer believed in religion and its transcendental values. Nitei Dhobuni of Suvarnapur lapsed into folk lore. But in the 11th century she was known as one of the seven major lady prophets and last seven Sahajayana disciples of Lakshminkara. The Sapta Kumaries (seven spinsters) were Madana Maluni (a garland maker florist), Nitei Dhobani(a washer woman), Luhukuti Lahurani(a black-smith woman), Sua Teluni(an oil woman), Patra-pindhi Sauruni(a saura tribal woman who clad herself in leaves), Sukuti Chamaruni(a cobblers' woman) and Gangi Gauduni(a milk maid).These seven low-caste subaltern women were famous Buddhist tantriks who could generate miracles in terms of their power. Madala Panji records how Nitei was able to enthrone Choda Ganga Deva safely and enshrined Lord Jagannatha on the Bhairavi chakra which was brought from Oddiyana(Suvarnapur) and installed in the sanctum. The installation of the Bhairavi chakra transformed the puja offerings of the Lord Jagannatha into Mahaprasada which can be shared by people from all castes and religions. The present Brahminic norms with regard to the entry of non-Hindus may be a new norm for security reasons, but in fact, Bhairavi Tantra did not admit caste distinctions in Jagannatha temple.

The contemporary critics discover an element of fantasy in the records of Madalapanji: the episode, for example, relating to Nitei Dhobani (The great Washer woman Sahaja prophet from Oddiyana who was the architect of the career of Chodaganga Deva). She was found cooking in an oven putting her own leg into it as a piece of wood. This episode should not have been criticized as an exaggerated 'fantasy' by the modern professors who are educated in colonial times and began to advocate "scientism" immediately after independence.

The episode of Nitei Dhobani mentioned in Madala Panji is neither a figment of the Panjia Karana's imagination, nor did it have an element of fantasy. If the temple of Lord Jagannatha is not to be marginalized, it has to be accepted that the entire Jagannatha-culture of Odissa is based on Tantra. The technocratic societies viewed it as a threat to their survival. Tantra is antithetical to their capitalistic notions of production, consumption and liberty. The prose of Madala Panji presents us with a free combination of history and legend, sharing a system of belief interchangeably with each other.

It does not matter at all whether our historians with colonial mindset believed in the textualized accounts of Madala Panji or not. What is remarkable here is that writing, as Derrida defines, brings home the "logic of the supplement:"The invention of the scripts in Urjam (1051 AD- Kalinga) and those reinvented during the Somavamsi kings in Suvarnapur area are different, though a keen observer would discern hieroglyphically angular shapes as a common feature in both the scripts.

The shapes and the varieties of sign system used in different areas do not concern us at this point. Textuality, whether in the shape of stone inscriptions, and copper plates or, in the records of Madala Panji has engendered interpretative complications, The description of a single historical incident, be it the childhood records of Choda Ganga Deva, or, Kapilendra Deva, is textualized differently. Paramananda Tripathy's Odisara Pratna Tattva-O-Anyanya Prabandha-Part-II (1972) records how Jagabandhu Singh's Utkalara Itihasa and Harekrishna Mahatab's Histrory of Orissa quote Madala Panji extensively to substantiate facts about Odissan history. Our postcolonial historians do not believe in what has been textualized in the Panji. In stead of making a faithful representation of the belief-system of the 12th — 13th century culture, we cast them into the dustbins of legends. The story of Natei Dhobani would be quoted and translated from Madala Panji later, while discussing about the Odia scripts and culture of the South Indian Ganga Kings.

The next chunk of Odia prose can be discerned in Chakada Pothi, and Chakada Basana the writing of which begins with king Pratap rudra Deva (1467-1540). A series of stories are contained in Chakada Pothi: the story of the Brahmin of Dagarapada, the story of the conquest of Kanchi, Anikia Adikanda Misra Katha, and the five accidents that occurred in Bamadeva Pani's house etc. The Chakada pothi narrates how the king and the queen gifted the villages for the Brahmins, how tanks were dug in Agrahara villages and other details. These are, to use an indigenous Sanskrit term, historical akshyayikas and they reflect a large part of the sociological practices of the mediaeval Odissa The Chakada Pothi narrates many such sociological happenings that occurred from the time of Pratapa Rudra Deva to Divyasingh Dev-1. It is interesting to note that all these prose writings from stone inscriptions, copper grants to the palm leaf writings in stylus endeavoured to record history, either the accounts of the kings or of the common plebians.

The next evidence comes from a book called Ghumusara RajaVamsavali, but that was written much later, during the eighteenth century. The language of this palace chronicle has tinges of Southy Kalingan Odia and the scholars of Odisa refuse to officialize the dialect. It is an irony that though the Odia scripts, language and literature were nourished in Kalinga, the postcolonial academicians tend to put all emphases on the Utkala brand of Odia, marginalizing those of Kalinga and Kosala. In fact, the linguistic signs developed in Bikramkhole and

Urjam paved the way for its nourishment in Kosala, during the period of the Somavansi Kings and the era of the Gangas. The subsequent phase of the evolution of Odia prose can be traced in the literature of the "vows-and-the rituals" (Osha-Vrata-Katha) presumably written by the diaspora Brahmins who came either from the South or from Kanyakubja during the Early Gangas. They learnt the scripts and wrote these books of folk-religion. Some Brahmins had also come from adjacent linguistic communities during the reign of the Somavamsi Kings of Suvarnapur between the 5th and the 10th century A.D. But these Brahmin Diasporas were treated with a touch of mild derision because of their daily dependence on the other castes, and since they were neither erudite in Sanskrit nor in Odia. They were never the elites of the community. But their advice was sought on mundane matters. So, they wrote these folk religious Vrata Kathas, prevalent in their regions and culled from other languages, to be recited before illiterate female folks. That was perhaps a sociological necessity and this literary art promoted their earnings.

The language of Somanatha Vrata Katha, Savitri Vrata Katha, Trinath Mela and Mangala Osha etc. are still spoken in North Kalingan villages. The Osha-Vrata prose was carried over to the non-metrical, unrhymed/rhymed prose of the Pancha Sakha age (16th century). Thus, one traces the continuity of the Nathist trend till the Panchasakha's period. It also merged into a part of the National Bhakti movement.

Jagannatha Dasa's Tula bhina and Balarama Dasa's Brahma Gita provide illustrations for such prose:

"Kanare Sunila Katha putare manare na ghenibu xxx Sugandha durgandha emananku eka kari ghenibu." (Tulabhina meaning ginning cotton) [My son, trust the words you hear (by ears). The bipolar notions of fragrance and foul smell are to be erased). Similarly, In Brahma Gita, Balarama writes "Srikrishna harasa hoi Arjunanku gyana kahanti vichara. E gyana muni mane suni joga sadhile" (Sri Krishna was pleased to impart some jnana to Arjuna. The sages heard the words of this jnana, practiced yoga and emerged as saints).

Sisu Ananta Dasa's Kumara Bodha is a prose treatise that explains the teachings of Samkhya in colloquial prose. But the most important of the prose writings of the medieval times are Vatrisa Sinhasana and Rudrasudhanidhi. A 14th century writer named Kshemankar wrote the stories of Vatrisa Simhasana (thirty two thrones) briefly. In Odia, two prose translations are available: one by Siva Das and the other by Jagannath Sinha. The Odia title is Vatrisa Simhasana. In Hindi it is Simhasana Vatrisi and in South Indian languages, it is captioned as Vetala Panchavimsati.

Narayanananda Abadhuta Swami's Rudra Sudhanidhi excels other prose writings as a debut in our prose romance. The text was not available in its entirety till 1930s. The verse romances written in Odia since the composition of Ushavilasa and Sasi Sena could, despite all their rasa and alamkara, be assigned only to oral literature since the kavyas were only sung to. Perhaps, Rudrasudhanidhi was also read out, but the Odia plebians were already used to listening to the recitals of Savitri Vrata Katha and Somanatha Vrata Katha during ritual pooja ceremonies.

Rudra Sudhanidhi, the first serious venture in Prakrit Odia, is comparable to Sarala's Mahabharata in its effect. But the oldest of our prose writings, Rudra Sudhanidhi has been periodized in between 12 th and 13 th centuries. Dr.Krishna Charana Sahu dates the manuscript around 1473 A.D. But Kedarnath Mahapatra, an authority on Orissan history and manuscripts, dates the book as a post-12th century treatise. Thus, its influence on Sarala Das is discernible (Baliar Singh 117-118). (18) Jantrana Parikshit's book Rudra Sudhanidhi: :Sailee-O-Saundarya (2009) makes an extensive and scholarly discussion on various aspects of its unfinished text. Artaballava Mohanty categorizes the genre as "neither prose nor poetry", but written in a running metre (Dandi-Vritta), while Dr. Prahallada Pradhan identifies that Dandi-Vritta style was introduced in post - Sarala Das compositions. The concepts that are discussed in the text signal that it was an early Panchasakha writing, states Jantrana Parikshit, "but written before 1510". But the philological symptoms (use of the word 'Mughal') of Rudrasudhanidhi show that Madala Panji was written 40/50 years after Rudra Sudhanidhi. Dr. Karunakar Kar's research has lead to a notion that the poetic prose was written after Sarala Das and before Balarama Das. Kedarnath Mohapatra reads Udayana Acharya not only as a wise scholar living in Ananga Bhima Deva's court, but also as the author of explanatory notes on Nashadiya Charita and Gitagovinda.

The stylistic peculiarities of Rudrasudhanidhi are the contributions of its author Narayana Abadhuta Swamy, a saint of that period who worshipped Rudra, Jagannatha and Lord Vishnu.

But the prose narrative does, in no place, authenticate that its author was a saint; except that he attempted to blend the Saivite and the Vaishnavite differences into a syncretic concept. Perhaps a poetic soul was lying hidden within this saint. Otherwise, he could not have created the first 'romance' of our literature. It seems Abadhuta Swamy had a feel for Sanskrit works and mode of classical representation. Hence a very powerful romantic story was presented to the audience of his time under the mask of religion. It was obviously an experimental literary engagement and St. Narayana had the guts to face the society in which vernacular literature was looked down as a degraded practice.

That was the requirement of early Odia mediaeval period. The writers could seek a license from the gods of invocation to articulate stories and real events, which would have been rejected by the public as impolite representation. The romance, though laid the foundation stone for the riti romance that would emerge after more than 400 years , sublimates Abadhuta Swamy's repressed wishes. Rudrasudhanidhi's use of uncanny, magic and supernaturalism pave the way for Dhananjaya Bhanja's Anangarekha and Devadurlabha's Rahasyamanjari.

Narayana Abadhuta Swamy has, as a Sanyasi, pulled down all tantric yogic and magical features to the ordinary people and proved that the Odia saints did not stay detached from the world, but could come to authenticate that their powers do relate to the grass roots.

Although it embodies concepts about jnana(knowledge), bhakti(devotion) and yoga (focused meditation for the union of the concrete and the abstract), Rudrasudhanidhi can be categorized as a katha, not an akshayika. But it seems, the manuscript has not been retrieved in its entirety. The five chapters of Rudrasudhanidhi reveal the birth of Rudrasudhanidhi, the growth of the hero, the quest for a bride, the arrival of a Kapalika named Kamananda, who plans to kidnap the girl by deploying tantra. The rest of the story is not available to us.

The format of the romance reveals that it has been inspired by Sanskrit romances like Dasa Kumara Charitam, but it has already been discussed how a number of such romances have been written in post-Rudrasudhanidhi period, the riti-kavya verses. The persistence of romance, perhaps, poses problems even graver than those generated by the childhood of Odia prose-its archaic nostalgia with which Rudrasudhanidhi becomes associated. It raises something like an aesthetic counterpart to the problem of ideology. It could have been rescued through fresh interpretations form its trivialization at the hands of taboo ridden, modern aesthetes.

The discovery of the manuscript of Sarana Dasa's Chacheri Lila provides another instance of medieval prose. The palm leaf scripts do not provide any hint about its author Sarana Das. But the story hinges around the Dola Jatra (Holi Festival) in Sri Mandir (Jagannatha Temple). The temple chronicles (Madala Panji) reveals that the festival was introduced in "Sakabda 1483 or, 1571 A.D. (Baliar Singh 149).

So, Chacheri Lila is expected to be a text of 16th or 17th century, a medieval text, anyway. The story of Chacherilila, described in half poetic style, is set on a background of the Holi festival in the temple of Jagannatha, when the images of Madan Mohan appear on a palanquin to be worshipped outside the sanctum sanctorum. The historical records inform that the celebration of the Dola Utsav (Holi) started in the temple much before the ascension of the fallen king of Khurda (Ramachandra Deva II who married a Muslim girl and was debarred from entering into the temple premises). Others claim that it started in 17th century.

Chacheri Lila is a romance embodying the story of Radha's birth, growth, and her marriage with Chandrasena. The astrological records of the pair were calculated to be inauspicious. Radha's father was upset and he went to Gobardhan hills to meditate. A blue coloured divine person (Krishna) appeared and consoled that he would marry Radha in disguise.

This wonderful romance, perhaps not known to any commoner, has episodic connection with Achyutananda's Gopalanka Ogala, Narayana Dasa's Panchamrita Sindhu Bindu and Bipra Kantha Dasa's Na' poi and from such extrapolations it leads one to believe that Chacheri Lila might be a prose text of eighteenth century. Leaving the dispute to the historians, let us examine the prose style of the book. The sentences are found to be telegraphic sentences: "Nabajuba bali, Mane bhali, Kemante Kama Keli." (Young girl. Thinks. How to play the game of sex.)

Another major text of Odia prose written in eighteenth century is Brajanath Badajena's Chatura Binoda (C.1755-1765), a text that is supposed to entertain the court pundits. It is a collection of short stories under four chapters:

Hasya Binoda, Rasa Binoda, Niti Binoda and Preeti Binoda. The prose of Badajena is more matured and developed than that of Rudrasudhanidhi and Chacheri Lila. A central story branches off into

History of Ancient Odia Literature | 77

17 episodes of sub-stories in various ways. In Hasa Binoda, a subplot extends into another. The stories of Rasa Binoda are different. A substory expands into three branches and in PreetiBinoda into six branches. The descriptions would appear slightly vulgar now, because of its permissive narratives, but the prose is fully developed and the plots seem to have been structured dramatically. The present author has scripted these stories in screenplay form and they have been telecast in 2000 A.D.in Doora Darshan, Cuttack

The sporadic prose writings of the medieval period available to us are considered as a treasure-house of worldly wisdom, but the essays never speak of subjects like shrewdness, sagacity and tact etc. as one would notice in the essays of Francis Bacon. The writers were mostly saints and they talked about high ideals, moral issues and about the problems of yogic practices. These prophets wrote well-knit and compact poetic essays with no digressions, The essays reflect the religious, moral and philosophical issues of medieval Odissa. Religion was a binding force in that society. Although different branches of religious systems had already confused the kings and the ordinary men, the medieval prose writers endeavored to put forth the wholesome logic, common to all sects so that conflicts owing to dissensions would be avoided.

An extensive survey of early mediaeval prose reveals how it crosses the chronotopic boundary of Nathist literature and extends up to 18th century through linguistic and syntactic affinity. The readers must have noticed that the metaphysics of Charya songs lapsed into Sahajiya pornocracy and the people during the Nathist mode of society felt more responsible and civilized not to democratize sex as was done during the Madana pooja celebration.

A war between philosophy and poetry had already started as it happened in Plato's Republic (10.607). Poetry was almost banned and drab prose narratives for religious propaganda replaced the porno metaphoric poems. But even after the invention of alphabets and palm-leaf textification, the creative people did not dare to exercise their imagination. The guardians of literature were prophetic in temperament and the prose that was produced with neoclassical discipline could not appeal to the ordinary listeners (the readers did not emerge by that time). Rudrasudhanidhi, or Chacheri Lila, or even, the 18th century Chatura Binoda could hardly keep the listeners spell bound. In short, it was a period of literary uncertainty.

The question of relationship between the popular and the ecclesiastical/learned cultures also raised new complications about the relationship between the oral and the written traditions of early mediaeval period. But the oral traditions of the distant past could not be directly recorded in mediaeval Odissa.

One feels proud to comprehend that the tendency of the medieval prose writings was to signify a civilization founded on religion and notions of immortality. But they carefully avoided the sophistication of the feudal/institutional saints. That was a period of a welter of spiritual belief systems in which many people believed that they were capable of exercising their own free choice,- that physical objects exist independently of perception, that there is a creator of the universe, that they have a soul and so on . Still other people held that such notions were also the denials of some, or, most of all of these beliefs. The prose writing of the period, especially those written by Jagannatha Dasa, Balarama Dasa, Achyutananda and Sisu Ananta Das were so colloquial and seemed so naïve that it can be argued that they seemed to resemble the thoughts of ordinary men. These saints revealed themselves in the most uninteresting and uneventful life of the ordinary man-on-the-street and these masters, like the Zen Buddhist Philosopher, Suzuki, discussed such subjects as appealed to the common man. It is interesting to note that the made of life lived by the Nathist Yogis can be rediscovered in the lives of the Pancha Sakhas (the era of five ascetic pals writing almost as contemporaries).

It is unfortunate that our contemporary critics could not take the advantage of discussing these prose writings in the light of Zen Buddhism or of Madhyamika Philosophy. Odia medieval prose, otherwise, would have offered to the world a new school of philosophical thought, embodying a syncretic realization of life, so prominently over-shadowed by the perennial polemics of empiricism.

With "text" and "writing" conceived as modes of discursive engagement, the importance of so-called literary texts and writing becomes obvious : they are among the most highly achieved, most economical exercises of discourse we encounter everyday in sloppier, less visible versions, they make the premise of discourse evident.

The Nathist corpus of literature focuses on practices and refuses in so many ways to accept the distinction between practice and thought, between the material and the transcendental realities. Such narrative literally recalls readers to their senses by focusing attention on the yogic practices of sharpening the levels of consciousness and sensibility.

We may also argue that textification that began with Nathist literature since about 11th century (post-1051 A.D.) reveals to us a large discursive frame of discussion, mostly on history, history as the most powerful construct of realistic convention.

But despite all these complex booms of civilization harvested from the fields of textuality, there existed a reverse in the countryside Orissa, where people did hardly know and master any script. They still continued to play their roles only as listeners of literary compositions. The diaspora Brahmins who were brought from Kanauj area mostly by the Kalachuri kings of Western Odissa wrote some Vrata katha stories (stories of vernacular religion) to be read out to the naïve villagers on the days of those ritual worship in a typical indigenous mode. Gradually, these texts (Lakshmi puja, Khudurukuni osha, Trinath mela etc.)

Osha-Vrata Katha

Osha-Vrata -Katha refers to narratives pertaining to folk religious vows and rituals, written in prakrit-mixed colloquial Odia. These narratives may be accepted as substitutes for Puranic litetature. Our ancient sages have attached more importance to the passages in puranas than those of the Vedas, in which the puranas were treated as part of them and not as separate literature. The puranas were, in fact, intended to explain the Vedic doctrines to lay minds. But with our faulty education system and emphasis on western logic, they have been devalued and being treated as childish stories.

Max Mueller treated the language of the Upanishadas as "child's babblings" and excepting Sri Aurobindo, no one in India had raised a voice of protest for such derogatory remarks. Like the Indians, the Odias also had a naïve, servile, obedient, mindset that digested the abusive, uncultured and prejudiced remarks of Max-Mueller. Rather we have accepted such immature, nescient remarks as some semaphore of Western wisdom that has highlighted Tragedy as the worthy drama of life. There is no tragedy in Indian Natya Sastra.

The literature of the Osha and Vrata (vows and rituals) rituals are partially folk versions of the Puranas with axiological endings. Contemporary ritologists support the notion that ritual is an important variable not just in tribal cultures, but also in modern industrial cultures. The study of the literature of the vows like Somanatha Vrata Katha, Khudurukuni Osha, Sudasa Vrata Katha makes serious inroads into the traditional preserves of our cultural studies.

The word Vrata is a folk version of the Sanskrit word 'vratya'. An entire book of the Atharva Veda (Book XV) is dedicated to the vratyas and their transfigurations. The Vratyas were a host of consecrated people within the Vedic traditions. Little is known about them to us today apart from what is recorded in the Atharva Veda. They were clad in a black, fringed garments; the black colour distinguished their attire, and it similarly did portray also Rudra when he appears on the sight of the sacrifice by the Angirases. The Vratyas wore turbans and carried lances and bows (Atharva Veda, 15.2.4.). The name is derived from Vrata, a host, which in turn, might have connection with Vrata, a vow or observance of a sacred ordinance. In the Satarudreeya hymn to the hundred forms and powers of Rudra, the leaders of hosts (Vrataspati) are invoked. This ecstatic litany imbued with the presence of the god opens with a homage to his wrath, to his arrow, to his bow. A Vratapa is the guardian of the Vow and ordinance (Vrata)whom the Rudra Brahman lauds.

In a state dominated by tribal cultures, the Brahminic and Buddhist rituals of drawing yantras and mandalas (geometric triangles and circles as surrogate forms of mother energies) are reduced to simple drawings of alpana (mostly floral designs drawn in rice- paste or chalkstones in front of homes). These are as much concerned with the mythic and symbolic repertoire of our common existence as with doctrinal pronouncements, litterae divinae reliquaries containing particles of the yantras, denominational affiliation, or ecclesiastic politics associated with organized bodies of religious worship.

The names of the authors are kept hidden since these folk versions of religious worship are intended to be given an eternal and impersonal dimension. The Savitri Vrata Katha is recited even today by every Odia married woman on the day of Savitri Amavasya, falling on the month of Jyestha. The husbands would be deified and worshipped and the Savitri Vrata Katha would be recited on that day. The languages of these Kathas are quasi-poetic, lyrical and lucid, but the anonymous, diaspora folk poets could not write metrical lines.

The Sudasa Vrata Katha is about the worship of Goddess Lakshmi on the 10th day of the bright fortnight of the month of Magha.

A Brahmin Lady named Lakshmivati from Avanti Nagar prepares a ten knotted thread to be tied on her arms to please Lakshmi, but an eagle takes in away the knotted thread from the pond that was in the forest. The Brahmin Lady was weeping since the Vrata, or the ritualistic ordinance could not be ceremonized without the thread. King Nala was passing by that route and he stopped near to ameliorate her distress. On being asked, the Brahmin Lady narrated her plight and King Nala promised her to bring back the ritual thread.

The king begged a thread from his queen. The reluctant queen was compelled to give the thread since the king had to keep up his promise. The event led to king Nala's financial deprivation etc.

Similarly, the tales related to Khudurukuni Osha, Trinath Mela, Sarba Mangala Osha and Sanischara Mela have probably been written by the diaspora Brahmins who neither knew Sanskrit nor learnt Odia. They attempted poetry, but failed and wrote some half-rhymed prose. They migrated to Orissa from Kanyakubja. They would have taken some time to settle and learn the language, alphabets and then they would have written these stories in quasi -poetic language that created a genre by their typical metered prose bordering on poetry.

The literature of Vows and rituals which the ladies observe mostly and occasionally by some men in the rural Odisa, gradually has transformed as a part of the ritual. Such literature has become, inter alia, the symbolic code for interpreting and negotiating events of everyday existence. Such literature, which is often neglected by the academicians, may be investigated through psychological, sociological and anthropological disciplines. Ritual and Vow literature is more than mere symbolic expression in some kind of socio-cultural semaphore. On the contrary, such literature forms the warp on which the tapestry of culture is woven, thereby opening a vista for the medieval, illiterate women.

The Charya and Nathist poets were highly symbolic since they articulated on an eco-feministic milieu. It was difficult for Odia mass of the subseqauent period to follow its prestine, tantric metaphysics. The subsequent period of sanskritisation was concerned with Brahminic minds only, confined only to courtly elites. The Sudras, who subsequently emerged as a caste out of the marital relation with the tribals, did never get a scope for developing a world view of their own, though they have one. Sarala Das's Mahabharata opened up a channel for articulation of such a world view. Let us examine one item of such knowledge: "Sapata Dina jebe hoiba suddha anga/ stiri purusha je hoibaka sanga." (On the seventh day after the periods, when the woman's body shall be pure again, a man can sleep with her).

Such micro rituals of everyday existence provided in Sarala's Mahabharata created the grammatology of everyday living, which our tribe-based Odias did not obey. The vernacular Mahabharata generated such axioms for the underdeveloped society. The documentation of this ritual literature served as the cultural matrix for the Odia Sudra world, as the hinge for mass culture, as the linchpin of mass society. Literature, we may conclude, paved the way for the foundation of institutional family life.

Jagannatha Dasa's Bhagabata (Translation) was recited by the Purana Pandas in the Bhagabat Tungis (derived from the tribal 'common houses' for the bachelors of the village). The Sanskrit word Upasana (worship) was reduced to Usha/Osha in rural/oral Odia and the Diaspora Brahmins tried to compose poems about the Vratas (taking a vow to worship with greater determination of mind. The term is authenticized in Atharva Veda). People who were not well versed in the Vedic rituals were directed to observe the Vrata(s). The process of such religious observances, and their axiological consequences etc. were testified through an imaginary story and the Diaspora Brhamins composed them in a poetic form that was worse than prose, a language that had great affinity with medieval Nathist literature. Rudra sudhanidhi embodies some such diction. An example would help us to conceptualize this linguistic evolution.

Emanta se Laxmi devi apanaku apane aparate pai paribari mananku pacharile. Agae mu e Kanyara prayeka disai ki. Eha suni boile semane bho devi Jagatara Lakshmi Narayana ra patamahishi ti. Tumbhanku tulaibaku nahin. Puni ehi tora duhita praya disai". (19).

The language of the different Vrata kathas (the stories embodying vernacular religion in Purana style) is almost similar and their authors did not mention their names. However, the following vratas are observed popularly in countryside Odissa event today; and the tradition is handed down to the Odia societies of 21st century.

Prof. Kunjabihary Dash (1914-1994), in his Lokagita-O-Kahani (20) mentions the list of the vratas observed in folk loric Odissa: Somanatha Vrata, Kukkuti Vrata, Kedara Vrata, Vajra Mahakali Vrata, Rabinarayana Vrata, Sudasa Vrata, Rai-Damodara Vrata, Ananta Vrata, Risi Panchami Vrata, Kaudia Vrata, Gurubara (Thursday) Vrata. Besides these Vratas, the Odia's Observe the following Oshas (folk-religious ordinances in which Upasana or worship is done on a non-vedic, folk level as it belong to the folk religious belief system): Janhi Osha, Budhei Osha, Khudurukuni Osha, Shathi (Sashthi) Osha, Kanjianla Osha, Bali Trutiya, Dvitiya Osha, Chaitra Mangalabar (the Tuesday of the month of Chaitra and Pousha Ravibara (The Sundays of the Month of Pousha: Sun-worship). These authorless texts may therefore, be put under the rubric of folklores.

For every Osha and Vrata there is a recitative literature that is read either by the observant woman or, in emergencies, by a touring Brahmin who makes a living by functioning as the head of such Vernacular religious ceremonies. They were diaspora Brahmins from Kannauj (must be inexperts who could not compete with others in Caste-specific profession) who were not properly trained in karma kanda and the Vedic science of different modes of religious worships). Probably, they were not yet engaged in learning Odia. Yet like the Nathist mendicants, (most of whom came from Gujarat and Jalandhar), they, too, started writing vernacular religious stories called Osha-Vrata-Katha with folk religious slant).Odia prose and poetry, in general, the entire vocabulary was enlarged and attenuated, no doubt, under the pressures.

However, our folklorists like Prof. Kunjabihari Dash have identified a relationship between the folk religious life and an inherent reflexivity entwined psychologically with it. Such vernacular religion-related literature had been emphasized after the Nathist mendicants started writing on Yogic practices etc. The Vernacular religion and its literature followed the line of the Nathist Mahaveena Vratakatha style.

Late Prof. Kunja Bihari Dash had often encountered such religious beliefs during his field studies and some of the next generation folklorists like Dr. Prasanna Kumasr Mishra (Poet, playwright and novelist) were found engaged in theorizing vernacular religious belief system and practices. Literature has always reflected the sociological practices of a particular age.

One of the hall-marks of the study of vernacular religion has been its attempt to do justice to belief and lived experience. The folklorists have done much to open scholarly eyes to the experiential factors that lie behind many such folk belief systems. They have done this not by psychologising beliefs and believers, but by taking seriously what people say, feel and experience.

The literature related to these vernacular religious ceremonies might not be of great literary value but they transpire the Odia tribe's cultural existence. Such literature was included in the academic courses in 1950s. The Somanatha Vrata Katha, edited by Prof. Janaki Ballav Mahanty (1968) (21) appears modern in its language. Perhaps the refined stage has been reached because of subsequent modifications made by academician-editors every time it was prepared for the next print.

Folklorists have followed a two-tired model separating the folk and the institutionalized religion. Folk religion has not opposed the central religious body in an organized form at anytime. The literature of the vernacular religion (22) might have been marginalized by the new-fangled colonial scholars and the espousers of avant-gardism, but in small pockets, groups of women in a locality still observe "Budhei Osha" or "Khudurukuni. A senior woman, who still trusts in her tradional folk wisdom, recites these vernacular poems. The poem's recitative efficacy can only be realized in their ritualized and sacramental observances. Such literature becomes operative in relation to a class-structured view of society; in relation to power evident in social divisions of class, economics, race, ethnicity, gender, sexual performance etc. These factors do profoundly influence the life of such literature. It is evidenced by the fact that they are read and honoured during these seven/eight hundred years.

The literature concerning vernacular religion embodies parables. But with all our modern gadgets and gizmos, computerized techniques and advanced space crafts, we could neither erode nor delink those systems of folk beliefs. Whether the Odias are conservative or not, some of us have definitely crossed boundaries and strangely our literary culture nostalgically preserves them to redefine them as instances of postmodernism. Colonial scientism has also failed to nullify such beliefs as outdated. However the Vrata-katha literature has transited now from the palm-leaf collections to the printed pages.

Half of the Odia gods and goddesses have come from Austric culture and a recent survey also shows that the tribal oshas which had been appropriated by the urban folks have become extant in the tribal societies now. The parties in power have sold the tribal men and their culture to the multinational companies along with their mountains containing rare and precious minerals. The tribal people do no more like to be sold as anthropological curiosities, and have been constantly migrating to the urban, multicultural sectors of living. The Aryans who came from middle-east, appropriated some traits of the folk-tribal religious practices and consequently some Brahmin families also began to observe the vratas and Oshas (Ordinances). A compendium of these Oshas and Vrata-kathas record around eighty such rituals. A parable in prose or poetry is added to each one for spiritual recitation. Literature acquires here a spiritual status and the stories are believed to be as trustworthy as the mythologies.

Nagalu-chauthi Vrata is observed to worship the cobra and the lady cobra. A sterile woman from a merchant's family worshipped the cobra and prayed, "Have pity on me O, god Naga! Be kind to my family! Bless me with a son." The sacred snake couple was pleased to bless the merchant's wife. They said, "We' are pleased with you Merchant's wife, you have conceptually elevated our position. We would bless you now with seven sons in the coming seven years. Keep up this devotion, believe us unshakably and observe our vrata with utmost care. How arduous it might appear is" needless to reiterate here, that the lady's periods started thereafter regularly and a son was born to her. The sons grew up gradually, got married and they bred children. The grand children grew up and got married and so on. One year, the youngest grand-daughter-in - law, while preparing sweetmeats and cakes of different varieties for the pooja offering tasted small bits from every item and the cobra gods were angry. The same day she was blinded. They punished for her greed. The old lady and the other members of the family prayed to the cobra gods and the daughter in law's eye-sight was restored. The moment her sight was restored the cobra gods commanded, "Those who would observe this Vrata would keep their conscience clear. Those who would flout would be punished. Those who would criticize the observants would be maimed; leprosy would infect them, and they would be rendered sterile and impotent.

Those who would obey would thrive, the flouters would be doomed. The same thing happens in Somanatha Vrata Katha. The ardent practitioners are blessed to lead a life without diseases, their life-span increases to infinity, poverty stays away, and victory comes to them in every step. The number of such Oshas and Vratas are not less in our neighbour state Bengal. The helpless, lonely simpletons of the society live by such observances, observances which keep one women as the queen of the land,

and she prays the other woman to be a childless beggar and a maid servant to her. No one knows how many Odia women have led the life of a queen, but such Oshas and Vratas communicate how unhappy and unfulfilled life can be in a state perennially neglected by the Centre. Our Puranas and the parables of the Vrata are more precious to the four Vedas. The Odias are Vratyas (Observants of Vrata) after all.

If a deshi-margi polarity is allowed in literature, the Osha-Vrata parables in quasi poetic prose would be put taxonomically in the category of deshi. Today the categories interpenetrate and the margi is getting indigenized. The anonymous poets of our soil have enriched our literature by pouring down their liquefied life on the grass roots of the land on which generations of future Odias would tread and take final rest. Probably we are not fit enough to assess them through our postmodern logorrhea.

The intellectual dilemma that we have inherited from the British colony has its roots in understanding literature by their authors, while the literature of Vernacular Religion belongs to the entire community. The notion of "folk" has conjured up almost invariably an image of community. Tradition, being the key ingredient in triggering off folk cultural activities and ritual observances, these literarary works are equated with communal creation and recreation in an atmosphere of anonymity and the emphases has been laid on the transmission of knowledge, customs and beliefs through such anonymans channels in a mystical fashion." (Nicolaisen, 268). (23)

Prof. Bansidhar Mohanty had retrieved some folk songs of this period that are related to Natha religion. (24) He cites some examples that depict the origin of bibhuti, sacred thread (given to the male children in Brahmin families) and Rudraksha. There are interesting legends that had been created for the origin of such things. A fifth Veda has been created as Sisu Veda, and the aim of writing such stories of origin was to popularise these Nathist legends. Prof. Mohanty places Sisu Veda as a literary work of the 16th century.

Along with these specimens of literature we need not conclude that poetry was totally neglected after the invention of alphabets. Rather it has generated a lot of subgenres. One more subgenre of poetry, the historians have recorded is constituted of retelling of folktales, proverbs, riddles and the prophetic adages. Folk adages of mediaeval wisdom probably authoured by Khana and Daka are famous. Probably

Khana and Daka were touring Nathist Mendicants who traveled through Assam, Bengal and Odissa.

Proverbs and prophetic words continued as bits of oral tradition till the mid 1960s in rural Orissa. The granny used to titillate the cognitive state of young kids by asking them few ancient riddles. They were given/stored in children's grammar books at the end, but originally belonging to the oral tradition. These adages and proverbs make an entry into the boundary of our literature through two sources: (a) Tribal Tradition (b) Nathist scholastic tradition.

Pt. Suryanarayan Das, one of our famous early historians of literature dichotomized our literature into folk and elitist categories and has classified the folk literature of Odissa into the following categories. Since we concentrate in this chapter on the transition from Oral to the textual state of literature, the categories of Pt.S.N.Das would help us : i) Songs and ballads relating to festivals, celebrations, folk dances, songs of the Yogis, songs of fertility rituals/harvest rituals, Children's songs ii) Songs mixed with prose statements iii) Weeping songs (when the bride leaves her parental house or someone is dead) iv) Farmer's songs v) Folk tales vi) Proverbs and Adages. We would take up some proverbs, riddles and prophetic words as the 7th category of Pandit Surya narayan Das's parameters of folk literature.

Let us take up some translated versions of these untranslatable proverbs just for providing an impression of their existence as a subgenre of literature.

i) She started quite late
a business, (that's) never fortunate
It's like an old lady's elephantiasis
A diseased growth, that's her accrued profit
And the rest is Gnawed by the rat.
ii) Let me not regret
for my own thought
Rather, I must Dwell upon it First
I must sow that Later I'd harvest.
iii) The whore lives in luxury
while the chaste woman labours hard
To collect her food
The milk-man must vend
Hawking on the street
while the wine seller'd sit

selling his product in his own hut.
iv) There's no mango on the tree
Why do you shoot?
Your catapult, for no effect?
There's no money in the wallet
Why do you fix a tart?
And negotiate to cohabit?
v) He who beats his son In
front of his mother Is
called a true father She,
who pounds her legs On
the courtyard
Is a true older sister

The mediaeval folk conversationalists of Odissa, it seems, employed relatively coded vocabulary. They intended to hedge their lexical choices and remain referentially inexplicit. These are coded metaphoric sentences in which the signifiers obliquely relate to the signifides.

This mediaeval proverb related to family and society is loaded with Nathist philosophy. The Nathists emphasized the body, its transformations through yoga, its purification and rejuvenation. The wise man who wrote these adages anonymously, aimed at two things: the discovery and demonstration of truth and expressing it in coded metaphors. A continuous exposure to Buddhist and Nathist metaphysics through ludic use of language was a useful orientation for the rural folks of mediaeval Odissa. Their levels of comprehension could be sharpened so that the conceptual formations of Nathism expressed through multiple linguistic games could be communicated properly.

The proverbs and the adages, in a way, were appreciated in those days as a treasure-house of worldly wisdom. Worldly wisdom does not imply any deep philosophy. It did not impart either any ideal, moral knowledge. It simply meant that the art or the technique that a man should employ must achieve success in life. The proverbs, thus, embody shrewdness, tact, sagacity, foresight, judgment of character and many other things in a ludic mode.

The early mediaeval phase of Odissan history witnessed all round changes in the form of agrarian expansion, increasing rural settlements, feudal land tenure, new pattern of agrarian relations, and relative decline in trade, urbanization and deeply penetrating monetary economy. It also experienced the growth of social hierarchies due to fragmentation of varna and proliferation of castes, rigidity in the Brahminical order and the growing importance of the kayasthas and karanas after they mastered the scripts. Revolutionary changes took place in the structure of polity and the state achieved stability under a stronger monarchical form of governments allied with Brahminical order, with the help of massive land grants, and their consensus to obtain sanction to their exalted genealogies and divine Origin...(Panda, P.62) 25(a) The archaic prose of MadalaPanji records about one Basudeva Ratha, a Brahmin, who fell out of the grace of the Kesari kings and started worshipping Bhubaneswara Deva. The Panji records," A divine message was dispensed; "Go to the South. One chora (thief) Ganga is already born to a widow by the grace of Gokarnesvara. Meet him, bring him to Puri, and coronate that widow's son as the king". (Ibid)

The Brahmin set out for South and found Chora Ganga. The boy was playing a game with his friends donning the role of the king. The Brahmin sent a messenger. The game-king answered, "I've little time to talk to the Brahmin from Odissa. Ask him to wait. Let him give this token (he presented a broken pebble) to the sweetmeat shop. He'd feed him free. Fifteen days passed like this...then the boy, donning the role of a king summoned the Brahmin. The Brahmin reported, "Lord Bhubaneswara has commanded me in a dream that you'll have to be coroneted as the king of Odissa. Kindly come with me" (Madala Panji. Prachi edition, P.21-22) 25(b)

A similar story is also available in relation to Kapilendra Deva (1435-1467), the founder of the Suryavamsi dynasty in Odissa. This Panji Chronicles establishes the extra human powers of the Hindu Brahmins. Chodaganga Deva, though a Saivite by faith, built temples of Vishnu at Srikurmam and renovated the temple of Lord Jagannatha.The renovated Jagannatha temple was inaugurated on the day his son Kamarnava Deva was coroneted (1147 A.D.). Chodaganga Deva invited a performing troupe from Sri Kurma pataka to stage a dance drama captioned 'Hari Lila'. The poet Sri Jayadeva, the then principal of the Sanskrit School of Srikurmam pataka had come here to stage Harileela, written, composed and directed by him. The dancers, who performed were settled in Chudanga Street, Puri and the "mahari seva"(a ritual in which a dancer would dance in front of Lord Jagannatha in the night before the Lord retires to sleep) was started in the temple.

The dance presented by the Maharis of Srikurmam was known in 'Odissa Rajya' as Rahasa or Rasa and Jayadeva, by virtue of a copper grant was given a big area of land at Kenduvilva. (The total account is lifted from Sri Jayadeva- O-Sri Chaitanya, by Ajit Kumar Tripathy,I.A.S., Books India National, Bhubaneswar).

Prof. Nagendra Pradhan has traced two Odia songs written by Jayadeva: (i) Navina Sundara Syama nindita kotiye kama/ Hari-suta pati koti Srimukha Thani/Katire Pita basana Sakra Chapa neela Ghana dalita Ajna tanu markatamani gosthe rahile Hari godhana pala abori/ Bhane Jayadeva Kavi se pade sira.

(ii) Braja sukha sagara prema ujagara nagara bahu rasa ranga Nabaghana sundara sarasa manohara sulalita lalita tribhanga Rasi rasayanarasavati jeevana rasamaya rasa bihari Puchha mukuta sira pitambaradhara muralidhara giridhari.

Such compositions testify the process of Sanskritization in Orissa initiated during the Ganga dynasty. However, the larger group of the Odias living in other tracts stuck to their folk songs. Indonesia, whose material base was of such a stranded space that it could assimilate elements of that culture. Dr. Patitapaban Mishra provides an interesting example from Balinese system of religious belief. (26) "Siva is the elder brother of Budha and on ceremonial occasions four Saivite and one Buddhist priest perform the rituals. To the common people, the saying is: "He who is Siva is Buddha" (Ya Siva sa Buddha) (27).

The temple chronicles called Madala Panji (Prachi edition, p.36) records that the king Kavi Narasimha (W.W.Hunter identifies him with Kesari Narasimha (1282-1317 A.D.) inaugurated the Gitagovinda in the liturgyof the temple.

The practices of the Nathist sect and its characteristics of a religious syncretism had again been re-circulated here. We do not know how with these reformative attitudinal changes passed four hundred years and the Ganga dynasty gave way to the Suryavansi Gajapatis. The collapse of the Ganga dynasty is ascribed to repeated attacks of the Muslims.

The Bahamanis from the South (later dismembered into five new kingdoms which included the Sultanate of Golkunda), the Muslim conquests of Bengal and Bihar and finally, the lonely existence of a Hindu state in Orissa provoked the Muslims. The reign of Kapilendra Deva (1435-1468) completed the early mediaeval period of Odia literature.

The history of this period is mostly retrieved by the scholars from the epigraphic sources, in which Kapilendra circulated a story that he was chosen by lord Jagannath as the successor of the last Ganga king Bhanudeva. Late Manmohan Chakravorty has translated the relevant portion in the Journal of the Asiatic Society of Bengal. The epigraph from Madala Panji reads as follows:

"By the order of the Lord of Nilgiri (Blue Hill) (Who is) the Lord of the three worlds (Jagannatha), there was born in Odra desa a king named Kapilendra, the ornament of the Solar Line." (28) Thus, Madala Panji offers us the first history of Odissa as it was understood by the chroniclers' of mediaeval times. The Madala Panji pages of history traced the religio-socio-political upheavals of the 'dark age' (called by the historians). This poetic prose extract from Madala Panji, becomes central to our Mediaeval literature for two reasons : (a) K.C.Panigrahi in his History of Orissa (1981) writes a Chapter on literature, captioned 'The Sarala Mahabharata and Kapilendra's conquests' (Appendix- vi, p. 234) (29) and (b) Late K.C.Panigrahi has also written a monograph on Sarala Dasa for Central Sahitya Akademi, New Delhi. (30)

There is, perhaps, one more reason: the Odia scripts have undergone one more stage of transformation during the Suryavansi rule headed by Kapilendra Deva. The earlier scholars have branded this sign system as the "Suryavamsi scripts".

A comparative chart of the previous Odia scripts of the Gangavamsis may transpire as to why the alphabets changed so frequently.

The angular geometrical Shapes were slightly innovated. The tops of the alphabets were now slightly rounded.

N.B (i) The specimen of Ganga alphabets are found from the bilingual inscriptions (Oriya and Tamil) written during the reign of Vira Narasingha Deva. The language is Odia, but the script is in Telugu in Lakshmi Narasimha temple of Simhachalam.

(ii) These inscriptions do not provide evidence that there existed a literature in Oriya.

(iii) Folk songs existed since they were transmitted orally from earlier times.

Whether the alphabetic symbols of a literary culture are stuck up to the instincts of a race or to their collective unconscious is to be decided by the psycholinguists. But the Proto Eastern Indian alphabets of the Somavamsis and the Gangavamsis were abandoned after Kapilendra Deva adorned the throne, "by the order of the Lord of Nilgiri".

Alphabets symbolize the image of a race. These images are valued as signifiers of a particular culture, and Kapilendra Deva occupied the throne of a state that was divided by multiple cultures, having multiple taxemic features. The previous Gangavamsi scripts borrowed some of the geometric features of the Somavamsi alphabets and after uniting the areas of Kosala, Kalinga and Toshli, the Gajapati needed a different insignia of his own scripts images to mark the advent of a new era. The impulse was altogether different. The emperor was completely caught up in the excitement of the moment, -political, spiritual or cultural. Literacy, and to some extend, the habit of reading seemed to have been comparatively wide spread through society, keeping pace with Kapilendra Dev's territorial expansion By 1464A.D. Kapilendra had become the master of an empire stretching from the Ganges in the North to Trichinapalli in the in the South along the coast and we find from the epigraphical records that he had assumed the proud title Gajapati Gaudesvara Navakoti Karnata Kalavargesvara.

Such an emperor wanted to have an improved indigenous system of alphabets capable of encoding the pride of Odia nationalism. The entire Odia speaking country was called Utkala for the first time. The alphabets therefore symbolized the cultural cognition of Utkala.

The comparative chart transpires that the Proto-Indian alphabets of the Somavamsis and the Ganga dynasty were angular ones with straight lines on their heads that lacerated the leaves. Hence for practical reasons, this Odia emperor (who emerged from the grass root level) abandoned these angular ones to begin everything fresh.

The Suryavamsi scripts appear as more refined than the angular ones. The 'lines' on the top were replaced by pin-head shapes. This facility allowed the soldier poet Sarala Das to venture for a grand epic called Mahabharata to be written on the palm leaves with a stylus. The epic is considered an admirable achievement in a newly formed Odia state with a recently formulated "written language" with a new brand of alphabetical images.

The Suryavmsi Emperor needed a vast political territory and the poet, a soldier in Kapilendra's army, needed an energetic culture to represent the collective unconscious. It became urgent therefore, to consider Sarala's Mahabharata more as a linguistic construct and a cultural symbol than a literary work. The Mahabharata is an epic of the Odia folks, perhaps the first in India to textualize the folk mindset, deviating from the Sanskrit version.

The Odia language was yet limping toward poetry. The newly born alphabets were undergoing quick phases of transformation. The epic, instead of following the great myth, became an assemblage of small 'mythemes' narrated in more than thousands of street ballads. The language appears, however, to be a continuation of Rudrasudhanidhi, and the folk proverbs and adages carrying the axiological import of Odia folks like including those in Kalasa Choutisa also...

It seems Odia language was warming up with chautisa poetry before launching its first epic. Bachha Das's Kalasa Choutisa, Balunkeswara Mardaraja's Budha Kalasa, Rukuni Kalasa and Biruli Jagat Singh's Budhi Kalasa are given a scholarly recognition in Odia literature. Some Kalasas (Old Oriya poems), compiled and edited by Dr. Padmanabha Sahu and published in Eshana Vol. xxxvi, June, 1998 helps this writer to place the Kalasa (Song of the Old bride) as a comic poem that describes how an aged ugly looking girl was married to a handsome groom and a quarrel was raised by the groom's friends. The king finally interferes and settles the dispute.

Balunkeswara Mardarajs' Rukuni Kalasa (A kalasa song on Rukmini's marriage) is a social reprobation to Rukmini for getting forcibly married to Srikrishna by her own choice. Budha Kalasa is also a funny poem in which a beautiful girl is given in marriage to an old man. One Guru Kalasa written by Bansi Das is included in the compilation edited by Satchidananda Misra.

To be precise, Kalasa poems are popular folk songs of Medieval Odissa. Dr. Manasingh writes, "This Kalasa Choutisa is a panegyric to Siva, though cleverly composed as a satire". Siva is depicted here as a farmer and an old man unfit for marriage.

Prof. Artaballav Mohanty, in his English preface to Kalasa has written," ... it is clear that the Kalasa Choutisa had grown popular in the time of Sarala Das and it must have taken at least 100 years to have attained such celebrity. So we can safely place Vatsa Dasa in the 14th century" 30 (a), Kalasa is the name of a raga or Vani, it is not a special genre of poetry.

This author does not intend to give his opinion with regard to such historical positioning of the Kalasa poets. This author does not also choose to evaluate these Kalasas either as an important genre of poetry or as great literature. The Kalasas are popular folk songs depicting mismatched marriages and some such comic happenings of the time. However, these poems might also have a role in shaping Sarala Dasa's Mahabharata. Sarala Das uses the word "Kalasa" thrice in his Mahabharata.

The Kalasa poems might have been written little earlier (never one hundred years, though) or we may imagine Baccha or Markanda as Sarala's minor contemporaries. However, the folk Odia signifiers built up by this time were capable of denoting the signified. Beyond that it could also build a poetic diction. The epic written by Sarala Das or a small poem by Baccha Das or Markanda Das was an exploration rather than a disquisition. It is not a way of starting effectively an already known idea or message. It is a way of struggling with the excitements and tensions of the words surrounding and embodying one's attitude towards a particular subject until those excitements and tensions result in the creation of a pattern and at least a temporary conviction of having achieved some kind of resolution.

It is needed therefore to switch over to Sarala's epic that appears to be a fusion of various horizons, cultural and literary.

The Fusion of Different Horizons: Sarala Das

Odia scholars and academicians seem to have generated a plethora of critical works on Sarala Das that is either euphemistic or polemic in nature. Our critical oeuvre on Sarala seems to suffer, thus, an ostensible polarity based on regional, ethnic, caste-centric, religious and cultist biases. We would, therefore, prefer to study the Epic as a cultural representation. Julien Greimas included in his study of culture large areas such as literature, myth, folktales etc based on "the science of signification" so that our semantic study of Odia culture of 15th century through Sarala Dasa's Mahabharata would also be placed under the rubric of linguistic studies called "structural semiotics" Sarala's Mahabharata reflects Odia culture as an area of cognitive system. Our society's culture consists of whatever one has to know or believe in order to operate in a manner acceptable to all members of the-then Odia society. The Mahabharata embodies shared codes of meaning underlying this symbolic action. The text of Sarala Das, therefore, is to be seen as an assemblage of multiple shared codes. In other words, Mahabharata with its re-created and indigenous mythemes becomes a collage of texts to be shared by a million Odias, the entire population of a linguistic community.

The verbal thought and the mythemes of Sarala's Mahabharata emanated from the historical cultural evolution of the Odias. From the time when human activity and speech came together, in the growing Odia child, or, in his human evolution, he left behind his purely biological course of development and entered the stage of cultural- historical development. According to such a premise, the Mahabharata proposes to link language, culture and the cognition level of the Odias. The mental representations of Mahabharata are not arbitrary, discrete, and propositional structures belonging to an ideal mental world, formed independently of the activities of the individual subject. These epical representations fully endorse the position that they have a natural and social and folk world.

Certainly, when we consider culture, it is not the individual schema of Sarala Das but his inter-subjective schema pertains to the 'consensual domain' that are relevant. Applying D' Andrade's words to the Mahabharata one may conclude that the text of the epic is a "cultural model" and its cognitive scheme is inter-subjectively shared by the social group called the Odias. Such models typically consist of a small number of conceptual objects and their relations to each other. Further, a schema is inter-subjectively shared when everybody knows the schema, and everybody knows that everyone knows that everyone knows the schema..." (31)

It is tempting to think that the Mahabharata's 'Cultural Models' or 'Schemas' underlie culturally embedded actions and use of language that we are routinely engaged in. And moreover, there is evidence to think that these cultural cognitive 'models' are at the best of our use of conventional metaphors, of the sort unearthed and analysed by George Lakoff(American linguist), Mark Johnson and others.

Furthermore, the cognitive point of view that the culture and all that surrounds Sarala's Mahahabharata result from mutually orienting behavior and that they are ultimately derived from sharing of Odia individuals' lived experience. That is the site that presents us with a micro perspective. We would take into account the contestations also as part of the cultural sphere as are agreements. Rather noise-free acculturation can perhaps be seen only in the limited context of cultural acquisition by the Odia children of the fifteenth centuty. Sarala had travelled up to Tiruchinapalli as a soldier, perhaps witnessing the recital of Mahabharata in Telugu, Tamil and Kanada languages. The cognitive domain of these fighting Odias was expanded without doubt.

The reflection of Odia pride, nationalism and the fusion of cultural horizons as discerned from Sarala Das' Mahabharata is founded experientially as well as cognitively, and abetted linguistically. They amount to a cognitive materialism of culture. This folk epic, therefore, would help us to do away with the archaic idealist notions. Culture often spoken of either as an essence or an abstraction belongs to the transcendental realms. But in Sarala's work the cognitive parameters of culture are easily available for discursive purposes, while the experiential base buried under thick crusts of apparently ideal constructions; such as in the localized mythemes and folk tales, as deep- psyche allegories.

Sarla Das did, for some time, serve under Kapilendra Deva as a soldier and acquired a locational knowledge about different places/ cultures of Dakshinapatha (South India) as well as Uttarapatha (North India). He could absorb cultures/systems of belief, and could acquire a fair idea of our National geography before he retired to his village Kanakpur, on the bank of river Vriddha where he worked as a cultivator, amid his neighbours. Thus he was able to produce the largest of the vernacular Mahabharatas of India that runs into 8000 pages of demy size in print. (The Department of Culture, Government of Orissa has published the volumes).

The author, as he declares through out the epic, is a Sudra Muni (A saint of the Sudras) and he took up this literary enterprise with the blessings of Goddess Sarala. Sarala is a deity or a Goddess worshipped on the northern side or river Chitrotpala. As we are not sure of Homer's place of birth, so are we ignorant of Sarala Das and his biographical details. Dr. Krishna Chandra Panigrahi, in his Sarala Mahabharata: Aithihasika Chitra (Ch.XIV) provides us with the authentic historical data about Sarala Das's life and talents. We don't have space for recording biographical details here.

The epic informs that his real name was Siddheswar Parida and he was born in a village named Sarola of Kanakpur, included in Jankherpur patna. Goddess Sarala was worshipped as Vak-devi (The Goddess of Speech) and Chandika (of Durga Saptasati) even till today, but it is not the same temple in which the Sudra Kavi wrote this epic. Siddheswar declares himself as an "illiterate, uninformed, foolish and stupid person" and the poet acknowledges how this literary epic could be written in an epiphanic state with the supernatural grace and blessings of the Goddess Sarala. Initially, the goddess was worshipped as the deity of the Vajrayana cult of Buddhism and its worshippers belonged to the Hindu scheduled caste. Later with the Hinduisation of the temple, the Brahmins took over and institutionalized the Goddess (Ref. Gopinath Nanda, Sri Bharat Darpana, P.341). (32)

The original Mahabharata in Sanskrit exudes an impression that the epic belonged to the Brahmins and the Kshatriyas (the ruling class) only. But as Dr. Mayadhar Mansingh points out in his book Matira Kavi Sarala Das (1958) "The Mahabharata of Sarala Das is essentially a literature of the Vaisyas and the Sudras. The secular aim dominates the book from the beginning to the end" (P.3). (33)

As a contrast to the poets who represent civilization and refinement, Sarala Das, the half-baked mystic of our vernacular literature, wrote with abandon, of impulse and epiphanic inspiration. He was our only primitivist without a peer, though Surendra Mohanty, in his Odia Sahityara Adiparva places Arjun Das as his contemporary.

Sarala Das, it seems, was a rebel against the Vedic as well as the Brahinical order, and in a brazen fashion parades his anti-intellectualism and alternative vision. He expresses as well, his disdain for literary pretensions shown by the mainstream classicists. His self categorization as a wild-man rhapsodist is revealing for he has been given the status of an outsider and a visionary standing on the edge of the mainstream culture, and yet is lionized as a writer of the native soil by critics like Mayadhar Mansingh. Sarala Das made his initiatory attempt at institutionalizing an evolving vernacular language liberating itself from the shackles of Sanskrit and subsisting only on the folk usages. He most ably captures the Odia country's collective dreams, manners, attitudes, fears and desires along with its Vratya as well as Buddhist, Nathist and Jain belief systems.

Sarala recreated and reinterpreted Mahabharata, deconstructed its Brahminical ideology, and incorporated everything that was valuable in Jain, Buddhist and Nathist yoga and tantra. Two hundred years before Sarala, during the 11th and 12th centuries the Jains had used a measuring rod called Jnanakola in Kalinga and it was also in practice even during the Suryavamsi rule. Yamaraja, in the Svargarohana Parva advises Hari Sahu, a Vaisaya of Jajpur, the Jain percept of kingship. A saint named Sujaneswar in the same parva appears like a degraded Jain saint of Orissa of those days, like Kamananda of Rudra Sudhanidhi, a degraded Sahajajyana Buddhist.

He was able to do so since he grew up in a period most often regarded as a time of prosperity and national well being. The era of Kapilendra Deva (1435-1467) nurtured a strident Oriya chauvinism. The unsophisticated Odia Vratya view of life was held and hailed beyond reproach. It was a sanitized Utkala, free of dissent, despite its multicultural polemics. The era with the political and military prowess of our Suryavamsi emperor (Kapilendra Deva) illustrated a melting pot dynamic in which people of diverse origins opted to get odianized by moving up with middle class populist culture. The Odia Empire spread from Karnataka to Gouda. The officials who had administrative affiliation with the headquarters had to learn Odia and thus, Sarala's Mahabharata had later influenced the neighboring epic writers to attempt their own vernacular versions of the epic story.

Siddheswar Parida's eclectic career as a soldier, as a widely traveled and geographically exposed Wiseman (though he calls himself a stupid, uninformed person), as a cultivator at Jankherpurpatna lent him the psychic dimension to invade into the exotic lands of liberty. The pan Indian attitudes infused into him an ambition of launching his literary expeditions into the thick terrain of Mahabharata. Thus, Sarala's Mahabharata, as I gather from a rough and rapid browsing of its contents with the guidance of Prof. Niladribhusan Harichandan and Dr. Sricharan Mohanty, appears to this author as a signifying break with the past that was more personal than cultural. But in the process of writing this gigantic literary project, Siddheswar seems to have explored one of the most tumultuous, exhilarating and anxiety-ridden periods of his cultural self, his "being-for-the-other".

The radical shifts in his social, political and spiritual status also seem to have been attended to by a "liminal" period, an interlude of anti-structure, where the individual author experiences an exploratory investigation of self, role playing, and community. His bold choice of secularizing Mahabharata as an "entertaining, national epic" (Mansinha, 13) (34) indicates an inner desire to produce a new art in dandi britta (a meter used in farmers' songs). It is a rhyme-scheme that allows a free play of the metres and cuts through the numerical account of the words. Siddheswar Parida's revolt against the supremacy of Brahminism, Vedic and Upanishadic learning and the Vedic interpretation of life becomes conspicuous in his Dandi Britta that turns out to be a mélange of prose and poetry. Such a quasi metrical form is a direct revolt against Brahminical tradition that espoused the genealogical lores of the royal families. Sarala Das invokes the unconscious of the Vratya Odias. As such one discovers indigenous eidons, motifemes and mythemes within his grand epic.

Sarala's Mahabharata is not a debasement of our culture as argued by Gopinath Nanda in Sri Bharata Darpana, but rather a literary and cultural enterprise to acquaint and inform the illiterate Odias about the national epic. He generated a space to embrace the popular taste of the suddenly expanded Odia country. The Dandi-Vritta was used to re-establish the relationship between the performer and the listeners. (It was read out initially from a palm-leaf script.) Pt. Gopintha Nanda was a polyglot from Parlakhemundi and had read most of the Telegu puranas, written in the classical Sanskrit model. Therefore, Sarala's underformed folk language and liberated extrapolations with Buddhist-Jainist-Nathist intellectual mockeries appeared as radical Violation and blasphemous to this orthodox classicist. It repelled him since he was an orthodox Brahmin searching for purity everywhere. Sarala Das did not prefer to separate purity from creativity and the strong Buddhist-Jainist-Nathist logic supported him.

Siddheswar Parida (Sarala Das) rejected lots of subplots and aspects of characterization narrated in Vyasa's Sanskrit Mahabharata re-written most probably in the Gupta Age (2nd - 4th century). The book, 'The Classical Age' published by Bharateeya Vidya Bhavan, mentions in its introduction: "it (The Gupta Age) saw the final development of the two great epics: The Ramayana and The Mahabharata xxx the vast puranic literature, which originated or at least took default shape during this period, completed the break from the Vedic Age and set on a solid foundation of what is now commonly known as Hinduism, the culmination of religious movement, which had behind in the rich heritage of the diverse peoples of India". (qtd. in Adi Parva) (35)

The Original Mahabharata that existed in the tradition of Sruti of the Aryans (in oral form) is lost to us. During the Gupta Age, it was documented and enlarged into one lakh slokas. A lot of creative stories were added into the original epic. These stories have been culled from different sources including the interesting ones from the pre-Aryan sects. A comparative study of the mythologies would show astounding similarities between these Mahabharatas and The Odessy and The Iliad. One can easily compare Arjuna's archery during the Svayambar of Draupadi with that of Odessyus in the Svayambar of Penelope. We do not know whether such stories are edited/ mutilated /substituted /expanded versions or later inclusions, taken from the legends and oral stories of the tribes of those days.

The Mahabharata of Sarala Das was written during the 15th century in a Vratya motif. Therefore, the author felt the necessity to delete/ alter/ devaluate most of the stories that depicted the Brahminical ideology. The author, as per the trends restated, transformed and Odianized the stories to suit the cultural requirements of the folk society/ listeners of Orissa. This technique of transmission is encompassed by the folklorists as the "Theory of Devolution".

The character of Sri Krishna appears, for example, totally transformed as a debauch engaged constantly in sexual cohabitation.

The Siddhacharyas of the Sahaja-Yana of Buddhism had also conceived Srikrishna as a character merged in licentious acts of free sex and physical pleasure Srikrisha in Sarala Das is no more the embodiment of ultimate knowledge, but he is only a Sahaja-yana Saint, who searches for salvation through all kinds of sexual aberrations and indulgences with low-women (dombis of charya songs).

The Odia society from the 12th to the 15th century underwent severe moral trauma of liberal sex exercises of the Vajrayana Buddhists. Common folks were inducted by the Sahaja yana yogis who practiced adultery as a spiritual mode of the attainment of moksha (salvation through sex). Kamananda Swamy of Rudra Sudhanidhi stands as a literary evidence of the practices of those days, when Madana Pooja became popular in the society because group sex was allowed in which the king and the dombi participated sharing each other's body.

Sarala Das, after his retirement from Kapilendra Deva's army, returned to his fields and to his hereditary services of conducting the pooja rituals of Goddess Sarala, who was worshipped as an eight-armed Mahasarasvati. In Chandipurana Goddess Mahishamardini embodies the potential energy of Vakdevi (the goddess of speech) and is mentioned as Sarala. Perhaps no where except in Odissa Mahasarasvati is worshipped as Durga/ lMahishamardini/ Chandika. The 16 names of Sarasvati as mentioned in Jain scriptures include Sarala (perhaps a devaluated from of Sarada). The cultural affinity between the Jain countries (Gujarat) and Odissa seems to continue from 9th Century B.C. The tantric. Buddhists worshipped her as Sasana Devi and later, in the Jain temples near Khajuraho, Sarasvati is worshipped as wonderful sculptural icon of beauty. Sarala Das visualizes her image in the psychic space as "Dhavala Kamakshi Se je Karpoora Varana" (She is white colored Kamashi with the colour of crystalline camphor. Siddhesvara Parida (Sarala Das) has written:

Nisithe Prasanna Thai jaha se Kahai
Aruna prakase muhin ta sabu lakhai
[Whatever she says in the night in blessed epiphany, I write when the morning dawns].

Thus he envisaged Bhima as the Chief protagonist of his epic, not Arjuna. He is an embodiment of 'hunger'-metaphorical as well as real. Draupadi's physical beauty is his 'hunger' and he is the only character who can laugh at Yudhisthir's lack of manliness and imperfect normal decisions. Bhima is the driving force of Sarala's Mahabharata and the other ones seem almost to have stemmed from the Vratya soil Orissa.

The Mahabharata in simple peoples' language was to be read by a Purana-panda (a worshipper and he who recites the epic, a Brahmin who recited from the palm-leaf script with dramatic modulation) These readers were not able to correctly interpret the text in the temple or Bhagavata Tungi precincts during the evenings. The epic mirrored attributes and sentiments which were already there, and at the same time provided an expressive/ performative field and a set of symbols through which (take for example, Bhima) these attitudes could be projected.

In Chaucer's Canterbury Tales, too, (Chaucer was a contemporary of Sarala Das) we get a corrupt picture of the hierarchy of the medieval church that had a complicated structure. Chaucer treats the Prioress and the Monk, the Friar and the Clerk and also the Summoners and the Pardoners as characters "wanton" in nature.

They are people in need of luxury, rejoicing in hunting games, fond of jewellery and fashionable make-up material. So were the Brahmin Pundits of Siddheswar's milieu dominated and targetted by the Sahajiya mendicants and the Natha yogis with tripundra marks on their foreheads who populated the streets.

The picture of Sri Krishna available to us is neither the embodiment of divinity nor that of the Ultimate in Anguttar Nikaya "He is neither a god, nor a gandharva, nor a Yaksha, he is Buddha" (Vol-II, P.38). (36) Sri Krishna is painted as one such substitute of Buddhist Maha yana saint(Upaya) and the gopis are reflection of prajna(s) of Mahayana sect of Buddhism. Buddhist texts like Astasahasrika Prajna Paramita are corroborated by Taranath (The Tibbetan Historian) and Hieuen-T'- Sang (629 -695 AD) who mentions about the "Mahayani Sthaviras in Kalinga' (37)

Our traditional Brahminical critics like Mrutyunjay Rath and Gopinath Nanda must have been annoyed to find the characters of the Brahmins like Agnika Maharshi, Parasara/Pareswara, and Durbasa as morally fallen bipeds, who deserved a pungent satirical treatment from Sarala Das. Similarly, Dr. Mayadhar Mahsinha emphasized on the "Sudra" aspect of the epic" and later tried to justify its writing as a matter of 'epiphanic down pour', indirectly dragging the issue to a filthy caste-centric satire.

But in our close study of the spiritual vision of Sarala Das with obvious influences from Mahayana, Hinayana, Nathist and Jain Tantric norms, we discover the self-professed "stupid" author to be one of the wisest authors of Odia literature with deep knowledge of Tantrik- Buddhist epistemes, substantial experiential cognition and a ceator with a flair for research.

The sexo-yogic lives of the Buddhist-Nathist Saints came to be regarded as one of the most important esoteric practices, held as "preparatory accessories" (Maharana P.50) (38) for the attainment of the final state of supreme bliss . Thus, Surendra Mohanty's conclusion that the milieu portrayed the ultimate moral degradation of the Odia social life be re-examined.

We should accept that Sarala delineates Srikrishna's character as a prototype of the "Sahajia kanhu" (of Kanhupada of the Charya poetry, who was also a Nathist saint). This repels the later Brahmin critics like Gopinath Nanda and Mrityunjaya Rath (Ref. Surendra.Mahanty, Odia Sahityara Adiparva: P.143). (39) Srikrishna's felonious sex with the old "Sahaja Sundari" in "Khanikara Janmavirttanta" episode is a pure invention of Sarala and the act of sexuality has nothing immoral; it is one of the six abhicharas (esoteric rituals) of Tantric Buddhism. The Khanikara (a digger) is deployed to dig a tunnel that would lead to the bed room of Radha so that Sri Krishna, from his Kadamba Tree, would be able to reach Sri Radha's bed room eventhough Chandrasena locked her up from outside.

In another incident Yudhistira had to ceremonize the annual Sraddha ritual for his dead father during his exodus into the forest. A Brahmin was an essential "requisite item" for the Sraddha ritual Sri Krishna brings a backward class untouchable named Kapila Bauri (he was an untouchable in the 15th century society) and puts a wild creeper around his shoulder like a sacred thread. The untouchable (Kapila Bauri), Srikrishna declares, "Is fit enough to perform the Sradha ritual since there is a sacred thread on his shoulder". What Sarala Das builds up in this indigenous episode is a raillery against the decadent Brahmins, who recited "any thing" as "mantra" because the Hindu society had empowered them with a sacred thread on their body as a symbol of sanctified higher caste. This parody as well as the burlesque of the Brahmins of those days not only reveal the wickedness of the Brahminical society, but also is to be considered as an attempt to censure their follies.

Again, in the episode of "Siba Das Brahmin", we encounter more of a cultivator than a Siba Dash having no qualities of a professional Brahmin for earning his livelihood. Siddheswar Parida's purpose as a satirist was to move his readers to criticize and condemn "through ridicule, contempt anger and hate". (p.74) (39)

A major deviation that needs mention in this short discussion of Sarala's creative extravaganza through these mythemes allegorizing the Buddhist points of view constitute the imaginative depiction in the Svargarohana Parva. While Yudhisthira, the ethical/moral model of the grand Brahminical epic is transformed into a cruel, selfish seeker of salvation, Bhima displays extraordinary humanitarian feelings for his brothers and the mother. He weeps when his brothers fall one by one and Draupadi dies. He remembers their positive qualities and implores Yudhistira to come to their rescue as the responsible elder brother. But Yudhisthira, who had, of late, married a Vaisya girl from Dharampura (modern Jajpur in Odissa), on the bank of river Vaitarani, ignores Bhima's implorings and marches ahead on the uphill journey toward moksha (salvation). This funny story of Yudhisthira's marriage with the Dharmapura girl might have appealed to a lot of Vaisya listeners of Jajpur area and the naïve villagers of Kanakpur, who in turn, would have believed the episode to be a real story of their epoch. They would also have nurtured a grudge against this morally elevated elder brother of the Brahminical Purana. Sarala's Buddhist radicalism has still a sadistic appeal for the common folk, who enjoy such gossips, but Gopinath Nanda, the author of Sribharat Darpana, condemns such a story as "absurd babbling" of Siddesvara Parida.

Chaucer, the beginner of English literature, too, devised such gossip-like framework for his stories, which are as unique as those of Siddhesvar Parida. Chandi Das (in Srikrishna Keertana) has also painted Srikrishna as a Sidhacharya. Krutibash Ojha and Kashiram Das of Bengal have included such local stories within their Bengli epics. Kamban in Tamil, who wrote Ramayana, has incorporated the historical pictures of the Chola era (9 th century). Pampa's Mahabharata (941 AD) in Kannad literature has many such devolutionary stories. Nannaya in Telugu (1019-1061 AD) and Kumudendu (1275 AD) in the Ramayana of Kannada (treated the epic with Jaina epistemes) have also deviated from the original Sanskrit texts. All these comparative statements are given from secondary sources.

Saralas' Bhima may be compared with that of the Bhima Charita in Assamese. This leads to a presumption that the treatment was similar in all the three Vratya countries: Anga, Banga and Kalinga. The Mahabharata of Sarala, in a sense, falls under the category of vernacular religion that celebrates the popular culture of the fifteenth century. The Mahabharata, in its description of nature, deployment of metaphors, in its description of the picturesque geography of Orissa, and in all its literary aspects deserves a high position amongst the other ancient works of India. It also carves a niche for Odia literature since it could reach heights of wisdom with its initiatory epic, both in its content and characterization. Besides, Sarala's Mahabharata acquires the qualities of pop- literature for the ordinary men and women in a Vratya country that did hardly receive any Vedic recognition at any point of time.

The fifteenth century Odias did not accept the Aryan version of Mahabharata without feeling a complex mixture of attraction and repulsion toward it. At times the clacisists felt disenchanted because of the tantric-Buddhist stance of Siddheswar, who attacked Brahminical tradition. But the author was never worried about a nation called India or a civilization that grew on the marshy, slimy land around river Ganges and claimed its superiority over the Dravidians and Vratyas of this native land castigating them as the Asuras and slaves. Sarala was a soldier in Kapilendra Deva's army, a regiment that devastated the areas from the Ganges to Karnataka. So he attacked the imaginary stories of idealism spun by the Brahmins of the Ganges valley like a courageous cultural-secular soldier. More important were the multi cultural, heterogeneous people of Kapilendra's Odia head quarters. They must listen to some practical and relevant, logical and empirical experiences of the past, not to esoteric and schizophrenic idealism; they showed violent distrust toward a culture that was imported from the Middle East by the alien Aryans. The Odias considered themselves as pioneers of secularism through Sarala's epic, and they voiced their cultural protest by reacting through this national epic. They reacted against the aliens who named them as Vratyas and asuras.

It is true that Siddhesvar Parida could not provide us with the exact translation of the Sanskrit text in 15th century and thus, Krishna Singh (1781), the king of Dharakota and Phakirmohan Senapati (1843) had to work hard later to give our literary tradition two exact translations from Sanskrit in addition to one of Jagannath Dasa. Jagannatha Dasa's Mahabharata was published in 1928 by one Bhikari charana Das, a former Subdeputy Collector living in Khatbin Street, Cuttack. It was an exact translation from Sanskrit. But Siddheswar (Sarala Das) in his recreated version could influence the Odias of the country side. His imaginary episodes appeared real to people. In fact, Sarala Das has incorporated all the popular legends of Odissa into the puranic narrative and at this distant date, the legends and the recreated tales have turned into folk beliefs. The lines of this Mahabharata have turned into maxims, aphorisms, precepts, and finally accepted as mythical truth.

One such creative story concerns the death of Srikrishna. He suffered from continuous injury and unbearable pain after Jara's arrow pierced into his foot. He summoned Arjuna from Hastina and Arjuna could sense that Srikrishna would pass away as soon as he would touch him. But despite his unwillingness to do so, he could not bear with his friend's pain. So, tactfully he handed over his bow to him and touched him so that he died immediately.

After the death of his divine peer, Arjuna chased Jara to kill him. Then suddenly a voice echoed from the heaven:

Proceed thou hence with Jara
To mountain Neelasundara
Light the funeral pyre
And put the body of Srikrishna there".

Incense wood was needed to burn the pyre, otherwise the 'Pinda' (heart) part of Srikrishna's body would not burn. Jara tried his best to find some incense tree (locally called Aguru wood) and finally procured some. But Krishna's pinda could not be burnt. Sarala Das satirizes:

Many a women he ravished
No sin could stain
His body divine
But his pinda after he was dead
Was tarnished: it's a soul blemished
Its lustre lost It couldn't be burnt.

Arjuna had to consign the rest of Srikrishna's unburnt pinda to the ocean. After Arjuna's return, Jara retrieved it from the ocean, but it was petrified and it had turned into a rock. Jara worshipped the stone. He named the stone as Sabari Narayana and Nilamadhaba etc. Years after that, a king named Galamadhab deputed a willing Brahmin to the jungles of Jara to bring Nilamadhava to his capital, Puri. He lured away Jara's daughter and smuggled the secret stone from the Jungles to Puri. The king built a temple, built abstract icons and that was the famous Jagannath temple. Thus, Sarala connected Srikrishna with the Odia country, and its central god, Jagannatha. The home-made poetic lie is accepted by the folks and the scholars of the vernacular department as a legend and very often they quote these lines in their essays.

The entire story is extraneous to The Mahabharata and Sarala Das's skillful contrivance of the episode metaphorises the national theme of Utkal. Jagannatha, the cult God, therefore, signifies a convergence of different religious sects including Buddhism that matches with Sarala's radical yet innovative mindset.

Perhaps the world needs shreds of such falsehood to construct a Truth. Legends are, after all, a major part of our collective unconscious. Here is built an epic and it fulfils the definition of Paul Merchant (An epic is) "a chronicle, 'a book of the tribe', a vital record of custom and tradition, and at the same time a story-book for general entertainment'. The later aspect of epic, its value simply as a story, needs no elaboration, but epic itself (here Sarala's Mahabharata) may have originated in the need for an established history" (40). For Homer the background of his Illiad is the fall of a great civilization: for the Mahabharata of the vernacular tradition is the origination of a spiritual identity for the Vratyas of Odissa whom the Vedic people sabotaged and subverted culturally, the Origin of an indigenous literature.

No debate is required with regard to Sarala's education and scholastic accomplishments. Homer, too, like Sarala Das, writes:

You will regret it afterwards if you kill
A bard, the singer for gods and men.
I am self-taught, and God planted in my heart
The various ways of song (22,345-8,Odyssey 8).

Gopinath Nanda and Mrutyunjay Rath's classical criticism do not apply to Sarala's pop-cultural epic. Mansingh and Prof. Niladribhusan Harichandan's critical interpretations are hinged only on the anti-Brahminical motifs of Sarala. That is like missing the forest for a tree. Surendra Mohanty in Odia Sahityara Adiparva (1963) appears broad and excellent with cross reference to Tantric Buddhism. The common men were influenced by Tantric Buddhism. Sarala was one of them and his tantric Bhudhist stances (like those of the secessionists like the Jains and the Nathists) are anti-vedic/ Brahminical) stances suited to the fifteenth century Odia folks.

But this author chooses to classify Sarala's Mahabharata as one of the grand epics of our literature. All classical epics of the world have been accepted as "Oral" since they were meant for recitation. Homer's Odyssy, Virgil's Aenied and the Old English Beowulf were sung to the people, and thus there is a direct relationship between the bard and his material. Sarala's Mahabharata too, offers valuable evidence for the actual conditions of performance. It was not read initially. The poet recited the epic to common folk listeners and thus, he was to cater to the pop-taste, to "stimulus-response" linguistic situations.

The scholastic demand for an exact and authentic translation is a matter of academic purity and the demand of the illiterate vratya audience was entertainment, pure and simple. The epic needed to contain appealing stories. At the heart of Sarala's enterprise was a revolt on behalf of the common men for their rights of access to the National Epic-(Mahabharata) that embodied the greatest possible diversity of information, knowledge and experience. The bard had also struggled for their right to participation and expression in the epical sites of meaning-making, the educational and communication systems of those days. At times, his words reveal immanent analysis, in which we take account only of the internal relations of the mythical and ethical epistemes. This leads to the consideration of the value-system, the nature of values and finally the comparative value system with reference to Siddheswar Parida's academic certificates in learning and his creative wisdom.

Most of the critics have confused ideas with regard to the distinction between the world of values and the world of facts, but the world of value exists side by side with other philosophically discovered words- such as, the 'physical world', the 'world of essences', the 'psycho spiritual world' and others. Gopinath Nanda, Mrutyunjay Ratha and Mayadhar Mansingh have confused the values of Mahabharata with facts and characters; that is, the characters (Draupadi, Srikrishna or Durbasa) plus the value they have taken on. Surendra Mohanty confuses the non-reality of the value with the identity of essence (Tantrik Buddhism), a confusion which converts values into ideal objects. At times, he equates the valuational state of Srikrishna with a psycho-physical state. The most interesting point about Dr. Mayadhar Mansingh's criticism is that by the time he wrote his book on Sarala Das, he had already changed his own religion from Hinduism to Buddhism and Sarala's vision suited that of his own. This critic-historian prefers, therefore, to quote Risiri Frondizi's essay on "The Nature of values" (1958) in which this French philosopher interprets: "Therefore, values are neither things, nor insights, nor essences: they are values (p.11) (41).

Sarala's delineation of the character of Srikrishna as a "licentious debauch" is a Tantrik-Buddhist attempt at subverting the Hindu mythic contents. This author has discovered an extant jataka text of Ramayana in Mr. Hadibandhu Hali's library (at Bargarh, Bhubaneswar)Late Sri Hali was an educationist, advocate and historian). The extant book is captioned, Dasaratha jataka in which "Sita Pundit" is "Ram Pundit's" sister. Although we do not know about the authorship and period of this book, we can guess that the interpretation belonged to 15th century Orissa, under the influence of Tantrik Buddhism. The Buddhists distorted the Hindu mythologies to suit their vision of Sahaja Yana, practiced through out the Buddhist belts of Utkala. Though it was in a declining state during Siddhesvar Parida's time, the sexo-yogic practices were rampant in Orissan folk life. So, the sexual side of the characters of Mahabharata cannot be interpreted with the moral vision of the British Calvinists, imported to India during the colonial times. Srikrishna indulges sexually with an old women; this constitutes another example of the sexo- yogic manifestations of the Sahajana sect. We cannot interpret them from the Aryan as well as Brahminical point of ethics, or, from Freudian perspectives.

Sarala Das defends himself by naming himself as "illiterate, "apandita", "wisdom-less fool" etc. But such expressions of humility May be facetious humour. (that he is not a Brahmin pundit, but a Krishikari, farmer").These may also be only tongue-in-cheek expressions. He insists through out his epic that culture was everywhere implicated in the play of power,-be it political, military or religious. It cannot always be searched only in Hindu puranic authenticity. Sarala Das was a Vratya, not an Aryan who intruded into India and marched from the banks of Caspian Lake with grazing cows.

His extrapolations of the creative episodes in his Mahabharata make the epic stupendous and bigger than the Sanskrit original. Sarala's deviations are two fold: structural and episodic. Structurally, he changes the order and names of the Parvas. He collects the materials from the Adiparava and Sabha parva and divides them into three chapters adding a Madhya Parva of his own. The Anusasana Parva and the Mahaprasthan parvas found in Sanskrit are not available and the materials are included in a new parva (chapter) called Svargarohana parva. The Sauptika parva has been renamed as Aishika or Kainsika parva. The materials of Salya parva are divided and a Gada parva is created.

The projection of the episode that Srikrishna (the Siddhacharya in characterisization) after his death was transformed into jagannatha is a major contribution o Sarala Das in fictionalization of an anti-vedic Buddhist God merging with Jagannatha. The Buddhists of those days believed strongly that Jagannath was an incarnation of Buddha.

The rituals still prevalent in the temple of Jagannatha are mostly taken from Mahayana practices. The deities are not anthropomorphic and are mostly symbols of the concept of void. The use of mantra,

History of Ancient Odia Literature | 111

mudra, mandala and dharani are Buddhist devices of the worship of the void (Also Vajra). We get such evidences from Nagarjuna's (in 1st - 2nd century B.C) Vaipulya sutra. Though the script of this book is not available, portions are given in Manjushree Mulakalpa, another Buddhist text. The principle was imagined to be a form of Bodhisatva during Ashoka's regime. Before he merged into void, Avalokitesvara imparted his knowledge as Siva, Vishnu and Ganeshwara etc. The deities of the Jagannatha, Balabhadra and Subhadra are decorated in those shapes during different festivals of the year. This Nepalese legend is substantiated by a car festival of Avalokitesvara and Gorekhnath.

The concept of the car Festival and its different rituals are directly taken from Buddhist practices. The Gods and Goddesses of the Brahminical religion are depicted holding different ayudhas (weapons). Jagannath does not hold any.

Indrabhuti's (c.705 A.D) Jnana siddhi proves jagannatha neither as a presence nor an absence, rather as a void that pervades; and an entity without having any conceivable beginning, middle or end. He is there only to emancipate the fallen ones, a spiritual power-centre only, which connects the virtual border lines between the inner and the outer.

According to Advaya Vajra Samgraha all the Buddhist deities are symbols of the void. The Buddhists, while worshipping Vajra, the main God of Vajrayana, use flowers, flames, sandal paste, flowers, and many such ingredients are also used in Jagannatha's worship. The deployment of songs, dance, choreographic gestures and musical instruments must have resulted in the creation of a sect of "dancing women"(Mahari) who, virtually, offer themselves for Mahasukha (indescribable transcendence through sex), or a sexo-yogic ritual of the symbolic gods practiced by the Buddhist Siddhacharyas of the Sahaja Yana.

The Vajrayana Doha songs in their most naked form are deployed by Dahuka(the charioteer in the car festival) during the car festival at Puri in which the bard sings obscene songs (the content being sexual cohabitation as the ultimate mode of salvation), nirvana and the attainment of the void. He Vajra Tantra accepts pleasure (maha sukha) as the ultimate goal of life.

The colour scheme deployed in Sarala's Mahabharata is almost like the worship of Goddess Tara, who is symbolized in pure white full moon, the newly bloomed blue lotus and the inclusion of a veeja mantra(the seed mantra) 'Tam' with yellow colour. These colours are also the major symbols: Black or Blue (Jagannatha as Happiness; the colour of happiness is black in Sexo-Yogic practices), white (Balabhadra who is the embodiment of void) and Yellow (Subhadra also represents void). In the symbolic descriptions given in Hevajra Tantra Samputika about the colours blue and black denote Union, Prajna, existence and non-existence. Green, Yellow and Red are also colours of Vajrasattva. Thus, the three deities are conceived by Sarala Das as his favourite non-brahminical symbols that transcend all kinds of narrow brahminical, orthodox caste division, introduced by the Aryans of central Asia, only with motifs of power politics and social domination.

Sarla Das built up the story of Lord Jagannath as an incarnation of Sri Krishna. That was the interpretation of Samkaracharya to save Hinduism from the grips of the Buddhists. But in Sarala's story Srikrishna is depicted as a Sahajia Siddhachrya. Hence he builds up believable legends because of which the Lord has been identified as the Natural God of the Oriya race. But Sarala's endeavour is more diplomatical and religious. He intended to emphasize the authenticity of Buddhist logic present in the icons of the deities, and at the same time, refuting Samkaracharya's logic in interpreting Jagannatha as Srikrishna.

But beyond the poet's religious convictions, one notices a fusion of the disparate horizons. His epic encompasses subjects like astrology and Kamasutra, Vajrayana and National geography, costumes and cullinaries, the "raw" and the "cooked". (See Claude Levi Strauss, 1964) A little beneath this grand literary mythologiques one notices the epiphanic moments of the Sudra -Muni whose epic genre combines comedy, romance, tragedy and irony (satire) and according to Northrope Frye's theory, these are the four "displaced" models or the four elemental forms of myth.

Finally, Sarala's Mahabharata is a positivist attempt to impose an order through literature on the chaotic cultural climate of a fifteenth century Odissa. It demonstrates universal significances which are uncalled for in other vernacular literatures in such a grand epical style. If not a centre, this may be considered as an empirical plentitude that seems more than hypothetical, a total cultural data, which, if it could be grasped, would guarantee even today an "ultimate state". Further, the epic embodies anthropological knowledge about Indian myths, Odissan religious practices along with the folk belief-system.

In the distant 15th century recitative performance programmes of Mahabharata the individual listeners must have received a message as to their cultural and religious identity. Yet, the credit is not taken by this great nation builder. He enacts, like Homer, the game of humility by assigning his literary art to supernatural inspiration and origin. A stray reading of this epic would convince the Odias about their manifold operations of power. It would stand as an evidence of the 15th century Odia cultural praxis and religious discourse. In a way, it is the "archaeology" of Odia cultural knowledge.

It would be more befitting to categorize Sarala Dasa's Mahabharata as a "folkloric" epic rathar than a "literary" one. This shift in approach would imply an agreement to include conceptions of tradition, society and culture into a single fold. If the text of Mahabharata can be approached through the disciplines related to the folkloristics, a rhetorical analysis of the work can be carried out by examining the three major aspects- 'text', 'context' and 'texture' of sarala's Mahabharata. That would be, in fitness of things, a real transit from orality to textuality, yet retaining some features of oral performance and a stimulus-response paradigm that would constantly have improved Sarala's representation on a semantic level

Other works of Sarala Das

Four more works are retrieved subsequently the authorship of which is ascribed to Siddheswar Parida: (i) Chandi Purana (ii) Bilanka Ramayana (iii) Lakshmi Narayana Vachanika and (iv) Vichitra Ramayana. Sarala has followed the Devi Bhagabata (Sanskrit) in Chandi Purana.

Sarala Das deployed a typical prose style in Chandipurana which is epistolary in nature. We are compelled to quote few lines to substantiate our point: "Srimukha bhasa chitau, srikara Anathanku namaste, Namaste. Anadi adi kasyapa gotri. Sri Rahu vamsare utpanna. Simhanka guna. Karme kula utkrma. Kashyapa rushi adipata. Tahanka vamasare utpatti Paramananda Madhurya. Krupalu srabana srata, Chaturdasa bhavanara adhipati, Bibhuda bhuvana patala bhuvana udaka patana sakala patana Sri Mahaprabhu, Viradhi-virabaranka prasade...etc.

The prose resembles that of Madala Panji and occasionally it appears like a continuation of the language of inscriptions. Although the prose is suitable for recitals, its style evidences the culminating point of a textuality that started with the Urjam inscriptions in 1051 AD.

Bilanka Ramayana, though not a direct translation from Sanskrit, embodies the ideas and episodes of the Sanskrit text. The puranic story depicts the existence of one more Ravana with one thousand heads, who reigned in Pushkara Island. Rama had come back to Ayodhya and was coroneted. Then he discovered that one more Ravana with one thousand heads had started ravaging the swarga. Rama Chandra, then implored by the gods, set out to kill him, but he failed. As the war continued Sita prayed Chandi and emerged before Bilanka Ravana as a nude, enticing female energy. The thousand headed Ravana was enthralled and was trapped and killed.

Lakshmi-Narayana Vachanika is a small composition with 79 couplets only written in Dandi vritta. Lakshmi steps into the house of an untouchable woman called Shriya Chandaluni and Lord Jagannatha drives her out of the temple premises for infringement of the ritualistic codes of the temple. Lakshmi was insulted and Lord Jagannatha and his elder brother Balabhadra could not get a morsel of food for daily sustenance. Finally she was invited in and the crisis was over. This legend concerning the temple of Jagannatha is rewritten by Balaram Das after hundred years,.It was dramatised and presented as a film subsequently and the women folk recite the story on the Thursdays of the month of Margaseersha (December-January) while observing the vrata of Mahalakshmi.

The text of Vichitra Ramayana has generated controversies about its authorship since it has been translated into Telugu during 17th -18th centuries for five/six times by different authors. (42) Late Prof Benimadhav Padhi doubts whether the two Siddheswaras are one since the language of Vichitra Ramayana looks more archaic than that of the Mahabharata. The description of Lava and Kusa, in comparison to that of Draupadi of Mahabharata seems very condensed in Vichitra Ramayana. Padhi also suspects as to how Sarala Das could arrange translators from Andhra. He has probably forgotten that the empire of Utkala was spread upto Tiruchinapally during Kapilendra Deva (1435-

1468) D.Gopinath, the first translator of Vichirta Ramayana was a Telugu scholar and a minister in Nandapur (Jaypur,Koraput) between the last part of 17th century and the beginning of 18th century. But D.Gopinath mentions that an odia "Vipra yogi" called Siddheswar Das had composed the epic. Prof. Padhi suspects that there might be another Siddheswara in Kalinga region since Sarala declared himself as a Sudra Muni. D. Gopinatha was a bilingual pundit and he should not have taken him to be a "Vipra Yogi" (a Brahmin Saint). The argument does not seem tenable since the Telugu Pundit of Nandapur might be one more creative genius and would have extrapolated the phrase "Vipra Yogi" to make the Purana more acceptable in Kalinga and Andhra Desa.

The Telugu pundit had settled in Odissa since the days of Choda Ganga Deva. Kapilendra Deva had also become the master of an empire that stretched from Ganges in the north to Trichinnpalli in the south along the coast by 1464 AD. But the last part of Kapilendra's life was not smooth. Entropy had started to engulf the vast empire.

While his eldest son Hamvira was busy subduing some uprisings in the South, Kapilendra enthorned his son Purushottama. The Madala Panji records reveal that Kapilendra prayed seriously for a divine dispensation in this regard and Purushottam Deva was nominated after a dream-command of Lord Jagannath. However, this autocratic political decision paved the way for the dissolution of the Solar Dynasty after his death. Kapilendra's defeated enemies began to retaliate from the south. Saluva Narasimha Deva emerged as a great opponent around 1470. The Afgans and the Muslims attacked Odissa from the North and finally after around 91years of independence Orissa fell into the hands of Mughals, in 1568.

Chautisa Poetry Our literature, to some extent, kept its doors open to Sanskrit influences and a distinct phase of court literature developed during the rule of the imperial Gangas. Following the cultural foot prints of the Ganga kings at Varanasi Kataka (present Cuttack) the feudatory and Gadjat states also began to nurture Sanskrit literature by granting agrahara villages to the Sanskrit pundits. Athagada (173 AD), Ghumusur (961 AD), Khidisingi (1168 AD), Jeypore, Manjusha (9th century), Paluru, Birula (1489), Khallikote (1374), Surangi (1465), Budharsingi (1443 AD), Tarala (1476), Tekkali (1423), Chikati (881 AD), and Paralakhemundi (1465) are the estates in which Sanskritisation continued with rapid progress. At the same time, the Somavamsi King of Suvarnapura, and Jajnagar promoted elitist poetry with the new settlements of the Brahmin diaspora.

Thus an immediate divide was created between the elitist court poets and the folk poets of central Odissa. The Chautisa poetry generated during this period seems to have bridged the gap. Chautisa poems are written as a string of poems, each embodying an elaboration of a particular theme. Structurally, each poem begins with a consonant from 'Ka' (the first consonant) to 'Kshya (the last alphabet)'.As a genre Cautisa is derived from Sanskrit chatrisa(34) denoting the 34 consonants of Odia language(from 'ka' to 'ksha' There are eight varieties of chautisa found during this period, classified as(i) poems of union and separation,(ii) chautisa of Self-reflection(iii) ofRomances (iv) Chautisas of the Alamkar School, (v) Narrative Chautisas, (vi) Chautisas recited with ritual weeping (vii) Chautisas of renunciation and (viii) Mystical Chautisas.

Some of the Chautisas were rewritten by different authors at different times. Sakuntala Chautisa, for instance, has been written by Raghu Arakhita, Balaram Das and Kanhu Das. It was written at the time Madala Panji was scribed (11th Century). Jnanodaya Chautisa was also written by these three authors. Dasadhua Chautisa was composed later by Jagansnatha Das, Bansi Das's, Goura Chautisa, Bachha Das' Kalasa Chautisa, Syamaghana's Koti Brahmanda Sundari Chautisa, Raghunath Harichandan's Chandradoota Chautisa, Kavi Surya Brahma's Sangini Chautisa, Narayana's Rasala Chautisa, Bishnu Das' Patasagara Chautisa, Bhakta Charana's Manabodha Chautisa, Mukunda Nanda's Sasimukhi Chautisa, Bhramarabara Chautisa, Dhananjaya's Panditabodha Chautisa, Danai Das' Chautisa, Balukeswar's Gurumandala Chautisa, Hari Das' Disamegha Chautisa, Rajendra Deva's Purabi Chautisa and Krishna Das' Mageni Chautisa need to be enlisted here. One Chatutaranga Chautisa is retrieved from the palm-leaf manuscripts, but the name of the author has not yet been determined by the scholars.

Most of these Chautisas have been written in Kalinga. It is interesting to note that the first developed alphabets of Odia were invented in

Kalinga, the process of sanskritization started in Kalinga and most of the Chautisas were written there. Perhaps Kalinga was the womb of classical Odia literature, but unfortunately the most prolific part of it is now in Andhra Pradesh. The Odias do not care even for Urjam, where the first Odia alphabets were invented. Our Sahitya Akademi has never held a meeting there to commemorate the birth of its alphabets. However, with the writing of a Chautisa, Odia literature appears to have reached a culminating stage of development. The new language has discovered its strength and inner energy that manifested in the verse narratives that were capable of reflecting the standards of classical cultures. Chautisa was a genre on which the new creative and intellectual impulse was nourished.

The prolonged tradition of Chautisa poetry needs a special discussion since the authors, under the influence of elitist court poetry, have taken an interest in verbal calisthenics. The Chautisa poetry uses the Odia alphabetical oder to write songs basing on each alphabet and at times, composing Chautisas using the reversed alphabetical order (Olata Chautisa). One more variety of chautisa is written using both the vowels and the consonants as their beginning syllables.

Our ancestor critics have classified chautisa under the lyric genre because of their emotive expression, but an analysis of the vocabulary shows lots of archaic folk words: 'tamba' for grass, 'takara' for bald heads, 'dhokara' for the big-bellied people and 'formana' for the orders of the king etc. The language is borrowed from tribal and folk languages too.

Plenipotentiary Poems

Plenipotentiry poems or messenger poems also need a special mention as these constitute a sub-genre of the Chautisas. Alternatively, these poems are also known as Koili Sahitya (Koili or the Cuckoo as the messenger in the poems). In Odia folk tales and the literature of the vows and rituals 'crows' and 'black bangles' are also deployed as messengers. Following the Chautisa style, these plenipotentiary poems are also written in syllabic order. Markanda Das' Kesaba Koili is a famous poem of this genre. Krishna and Balaram's journey to Mathura leaving Yasoda forlorn and the mother's thoughts of separation and filial sentiment is exteriorized in the poem addressed to the Cuckoo. The mother pours out her heart's sorrow in the absence of Krishna and Balarama, who were her source of permanent strength and joy. The authenticity of Yasoda's motherly emotions, the quiet, religious acceptance expressed in the simplest feminine idioms, make the messenger poems more popular than the Chautisas. The 'Koili' poems used to haunt the teachers and students till 1950s, and every beginner in the school was asked to get the poem by heart and recite it every day.

With Sarala Das and the poets of the plenipotentiary school, the doctrine of simplicity and colloquial idioms enter into Odia literary genres. That was true reflection of the simple life of the folks and the test of the power of our expressivity in folk Odia; the illiterate folks' lived experience throughout the state. Literature was not different from the lyricism of the everyday life of the Odias and their language.

The plenipotentiary poems come closer to the Italian imaginatio and phantasia. I seems the entire mediaeval tradition rested on such a trend, in different themes though. The creative capacity of imagination and loftier functions of phantasia are to be examined here. Imagination is that intellectual lens through the medium of which the poetical observer sees the objects of his observations, modified both in colour and form; or it becomes an inventive dresser of dramatic tableaux, by which the persons of the play are invested with new drapery, or placed in new attitudes. Bachha Das or Markanda Das's poetic personas in the plenipotentiary poems can be viewed even from this English angle of 'imagination' and 'fancy'. The Koili (Cuckoo) represents a primary creative innovation, allows the poetic self a willed activity of the spirit, a self consciousness, and a self-realising intuition, joining and coalescing the otherwise separated notions of the addressee and the addresser.

NOTES

1. Michel Foucault — The Order of things: An archaeology of the Human Science, Newyork, 1978.P.296
2. K.B.Tripathy — PrachinaOdiaAbhilekha, Bhubaneswar, 1962 Pp 1-2.
3. Sudhakar Das — OdiaLanguage, literature and Culture, Prajna-Siromani Pratisthana, Mahanadi Vihar, Cuttack, 2006, p.2.

4. I bid p. 19.
5. Elezabeth Deeds   Ermarth Sequel to History, Princeton, New Jersey:Princeton University Press, 1992
6. Mayer Shapiro   "Nature of Abstract Art", Marxist Quarterly, No 1. (Jan-March, 1937) P.85
7. L.A.Weddell   Tibbetan Buddhism, Newyork, 1972.
8.   S.B.DasguptaOpcit. P.72.
9.   Quoted in SB Dasgupta Opcit.
10.   Kalyani Mallik "The philosophy of Nath Cult", The Philosophical Quarterly, Vol xxv, No.2, July, 1952, Pp 101-106.
11. Sribatsa Prasad Nath-   Natha Dharma-O-Nath Sahitya (Oriya) Published by Kasturee Nath Sarma, Po Gopalpur, Via: Nischinta Koili, Cuttack-754207, 2004.
12. Op Cit. P. 85.
13. Shirley Nicholson (Ed)-Shamanism: An Expanded View of
14. Sribatsa P.Nath-OpCit. P.241.
15. Chintamani Baliarsingh- Prachina Odia Gadya Sahitya, Rajarani Prakashini, Bhubaneswar,
16. A.A.Mc Donell-A History of Sanskrit Literature, Vol-III, P 307-329.
17. M.M.Chakravarty-The Journal and Proceeding of Asiatic Society Bengal, Vol-XI, P.216.
18. Chintamani Baliarsingh-OpCit. 117-118.
19. Rudrasudhanidhi (Ed)-Dr.Karunakar Kar, 1965-P.135.
20. Kunja Bihari Dash (Ed) - Lokagita-O-Kahani (Folk Song and stories) 1958, P 43434.
21. Janaki Balava Mohanty (Ed.) - Somanatha Varatakatha (1968) quoted by Pathani Pattnaik in Odia Sahityara Itihasa, P.139.

22. Leonard Norman Primiano–" Vernacular Religion and the search for Method in Religious Folk life," Western Folklore – 54, January NB. Premiano states" since 1984 I have been using the term" Vernacular religion" first as a cautionary alternative to "folk" and "popular" religion and then as a term representing my own understanding of cave dwellers' religion in both publication and public presentations" (p.41)
23. Wilhelm F.H.Nicdolusen "Names and Narratives" Journal of American Folks, 97 (1984) P.268.
24. Bansidhar Mohanty-Odia Sahityara Itihasa, Friends Publishers, Cuttack, 1970. P.234.
25. Harish Chandra Panda.-"Military system in Orissa in the so called dark age", Exploring OrissanHistory. Edtd. Nihar Ranjan Pattnaik, Kitab Mahal, Cuttack 2005. Pp 6-71. 25 (a) Ibid 25 (b) Madala Panji,Prachi edition P.21-22.
26. Patitapaban Mishra"Orissa and Bali: A Study in Cultural Transitand approchement, Exploring Orissan History, Op Cit. 89-97.
27. 'D.Daweenwarn Brahminism in south East Asia, New Delhi, 1979, p.197.
28. Manmohan Chakravarti. Journal of the Asiatic Society of Bengal, Vol. LXIV, 1901. P.175.
29. K.C.Panigrahi 30. History of Orissa, Kitab Mahal, Cuttack, 1981.
30. Sarala Dasa (Makers of Indian LiteratureSeries) Sahitya Akademi, New Delhi, 1975. 30 (a) Quoted in History of Odia Literature, Pathani Pattnaik, Nalanda, Cuttack, VIII Edn. 1997, P167.
31. R.D'Andrade "A Folk model of the Mind" in Cultural Models in Language and thought, Holland,D and N.Quinn Ed. Cambering Unit Preen, 1987 (Pp 112-148)
32. Gopinth Nanda, Bharata Darpana
33. Mayadhar Mansingh, Das Brothers, Behaupur, 1968.
34. Matira Mahakavi Sarala Das (Odia) 34. I bid.
35. Surendra Mahanty Odia Sahityara Adiparva, Students Sltore, Cuttack, 1963.
36. Anguttora Nikaya (Vol.II) is and extant Buddhist text and the quotation is collected from. Ashok Kumar Rath Jaina Dharma-

O-Sanskruti, Taratarini Pustakalaya, Bahaupur, 1991. T. Watters On Yuan Chwaing's Travels in
37. India, Vol-II, London, 1906. P.198. Surendra Kumar Moharana.- "Tantrayana in Orissa" Religious
38. History of Orissa, (Ed) Nihar Ranjan Pattnaik, Kitabmahal, College square, Cuttack. 2004. P.50 Arthur PollardSatire (Critical Idiom series), Methuen and Co. Norfolk, 1973.
39. Paul Merchant The Epic (Critical Idiom series) Methuen and Co. Ltd, London 1971.
40.
41. Risiri Frondizi "The Nature of Values" (1958) quoted in Robort S.Hartman's essay "the logic of Description and valuation, The Review of Metaphysics Vol. XIV, No.2 (Dec.1960)
42. Benimadhav Padhi "SiddheswarDas-O-Vichitra Ramayana" in Sandhana-O- Samikshya, Taratarini Pustakalaya, Behampur, 1997. Pp 25-33.
43. Krishna Chandra Panigrahi" Sarala Sahityara Aitihasika Chitra" (Odia: the historical picture in Sarala Literature) Prajatantra Prachara Samiti, Cuttack, 1977.

P.174-5.

■■■

CHAPTER-III

LITERATURE AS SUBSTITUTE RELIGION: THEOSOPHICAL POETRY OF THE PANCHASAKHAS

Inevitable reactions are always followed by inevitable ends. A period of glory fades after a few years. Time erases its hollow, and it passes from bright sunlight into the sunless shadow of history. The palm leaf epic of Sarala Das was new, to be studied in perspective with the rest of the epic literatures. Comparative studies began to emerge and the vernacular epic was to be evaluated either subjectively or objectively, as was done by the Sanskrit Scholars, the Siddhacharyas and the Natha saints. In the midst of such polemics and contradictory versions of opinion, Sarala's Mahabharata, no doubt, fuelled the Vratya folk sprit of the illiterate Odias to some extent, but the people's estrangement from the mainstream classic culture generated a space also for falling into the traps of folk religions including the powerful Buddhist Sahaja Yana.

The Mahabharata of Sarala Das was a grand Sahaja Yana brand of epic story, and it could neither promote a transcendental vision nor could retrieve Odias from their deep seated spiritual vulgarity. In an era of imperial expansionism and a society infested with sexually liberated Sahaja Yana syndrome, the vernacular epic entertained the baser Odia minds and they extolled it as a magnum opus. However, it was a great attempt to exercise with the expressive affectivity of an under-developed language.

The academic disinterestedness of the naïve folks of Odissa with their reluctance to engage in contemporary politico–cultural process

History of Ancient Odia Literature | 123

was a barrier on one side. On the other hand, a conservative resistance to the pressures for a socio-ethical change had turned the Odias into a frozen and petrified race. A purported intellectual stand about the past glory induced by the Mahabharata was, to some extent, an inspiring way of living in the present. But, competing versions of national epics were in considerable conflict and Kapilendra's last regnant years were full of rebellions. The cultural and political irreverence had already started from the southern tracts. The Moghal- Afgan raids from the north kept the Emperor diverted and instability crept in.

New critiques of Odia imperialism and the continually circulating news of Mogul destruction induced cleavages within the folds of racism that appeared rampant during Kapilendra's last regnant period of history. Others like the Moguls disregarded the linear progress of Odissan model, providing thereby at once a convenient target for traditional, conservative critics.

The prejudiced selection of a successor by Kapilendra to the throne by installing his son, Purushottama was met with severe resistance from his eldest son Hamvira, from the Southern tracts of the Odia country. Purushottama, it is mentioned, was the son of a Brahmin woman whom Kapilendra promoted as one of his queens and this furthered the racist antagonism in the state. Purushottama issued copper grants donating lands liberally to the Brahmins. The Brahmins, almost decadent by that time because of Buddhist empowerment, were unable to keep up their dignity while the Afghans and the Muslims started destroying the temples and sacred books of religion, art and architecture written in Odissa. The Buddhist monasteries had already been destroyed. Nagendranath Basu, in his Modern Buddhism and Its Followers in Orissa mentions "...after the invasion of the country by the Mohamedans in A.D. 1200, the monasteries of Odantapura and Vikram Cila were destroyed and the monks were killed and some fled to other countries. The learned Chakya Cri (Sakya Sri) went to Odissa and afterwards to Tibbet." 1 {P.13,, quoted in Pathani Pattnayak, p.233)

However, it could be obvious at least by this time that the experience gained through military conquests and geographical annexations did, in no way, improve the standard of the people. Perhaps the loudest manifestation of the erosion of culture lay in the catastrophic failure of education in the state. Education, to begin with, cannot be an arithmetic concept as culture is not so. Ironically, culture, to which we trace our wisdom and literature, and on account of which we designate ourselves as human, could not protect the Odias from falling into axiological doldrums. The folk epic of Siddheswar Parida (Sarala Das) did embody no moral force, as such, to contract the folk's Buddhist perversion into an inverted value system. The grand epic could not ensure compatibility with the deep-psyche eco-system. The Odia folk, as a species got into exceedingly serious moral trouble.

The poets of this period, therefore, referred to and led the life of the Saints as it was needed to show a model to the fallen folks. They proved that the written words could pull them up from the quagmire of libido, and that poetry had the power to enrich the imagination of the people, and to clarify thought and feeling. They offered literature as a substitute of religion; they provided a philosophy of life which the folk-Mahabharata failed to inculcate.

Could it define the total world–picture of a human culture, summing up the several ways in which men may relate to the cosmos in a single dramatic instance? Could it provide a scenario, or a prescription, at least, for action, and limit the possibilities for human response to the universal? It could neither represent a national myth nor an Odia archetype; nor could it amalgamate Odia consciousness with the universal, to the extent that there are universalities in the human condition which the Odias should be conscious of. In such a period of cultural inversions and spiritual fragility, the temple of Jagannatha provided a refuse to all saints and their followers, Buddhist and Jain, Saivite and Vaishnavite, Vedic and Tantric. A centre of integration was needed for Odissa that sprawled from the Ganges to Tiruchinnapalli and now being dismembered by the enemies. At home inter-dependency between the Hinduized Rajahs and the tribal population of the periphery sought some kind of integration in the temple precincts. The peculiar iconography of its main deities testified their tribal origin.

Jagannatha was worshipped as Vishnu Purushottama and Vishnu Jagannatha by the Brahmins. The non-Brahmins also conducted different rituals on special occasions. But the non Brahmin tribal priests were not adept at Brahminical rites. Prof. Basant Kumar Mallick, in an essay captioned, "Patronage, legitimacy and cultural assimilation in Medieval Orissa" notes, "The King –Brhmin alliance reached a climax during the rule of the Gajapati. Since the Brahmin (priests) were the custodians of lord Jagannatha and they monopolized over the "Spiritual domain" and the kings derived their legitimacy with the help of the priests, the interdependence or so to 'Sayan' alliance developed between them. This alliance has been explained by different traditions still prevalent in Orissa (P-207) (2)

This period of transition was a strange mélange of tolerance and jealousy; and their borders meeting tangentially formulated an art of living .The Brahmins tolerated the tribal people of Sonepur, Baudh and Koraput since the Bhairavi Chakra on which Jagannatha was installed had come from that centre of Oddiyana, Suvarnapur. Secondly, they tolerated the 'Others' since they did not threaten to disturb their inner territory, their singularity and their cultural memory.

But this compulsive alliance was often an untenable position for the reason that the conflict between real or imaginary territories was a relation of powers, either "implosive" or explosive "or "alternating" The implosive movement of the memory of the Siddhas and the Nathas or even of Sarala Das referred to a past that was no longer sustained by today's reality. Sarala's Mahabharata and its quasi-vulgar folk devolutions of the plot line was a lost model, though not forever. A theological unity between the temple precincts and the Grand road of Puri, the city of God and the city of men, or, a "strict equality" between the forces of life and death had become the new order of the day. The Moghals and the Afgans perpetrated pillages and devastation. It was a motif of unbridled greed threatening the fabric of human relations and the life value underlying it.

The new poets who set a model by living a saintly life identified themselves with the new model of civilization, radical and exploratory. Instead of totally transforming themselves, they evolved and tuned themselves with the reality of the world. Their memory (of the Siddhacharyas and the Nathists) found its strength in the nostalgia of the past, but that was a past without a past. In other words, the memory survived in moods of melancholy only.

The social structures during the reign of Purushottama Deva (1467-1497) admitted caste-centric divisions. His legendary war with the kingdom of Kanchi issued because of his proposal of marriage with the daughter of the king of Kanchi (Rupambika,or, Padmavati). The incident turned also into a sensational story for the Kavya- romances of later days. The king of Kanchi refused to give his daughter in marriage to Purushottama Deva, who had to perform the menial duty of a scavenger on the occasion of the car festival of Lord Jagannatha, every year. The Odia king took it to be an insult to both Lord Jagannatha and himself and took a vow to capture Kanchi and its princess (Rupambika/ Padmavati) by force. (3)

Purushottama was a learned man and a patron of learning, especially of Sanskrit Studies. He had also authored some Sanskrit texts. His son Prataprudra's accession (1497) was smooth and there was no hitch at the outset, but troubles did shoot up later. The campaigns of Krishnadeva Raya were successful and the Gajapati Empire broke up into pieces. Prataprudra was defeated and he gave his daughter Jaganmohini in marriage to Krishnadeva Raya.

It would be sufficient to state precisely that Prataprudra's period (1497-1540) was one, full of unrest and destabilization, but the most remarkable event of his reign was the visit of Sri Chaitanya to Puri in 1510. Sri Chaitanya's stay at Puri transformed the entire atmosphere and a new wave of theological feeling, a wisp of metaphysical steam began to charge the milieu. Five Odia saint poets-Jagannatha Das, Balaram Das, Yasovanta Das, Achyutanand Das and Anata Das were found to be associated with Sri Chaitanya and they are affectionately designated by the Odia literary historians as the Pancha Sakhas. (The five Associates of Sri Chaitanya)

However, it is difficult to bracket these five associates under the rubric of Gaudiya Vaishnavism (The Bengal school of Vaishnavism, which Sri Chatanya inculcated). Odissa had a long tradition of Vishnu worship that began with 4th century A.D, the time of the reign of Mathara dynasty. Dr. Hemant Kumar Parija in his essay,"Vaishnavism in Orissa," mentions, "the Matharas, who came to power in Kalinga in the later part of fourth century A.D, established their headquarters at Pistapura and Simhapura. Except Ananta Varman all the members of the family were more or less connected with the worship of Vishnu."(p.127) 4

The advent of Sri Chaitanya's group in 1510, his association with the Panchasakhas and the patronage Chaitanya manouevred from Prataprudra Deva, gave a new twist to Vaishnavism in Odissa. However, the 'Sadhana' of the so called Panchasakhas included Buddhist, Nathiest and Tantrik modes for which Surendra Mohanty designated them as "Jaga-Khichdi", a 'Jagannatha-risotto' in a light humoured idiom. Their multivalent yogic powers were merged into the Jaganatha school of thought. It was a fusion of Tantricism, Vaishnavism and Srividya Sadhana incorporating few Jain and Buddhist features too.

Dr. Mayadhar Mansingh has a point of his own. He mentions, "But as Chaitanya and his Oriya literary friends and disciples, who are now described as five associates had already been moulded in their own process of spiritual and literary strivings, they were unaffected by Chaitanya's religion. Up till then Orissa had a religious culture of her own. It was an indefinable combination of the Vedic, the Buddhists and the aboriginal or tantric streams of thought and all were symbolized in Lord Jagannatha.

From widely current sources it has been asserted that Jagannatha was originally a tribal god of the Savaras. Later on, this God has had Buddhistic and Brahminic metamorphoses. As a Brahminic God, Lord Jagannatha at Puri represents the reappearance of Krishna in Kaliyuga. So, the Krishna-cult has practically turned out to be the Jagannatha-cult in Orissa. The beatific realization continued through a sort of Vedantic self–examination till Chaitanya came on the scene. Intermittently, the Buddhist mode of self purification and some esoteric tantric practices did also continue...

This is what we find being held out in the writing of Jagannatha Das and his associates." (5)

The Panchasakha School of Poetry

The Pancha-Sakha, or the five pals, named Yashovanta Das (1470), Balaram Das (1473), Jagannatha Das (1487), Achyutananda Das (1482) and Sisu Ananta Das (1493) have lived in Odia literarary history as much by their miraculous Vaishnavite tantricism as by their spiritual poetry. Vaishnavism with a Tantric core thrived and controlled the socio-political destiny of Odissa during the time of the Pancha Sakha and its centre was the temple of Jagannatha, where the deities were re-enshrined and consecrated as Purushottama Jagannatha since the time of Chola Ganga Deva in the twelfth century. The Panchasakhas wrote Vaishnavite scholastic poems during the time of Prataparudra Deva (1497-1540).

Much water had flown down the river of time during the years that invested Vaishnavism with the practical energy. A bit of heat from the echo of the Sankeertana, a drop of love from the ocean of humanity, a patch of saffron sky and a flicker of genuine prayer shaped the inner geography of the Pancha Sakaha Poetry. The great Kapilendra

Deva, during whose imperial era flourished Sarala Das and his 'epic' for the Sudras', was himself a usurper and a king of dubious origin. He harvested every possible political benefit from the tripartite power conflict among the Somas, Bhaumas and the Bhanjas and focused on Lord Jagannatha as a unifying icon of political turmoil as much as Sarala's Mahabharata highlighted the concept for his own literary popularity. Kapilendra belittled Chodaganga Deva in the records of Madala Panji (the temple records) and did not acknowledge him as the renovator of the temple. He did not get his due since he was from South Kalinga. Kapilendra, in order to espouse a false secularism and diplomatic nationalism, had tortured the Brahmins of Jajnagar, manipulated the temple records and encouraged regional and caste-centric politics among the Odias. Sri Chaitanya's family had finally made an exodus from Odissa being tortured by Kapilandra Deva.

A Saivite -Vaishanavite conflict had already continued to create a schism in the Odia society since the 9th century and it was Ananga Bhima Deva-III (1211-1230) who resolved it by renovating the temple of Jagannatha and enshrining Jagannatha as "Purushottama Jagannatha", a Vaishnavite God. As the monarch of the Ganga dynasty, he declared himself as the 'Rout' (servant) of lord Jagannatha and administered the country on His behalf. (Epigraphia Indica Vol. XXX 6 PP.96-98 and Kulke.1978.150-155).6

Ranjan Gurukkal, in his essay," The Socio economic milieu of the Kerala Temples: A functional analysis" provides a nice analysis which would be applicable to the temple of Jagannatha also. Ranjan observes : "The temple gained a great deal of control over society through agrarian management by integrating the landed intermediaries, tenants, subtenants and the tillers into a system of production and distribution based on ties and obligations from the base to the top. By making the temple the nucleus of such an integrated society the corporate Brahman oligarchy was establishing control over the people at various social levels. The kings were drawn to the temple as chief patrons for the legitimization of their powers and the landed aristocracy for socio-political ascendancy" (Ranjan, 1980)7

The Saivite and Vashnavite conflicts were not only reflected in the Puranic literature of the age of Sarala Das, but the conflict also provided opportunities for the monarchs to reap strategic advantages out of it. The Skanda Purana (Purushottam Khanda) composed towards the last phase of Ganga Rule and the Mahabharata of Sarala Das, composed during Kapilandra Deva embody such conflicts and fictionalize the ultimate victory of Vaishnavism.

None of the inscriptions belonging to the Soma Kings mention about the Purushottam Kshetra of Puri. Chola Gangadeva's inscription available in the Nrushmha temple of Jagannath Temple precincts mentions about the rituals of Purushottama worship and the inscription at the Markandeswar Temple, built during Chola Ganga Deva's time. It also mentions about Purusottama. Chola Ganga Deva has also inscribed in the temple at Mukhalingam the name 'Jagato natha' for Madhukeswar (Inscriptions of Orissa P.25) Eschmann, Harman Kulke and G. C. Tripathy in their co edited book ,The Cult of Jagannatha and the Regional Tradition have also concluded in the first chapter that Chodaganga Deva declared himself to be a Vaishnavite for political benefits. Later, Chandrika Devi, a widowed daughter of Ananga Bhima, explored possibilities of elaborating on the concept of the Trinity: Jagannatha, Balabhadra and Subhadra.

It is also interesting to observe that Jagannatha as a deity has evoked multiple varieties of poems and concepts at different periods of our literary history. Indrabhuti, the great king of Uddiyana, (of the Charya period), in his Jnana Siddhi invokes Jagannatha in the following lines:

Pranipatyam Jagannatham Sarva Jeena Vararchitam
Sarva Buddhamanyam Siddhi vyapinam gaganopamam

The Lord is Jeena, Buddha and Vajra simultaneously. Sarala Das, in his Mahabharata, has used the word Patitapabana for Jagannatha to imbed the concept that Jagannath is a God for the fallen people. But Dr. Kailash Chandra Dash attributes this not to the deities on the sanctum sanctorum, but to a Patitapbana relief at the Lion's Gate.(Das:76-91)8

Kapilendra Deva followed the strategy of the Ganga Kings in nationalizing Jagannatha for diplomatic purposes. But after the vaishnavization of Jagannatha, the first poetic upsurge is evidenced during the Pancha Sakhas. Reformers like Shankar and Ramnuja had already visited Odissa in the 9th and 12th centuries respectively, and then came Madhvacharya to Puri to propagate his dvaitavada (dualism).

During the Ganga rule Nimbarka had also come to Odissa to propagate his visista-dvaitavada. Students from different parts of the country used to come to the Vishnu temple of Sri Kurma Pataka to study dvaita and advaita philosophy, music abhinaya and Sanskrit literature .the famous poet Jayadeva, belonging to a Brahmin family of Kalinga (before their migration to Kenduli) was a student in this temple school. He used to compose musicals based on Krishna themes and directed them. Sanskrit was the medium of performance. (Tripathy, 58). (9)That was how he used to propagate the philosophy of Nimbarka and Madhvacharya.

The Pancha Sakhas, it seems, should also be treated less as poets and more as propagators of Vaishnavism, but of a Vaishnavism of a new order, called the Vaishnavism of Utkal as opposed to that of Bengal. This new umbrella under which stood Balaram Das, Jagannath Das, Achyutananda Das, Ananta Das and Yasovant Das wrote as they understood Vaishnavism. The concepts were imported from the South by Nimbarka and Madhavacharya and Ramanuja, but they appropriated the entire philosophy to create an Odissi school of Vaishnavism with some difference. Finally, Sri Chaitanya had to meet Ramanuja to clarify his own concepts.

The difference was asserted the moment Jagannatha was conceived as Srikrishna. A Shakti named Sri Radha was introduced later, linking the concept of Vaishnavism partially to 'dual '(dvaita) and nondual ((advaita) dichotomies of philosophy, and also partially to the charya and Nathiest traditions of Mahayana Buddhism. The religion of Purusottam Jagannatha was established first when the deities were enshrined and installed on the "Bhairabi Chakra", brought from Oddiyana (Sonepur) by Jajati Kesari. The temple, it has been already reported, was renovated by Chodogangadeva when he retired from administration delegating all powers to his son, Kamarnava deva.

Reality in Advaita Vedanta, to tell it in technical terminology, is an undifferentiated, uni-patterned, whole, a self-referral field. In Vrihadaranyaka Upanishada it is defined,"sa yatha saindhava Ghana"(IV.5.12) and Chhandogya Upanishada says,"Tat poorna aparivarticha"(III.2.4.). The reference to taste is a clear testimony that in advaita, the Vedantists approach a concept by an intuition free from all differences, not by a concept of postulation. Every differentiation is a differentiation within one and the same intuited continuum.

The Upanishada attests to such equation in its understanding of the reality of the world and Brahman as poornamadah poornamidam. Thus Maya, (nescience) presents no duality. The microcosm and the macrocosm are built on the same plane- explained Vivekananda. Advaita keeps it clear which is often misunderstood: that it is not identity between the Brahman and the world that is asserted, but the independent reality of the world that is denied. Vachaspati Mishra clinches the issue:"When we say that the world is non-different from Brahman, we do not assert and identify, but only deny difference" (na khalu anyanyatvamiti avedam bramhah, kintu vedam vyasedhama) 10

The position of Advaita is clear as it formulates the reply to the charge leveled by Samkhya that attribution of omniscience (necessary knowledge of all things) to Brahman makes him dependent on the objects. Vedanta ascribes no contrariness in this. Bramhan can remain alone to shine and warm even if it has nothing to shine upon. Illumination can have no reference to the presence or absence of objects before him. But if the question is insisted that the Intelligent Sun, has always Something to know and think upon, Vedanta replies that the object of His eternal thought are nama-rupa (Names and forms). The idea of the Supra Being meditating on "words "and shaping worlds by mean of "word" cannot be taken as outlandish because we can perceive an extraordinary similarity between this theory and the Platonic theory of idea and the Stoic theory of the 'Logos'.

The Pancha Sakhas have, therefore, found it suitable to meditate on the "mantra" Klim Krishnaya Namah" and intuit Jagannatha as Krishna /Vishnu/Narayana. But the difficulty arises when we combine the five mendicants under a single category and link them with advaita school of Vendanta that was originated in the South and was propagated in Northern India through Odissa. The literature of Odisha, is situated somewhere on an interface, imbibing the cultural trends of both the regions and yet striving for an identity of its own through the temple of Jagannatha. The literature of the Pancha Sakha has been treated with a special status because Balarama, Jagannatha, Achyuta, Ananta and Yasovanta carved out a discernible cultural identity for the Odias in philosophy and in literature as well.

In Pancha Sakha literature, we discover Odia poets joining the mainstream literature of India for the first time. For the first time they seem to have been inducted into Vedic philosophy that had come to Odissa from South India. Jagannatha could not have been consecrated in consonance with the principles of Narayaniya (the Tantrik mode of worship combining Narayana as Purusha and Lakshmi as the Sakti) had there not been a king from the Chola dynasty of the South. The euphoria of nationalism created by Kapilendra and Sudramuni are later constructions, played through ethnic and caste-centric cards, and, the anti Ganga propaganda made by Kapilendra did not last long. One of his grandsons, Pratapa rudra Deva however, converted himself into a dedicated Vaishnava and created a forum at Puri for the discussion of Advaitic philosophy.

Around 1510, Sri Chaitanya came to Puri and stayed there for two years. This great Saint's grandfather Upendra Mishra had migrated to Nava Dvipa (Nadiya in West Bengal) because Kapilendra Deva had tortured and coerced the Brahmins at Jajpur. Sri Chaitanya, now a great Vaishnavite Saint, came to Puri and went to the temple alone to have a 'darshan' of Sri Jagannatha. A miraculous intuition of the realization of the Supreme Being made him unconscious in the temple . Vasudeva, the sovereign worshipper of the deity, took him to his home and Sri Chaitanya stayed in Puri for a month. Then he went to South to take some lessons on advanced Vaishnavism form Raya- Ramananda and came back to Puri in the month of July 1512. Sri Chaitanya was a twenty four year old young man by that time.

In July 1512, when Prataprudra Deva was performing the sweeping ritual; on the chariot of Jagannatha during the car festival, he was amazed to find young Chaitanya performing the Mokshya Nritya in a frenzied style with Samkeertana. In that keertana and dance performance were the Panch Sakhas along with Raya Ramananda, Raghu Arakhita, and 'Kanhei Khuntia and Sivananda Sen (Tripthy, p.127) 12 The Pancha Sakhas joined Sri Chaitanya in the Keertana marches to Bhubaneswar, Cuttack and Jajpur, Chitanya's ancestral place. The Bengalies had formed their own Gaudiya school of Vaishnabism and the Pancha Sakhas belonged to the Odissi school .There was hardly any metaphysical difference between the two groups. The Pancha sakhas, in addition to their saintly life style were engaged in writing puranas and Samhitas in Odia and Sri Chaitanya was famous in Puri as the incarnation of Sri Radha.

Yasovanta Das (1470)

Nurtured in a culture of verbal folk art at Adhanga that gave durability to his understanding of the world, this senior most of the Panchasakhas, Yasovanta Das related literature directly to his folk belief system in which the genesis of all writings is to be dissociated from time or history. Poems, as works of art, were self-sufficient totalities produced simply to be contemplated for their own sake. That is disinterestedly, purely for the enjoyment of their internal attributes and relationships. The author was not important at all as it happens in the folk and fairy tales. Hence he has nowhere mentioned about himself as the author. He has perceived his poems as energies inventing directly in human life as imparting and empowering beliefs, as communicating truths (and of course, also falsehoods) in a phasing form and their value and excellence as works of art had been measured instrumentally, in terms of their success (or failure) in serving broad human purposes.

In other words, Yasovanta, through his writings created a space into which he constantly disappeared. This notion of total merger and self effacement also occurred in meditation. In meditation Yasovanta could divest himself of all material conditions and could feel his own divine nature. He thought himself that he was the spirit and not the body, and that the whole of this universe, with all its relations, with all its good and all its evil, is but a series of paintings; scenes on a canvas-of which he himself was the witness. For Yasovanta imagination was the window to inspiration and the basis of all his thought.

At the threshold of this state of "Samadhi" was his domain of literature: and this moment was automatically one of self effacement. Nothing about him could have been available to us if Achyutananda's Udaya Kahani, Sabda-Brahma samhita and Sudarsana Dasa's Chaurasi Ajna would not have alluded to Yasovanta's biographical details.

Pandit Suryanarayana Das takes a decision about his year of birth as 1487 based on Udaya Kahani. But Artaballav Mohanty, depending on the introduction to Siva-Svarodaya, guesses Yasovanta's time of birth to be between 1495 and 1500. The research scholars of Bengal - like Nagendranath Basu, Sasibhusan Dasgupta and Biman behari Majumdar calculate Yasovanta's year of birth basing on Sabdabrahma Samhita (Charikhani) to be some times between 1470-1550.

However, this author accepts 1470 as the nearest probable because of three simple reasons: (i) Staying far away from the cultural capital (Puri) Yasovant was nurtured in the sub-cultural agrarian milieu. The memory of Kapilendra's last years was very fresh (Kapilendra died in 1467) and the influence of cultural populism was strong on Yashovanta. All that he understood by literature was taken from the practices of folk literature. None of the folk literary works imprint the name of the author. So did Yashovanta. He never mentioned his name. (ii) His literature reflects the memory of Kapilandra's heroic conquests so vividly that one would believe he was born and nurtured during his time. The gap between Kapilendra's death (1467) and Yashovanta's birth (1470) is negligible (iii) Thirdly, Achyutananda (b.1482) had married Yasovant's niece. It is probable that the uncle –in-law was 12 years elder to the Son-in-law.

However, Yashovanta's disciple Lohi Dasa's 'Sasthi Mela' and Sudarsana Dasa's Chaurasi Ajna (The Eighty four commandments) are too reliable, extant texts that provide details about Yasovant's life and time; Chaurasi Ajna informs:

"First Bhagaban Malla and then his two sons. The second one's son Niranjana and his son is Purushottama, Whose son was Nanda Malla. Nanda Malla's son was called Balabhadra and his son was Yasovanta" (Tr. R.Panigrahi).11

Yasovanta's father, Balabhadra was a military officer in the Army of Kujanga estate. Yasovanta did never serve the king of Kujanga and was working as a watchman to the feudal lord of Adhanga, a nearby place in Jagatsinghpur district. He was convicted in a theft case of a granary and Raghuram Champatty threw him behind the bars. But later, he was taken aback by the supernatural power of Yasovanta and was fully impressed by his personality. He gave his sister Anjana in marriage to Yasovanta.

Achytananda married Yasovanta's neice and in Udaya Kahani, he eulogizes Yasovanta:

Born in Lunar dynasty
Yasovanta sanctified his clan
Being a Kshatriya he was
A Saint, a Vaishnava with
The sect-mark on his forehead
He made his heart a temple of Vishnu
Frenzied was this saint in Love. (12)

Yasovanta accepted Lord Jagannatha as his Preceptor and mastered two seminal mantras for his sadhana: "Om Namah Sivaya and Om Klim Krishnaya Govindaya, Gopijana Ballavaya Svaha" He had to appear for a test for his accomplishment in the court of the Gajapati king and after he was accepted as an authenticated saint, Yasovanta was given an independent "Matha" (Monastery) which still operates in

Heragohiri street of Puri. Prema bhakti Gita was his seminal work in which 'Prema', or Love is extolled as pure knowledge mixed with 'bhakti'(devotion) But before we analyse the tenants of prem-bhakti, we need a short preliminary discussion on Vaishnavism as propounded by Sri Chaitanya (Gaudiya Vaishnavism) and this may be juxtaposed with the Utkaliya Vaishnavism centered round the temple of Jagannatha.

In Chaitanya Charitamrita, Krishna Das Kaviraja has elevated Parakiya Prema (extra-marital love) to an unstinted height and Sri Radha stands as the emblem and ultimate embodiment of this kind of devotion. Thus, Vaishnava theology is replete with illustrations of Krishna's sportive dalliance with Sri Radha called 'Lila' (a process of self-sacrificing emotion of total surrender in devotion) in 'Nitya golaka (a perpetual paradise). Thus, the literatures of the Vaishnavas of Bengal (Gaudiya Vaishnavism) elevate the eternal erotic sport of Radha and Krishna to mystic heights. The state of mind in such a perpetual erotic syndrome is called achintya-bhedaa-bheda (total dissolution of the 'I-you' conceptual differences). This idea of devotional engulfment is exemplified in Sri Radha's complete erotic surrender, which, in Vaishnava theology is also called 'Suddha (Pure) – Bhakti (devotion). Radha becomes the ultimate preceptor. Sri Chaitanya identified himself as 'Sri Radha' in terms of achintya-bhedaa-bheda (undifferentiated devotional surrender) bhakti.

The Utkaliya vaishnavism, however, does not accept this libidinal perpetuation as the highest order. On the other hand, they espouse jnana-misra-bhakti, devotion related to the spiritual philosophy of Vaishnavism, based on knowledge and cerebral realization. This technical knowledge is imparted by the right preceptor.

Yasovanta therefore, accepted Lord Jagannatha as SriKrishana and as his preceptor. The libidinal state is a prolonged state of ignorance, though in moments of epiphany sparks of ultimate ecstasy appear as spiritual euphoria. The beatitude experienced in such a state is as elusive as psychedelic.

Yasovanta was engaged in a continuous yogic endeavour to dispel such libidinal esoteric through the love of the eternal Brahman within. His Prema-bhakti-Gita stands as a radical challenge to counter argue the trend of Raganuga bhakti. (Emotional and sensual spiritualism) of the Gaudiya Vaishnavas.

The Preceptor in Prema bhakti Gita is Lord Srikrishna and he awakens the self knowledge in Arjuna. This literary text in five cantos is regarded now as a major theological treatise of the Jnana-/misra devotion. (Vaishnavas who consider love as a major component of devotion) Superseding Surendra Mahanty's remarks that the literature of the Panchskha period is "non-literature ("these are theological doctrines only"), this author ventures to provide a detailed synopsis of Yasovanta's Prema Bhakti Gita, partially following the tenets of Kant's Critique of Judgment reinterpreted in Jacques Derrida's 'Economimesis.' The Kantian judgment about art is a "self– sufficient totality." It is produced simply to be contemplated "for its own sake", 'disinterestedly', purely for the enjoyment of its internal attributes and relationships independently of any external relationships or effects it might have.

Jacques Derrida writes, "It is merely an accident of construction, a chance of composition that the whole Kantian theory of mimesis is set forth between these two remarks on salary...the definition of free (or liberal) art by opposition to mercenary art (and the statement) that in the fine arts the mind must occupy itself, excite and satisfy itself without having any end in view and independently of any salary." (13)

Whether Yashovanta had any end in view or not is not clear. But born in Kshatriya caste and following the foot prints of Sarala Das, he had to encounter a number of mainstream pundits and knowledgeable people starting from the Brahmins to the king at Puri. We don't have adequate space to mention them .But those who read Odia are advised to go through the monograph on Yashovant Das written by Dr. Lavanya Nayak (14)

Premabhakti Gita

By the observance of strict continence, Yasovanta could master up spiritual knowledge in a very short time. Yasovanta was an adept in the science of Raja-Yoga that gives the means of observing the internal states. He believed that the power of attention, when properly guided, and directed towards the cosmos within, would scan the mind, and would illumine facts sieveing out illusions.

Son of an army man and working for some time as a watchman, Yasovant dons the robe of Arjuna and questions Lord Krishna. The dialogue between the preceptor (Sri Krishna) and the disciple (Arjuna) brings home the theories of Jnana bhakti.

The chapter –one explicates the myth of origin of knowledge. What was the state of Param-Brahman (Supreme consciousness) in that primal era, before the creation began."-when nothing existed except a void? Srikrishna, in this dialogic discourse, explains that the Paramabrahman was in a state without attributes. The nature was born out of this supreme desire. Urma, Dhoorma (layers in the sky) Jyoti, Jwala and Bindu interacting with each other, created Yogamaya, but she was unstable in the fierce current of apocalyptic waters. The Supreme Being, then uprooted a hair from His body, created a post of thunder that stabilized Yogamaya. The thunder-pole metamorphosed and took the shape of the primal phallus. With the union of this phallic post and the Shakti of Yogamaya this Universe was created. The myth of creation envisioned in Yasobanta's Premabhakti Gita is epiphanic.

The Chapter -2 recreates the myth of the birth of Sri Radha and Sri Krishna. It reveals a folkloristic predisposition. Yasovanta tested the efficacy of such folk-myths of creation in the group discussions held with his followers at his matha (monastery) at Heragohiri Street, Puri. But he intended to overshadow the role of the author and to keep his myth alive. Let us examine the following mythopoeic account.

Parambrahma's omnipresence was symbolized by a speck in the void. From Him flowed a divine potion to the hands of Yogamaya and she drank it. She was pregnant after that and twins were born, a boy and a girl; and no sooner they fell down on to the earth, they were found dead. Yogamaya prayed the Almighty, and a command was heard from the void: "Recite the mantra "Gopijana ballavaya Svaha". They were resurrected after the mantra was recited, but their bodies could not be separated. Yogamaya blessed them: "Let your tender bodies develop into strong and youthful ones and let your attachment not be broken for million years." This Youngman and Young lady transformed into Sri Radha and Sri Krishna, a meiotic chromosome after separation of the two homologous members were born.

The Chapter -3 is devoted to depict the birth of Tripura, who was authorized to get an entry into the sporting pedestal of Radha and Krishna. The divine nectar of love spills out into the river Kalindi and Tripura is born. The poet addresses her with different names: Durga, Sasthi Devi, the head of the 64 thousand gopies, Vedamata and as the compound energy of Sattva, Raja and Tama etc. The three alphabets-'a' 'u' and 'm' (the phonic components of 'Om') were born from goddess Tripura. The creation was devoid of consciousness; now with the powers of Tripura Jnana (cognition) as a faculty was induced into creation.

This Chapter also constructs how the single phonic unit 'Om' split into the two-lettered word 'Rama' and then into a triangle, then into a hexagon and into numerous geometrical figures with eight, sixteen and thirty-two lettered mantras. and the geometric yantras. Srikrishna, then, offered Arjuna the enclosed sixteen syllable mantra of love: Om Hrim shrim Klim Gopi-jana- Ballavaya Svaha Klim shrim hrim. This is the samputa form of he mantra. (guarded by the veeja mantras Hrim-Shrim-Klim at the beginning and at the end.

The fourth chapter deals with the genesis of the universe and of the mantras, of the principle of eternity, the living Being and its relationship with the Supreme Being, the theory of 'Pinda' (body) and 'Brahmanda'(universe) and the methods of yoga etc. in a symbolic manner.

The fifth chapter of Prema-Bhakti- Gita describes the significance of Sri Krishna and his latest incarnation as Lord Jagannatha, who is installed as ParamaVaisahnva. Sri Krishna and Arjuna had arrived at the temple of Jagannatha at Puri riding on the wings of garuda (the bird and the vehicle of Vishnu) and have merged into the symbolic wooden images. installed on the bejewelled throne. Yasovanta describes:

Vedas on four sides exist
As steps; His gem-studded alter
dazzles over
This enormous vessel called universe
He's the Omkara,
the Brahma bindu, the passage through which flows
the nectar; our terminus
Timeless and endless
gods Ananta and Seshadeva
Constitute a dyad.

Yashovanta makes an attempt in Prema bhakati Gita to bring out a synthesis between the liquefaction of feelings and the total merger of identity (raganuga bhakti of Sri Chaitanya) on one side, and the logically, reasoned out concept of devotion (jnana-misra-bhakti) of the Odissan school of Vaishnavism on the other. The Odissan school of Vaishnavism generates a space for the study of the myths of creation and their theological explication. Yasovanta was committed to cater to the socio–religious needs of his time. He had not challenged the basic tenets embedded in Vedanta. But his capacity for explicating difficult concepts in folkloristic style for easy communication makes him a popular saint.

The narrative method of Premabhakti Gita, is, thus, a conscious activity that uses multidisciplinary theories to explicate Man's position in relation to the cosmos. Despite his deployment of every possible folk religious and mythopoeic style, Yasovanata's discursive content never opposed the institutionalized religions. His experience–centered approach and his application of it to occasions of supernatural encounter make it more authentic and acceptable. Its seriousness rests in the quest for truth. The course of this spiritual journey is rigorous and it necessitates strict moral discipline. Yasovanta emphasized moral discipline as the Sine-qua-non of realizing the Vedantic concept of Truth. So, he was acceptable to the commons and was capable of provoking the elite Brahmins of Muktimandapa.

To some, Premabhakti Gita is a folk version of Vedanta, a Vedanta in vernacular. It is a Prakarana Grantha embodying the philosophies of the Upanishadas as taught by Sankaracharya. But we don't have any proof that Yashovanta had studied Sanskrit at any time.

The Kshatriya subcastes were not allowed to touch Sanskrit texts, during the era of Gaajapati Purushottam Deva, yet it appears to have embodied an experiential inner voyage of the author from the world of material bondages to the point of spiritual illumination. His interpretation of Tripura (the name of a goddess) in Chapter-3 of the text as an energy born out of the fire of consciousness testifies his own spiritual illumination.

The idioms used by Yashovanta received their main impetus and their comprehensive definitions in the controversial debates of the circle of the Brahmins. Other spiritual exegete thereby was provided with sophisticated arguments to discuss whether the theological literature of the Panchasakhas tended to be scientific and had much to say about the nature of theology.

Yasovanta opens a discussion on the ontology of bhakti (devotion) and its positive results in Odissan context. He understands Sri Chaitanya's concept of empathetic surrender, but puts into practice the logic of devotion. His understanding of culture is not an innate genetic code. It is acquired by learning and socialization.

Bhakti (devotion) is alloyed with Jnana (knowledge and reasoning). Tripura dispels the darkness of Avidya (ignorance) from Yasovanta.

Instead of the libidinal continuity in the Raganuga bhakti, Yasovanta asserts the dominance of consciousness in his Jnana-misra genre of bhakti, which Tripura abides in that fire, but is not from it. Jnana (consciousness) is capable of consuming the entire universe. So, the poet-Saint does never assert the author within him. The total self effacement or dissolution of the self has taken place in that state. She is the de facto author in jnana-misra Bhakti. By disappearing into the realized strata of devotion, Yasovanta effaces the poetic self, consecrates writing and sacrifices the text for the posterity, for the unworthy bipeds claiming existence under the spell of avidya.

Prema bhakti Gita, touches the tangents of folklore. The folks including the Gajapati King understood him, however, as an 'expanded individual', as the creator and possessor of a focussed folkloric world view, who constantly interpreted and negotiated his own beliefs. This does not imply that Yashovanta Malla as an individual was not influenced by a number of physiological, cultural social and environmental forces; on the contrary, he understands that given the human capacity to interpret these influences, people develop their own folklore within as well as around themselves.

Regina Bendix, in her essay "Mormot, Memet, and Marmoset: Further researches on the Folklore of Dyads" (1987) discusses on the importance of "idio-culture" to characterize small group culture, defining it as a system of knowledge, beliefs, behaviours and customs particular to an interaction group to which members can refer and employ as the basis of further interaction."15 Yasovanta's disciples in his Matha (monastery), situated in Heragohiri Street (Puri) formulated this small group culture that believed the myths of creation and the tenets of Jnana-misra-bhakti brought out in Prema-Bhakti-Gita. It is worth noting that the difficulties of scholarly transmission of Utkaliya Vaishnavism can be removed by accepting the technical terminology or Regina Bendix. While the term "idiolect" seems to refer to the linguistic system of a single individual, the term "idioculture" (16) in the hands of folklorists like Bendix does not refer to the culture of single individuals (Like these saint -poets), but rather emphasizes the small group assembling at the Heragohiri Street Matha (monastery). Yasovanta was able to create a "uniculture" through which an Utkala brand of Vaishnavite culture could be created. Whether the current generation of critics would reconstruct through the text a thought or experience does not matter. Rather, to understand Prema bhakti Gita by a poet from the kshatriya sub-caste with no classical education is important for us. It is also important to assess the text through its structure, its architecture, its intrinsic form, its closure with overemphasizing Srikhetra (Puri) and finally, through Lord Jagannatha conceived by him as Sri Krishna.

The big gap between Yasovanta's literary creations (16th century) and its critical revaluation (Mid -20th century) facilitated Odia critics to extrapolate their fantasies and personal intuitions with regard to the year of the birth of the poet and the full list of his works. In our times, 'authors' are declared dead by Rolland Barthes (The death of the Author) (17) and if by chance, they exist, Michel Foucault in his 'what is an author' (18) would dispel all our misgivings about the author's creative esoteric. We would not devote pages to prove whether Surendra Mohanty was right or Sachidananda Mishra; whether Krishna Charan Behera was right by precluding Suryanarayan Das and whether Artaballav Mohanty was right with regard to Yasovanta's year of birth. Such historical investigations have become irrelevant for the present generation.While our earlier critics name one of Yasovant's works as Gobinda Chandra Gita, Suryanaraya Das, Artaballav Mohanty and Surrendra Mahanty named it as Gita Gobinda Chandra. This small book available on the foot paths is captioned Gobinda Chandra.

Gobinda Chandra is a Buddhist allegory on renunciation. The story establishes Yasovanta's link with the Nathist tradition because the original story has been culled from Nathist literature. Hadipa is a character in this religious romance. The story depicts how a prince named Gobinda Chandra, the son of the king Ripu Chandra renounced the glitz and glitter of the palace and two of his tender wives to join as a mendicant under the Nathist fold. Gobinda was extremely handsome and he was deeply indulged in the luxuries including carnal pleasure in his early twenties. Mukta Dei, the mother of the boy (probably a disciple of Hadipa) was extremely worried about her son's future and tried to protect him by imposing a disciplined living and a rigorous avoidance of pleasure on him.

So, she pulled her son out of the quagmire of sex (practiced by Sahaja Yana sect) and sent her son out as a mendicant. Govinda abandoned his two teen aged wives and took to begging as a means of livelihood. Mukta Dei, probably, had a fear that pursuit of pleasure would turn into pain at the end. Govinda lived as a mendicant moving across the county begging with Hadipa. He disfigured his handsome body by painting it with ashes, holding a bowl and clad in rags.

The mother queen, it seems, was possessed with an actual fear for pleasure probably because she was deprived of the actual pleasures of gratification. Gobinda went and begged in fair houses to collect the food for the day. Hadipa, a guru of the neo Buddhist Natha cult, lodged him in the house of a hoary fisherwoman aged about three hundred and eighty years. This workholic lady had 3000 goats and hundreds of milking cows. But despite being extremely rich and having no one to inherit the property, she woke up early in the morning and went on working till late nights. The young mendicant, one day, asked her as to why and for whom she was toiling so hard.

The 380 year old fisherwoman replied that she was also a yogin and a better one than him since she was able to work hard. Yasovanta's handsome hero thus was trained in kayasadhana or the practice of yoga through the culture of the body so that the body would attain the state of 'Jivanmukta' or, he would attain a state of liberty in which death, god of time (Kala-Yama) would not be able to overpower him.

Yasovanta's Gobinda Chandra was an axiological romance. The ballad appears to be a fantasy with an allegorical secondary level of meaning which reflected the debauched Odia society during the post Kapilaendra Deva era. As a knowledgeable prophet, therefore, he aimed at some kind of social reformation through literary-moral allegories.

Yasovanta has also written religious poems like Siva Svarodaya, Bana-bhoji (Picnic Poems), Mantra boli (The word as Mantra) and Atma parache Gita (A Gita on self identity) etc. These works are almost devoted to the theories of Yoga etc. His Padma-vana-rasa, Maalikaa and the devotional songs need not be analyzed since they repeat the same austere reformative principles of theology. Govinda Chandra's renunciation is accepted as a heart rending story still sung by the Nathist Mendicants with a Kendera (a one-string fiddle to be bowed to produce a tragic note, an indigenous musical instrument.) Atma Parache Gita extols the magic woven round the Lilas of Jagannatha Yasovanta's simple expression makes it extremely readable.

An account of Yasovanta's theological literature does not complete the history. On the other side of this poet, his sub-creations existed, of marvels and magic performances. Neither the justification of the era of the so-called Pancha -sakhas nor the full biographical historical criticism of Yasovanta's literature would be complete if we do not mention vignettes of those miraculous activities. The miracles by the Pancha sakhas kept the king overpowered and the administration was forced to acknowledge their power officially. The grant of the 'Matha' (monasteries) and position to Yasovanta Das in Heragohiri Street, Puri could be possible only because of Yasovanta's Tantric powers through which he could be able to assert himself as a prophet with supernatural power in the Brahmin dominated city of Jagannatha.

Yasovanta figures in history as well as in literature after his arrival at Puri as a prophet and poet. The story of his journey begins with a miraculous brahma-rakshas leading his way to Puri since Yasobanta did not know the road from Adhanga to Puri.. At times he was flying secretly riding on a broken wall to distant places. Such miraculous movement is possible in "Chhinmasta"sadhana of the Saktas. Probably Yasovanta had learnt and acquired such occult powers through Buddhist Vajra yana practices, which the Sapta Kumaris (the seven women tantrics trained by Lakshminkara in the 12th century Oddiyana) spread in the Orissan countryside through their innumerable disciples. The Buddhist Tantra was devoted to the cause of the empowerment of the Sudras and other low caste people who were abandoned by the Brahmins as untouchables in the citadels of Vedic religion. The mysterious occult power worked as a subversive force to overpower Brahminical religious autocracy. This religious rebellion had started since Kapilendra Deva usurped the throne.

The Panchsakhas promoted each other and had deep knowledge in Vaishnavite tantra. The Purusha-prakriti (the principle of male and female energy clubbed together to form an invincible syncretic force) paradigm was introduced into the Radha-Krishna format (instead of Linga and Shakti, Buddhist Prajna and Upaya) and it was extrapolated in the temple of Jagannatha after Choda Ganga Deva installed the Bhairabi chakra. Thus, they kept their real identities hidden from the mundane society; The Buddhist mode was not given a currency because Lakhshminkara's Sahaja Yana could not be accepted by the imperial administration publicly. The Scenario of decadence continued to pervade the sociological levels in which tantra was castigated as "non-vedic" and sexo-yogic debauchery.

The process of disintegration in Odissan religio-political sector had already started during the last few years of Kapilendra Deva's regnant period. The wisdom of the Odias, their confidence, morale and alacrity was at its lower ebb. The self-centered, caste based conflicts had entropied the so called Odia solidarity built by the shrewd tactics of Kapilendra Deva and his solar dynasty. The Gangas were caricatured as "Southies" by Kapilendra to divert the attention of the common soldiers. But they could survive in Odissa because of Nitei Dhobuni's Buddhist Tantras (Nitei is one of the famous sapta kumaries of Oddiyana who were the seven Sahajayana disciples of Lakshminkara). Buddhist Tantric religion had already made insidious incursion into power corridors. (Nitei Dhobuni is still worshipped in Oddiyana, i.e. Sonepur) (19) Kapilendra Deva's Odiya nationalism was too brittle and fragile an emotion to hold the religiocultural weight. It crumbled down because of the Brahminic incapacity to provide tantric-spiritual protection to the state.

The last straw to hold was the Temple of Jagannatha. But the god was worshipped on the Bhairabi chakra brought from Oddiyana by the Kesari Kings. Chodaganga Deva renovated the temple. Kapilendra and his successors attempted to play the game of power centering the temple. The enthronement of Purushottama (he was the son of a Brahman woman whom he married by simple exchange of garlands) created court intrigues. Purushottama's politics of "Jagannatha miracle" began with his invasion of Kanchi in which a rumour was circulated that Jagannatha and Balabhadra accompanied the king to fight with Saluva Narasimha Deva, a Ganapati worshipper of Andhra.

Purushottama Deva's victory over Kanchi and his capture of the Telugu princess Padmavati (Roopambika) generated one more trouble for the Odia country. Purushottama had strong faith in the Vedic power of the Brahmins. He wanted to replace the Buddhist mode of Tantric worship by the Brahmins who were relieved of paying all kinds of taxes and land grants were given to them during Purushottama Deva's rule.

The Tantric practices however could not be discontinued totally. The mode continued residually, limited only to some rituals to be performed by the non-Brahmin servitors. The rising Brahminical power, with the support of the king tended to cross boundaries. The Buddhist siddhacharyas were assaulted and killed. But the Brahminical forces were divided. The Odia Brahmins were underestimated by the ones who came from Kanyakubja, Ujjain and Andhra through the Kesari

Kings. The Brahmins who were invited from the South by the Gangas had their own opinion about religious issues. The king, especially, Prataparudra Deva (1497-1540) son of Purushottama Deva) was in deep trouble because of such Tantric-Vedic fights.

The records of Madala Panji (2nd edition) literature provides one more version of Purushottama Deva leading two expeditions to Kanchi. The second version states about the princess called "Padmini: The king of Kanchi about the marriage...After the victory over the throne of Kanchi, the king forcibly captured the Princess (Padmini) and did not marry her. The reason was discovered later. Purushottama Deva, after his victory and capture of the princess was exercised with some reprobate application of Buddhist Tantra that would not be the body of the king and his wound would be infested with worms if he cohabited with Padmini (Padmavati) after marriage. The Brahmans of the closer circle persuaded Purushottama to marry the princess and the recondite Tantric infection manifested in the body of the king. The suppurated wounds on his body were never healed The act of reparation started with habilitation of Brahmins in an agrahara (brahmin sasana) village called Dandamukundapur and a pond was dug naming it after Padmavati. (20)

This record of Madala Panji cannot be undervalued and sidelined as a hoax or an account of Odia superstitions. The suffering of Purushottama Deva was a consequence of the recondite Buddhist Tantra. It proved how the Tantra overpowered the imperial power gradually, and confirmed that the Brahminic modes could not protect the king. The Buddhists struggled since the 11th century to capture the political power. But the cultural religious centre had already shifted from the Tantric field of Oddiyana (Suvarnapur) to the temple premises of Puri.

The seven woman Tantric disciples of Laxminkara's Sahaja Yana School had grown powerful during the regnant period of the Ganga kings. They are worshipped even today as 'Sat–bahen' (seven sisters) 'at Suvarnapur. These seven Buddhist lady tantrics, known as Jnanadei Maluni (A florist woman), Nitei Dhobani (A washer woman), Patra Sauruni (A sabara woman putting on leaves only), Sua Teluni (An oil-woman), Sukuti Chamruni (A Cobbler's woman) and Gangi Gauduni (A milk maid) played a major role in Ganga power-politics. They had trained many non-Brahmin practitioners to generate an army of tantrics who would overpower the Vedantic Brahmin force.

The continuity of such a Tantric/ Sakta tradition can be traced back to the period of Charya poetry which seems to have been revived by the Pancha Sakha prophets. The Tibbetan sources inform that Saraha Pada was the founder of Buddha-Kalpa Tantra in Orissa. The Buddhist monasteries at Ratnagiri, Lalitgiri, Udayagiri and Jaipur were research centres of Buddhist Tantras. New tantric schools were founded and popularized throughout the country. Lui Pa's Yogini Sama charya Tantra, Kambalapada and Padmapada's Hebajra Tantra, Krishnacharya's (Kanhu Pa) Samputaka Tantra, Lilita Vajra's Krishna Yamari Tantra, Gambhira Vajra's Vajramrita Tantra, Kukkuripada's Mahamaya Tantra, Pitopada's Kalachakra Tantra and Jayadratha's Chakra Sambhara Tantra emerged from Oddiyana and probably Yashovanta had acquired some such powers from the touring mendicants of fifteenth century.

They are important to us since they produced volumes of Maalikaa Poetry (astro- predicton about the future happenings) and other mystical poems of the era. The Pancha–sakha poetry emerged as a modified version of the Tantric Charya poetry, but it was centered round the Temple of Jagannatha and was operating under the rubric of Utkaliya Vaishnavism. Yashovanta's Utkaliya Vaishnavism emphasized spiritual knowledge (Jnana) advocated by the Buddhist modes of logical quest for the truth.

The authors of Orissan history of literature engaged themselves in tracing the exact year of the birth of the poets. They could not study Yasovanta's early life at Adhanga village, prior to his exodus and arrival at Srikshetra (Puri). A monograph published by Orissa Sahitya Akademi informs that Yashovanta encountered a Brahma – Rakshasa/ ghostly demon on his lonely route to Puri. He conjured it up with a Tantric wand and commanded the ghost to lead his way to Puri. The hypnotized Brahma-rakshas obeyed his command.

The bizarre news related to supernaturalism invoked the curiosity of the king (Prataprudra Deva) and he came up to Atharanala (the entrance to Puri) to welcome the Saint, who after being settled in the Monastery granted to him in Heragohiri Street performed numerous marvellous acts to win the royal trust. The king was convinced at once about Yashovanta's recondite knowledge, which the Brahmins did not know.

The Sapta trimsa Bayana (The Thirty seventh Narration) of Yasovanta describes how king Prataprudra summoned Yasovanta to the banks of Narendra tank, where he waited under a Kadamba tree to meet him. Yasovanta paid a visit, generated a garland out of void and greeted him. The king was mystified once more since he could not conceive as to how Yasovanta produced a garland out of the vacuum. Little awed by the marvel, the king tested him further. He took a palmful of soil secretly and asked Yasovanta what he held in his closed hand. Yasovanta replied that the king held some gold and the king opened his palm to discover that the soil had metamorphosed into gold. Such miracles take place even today by the street mendicants of Cuttack and Bhubaneswar.

The Brahmins, one day, tested Yasovanta by keeping pebbles in a pot and asking him what was inside, Yasovanta answered immediately that it was milk and to their surprise, the Brahmins opened the pot to discover milk within.

The 39th narration depicts one more marvellous incident in which Prataprudra Deva(the King) gave him some scented sandal paste to anoint it on the icon of Lord Jagannatha. Yasovanta knew that he was Sudra by caste and the Brahmins would not allow him to touch the icon at the sanctum. So he did not go to the temple and painted the walls of his room with sandal paste. The news was immediately communicated to the king. The king summoned him immediately and asked him as to why he flouted the royal commands. Yasovanta replied that he offered and anointed the sandal paste on the icons of the Lord. The King verified to discover that the scented paste was actually anointed on the Lord.

The essential ingredients in all such Tantric marvels are to be regarded as miracles happening outside the normal space - time continuum of the everyday world. Yasovanta's yogic perseverance and Tantric accomplishments were so perfect that his will power could irrupt into the normal world and the kings as well as the Brahmins of his era were forced to be transported into another world.

The empirical mindsets and the occidental orientation of gross rationalism forbid the modern readers to accept these miracles of the saints. However, the countryside Odissa, even today, does believe in the mendicants and such miracles are performed in different festive occasions.

Balarama Dasa (1473)

Pt. Suryanaraya Das mentions about Balaram Dasa as a poet born in 1484 and others date his his birth between 1504 and1532. We have accepted here Prof. Artaballav Mohanty's calculation based on the introduction of Balarama's Bata-Abakasa. There were two poets during that period with the same name-one Matta Balarama, born in Bengal and the other Balarama Dasa.Pt. Binayak Mishra also supports Suryanaryana Dasa's opinion and concluded that both the names refer to the same person. But Surendra Mohanty in his Odia Sahityaara Itihasa, (Madhya Parva) proves them to be two different poets.

The search for an exact person and an exact historical date of birth was important in early theories of interpretation. The literary historians, therefore, made genuine attempts to prove their own historical authenticity. The inadequacies we notice in their findings are due to non availability of source documents, which are available to us through various research works now, published and unpublished. Besides a close reading of Balarama's poetic texts reveal some information about his personal details:

"The poet says he was thirty two years old when he finished the epic and that he versified the whole account of Ramayana as he learnt it from the narration of the story by the pundits."(22)

But B.C Majumdar, in his Typical Selection from Odia Literature does not specify when the epic was completed.. He refers to Balarama Dasa's magnum opus Jagamohan Ramayana in which the poet mentions:

There was a great minister, Somanatha Mahapatra I'm Balaram Dasa, his son", (Sundara –kanda) Achyutananda's Udaya kahani assigns 1484 as the year of the poet's birth. The new generation historians prove that Balarama was alive during Prataparudra Deva (1497-1541). Rama Dasa's Dardhyata bhakti Rasamrita states: "Purushottama Tara ghara" (His home is at Purushottama, Puri); but Iswara Dasa's Chaitanya Bhagavata reports that Balarama was born in Chandrapur, near Jajapur basing on what sources not mentioned, though. We do not have space for such arbitrary accounts and legends.

Balarama's Jagamohan Ramayana was probably recited by the poet to the public in the Jagamohana of Jagannatha temple. Bijoy C. Majumdar reports, "The whole poem was evidently recited by the poet by taking his seat in the Jagamohana, or the audience hall of the Puri temple, for the title of the book is Jagamohan Ramayana. Though Jagamohan Ramayana is the title of the colophon, the work subsequently acquired the name Dandi Ramayana by the listeners for two reasons –recited on the danda (street) and recited in dandi vritta (the 14 lettered rhyme scheme)."23

It is most probable that his father Somanath Mahapatra was an Odia samanta from Puri in Prataparudra's time and hence as a Sudra, he was rejected by the Brahmins to be admitted as a student. He was tutored by the Bhuddhist Siddhacharyas who taught him Hindu scholastic books (the Vedas and the Vedanta) along with Buddhist Tantra. The 37 books which he wrote gives us a general impression about Satya and Ruta (rta) Satya is the cause of the universe where as Ruta (Rta) is the rhythm of the later literature. The term Brahman replaced the term satya and the term Dharma replaced the term Ruta (Rta). Since these terms are frequently used in the Rig-Veda, we guess that Balarama got a formal training in Vedas also. The list of his works evidences his level of erudition and mastery over our classical religion:

(1) Jagamohana Ramayana (2) Bata abakasha (3) Bhava Samudra, (4) Lakshmi purana (5) Srimad Bhagabat Gita, (6) Brahma Gita or Gupta Gita (7) Vedanta sara Gupta Gita (8) Virat Gita, (9) Amarkosha Gita(10) Dipti sara Gita (11) Arjuna Gita ,(12) Jnana Ujjwal mani Gita(13) Garuda Gita(14) Manu Gita(15) Gaja nistarana Gita(16) Giita sara(17) Brahmanda Bhugala(18) sareera Bhugoal(19) Saptanga Yoga sara Gita (20) Ganesh Bibhuti (21) Adhayay Mahabharta, (22) Jnana Chudamani, (23) Mriguni Stuti, (24) Durga Struti, (25) Kamal lochan Chautisa, (26)Baramasi (27) Rama Bibha ,(28) Tula Bhina, (29) Malasree , (30)Brahma purana, (31) Gupta Tika (32) Sabha Binoda (33) Bhuta keli,(34) Brahma Puran, (35) Kural Puran (36)Panasa Chori (37) Kali Bhagabata

These works may be grouped under the following six categories: a)Gita (b) Malika(c) Purana (d) Stuti or devotional songs (e) Chautisa and (f) Philosophical Treaties.

Balaram Dasa has written 11Gitas for the benefit of his Sudra listeners. He knew it well that the mainstream Sanskrit scholars considered Gita as one of the Prasthana Trayas, the other two being the Upanishadas and the Brahma sutras. It has remained a perennial source of spiritual inspiration, whereas the Brahmins had closed the doors of knowledge for the Sudras. This caste-centric prejudice had caused manifold difficulties to the poet and he was determined to summarize the contents of the classical Sanskrit books for the consumption of the downtrodden people. The Gita was also popular since it embodied different systems of Hindu philosophy: ethics and religion that suited to people with different temperaments. This universality of the Gita, however, has puzzled the scholars, but the Brahmins of Kanyakubja and those of Andhra–Tamilnadu Karnataka had engendered different hermeneutic accounts. They had created walls not only amongst themselves, but between them and the non-Brahmin castes also. Balarama felt that the multivalent interpretations confused the Vratyas of Odissa. These were contradictory in nature, for instance, they created a division between monism and dualism, knowledge and action and devotion, and Samkhya and Vedanta etc.

The Brahmins of Puri, having migrated from different cultural and linguistic communities, had been trained by different Gurus who interpreted the religions with no endeavour for reconciliation. Balarama, himself trained by the Buddhist Scholars understood these inner contradictions of Hindu religion with sharp logic and reasoning and felt the urgency of presenting to the mass a simplified version of spiritual knowledge. He began, therefore, to put the essence of the Bhagabat Gita. in ten of his vernacular Gita texts: Balaram Gita/ Gupta gita, Virat gita, Amarkosha Gita, Diptisara Gita, Jnana-Ujjwala Gita, Garuda Gita, Manu Gita, Gaja nistarana Gita ,Arjuna Gita and finally one Gita sara (Essences of Gita).

It has to be borne in mind that the land of the Oda farmers called Odissa was a Vratya country and the North Indian Brahmin Diaspora who migrated from the Middle East were sanctifying themselves by sprinkling cow-dung water when they visited Anga, Banga and Kalinga countres.They felt that the Vedic norms were constantly being flouted in these three regions. So, the ordinary, naïve Odias were obfuscated about Dharma or religion.

Balarama takes the definition of Dharma from Rig veda which defines it is as "the upholder, or supporter or sustainer." In Atharva veda, Dharma is attained in the sense of merit acquired by the performance of religious rites. In Aiterya Brahmana, Dharma is the whole body of religious duties. The Chhandogya Upanishada mentions that dharma is constituted of three components: One is constituted by sacrifice, study and charity, the second by austerities (like one notices in the hermits) and the third is what the Brahmchari, sojourning in the hermitage of the Guru (teacher) attains.

Gradually, the word Dharma, by the time Balarama Dasa wrote passed through several transitions of meaning. It signified the privileges (that belonged to the Brahmins alone), duties and obligations of a man as a member of the Aryan community, as member of one of the four castes, and as a person in a defined stage of life. It is in this sense that Dharma is interpreted in the Bhagabat Gita. Balarama, trained in Buddhist Tantra and episteme, understood Dharma as a basic component of existence: of matter, mind and force, to stay in tune with the philosophical trends of the time. He explained the tenets of Yoga and human anatomy as the Nathists did in Kaya sadhana, Panchanga yaga, Saptamga Yoga and Astanga yoga.

Balarama revived the Nathist practices by propagating its tenets in terms of vernacular religion for the consumption of the ordinary men. But in fact, he attempted to impart the highest spiritual knowledge through the concept of Jagannatha, the Odia God that was simultaneously one and many. Indradyumna, who conceived of such icons, intended to cater to the five major sects of Hindu worshippers 1) the Vedic ritualists, 2) the Vaishnabas, 3) the Saivites, 4) the Saktas, and 5) the Ganapatyas(the sect believing in Lord Ganesha). All these cults are synthesized in 'Sri Vidya' and 'Sri Chakra' on which the deities are installed. Having understood this synchronic principle, Balarama composed the folk Brahmanda Bhoogola and Sareera Bhoogola. He related the body (pinda) with the cosmos to explain that the cosmos is contained in the body. It is a combination of the senses and sense organs. Balarama explained the properties, character and conditions of transformation in the sense organs.Yet, Brahmanda Bhoogola is to be considered as a radical text at a time when the king and the Brahmins of the sixteen agarharas declared Puri as the holiest of all places and the temple of Jagannatha as the only seat of God. Balarama persuaded the readers to believe that the entire temple and the temple city are contained in the body itself. The twenty two steps of the temple and the Jagamohan etc. are situated within the human body. A metaphor, thus, changes the whole concept and reinterprets the Brahminical /political meaning of Puri and its Brahman, he explains, is 'absolute intelligence' and 'bliss', the ultimate resort of one who bestows others with wealth, as one who is the knower of Brahman, and who lives in it. The Yogasastra of Patanjali is explained in the simplest terms.

The aim is to conceive what is eternal and immortal. In Balarma's definition the 'infinite' is in which one sees nothing else, but that in which one sees something else, Understands nothing else, but that in which one sees something else., is the finite that which is infinite, and is alone immortal and that which in faith is mortal.

Balarama's Saptanga Yoga sutra Gita refers to Patanjali's "tasya saptadha Pranta bhumih prajna (ii.27). Balarama does not only elucidate the seven limbs of Yoga practice (the eighth limb being Samadhi or a conscious death), but also he takes care to warn that awareness must be the hall-mark of all the seven limbs of yoga, otherwise yoga would end up as gymnastics. The light of awareness shines when the psychic impurities are cleansed and eliminated by the intelligent practices of the seven limbs of yoga. Balarama enumerates that discipline, observances, posture, exercise of the life force, and introversion of attention, concentration and meditation are the "saptanga" or the seven limbs of yoga or, the direct realization of oneness within. He alludes only to seven limbs or steps as prescribed in Patanjali's YogaSutra: yama, niyama, asana, pranayama, pratyahara, dharana, dhyan and Samadhi (the eighth step is not dealt with). In Balarama's book, this develops in to a doctrine. A practitioner of yoga shall have to ensure that these eight limbs are all intact together and that they are characterized by the light of wisdom. Balarama, in his works like Brahmanda Bhodgala and Sareera Bhoogala (Geography of the Body) summarizes the essence of Chhandogya Upanishada and Patanjali's Yoga Sutra.

The function of the arteries, the Susumna, the characteristics of the different elements are explained in Kundalini Yoga, one has to acquire a thorough knowledge of Susumna Nadi or what the westerners call a spinal cord has almost been translated in comprehensible poetry for public understanding.

The arteries which belong to the heart exist filled with the juice of a fine substance which changes to reddish brown, white, blue, yellow and red, like the sun that combines different colours. The sun is also reddish- brown, he is white,, he is blue, he is yellow, he is red.

After the arteries, Balarama explains the geography of the spinal cord. In the middle of that narrow space of the hollowed space of Susumna naadi (vertibra), remains the undecaying all knowing Omni faced, great fire, which has flames on every side, which enjoys the food presented before it which remains assimilating the food consumed (the rays of which spread scattering themselves vertically and horizontally) and which warms its own body from the sole to the crown. In the centre of that fire which permeates the whole body, there abides a tongue of fire, of the colour of shining gold, which is the topmost among the subtle, which is dazzling like a flesh of the lightening that appears in the middle of a rain –bearing cloud, which is as slender as a paddy – grain; and which serves as a comparison to illustrate subtlety.

Sushumna extends from the Muladhara chakra (Second vertebra of coccygeal region to Brahmarandhra. The western anatomy admits that there is a central canal in the spinal cord, called "canalis centralise" and that cord is made up of grey and white brain–matter. The spinal cord is dropped in the hollow of spinal column. In the same way, sushumna is dropped within the spinal canal and has subtle sections. It is of red colour like fire.

The Sareera bhoogola (the geography of the human body, explains Balarama, embodies the Brahmanda (The cosmos) within. Thus his poetry covers the knowledge of the Upanishada and all ancient scriptures. Balarama had written a number of Malika poems. The Malika poems foretell the future. He has written four popular mythological works called Puranas. Balaram has written Brahma Purana, Lakhshmi Purana and Kurala Purana in addition to his Magnum opus Jagamohan Ramayana. One is astounded to notice Balarama writing the Kurala Purana in Orissa since Tiru-K Kural of Tiru Valluvar is one of the oldest and extant Tamil books.

We do not know from which sources Balarama Dasa knew about Tiru Valluvar who wrote prior to 2nd century A.D. Purana is a document of moral doctrines embodying a thorough knowledge of human psychology. Purana intends to help imperfect men with practical wisdom that helps one to struggle against evil.24 Laskhmi Purana of Balaram Dasa is, thus, a precious possession in most of the households in Orissa. Balarama's Laskhmi Purana depicts how a woman (named Sreeya) from a chandal (untouchable) family keeps her household clean and tidy to welcome Goddess Mahalaxmi on the Thursday of the month of Margaseersha (November-December) whereas the women folk of the rich feudal houses sleep even after sun-rise and never care to do the cleaning work. Mahalaxmi, the goddess of wealth, was pleased with the devotion of the untouchable woman, went to her house and blessed her with riches and gold.

Balabhadra, as the elder brother and guardian of the divine abode (the temple of Puri), complained that Laskhmi should not be allowed to enter the temple since she had been to an untouchable's house and stained herself. Jagannatha does not dare to protest against this social orthodoxy and Laxmi was driven out of the temple precincts. But after that the Lords, Jagannatha and Balabhadra, did not get a morsel of food to eat. They begged from door to door, but no one gave them anything. Finally they reached a palace on the sea-shore and depicted their suffering. The lady of the house offered them food that tasted exactly like the temple food, cooked by Jagannatha's wife, Lakshmi. Lakshmi, the owner of the house, appeared finally, the two brothers begged excuse and the goddess was allowed after that to visit the houses of the untouchables and bless them. The Purana (myth) created by Balarama seems to be a powerful allegory against the caste-centric practices of the Odia society of the sixteenth century. This Purana is preserved in most of the households today, as a holy book, along with the other home gods of the family. The story is so powerful that it has been dramatized and filmed by several authors in the twentieth century.

Balarama Dasa's Jagamohan Ramayana, like Sarala's Mahabharata, was also a folkloric epic. In many places Balarama emulates Sarala's style of representation. Like Sarala Dasa, Balarama also wrote:

Born illiterate I was, young in age
I was thirty two years old
when this epic did I compose.

The Ramayana like Sarala's epic, is constituted of archaic folk words like hiya, layaka, garua, takara, ahanasi and gumana etc. Like Sarala Das, he also recreated the geographical details of Ayodhya and Lanka to suit the Odia plebians, who shared his recitals in 'Jagamohana' of the temple, Bijoy Chandra Majumdar reports, "Balarama Das, as a national poet, has sung for the people, and by making Orissa, a miniature world by itself has taught his countrymen to love the land of their birth. The Kailash of far north has been located in Orissa and the Kapilasa hills of Dhenkanal has been renamed as the Kailash Mountain. Even the hilly tracts of Orissa have been identified as Malyavanta (Malkangiri) of Jagamohana Ramayana. It was the dwelling place of the tribal army of Rama. The camp followers of Rama in the Kiskindhya Kanda, for instance, are rude tribes from Bamara and Bonai area. They have been mentioned as the soldiers recruited by Rama."25

Jagamohan Ramayana is full of creative stories, narrated in folk language. Popularly known as Dandi Ramayana. The epic, it seems has been rewritten many times by the later poets since it ran into several editions. When printed in Ganjam a different version of Dandi Ramayana (Jagamohan Ramayana) is sold to the Hindu Odias. Balarama Dasa's spiritual mission and imagination was so strong that he wrote popular vernacular versions of Gita, Upanishada, Vedanta and theories of Yoga. He had also written on the theory of pinda (the material body) and Brahmanda (cosmos). Although extremely imaginative and spiritual, Balarama's creative imagination does neither destroy nor insult reason. He ranked the creative ability of a poet as the peer of reason, not as its agent. Besides such migratory powers of imagination, Balarama's tantric sadhana actualized his creative dreams materially.

A story about Balarama's tour to Sri Lanka needs a mention here. Balarama prayed Lord Jagannatha to help him to see Sri Lanka so that he could describe it authentically. Jagannatha, as the Supreme Consciousness blessed him in meditation and the wise lore says the Lord commanded him to ride on the bejewelled golden bowl and visit Lanka. The Lord offered it to him in dream. The golden bowl belonged to the temple.

Balarama with his meditative power and the blessings of the lord flew to Lanka. Next day, the golden bowl was searched for in the temple and it was discovered in Balarama's house. He was taken to the king as a thief. The king, after Balarama's confession about the dream liberated him. The dream in this episode refers to tantra yoga, a state of supra-consciousness in which the human 'will' is concretized. The lore collected from the wise men of our times reveals to our understanding that Brahman is conditioned by knowledge and if one knows Brahman and does not err about it, one enjoys all enjoyable things. This is in tune with the jnAna-misrA vaishnavism of Odissan School.

The creation of caste-centric hierarchy, according to Balarama's pro-Buddhist Tantrism, was nothing but a nuisance created by the narrow-minded Brahmins. Once the Brahmins of Mukti Mandapa (a pedestal/shed in the temple precincts demarcated for the Brahmins to conduct spiritual discussions and to take decisions in times of crises) altercated amongst themselves on the issue of 'dharma' (duty) and Yajna (sacrifice) and the arguments reached a state of aporia. Balarama attired like a Brahmin reached there and resolved the controversy. But some of the defeated ones identified that a "Sudra" had no rights to make a fake appearance on the Mukti Mandap. He was taken to the king and on being questioned, Balaram replied: "I can create a knowledgeable Brahman and open his doors of consciousness only by putting my hand on my head." Balarama was kept imprisoned in the Koili Baikuntha (the graveyard in the temple in which the wooden images of the Lords are buried after twelve years. The ritual is called Naba Kalevara).

The Brahmins, next day, brought an idiot named Hari Das and asked Balarama to open the doors of his consciousness Balarama touched him on the forehead and transformed him into a pundit. The idiot started muttering the "brahma Sutras" (formulaic principles) immediately.

On another incident, he was thrown away from the chariot of Jagannatha during the car festival since the Sudras were not allowed to ride on it. Insulted and abused, Balarama came to the shore at Banki Muhana" (an estuary), built a chariot in sand and invoked Lord Jagannatha. The Lord appeared on the sand–chariot. The actual wooden chariot of Jagannatha, called "Nandighosha" did not move on the grand road. The car festival could not continue. The king was reported in a dream vision that the Lord made his presence felt in the sand–chariot at Banki estuary after his sudra devotee was assaulted. Next day, Prataprudra went to Balarama and begged to forgive him. The chariot called Nandighosha moved after that.

The inclusion of such miracles collected from the wise men's lore are included in this history of literature to assert that the tantric power of the poet was strong enough to bend the royal power and to bring it to submission. More so over, the purpose is to prove that the prophet Balarama might have in him a poet who broke out often into speech surrounded with the vivid atmosphere of life in the directness of his message. Our Upanishadas do not at all evidence philosophic thinking, but they are only "spiritual seeing;" its ancient stanzas are a rush of spiritual intuitions, flames of a burning fire of mystic experience, waves of an inner sea of light and life. Balarama's poetry and his mantra become one on a higher plane which at this distanced epoch appears unreal.

Balarama Dasa's experiencing psyche and the things he perceived, subject and object, literary and religious, melted and absorbed into one another. What resulted may be called a typical roma's one another. What resulted may be called a typical theological literature, more than what the English people understood by metaphysical poetry. His authentic pursuit was not the mode of poetry, but the course of salvation, a longing for God, and in the second sense, of inner communion with God. He wrote in that state of complete merger.

In Sanskrit it would be somewhat nearer to a samprajna-samadhi. The mind in the state of samadhi gets detached from all that 'the roving eye, the eager ear, the savouring tongue, the thrilled skin experience and deeper still, untiring recollection and seemingly wild imagination assail it with, like a tortoise tucking in head, tail and feet, turning inward, away, what may be battering at its shell."(26)

The lucidity of Balarama's poetry is, as such, of intolerable intensity; but once concentrated upon, it draws the mundane man's psyche heavenward. It is like the thread of the Spirit fastened to the sun in the Satapatha Brahmana, (a commentary on the Sukla Yajurveda) as also the thread of the cosmic necklace of the Bhagabat Gita.

Jagannatha Dasa (1487/90/91-1550)

Almost nine hundred years' quest (from Lui Pada to Jagannatha Dasa) for a standard Odia language ends with Jagannatha Dasa. Odia poetry, till this Brahmin pundit trans-created Bhagavata, embodied the colloquial diction, built images out of immediate real experiences and touched the tangents of mysticism. The Tantric Buddhist poets wrote allegories. An allegory is but a translation of abstract notions into a picturesque language, which is itself nothing but an abstraction from objects of the senses. The Nathists did not give language any emotional intensity enabling us to be surprised by perceptions which language itself provides when we indulge in verbal play. Sarala Dasa intended to ascertain how far the language of conversation in the middle and lower classes of society were adapted to the purpose of poetic pleasure. With Jagannatha Dasa's erudition in Sanskrit a neo-classical diction began to set the standards of Odia written language. Baccha Dasa and Markanda Dasa deployed a refined poetic diction and thus the Odia language showed two bifurcated streams: the crude and the refined. While Jagannatha Dasa ousted Sarala Dasa's plebian diction, he set the tradition for a standard written language.

Jagannatha's recitation of Odia Bhagabata in his mellifluous voice attracted Sri Chaitanya towards him in the temple. He was moved toward this 19 years old young boy with brilliant sparks of wisdom and his knack for making an excellent exposition of the Sanskrit Bhagabata in lyrical Odia. He could read into him and decipher a soul that merged the organ of speech into the mind; merging that mind into the intelligent self (ego) and then merging the intelligent self in the supreme Soul. Chaitanya's piercing observation identified this young Jagannatha's psyche resting in Samprajnata Samadhi, in which were synthesized reasoning, reflection, bliss and a sense of pure being. (27)

Jagannatha Dasa was not a Vaishnava by that time. Later, however, he was initiated into Utkaliya school of Vaishnavism by Balarama Dasa, his preceptor. One day, Prataprudra Deva met Sri Chaitanya in the temple and requested him to explain the principles of sensuous devotion (Raganuga bhakti) in Vaishnavism, and Chaitanya directed Jagannatha to help him and thus did Jagannatha negotiate the king for the first time.

Prataprudra asked Jagannatha to leave his ancestral village Kapileswarpur and stay at Puri. The small hut in which Jagannatha stayed little away from the sea shore is now known as Satalahdi Matha of Puri. Gouri Devi, one of Prataprudra's wives became his disciple.

Although Jagannatha followed the interpretation of Sridhara Swamy, he faced lots of opposition from the Brahmin classicists. Dibakara Dasa's Jagannatha Charitamrita embodies many such accounts of Brahminic wrath. He had to pass through several official tests conducted by the king to prove his worth. Sri Chaitanya designated him as Atibadi (too great) Jagannatha Dasa.

This extraordinary poet composed eight Sanskrit texts and fifty Odia books of poems. A list is provided below:

a.   Sanskrit Texts

(i)Krishna Bhakti Kalpalata ii) Sri Krishna Bhakti Kalpalata Phalamiii) Nitya gupta mela / Nitya Chintamoni iv) Upasana Satakam v) Nityacharadi Diksha-sahita-Upasana bidhih vi) Niladri Satakam and viii) Sri Radha Rasamanjari

b.   Odia Texts

1) Odia Bhagabata 2)Tulabhina 3)Daru Brahma Gita 4) Artha Koili 5) Mruguni Stuti 6) Gaja Stuti 7) Pashanda Dalana 8) Itihasa Purana, 9) Mahabharata 10) Manasiksha 11) Dahi Khela 12)Gupta Bhagabata 13) Deeksha Sambada 14) Saivagama Bhagabata 15) Shola Chaupadi 16)Sreenama Chandrika 17) Anamaya Kundali 18) Padmapada Sudhanidhi 19)Dhruva stuti 20) Soonya Bhagavata 21) Bhoogola

History of Ancient Odia Literature | 159

Ekadasa Skandha 22) Brahma Gita 23) Nitya Niladri Vilasa 24) Sudha Traya 25) Guru Pronali 26) Dutibodha 27) Nilagiri Dyana 28) Bhasa Parinaya 29) Kaliya 30)Pramoda Cheintamoni 31) Pahanti Abakasa 32) Akroora Boli 33) Uddhava Janana 34) Mala Nirnaya 35) Gopibhasa 36)) Kali Malika 37) Indra malika 38) Pasa Parva 39) Padma Kalpa Tika 40) Bhabishya Malika 41) Gupta Gita 42) Rukmini Malika 43) Gundicha Bije 44) Alankara Boli 45) Panchabhoota Gita 46) Anameya Kundali 47) Dvara bali 48) Sri Satsanga 49)Rasa Kreeda etc. Dr. Narayana Panda of Sea-Shore Sahitya Academy, Bhubaneswar has shown this author Jagannatha Dasa's Mahabharata in eighteen volumes. The present author has verified the Madhya parva of Mahabharata written in 9-syllabled rhyme. Bhikaricharan Das, one of the former Sub-deputy collectors of Orissa (belonging to Khatbin Street, Cuttack) had published it in 1928 and the volume is priced twelve annas. The Mahabharata was printed by Radhanatha Ratha in Satyabadi Press, Cuttack in 1928. Late Bhikari charana has written in the preface to Madhyaparva "We have taken utmost care to publish the six bundles of palm leaf scripts of the Mahabharata, but fiscal paucity stood as the major impediment on our way. We have taken some time to publish the Mahabharata one by one. The Adiparva was published first..."

The list, slightly longer through, than that of his guru Blaram Dasa's oeuvre, almost covers the same variety of genres of poetry:

Jagannatha's Saivagama Bhagabata presents the essence of Utkaliya Vaishnavism through a dialogic discourse between Siva and Parvati. As it is a text of Vaishnava Agama it extols the concept of Advaita of bringing out a synchrony between the sensuous (raganuga) and the reason- based (jnana –misra) modes of Vishnavism. The dialectic between Saivism and Vaishnavism generated since the time of Kapilendra Deva found its synthetic resolution in Jagannatha's Saivagama Bhagabata. It combines the tenets of Saivism, Agama and Bhagabata.

Brahma Gita is a text on spiritual anatomy that explicates the functional relation of the sense organs to the basic constituents of the universe. The book, in five chapters, explores how nature serves as a primary agent of creation and how it operates with the geography of the body constituted of eleven organs –hands, feet, the speech organ, and two excreting systems for discharge of solid and liquid waste matter, five sensory organs and a psyche. (The count is taken from Samkhya text) The five sensory organs open up outlets to the five elements of this macro cosmos: the ocular figuring the form, the gustatory discriminating the tastes, the olfactory discerning the smell, the auditory tuning itself to the wavelengths of sounds in ether, while the tactile experiencing the thrills of the touch are directly related to the sky, the wind, the fire, the water and the earth.

In addition to this micro-macro nexus (the Pinda-Brahmanda tattva), Jagannatha also alludes to the 'knowledge–devotion' binaries following the commentaries of Bhagabata Gita. The crux of the topic is neither deductive nor prescriptive. In Gita, Lord Srikrishna prescribes the four paths of action, knowledge, devotion and meditation. The purpose is to see the self either in the body or by the mind through meditation, or, by the path of knowledge or selfless action. Brahma is conceived here as an organic whole and a harmonious blending would result in all round development.

Jagannatha borrows the concept of the 'gross' forms from Brihadaranyaka Upanishad and defines that the gross forms are the elements other than air and ether (i.e. earth, water and fire). These are mortal, limited and perceptible. The sun is the essence of these three elements.

After the Pinda-brahmanda (the individual body as micro cosmos) and the universal body (macro cosmos) relationship is established, Jagannatha Dasa connects these elements with Lord Jagannatha, the vital force, the Brahman. He begins with the element of sky.

The first modification of Maya is Akasa (the sky). Its nature is space, i.e. it gives room to things to exist and expand. Akasa (the sky) derives its existence form Brahman, its substratum. The nature of Brahman is existence only. Brahman is space less whereas Akasa has both space and existence as its nature. Akasa also has the property of conveying sound, which Brahman does not have. Thus Akasa has two properties –sound and existence, whereas Brahman has only one existence.

It is not possible to summarize the 50 texts of Jagannatha Dasa in this small book. What we intend to outsource is the essence of Jagannatha's wisdom that trickled down into the collective Odia Vratya mind through his literature. It is obvious that he presented in simple Odia the philosophical concepts of Samkhya, Chhandogya and Brihadaranyaka Upanishadas. However, it should be noted that Jagannatha Das, as a disciple of Balarama repeated some of the tenets

History of Ancient Odia Literature | 161

of Brahma and both of them emphasize the feature of non-duality (Advaya), the theories of Pinda (the body) and Brahmanda (the universe) and the practice of Yoga.

The Natha mendicants had written about similar theological concepts since 11th century. Sisu Veda, written much earlier, Amara kosha and Saptanga Yoga of the Nathists were reinterpreted by Balarama Dasa in a different manner since his experiences changed, within these four hundred years. Patanjali had already gained importance in the Odia system of belief. Balarama's Virata Gita has already established:

Meander thou' not in
the labyrinth of this universe;
Take shelter in me before that endless
Circle thou enter; concentrate
Knowledge shall dispel your fear
The shadow of time won't engulf you thither.

This prescriptive mode dissolves in Jagannatha, Balarama's disciple.

In the xith S k a n d a of the Bhagabata Jagannatha has emphasized the "Absolute Brahma" as one without attributes:

He has an earthly frame
A material form, yet
Hari is without
Any attribute, He's colourless to paint.

This concept of the Brahma (The Absolute) as one without attributes is repeated throughout the works of Jagannatha. Prabuddha Maharshi and Pippalayana have explained in Ch. XI of Bhagabata.

He's the Truth, One without
Any attribute, never was there
A beginning never was an end.
He did neither grow, nor reduce
Big or small.

(Bhagabata (Odia) XIth Skanda)

Brahman is also defined in Brihadaranyaka Upanishada in a similar style. It conveys that the knowers of Brahman describe it verily as the Absolute: "It is neither coarse nor fine, neither short nor long, neither red nor oily, neither shadow nor darkness, neither air nor earth. It is without eyes and ears, without the organ of speech and mind, nor effulgent. It does not have a measure; it is without an exterior or interior, It does not eat anything, nor does anyone eat it," (Drihad.Up.3/8-11)

The Panchasakha poetry, thus, advances a step further from that of the literature of the Sanskrit classicists and the Nathist mendicants because of its syncretic nature. While attempting to define Lord Jagannatha as Sri Krishna, as a non-dual (advaita) entity & Absolute, they take the help of the Upanishadas. Jagannatha Dasa as a Sanskrit scholar had a deeper access to the Upanishadas. Thus, he defines the Absolute: "He is never seen, but is the seer; it is never heard, but the hearer; it is never thought, but is the Thinker; it is never known, but is the knower. This is Absolute. It pervades the un-manifested ether."

The consciousness witnesses the interval between the disappearances and the rise of different Vrittis. It witnesses the period when they do not exist, and which is itself unmodifiable and immutable. It is called "Kutastha".

Jagannatha got the opportunity to discuss Vedanta with lots of yogis and mendicants who visited Puri and versified the essence. By the time Jagannatha wrote Ramanujacharya had already introduced the Pancharatra Agama rituals (Tantric-rituals) in the Jagannatha temple. The stone image of all the twelve Alvars along with that of Ramanuja, the greatest of the Acharyas, are enshrined and worshipped in the compound of the temple of Srikurmanatha. A separate shrine of the Alvars exists in the southern wall of the Assembly hall of the temple of Varaha Nrusimha at Simhachalam. Chodaganga Deva had to build the temple of Lakshmi in the temple premises.(28)(Parija-135) .The Panchasakhas wanted to establish a new life according to this faith, a life free of the evils of a constricting society. The tensions and the conflicts of the Odia community were accentuated while confronting the new Panchasakha culture, but the artistic expressions of these conflicts were also explored. Their key messages were quest, survival, faith, hope, fellowship and endurance.

An account given in Bhakti Ratnakar alludes to the fact that Purushotama Deva sent an image of Radha to Vrindaban to be installed at the left side of the image of Govinda. The Yugala Upasana (Worship of Sri Krishna with Sri Radha) and the concept of 'achintyabhedabheda' (having no difference between Sri Radha and Sri Krishna) were already popular by the time. Jagannatha wrote his Tulabhina. (Ginning cotton)

> Engaged are they in a perpetual sport
> Of love; a desire infinite, yet
> Unable to manifest, until He got embodied in

Gopapura As the son of Nanda, endowed With the
sixteen artistic powers.
One was Krishna, and the other Was Radha
In perpetual union.
(Tulabhina: p-4)

In Rasakrida, Jagannatha provides a descriptive picture of this sport of love. This slender text in five chapters is one of the most popular reading materials for the country women of Orissa. Once prescribed for the beginners of education, Rasakrida presents Jagannatha as a poet of sensuous devotion (the cult of Raganuga bhakti) tinged with his guru Balarama's Buddhist sexo-yogic descriptions:

Govinda mused that may
I must play
A frolicsome game amorous
With these sixteen thousand gopika lasses
Today:
They invoked me, turned their hearts out
In meditation, I must
Appease their lust;
their randy desire." He played his flute, a fugue, enchanting
And posed in seductive Tribhangi,
Cajoled the maiden out of home
and hearth; coaxed them out one by one
The fugue in the flute hooked those women.
They stood dazed, bodies trembling in privation
Amorous rigour
"I must rush to him", said the lass
"Force him into a play of erotics".
(Tr. From Ch.i)
she heard
The flute, the tune pierced into her
Interjected, the arrow of cupid
did wound.
She looked intent
Krishna's body provoked,
Concupiscence overtook, another
Came out leaving her son behind
An uncle chasing the other

A husband overbearing caught his spindly wife
Locked inside, and flogged black and blue.
She wept and embraced Krishna
And fainted; uncontrollable urge engrossed her
She dissolved in Krishna with a kiss. (Chap.1)

These apparently sexo-yogic lines of Rasakrida, to cite Kenopanishada, form a text, "unknown to those who know well and known to those who don't know". (11.3)(29)

Krishna is Lord Jagannatha, the salvation point of all the Buddhas of the world, spread out above like the infinite sky of Indrabhuti's Jananasiddhi, the path of knowledge of the Odissan sect of Vaishnavism, combined with the sensuous devotional path of Sri Chaitanya.

The concept of the void (shoonya) originated in the Austrik (Nishada) religions and it was Hindu-ized in Nasadeeya Sutra. Jagannatha as the "worshipable icon of all the Jainas" is also void; and thus, 'Srikrishna is void (here blowing the void in flute and the sound permeating the void) too.

The particular gopika (the milkmaid women) merge in Srikrishna, for example, in Rasakreeda, transforms the lass into one complete "full" (poorna) and a complete zero simultaneously.In Bhagavata Jagannatha clarifies this concept of the Milk-maids' merger in Krishna's body. Krishna says:

See all these rivers, rivulets
They flow on and join the sea
Mingling with saline water
They forget their life and mind, in me,
They forget, the body, the samsara
And were delivered over
From birth and death (Mahapatra, 59) (30)

A similar concept is differently versified in Anamaya Kundali. The space into which the milkmaid of Rasakrida merged is also the space of perpetual emotional elation; the Maha (grand) Nitya(perpetual) Sthali (space) Padmapada Sudhanidhi depicts his relation with Sri Chaitanya, how he adored him by addressing as"Ati-bodi" (very great in wisdom) and how his intimacy geared off jealousy amongst Chaitanya's Bengali devotees etc.

Shoonya Bhagabata emphasizes Lord Jagannatha as Shoonya Brahma(the Supreme Void) in a quest for the roofs of voidness. From the sound of the voice was born Kama (desire). The third chapter of Kenopanishada, while searching for the chief protagonist (Pradhan purusha) of this creation discovers an woman named Haimavati. The Odisan Vaishnavas have accepted Haimavati as the root force of Brahman. Probably after a thousand or more years after that Varaha Mihira imagines in his configuration of three icons, the centre of which was a woman called Ekanamsa. Gradually the placement of Subhadra in the middle of the triad is conjoined with the void. The text of Shoonya Bhagabata is written in Chautisa style, in alphabetical chronology beginning with 'A' and ending with 'Ksha'.

Jagannatha Dasa's Nitya Niladri Bilasa is one more valuable text hinged on Jagannatha chetana (consciousness). The text embodies the daily chores of an ideal Vaishnava, his purification of the internal and external body, wearing the Vaishanava sect mark on the forehead and the four-tired mode of worship: Laya (Meditative concentration), Bhoga (otterings to Jagannatha), Lila (the rituals) and Bilasa, This includes the metamorphosis of the devotee to trans-genderic Sri Radha. Nitya NiladriBilasa, it seems, is influenced by the Nathist books on the daily chores of the Natha mendicants and their tripundra mark etc. as Sribatsa Natha mentions in his Natha Dharma-O-Natha Sahitya.

Artha Koili is a spiritual interpretation of Markand Dasa's poem Kesaba Koili. Odia literature of the medieval period embodies a great deal of plenipotentiary poems in which the bird Cuckoo (Koili, Koel) is deployed as an agent for the exteriorization of the protagonist's core feelings. Yasoda expresses her filial love for Krishna after he went to Mathura (Koili-lo-Kesava-je Mathuraku gala etc.). In Jagannatha's Artha Koili the interpretation is spiritual. Koili is Jiva (Pinda or the body) and 'Mathura' is Brahmanda (the Cosmos). However, this interpretation is proved to be philosophic euphemism since "Kesaba Koili" was written much later. Probably Jagannatha has interpreted it form a folk lore or a later poet has written in the name of Jagannatha Dasa.

Bhoogola Ekadasa Skandha elaborates the theory of Pinda – Brahmanda (Micro-Marco) separately. The body is metaphorised as a tree. Jeeva (the Being) resides there. The fruits of this tree are as juicy as the essence divine. The poet expressed these metaphorised ideas in a dialogic discourse between Hari and Arjuna..One more text that puzzles the reader is Tula-bhina (Ginning of cotton) because of its ludic narrative. Scholasticism admitted in medieval age hermeneutical battles. Dr.

Surendra K.Maharana reports in his history how Pf. Brahmananda from Kashi challenged the Odia scholars to join a battle of epistemological polemics. Jagannatha had defeated the scholar (Moharana,p.238). Perhaps it was because of such challenges that Jagannatha had introduced a metaphorical game of ginning cotton of epistemes to make it softer, cleaner and accessible to common readers.

However, Tulabhina embodies complicated interrelationship amongst its language, structure and reader perception, Structurally Tulabhina is a mixture of prose and poetry; one –third of the work is constituted of a gloss in prose. The text conducts a discourse on ontology and a new myth of creation. In an answer to Parvati's question, Lord Siva explains:

And ultimately, the void manifested
Scintillating with its immanent glitter.
The luminosity produced a gross sound
Then it was visible; a half–circular alphabetical mark
A dot on its head;
Faded in then an Omkara, the sound Transcendent.
Listen to me, Oh, Parvati:
This cosmos, world, the boundless space
Had nothing but this sound, the Omkara
In which all shapes dissolved, but a world there was
Full of smoke, bleary; engulfed
In darkness, it was an archetypal principle.

The revelation may be juxtaposed with Nasadiya Sutra (Rigveda.X.129.1-7) that describes the genesis:

"It was pre-apocalyptic darkness that encompassed the boundless space. The existents were buried in darkness. It was deep water all around, dark and quiescent. The binaries like the Truth and untruth were dissolved, there within. Nescience and darkness were in total fusion, without any finite intelligence. And one singular Brahman, the primeval Being, produced himself out of darkness, an outcome of meditation." (Nasadiya Sutra: 3)

The subject was popular in medieval hermeneutical circles. The text and the metaphor of cotton-ginning do not disagree, since both the text and metaphor, work and word, fall under one and the same category, that of discourse. Sree Nitya Gupta chudamani is a representative text on Odissan Vaishnavism alluding to puranic texts and philosophy. Dutibodha is a slender book depicting some events of Radha and Krishna's lila phase. The poet's self reflexive account in this text is important to us.

It is a paradox
I am born as Brahmin, knowing not
What is Brahman! Yet
Chaitanya Chandra considers me great.
I am named after my Lord
Thus could I express from my core!
Blessings are there,
Blessings of my Preceptor
(Trans. by the author from Duti Bodha)

Jagannatha Dasa remains immortal in Odia literature and culture for his Odia Bhagavata. A mélange of Sanskrit and prakrit, the nine–lettered Gujjari rhyme of Bhagabata (Navakshari Vritta) is as lyrical as spiritual, as lucid as communicable, To quote Sitakant Mahapatra, "The Oriya Bhagabata is not merely the magnum opus of Jagannatha Dasa as a poet; it is one of the finest classics in Oriya language. It remains unsurpassed for its combination of philosophical ideas and charming lyricism, it is not easy to translate it into English. (31)

This author expresses his inability to translate the untranslatable lines of Bhagabata. However, Dr. Sitakant Mahapatra's monograph on Jagannatha Das has a section of aphorisms and selected couplets. I would quote some brilliant concepts that would help a reader from outside the Odia linguistic community:

With the soul's well-being everything is achieved
And you cross the ocean of samsara
* The path of meditation is indeed tough
Even the Yogis panic away in fear.
* The saving acquired through pain
Are of no avail for happiness.
* The body suffers the pangs of karma
Like the python in the forest
* The mind is the give of pleasure and
pain The author of sin and guilt
* The sky is totally vacant
* In whom desirelessness is born
He saves his own soul

* With wealth, thrift and service
What is unattainable in this world?

The authentic literature in Odia began with Bhagabata; Sarala's Mahabharata was just an attempt that ended in failure. But Jagannatha Dasa's Mahabharata was an authentic translation in 9- lettered rhyme. The Odia language matured with the translations of Bhagabata. and Mahabharata. The subsequent poets of Odissa, even the late 20th poets are immensely influenced by the language of Bhagabata, simple and sober.

Jagannatha Dasa is important today as the he was the first poet whose Bhagabata premiered a socio-religious upsurge between the 16th and the 19th centuries till the Britishers pulverized the Odia cultural pride. The reading of Bhagabata was a part of the daily chores of an Odia woman. Bhagavata ghara and Bhagavata Tungies (clubs) were built in every village .Gopalila paintings were rendered on the wall of the mathas and the pilgrims' rest houses at Puri. Patta paintings, palm leaf paintings and ganjapa illustrations depict the chapters from Bhagabata. Bhagabata is recited when a child is born and is read out while an old person departs from this worldly abode.

Jagannatha Dasa describes God to the illiterate folk of Odissa. It is to be remembered that in every village of Odissa, a Bhagabata Tungi (A small community centre for the village where Jagannatha Dasa's Bhagabata was being recited) was built and every evening a Brahmin recited Jagannatha's Bhagabata. In Assam it is 'Namghar'. Now even after globalization, true Odias identify themselves by possessing a copy of Bhagabata in their house. Thousands of Odias are living in Andhra, Bengal, Jharkhand and Bihar in villages that could not be tagged to Orissa in 1936, when the state was formed. They show a text of Odia Bhagabata to a stranger like an "identity card". Jagannatha describes the features of the Supreme giver to his countrymen in the following words, at different places of Bhagabata Dr. Sitkanta Mohapatra has selected them in his book as aphorisms:

The sun and moon
are his two eyes
It's rising and setting
Enacted by the two eyelashes.
His wink is this samsara
And the jiva receives it directly.
The rivers are his veins

And trees and shrubs
Hair on his body
The clouds are his hair
The evening his true clothes
Prakriti is her heart
and his mind, the moon.
The birds are his grammar
The manas his intelligence
His nest is the human body
Woven out of illusory maya
(Mahapatra pp 36-59)

For Jagannatha Dasa, the importance of literature rests not merely in its mode of expression, but also in what the author says. Despite being a disciple of Balarama Dasa and an intimate associate of Sri Chaitanya, Jagannatha, as he is transparent to us through his spiritual oeuvre, can be grouped under the label of Neo-Humanists. He, like his peers, believed that man is a being who may be distinguished from the animal by his power of reasoning and his possession of ethical standards. He stands as a free being, prone to animalistic urges or egocentric yawps; but is responsible also to place these instincts away, in so far as he decides to cultivate his peculiar human nature, under the control of reason. Freedom is not only liberation form circumstances, but subjection to "inner law." So, the watchwords of humanism are order, restraint,' and 'discipline.' Jagannatha's realization with regard o this is:

Ever engrossed in material pursuits
They don't notice the erosion of life
Night takes away half of it
Or sleep, woman or company of friends.
The day devoted to anguished quest
For wealth to maintain the family.
Happy in the charmed circle
Of sons, grandsons and relations.
They take Vishnu's Maya as reality
And never notice Death sitting nearby.
(Mahapatra, p.45 (32)

It would be evident that though he belonged to Utkaliya cult of Vaishnavism, his literature incorporated the warrant of general moral standards. Some of the historians of literature, including Surendra

Mahnaty argue that the literature of the Pancha Shakas should not be viewed as pure literature since they are works of religion and theology. In this connection we may allude to T.S. Eliot's essay, "Religion and Literature," in which he enunciates, "The greatness of literature cannot be determined solely by literary standards; though we must remember that whether it is literature or not can be determined only by literary standards." (p.26). (33)

Jagannatha had to sing out the attributes of the Supreme Being to the native devotees of his milieu. He did not make his discourse heavy with scholarly allusions as they did in the MuktiMandap symposiums held every day inside the temple. He believed in simple poetic explanation of the attributes of the Lord.

> He is the Lord, the Time;
> Whoever can enumerate his attributes?
> He has no favorites, no foes,
> He destroys all the embodied beings.
> Afraid of that Kalapurusha.
> The wind ever blows Driven by the same fear
> The sun roams the skies alone
> The clouds send down rains
> Without punctuation;
> The stars shine in the Sky
> The trees, plants and creepers
> Flowers and fruit in time.
> The rivers flow ceaselessly
> The oceans never jumps the banks
> Fire consumes everything
> And the mountains stand
> Rooted to the earth."(Mahapatra, 47) (34)

What Jagannatha Dasa viewed was very vivid and vital things though he operated within the limits imposed by the two sects of Vaishnavism current in the milieu. Yet, he talked about human 'liberation,' of elevating the word to the level of emancipation. He did not intend to liberate human beings from empirical circumstances only, but in relation to their inner laws that govern them on the path of bondage.

Achyutananda Das (1482-)

Five years senior to Jagannatha Das, Achyutananda Mohanty/ Khuntia was directed by Sri Chaitanya to get indoctrinated into

Vaishnavism under Sanatana Goswamy. Dr. Kunjabhihari Mohanty, in his Sahitya Academy monograph on Achyutananda Das, has dealt extensively regarding the historical exactitude of his date of birth and assigns the above year as authentic.

His father, Dinabandhu Moahanty was one of the servitors in the defense department of Pratap Rudra Deva, but after some years of service he expressed his reluctance to get engaged in war activities further. The king, after that, appointed him as a general servitor (Tahalia) for the temple and conferred on Dinabandhu the title of "Khuntia." Dinabandhu Khuntia, a great devotee of Lord Jagannatha, was very often a victim of Imperial wrath and he had to suffer a miserable socio-economical life. But his dedication for the Lord earned him the blessings of Jagannatha. He was blessed with a saintly son, and a rare poet named Achyuta.

Achyutananda did neither accept the title of Khuntia, nor that of his ancestral title "Mohanty" He had chosen 'Dasa" instead like the other poet mendicants. Dasa as a surname connotes the feeling of devotional surrender, the feeling of a true Sudra servitor. Achyuta wrote in Varna Tika:

Blessed are the Sudras
Servants of the Lord;
Never did ego infect
their mind within. (Varna Tika)

This was the common feature in the cultural milieu of the five associates of Sri Chaitanya, who, including the Brahmin Jagannatha, preferred to identify themselves as "Dasas" (Servitors of the supreme Lord, Jagannatha).

Brahminhood never
Did I aspire,
Never did my faith I repose
In the Kshatriya, the warrior caste
Vaisyas I despise.
It's better, to stay low ranked
Inferior, rather I would prefer
To continue as a Sudra, Achyuta.
(Varna-Tika)

We remember that poet and prophet Yashovanta, twelve years senior to him. He was also alive by that time and he was instrumental in arranging the marriage of Achyutananda with the daughter of the king of Adhanga (Raghuram) Champavati, whom he considered as a niece. Achyuta's wife was also a versifier in temperament. Dr. Kunjabihary Mohanty, in his monograph on Achyutananda quotes Chamapvati's verse:

I am gopika, he's my gopala,
A team mate in Krishna's playground;
I was wheeling round with Radha
A dancer companion,
He took his birth in a family of "Ahokarana" (35)
I was born in Lunar dynasty
Marriage between a Kshatriya girl
And an Ahokarna
Is not culpable; no distinction
Between a sati (chaste woman) and Yati (a mendicant) (36)
A little elaboration is needed in relation to Achyutananda's

Versions on casteist prejudices of the Odia society of the 15th century. Achyutananda's literature has frequently allusions to the casteist conflicts of his time. Udaya kahani and Shoonya Samhita of Achyutananda report that the Brahmins of Mukti Mandapa of Puri temple were extremely jealous of these Panchasakha dasas. They used to make sarcastic remarks in small coteries that the Pancha Sakhas hardly got any scope to study the Vedic texts since they were prohibited because of their genealogical draw backs etc. That was the reason as to why they call themselves dasa/Sudras. Achyutananda used to answer them back that the Brahmins as cerebral creatures had studied too many texts and devoted their entire life to argue over hermeneutics and episteme of knowledge. But they had little space in their hearts to visualize and communicate with the Supreme Being. They are devoid of devotion. Thus, in Chaurasi Mantra he declares:

I am Achyut
A Vaishnavite by caste
To the servants of Vishnu
My time I devote
as a servant of the servant.

Achyutananda's humble surface was not that of true humility, it was an expression of intense resistance and at times an indictment on the Brahmins of those days who never cared to read Sarala's Mahabharata even for once and designated Jagannatha's Bhagabata as Teli (oilman's) Bhagabata,(meaning inauspicious and meant for the low ranked commoners). A born rebel and an active reformer, Achyutananda devoted all his time to yoga,Tantra and to different modes of attaining perfection in life. His inward journey was his pilgrimage. A performer of Rasalila, he began the performance of Lila in Orissa, became a social activist to eradicate the evils of caste-centrism and also worked for the emancipation of women. His aesthetic and ethical talents were utilized for the betterment of the society, to ignite the issues of cultural citizenship suppressing all sorts of class antagonism.

The growing power of the five associates and the support they received from the hegemony of the ruling class generated this Brahminic antagonism. Lots of people from the cowherds' caste accepted him as their Guru. This handsome prophet was an accomplished singer and he was staying away from Puri. He was the beginner to perform Rasalila in the company of his young milkmen mates. Nemala was his place of spiritual retreat. Achyuta did not repose any faith in Sri Chaitanya's school of Vaishnavism. He understood Lord Jagannatha as the 'shoonya,' the void of Indrabhuti and began to explore the concepts of the Lord through the hardcore Jnana-misra bhakti. (Devotion through reasoning). In Shoonya Samhita and Gurubhakti Gita Achyuta mentions the name of his guru as Sanatana Gossain and in Gurubhakti Gita he mentions about one Sri Charana Gossain.

Nabakishore's disciple
Siri Charana gossain
Siri Charan's disciple
I am Achyuta.
(Chhanda 1/30, Gurubhakti gita)
The son of Sachi looked
At Sanatan Swamy and said:
"Go and indoctrinate Achyutanada!"
(Shoonya Samhita)

Dr. K. B Mahanty is of the opinion that both the Gurus might refer to the same person. However, the milieu of Panchsakhas is full of inner divisions. By the time Yashovanta was indoctrinated, Vaishnavism had two categories: Gaudiiya and Utkaliya. But Achyuta in Gurubhakti Gita mentions:

Ananta sisu is Ramananda Vishnava
Yoshovanta is Madhwacharya Vaishnava

Balaram Dasa's Vishnu Shyama Dasa
Achyuta Nityananda "vaishnava"
(1: Chhanda, 32)

Achyutananda, as a young boy, had been to Puri with his father Dinabandhu and he joined the Nama Samkeertana (choral singing and dancing of prayer songs of the Vaishnavas) of Sri Chaitanya. Chaitanya immediately ordered Sanatana Goswamy to indoctrinate the boy.

Achyutananda, like the other three associates of Sri Chaitanya, did not stay at Puri in a monastery of his own. He came back to his village Tripura, as recorded in Shoonya Samhita. Two other works of Achyutananda, i.e. Harivamsa and Ananta Goi record:

I live in Madhya grama
Under Padmanabha Narendra of Ranapur
He nurtures me
Providing food and clothes'

No child was born to Padmanabha till late age and he led a lonely and remorseful life. Achyutananda asked him to read his Harivamsa and he got a child, the legend says.

After some years Achyuta came to Nemala (Nava mala) and his devotees built a monastery for him in that bucolic forest. Achyuta lived there for 105 years. (37)

Dr. Ratnakar Chaini, a reputed writer of fiction and plays has edited some of Achyuta's works and published Achyutananda Rachanavali. But palm leaf manuscripts of hundreds of his books are still unpublished and they are available in the houses of his true devotees. Mr. Kunjabihary Mahanty has provided a list of 269 major works and 101 small books written by Achyutananda. It is not possible either to enlist or summarize them here. Some important works central to his concept of void are hinted below:

Anakar Samhita defines Brahma in the following words:
Formless and beyond logos
He's without a beginning
Without an end.
This formless in the process
merges in some shape
and an iconic form emerges.

These ideas of Achyutananda link him with the Pancha Sakha School. He may also be linked with them through another route, of the Agama Sastra (PreVedic spiritual documents).

The Agama Texts are divided into four groups. The Charyas and the Mantra Sastra (logo-centric occultism), Jnana pada and Kriya pada that deal with the consecration of the images and its worship in four places-in the image, in the water pot, on the mystic diagram and the sacrificial fire-pit. Achyutananda, it seems, had studied or had participated in discussions related to the three Agamas-the Sakta Agama, the Saiva Agama and the Vaishnava agamas. His notions in Shoonya samhita leads one to presume that while partially rejecting the Brahminic practices, he partially accepts Saiva and Sakta agamas to formulate his own version of Vaishnava Tantras. Relying less on Advaita Mayavada (non dual concept of illusionism) he proceeds toward Pacharatra (primordial Tantra worship) and in the process he reached a state in which he believed in the principles of Narayaniya, in which Vaishnavism lapses into Vaishnava Tantra. His senior pal Balarama Das was well conversant in Vaishnava Tantra. Yashovanta was a greater Tantric who acknowledged the Brahman as the ultimate essence (parama tattva) – and accepts Him both as nirguna (non-attributive) and Saguna (attributive). Achyutananda was the fourth Sakha of the time who stayed at Nemala, accepted no mastery or seat in a monastery at Puri from the King, and yet was very popular as a Saint and was prolific also in literature.

In order to overcome this conceptual impasse (his confusion about Saguna, Nirguna and Shoonya), Pancharatra philosophy introduced the concept of Sakti (for Jagannatha the Shakti is Lakshmi). It is noticed that Brahman which is, in itself purely transcendent and motionless, has somehow been associated with a principle of creative potency called Sakti, or Laxmi.

Balaram Dasa allegorized this concept in the simple, tenable story of Lakshmi Purana for the ordinary mass. Dr. Mayadhara Manasingh, (salutation to his critical abilities), interpreted it as a "swang". The story depicts how Purushottama Jagannatha (Narayana) and his elder brother Balabhadra (Siva) suffered the process of de-potentialization in the absence of Sakti (Lakshmi).

Achyutananda, on the other hand, staying away from the city of the Vaishnavas, practiced the highest form of Vaishnav Tantra and had acquired unparalleled Siddhi. (spiritual accomplishment).The text of his Anakara Samhita quantifies that he had written 36 Samhitas, 78 Gitas and poems numbering around one lakh. As the post colonial government in Orissa did not care to invest money to retrieve the palm leaf manuscripts, and publish them, most of the palm leaf scripts have been destroyed in the houses of his ancient devotees who preserved them. However, his published books still make a long list: Harivansa Brahma sankuli, Gurubhakti gita, Sabda Brahma Samhita, Chhayalis (forty Six) Patala, Tattva bodhini, Garuda Gita, Varna Tika Purana etc. It is interesting to note that Achyutananda's Malika literature (Astrological predictions for the future in songs) is still sold in buses and trains and the vendors still sing his predictions even today. The super cyclone of 1999 that devastated Odissa was predicted in Achyutananda's Malika.written in fifteenth-sixteenth century Amara–Jumara Samhita deals with the myth of origin. Astagujjari extols the relationship between the godhead and the devotee. Agata Vabishya Malika belongs to the rubric of Tantric Astrology and his predictions about future happenings are still quoted even by the atheists when it comes true.

Achyutananda could foresee the future upheavals of Odissan civilization, and invasions of outsiders in his Malika literature. Shortly after his death, his poetic forecasts were proved to be true. The Afgans, Mogals and the Marthas had invaded the Odia country as predicted years before. However, by the time Achyuta concentrated on writing Malikas, it was an overused genre. Our research through the secondary source readings and browsing through the texts of Achyuta reveals that he, too, wrote six types of poems like his uncle-in-law (Yashovanta Dasa) and other two senior writers-Balaram and Jagannatha: a) Gitas b) Malikas c) Puranas d) cultural histories e) Yoga Sutras f)Spiritual realizations . The extra quality in Achyuta's poetry is his iconoclasm. His voice of protest clarifies the following three layers of rebellion:

i) Centre and the margin: He was not granted a monastery at Puri and he was not close to political power-centre. He operated from Nemala, one hundred fifty kilometers away from Puri, and the activities of his peripheral societies either at Ranapur or at Nemala has been evaluated as national cultural phenomena. Since he lived amid Rasa performers/rustic cowherd boys of the periphery, his voice had become feeble at Puri, but he grew bolder than the other spiritual writers of the center (Puri). Achyuta noticed keen political rivalry between the Sudra-prophets and the scholarly pundits/Brahmins whose force had already been spent in caste-centric and scholastic competitions to get close to political power.

(2) Caste-centric discrimination: Achyuta was informed about the struggle his uncle-in-law Yashovanta had to face after the monastery at Heragohiri Street was granted to him. He was aware of Balarama's open encounter with the Brahmins at Muktimandapa.

(3) Contests for Power: Spiritual power competitions and assertion of one's own political power was the real source of this antagonism with the mainstream urban forces. Achyuta's own cultural marginalization generated such problems.

However, he was an extraordinary prophet trained in the Vajrayana practices of occult and capable of performing tantric miracles. The number of his countryside disciples was large and many of them were minor writers. These trantrics were affiliated to autochthonous and Vajrayana goddesses. The disciples surrounded Achyuta either in Nemala or in Ranapur, places where Achyuta had his temporary hermitages. It is suspected that thousands of Achyuta's poems had been taken by his fake followers who published them as their own writings. Some of other fake writings are now available with the name of Achyutananda as the author. These verses are available in palm leaf bundles. The scholars suspect the authenticity of these writings.

Versification of the theories of Brahma as a Void, the theory of Pinda and Brahmanda, Yogic practices etc. and all other poetic discourses of Achyutananda seem to be in tune with the other urban writings of Puri, where other urban associates of Sri Chaitanya lived. In the process, he too wrote the Purana, captioned Harivamsa to match with Jagamohan Ramayana and Bhagavata written by his contemporary preceptors. But Achyutananda does not figure as an awarded poet of his time.

However, his literature has survived the test of time even after his sectarian revolt and his collective, organized endeavor against Brahminical hegemony. The Brahmins, for example, used to earn some money by interpreting Sanskrit Bhagabata to the common devotees inside the temple. Jagannatha Dasa's Bhagabata was therefore underestimated as Teli Bhagabata (Bhagabata for the oilmen, and therefore considered inauspicious by brahmins etc). Jagannatha, as a Brahmin of Kapileswarpur did not over-react to such scandalous remarks from the Muktimandapa.However the Gajapati king admitted his talents both as a poet and a spiritual leader. He was granted a monastery called Saatalahari Matha at Puri. But such a compromising attitude was not possible for Achyutananda. He never wanted royal patronage. His hermitage at Nemala was built for him by thousands of his devotees who came from the milkmen, blacksmith, carpenters, cobblers, farmers and to other sudra families, who were not allowed to touch the palm leaf scriptures of Hindu spiritualism. The casteist discrimination of the Brahmins kept a larger section of the Odia society away from spiritual knowledge. Achyutananda proved through his organizations at Nemala and Ranapur how thirsty these subaltern Odias were to come and merge into the spiritual mainstream.

The Mahayana tantric techniques of Achyutananda clicked immediately. The most revolutionary concept of his metaphysics was a blending of Jagannathism with madhyamika philosophy of the Buddhists. Achyuta's Shoonya Samhita, therefore, deserves to be his magnum opus, if not Kaivarta Gita, a mythical fantasy written in purana style to transcend the narrow boundaries of Brahminical discriminations with regard to caste and idolatry. Achyutananda, sheltered under Shankara's interpretation of Vedanta blended with it the logic of Buddhism (though they were opposite poles) and reached at the visionary Void, equivalent to that of Buddhist Madhyamika philosophy. Achyuta, it is obvious, was trained in Madhyamika and he superimposed the concept of the void on Jagannatha. Five of his books deal with the concept of the Void: Anakara Samhita (The Book of the Shapeless), Jnana Pradeepa Gita (A discourse on the flame of knowledge), Jnana Sagar boli (Verses on the ocean of knowledge), Sunya Rasa (The histrionics of the Void) and Sunya Samhita (The Book of Void). The Brahmins of Muktimandapa were silenced because they understood it as Shankara's hermeneutics on Vedanta. An elaboration on the point is, therefore, necessary. The central point in Shankara's Vedanta is that 'consciousness absolute'. It is the fundamental reality. Brahman is that consciousness. It is devoid of all attributes. It is one, and indivisible. Differences of class/caste/sect cannot arise out of it. Brahman does not admit any such differences. Each individual is essentially the same as Brahman, but it appears as other than Brahman because of adjuncts that arise out of nescience. The world emanates from it and subsists in it. Now the question is: how this meta-rational Brahman is to be linked with this relational world. Sankara says that it is possible. For him, the world, as it is, does not exist at all nor did it ever exist, nor will exist in future. The truly existing being is alone Brahman and all else is naught.(38)

This unreality has Brahman for its substratum. Ignorance is not based upon nothing-ness, for we could not then perceive phenomena at all. Brahman alone is real, and ignorance and the entire material phenomena of the world which one of its products are only superimpositions upon Brahman" (p.21) (39). Such a nature regulates all activities – a law that makes the world as it is. A man believes as that he is identical with his body and he never explicitly denies that he is his body and never feels detached from it. The notion of this false identification of the "self" with the "body" would never occur to a person who has an experience of himself as the supreme consciousness. He is only one who had realized such a distinction between "self" and "not-self"and he would wonder at this body-centered identity. An individual self means a self feeling itself as embodied. The illusoriness of the embodiment is the illusoriness of the body itself. Such a self identity is illusiory.

We can never conceive the illusoriness of the world unless we start with the illusoriness of "me." The illusoriness of "I" lead to the feeling that the "self" can never be identified with "not-self ". This feeling forms the very background on which Shankara establishes his theory of objective illusion, the avidya or maya, the principle of individuation. In other words, the individual feels that he is actually / really an individual because this principle exists in Brahman prior to the starting of this world as an object of experience. Due to such experience every individual thinks that there are as many individuals as there are beings. (40)

This principle of individuation is entirely independent because nothing can be conceived without being related to pure consciousness, which is Brahman. Absolute Brahman is independent. It has nothing to do with conditions and has no concern with the world.

Achyutananda perceived Jagannatha as Absolute Brahman who is eternal, and has neither positive nor negative attributes. In it (Him) there is a total extinction of empirical life along with the relative distinctions of subject and object. Freed from the limitations, the self attains oneness with Brahman which is undifferentiated consciousness and bliss.

Such metaphysical speculation in Madhyamika philosophy is Shoonyata (void). The word Brahma is substituted by Shoonya. The objects of the world have no existence at all. They are perceived as existing but in essence. They are not so. To exist in reality is not the same as to be perceived as existing .Appearance, though exists per se, subsequently dies out, and is discovered later on, as never existing. Yet it has its empirical value, an empirical reality. This reality is derived from the absolute where there is not even a shadow of distinction between "within" and "without". The removal of difference takes away from reality its concreteness and opens it to the character of pseudo reality. Madhyamikas, therefore, were forced to postulate an indeterminate reality, which presupposes instead a determinate universe.. But to be determinate and at the same time to transcend, ends up in a contradiction. To avoid this difficulty, the Madhyamikas had to chalk out the principle of avidya. It is not clear how and why the absolute becomes determined itself. The only plausible answer to this question is offered in the principle of avidya which does justice to the determinate and indeterminate aspects of existence. At the same time it avoids the error of either making the indeterminate determinate, or, installing determinate as reality.

Thus, "avidya" has its locus not in Shoonya .This is not possible, though possible form Shankar's point of view. Shoonya which literally means void-ness or emptiness is mostly misunderstood by those who are not well acquainted with the Buddhist phraseology.

Madhyamika considers Shoonya as the highest truth denying the existence of everything, conditional as well as unconditional, relative as well as independent. It is a perfect state of consciousness. What the doctrine of Shoonya positively insists on is the annihilation of the imagination that weaves the dwaita/dualistic conception of the world. (41)

The concepts of Anakara Samhita, Jnana pradeepa Gita, Jnanasagara boli, Sunya Rasa and Sunya –Samhita, in contradiction to the contents of Vedanta, perceived Jagannatha only as Void, i.e. the ultimate truth. Shoonya Samhita states:

The void-self is steady, indifferent
But throws a net
Of nescience, sits in every
Corporeal body, most compassionate
Politicking with it, a diplomat;
Dissolves you in the Void, then moves
Toward virtue. -Sunya Samhita-

Achyuta in the above stanza does not speak of the Vedantic Brahma or of any such thing mentioned in Brahminic religions. It appears to be a tantric energy. He advises some practicing saints in Prachi Valley.

I advised them to activate
The mantra for the yantra
Related to the Void
And the saints shouted in joy
They perceived the Void in it
Metamorphosing into light
Effulgent
Descending down into the body
He, the Void –bodied one.
- Sunya Samhita –

Achyutananda proves himself to be a powerful Buddhist tantric practitioner, but in his Ganesha Bibhuti Tika he utters a mantra: "Om dhling Veeja Sunya-brahman namah". We do not know whether this is the "Nirakara mantra".

The Nirakara mantra is enough
For this body, the void supreme
Almighty, a rescuer, brother
Of the oppressed
Blessed me, once.
-Sunya Samhita.

The Void, concentrated upon, manifests in an effulgent light. Achyutananda merges his ideas of "nitya–rasa" (The Vaishnavite concept of the male and his female energy in eternal union) into this Void and writes:

Lo, my friend, He lives
In an empty temple.
Perceive his effulgence
Your sufferings would end.
-Sunya Rasa.

He mentions about "seven layers of void wherein is the abode of Brahman.Seven layers of Brahman turns into Void Brahman/seven sticks joined generates a zero."(Brahma vidya). Here Achyuta does not deviate from what is written in Patanjali's Yoga Sutra, though he changes the jargons only to sabotage the concepts of Brahmana, Upanishada and Yogasastra. The seventh layer of wisdom is designated as Turiya by Patanjali. In Sri Tattva Chintamoni Sastra (Ch VIII, 40, 41, 42,) a yogin rises up through Sushumna (Spinal chord,which is metaphorized as "seven sticks" and "seven layers") It is called the seventh Chakra or the Sahasrara in Tantra Yoga.

Such metaphysical and metaphorical expressions very often recur in Panchsakha poetry. It confirms the postmodern notion that literary works are created by literary works and texts are created by texts. We can take for example, Jagannatha Dasa's Tula bhina, Yashovanta Dasa's Prema bhakti Gita, Chaitanya Dasa's Vishnu– garbha Purana, the devotional songs of Sisu Ananta and Balaram's Saptanga Yoga, and Gupta Gita etc. These texts generate such metaphysical discourses. Cliches, probably, appear talking among themselves celebrating the creative union of Panch Sakhas in a metasemiotic culture. As a result, inter-textual Yogic archetypes emerge from them.

However, Achyuta's theological texts constitute a social space which leaves no language safe. His position either as an enunciator, or, a judge, master analyst, or, as a prophet, is also not safe. Mutual influencing of textuality and subjectivity produces territorial religions, and though Achyuta was never a temple centered poet, he is grouped under the rubric of Vaishnavite devotional literature. By introducing the Madhyamika-void into the Vaishnavite notion of 'nitya –rasa (perpetual union of the male and female energies), he paradoxically, carves out a shape of the shapelessness. While attempting to image himself as an advanced modern thinker, Achyuta, iromically, returns to the same Vedantic sources. There was no alternative left for him. But he failed to comment about the state of "Turiya," the bliss of Sat-chit-and-ananda through his Tantrik enunciations.

Sisu Ananta Das (1486/1493-)

The youngest of the Panchasakhas, Sisu Ananta, reports Ms. Tanyaya Das Goswamy, his, great granddaughter and biographer, was born in 1486 (not in 1493) at Balipatana. We accept her assignment of the year of his birth because of genealogical reasons. Her father Mathurananda Sisu Goswamy stood as a proof that "Sisu" was their family name and the word does not denote anything etymologically ("Sisu=childishness").

He was the founder of the Sisu cult of Vaishnavism in Orissa and lots of gifted writers belonged to the Sisu family. Sisu Arjun Das (author of Ramabiva), Sisu Sankar Das (of Ushavilasha), Sisu Bananmali Das (of Rasa), Sisu Pratap Das (the poet of Sasisena), and Sisu Dayanidhi Das (Aswamedha Jajna) belonged to the Sisu family of the Vaishnavas. However the legend makers of Sisu Ananta's magic performances have attempted to create stories justifying that Ananta Das of Balipatana village, twenty kilometers away from Bhubaneswar, was not only able to fly riding a broken wall by his tantric accomplishments, but he was also able to transform himself into a baby child also by his occult power. (42) Tanaya Das Goswamy reports in her book that the Brahmins of Puri, who earned their livelihood by reading out the Sanskrit Bhagabata and interpreting it to the commoners, grew jealous of Jagannatha Dasa for he translated it into Odia. They complained to King Prataprudra Deva that the young Jagannatha was a libertine debauch and he was found always in the company of women. The king summoned him and asked to clarify his position. Jagannatha answered that he mixed with women folk as a woman. He could change his gender.

The king was annoyed and ordered to prove that he was able to change his gender, failing which the punishment would be more severe. The king ordered that the test would be conducted the next day. Jagannatha could not sleep and prayed Lord Jagannatha to save him out of the trouble. The Lord appeared in an altered state of consciousness and commanded him to appear before the king as a woman. Jagannatha went to the court dressed as a woman and while providing the evidence he squeezed out milk from his breasts. Real milk began to flow and the stream did not stop.

The king was awed and Jagannatha said it would stop if a real baby child would come and suck it from his breasts. The king was at a loss to understand as to how a baby child would be brought to the court. Just at that time a gentleman emerged and offered himself to transform himself into a baby and suck the milk. In fact, he turned into a small baby and sucked the milk to the amazement of the king and the court. He was Ananta Dasa of Balipatna.

Legends about him inform that he practiced some yoga and mantra-sadhana at Konark and Sri Chaitanya as a preceptor indoctrinated him with some mantra related to the Surya Upasana (Solar worship). Dr. Surendra Kumar Maharana identifies Ananta as the writer of the following books: i) Hetu Udaya Bhagabata ii) Chumbaka Malika iii) Anakara Sabada iv) Bhava-mukti-dayaka Gita v) Artha Tarini vi) Bhajana Tatva vii) Mantra Chandrika viii)Garuda –kesava Sambada ix) Pinda–Brahmanda x) Thika Bakhara xi)Ude Bakhara xii)Chhata Bakhara xiii)Parardha Bhavishya (xiv) Bhavishya Purana (xv) Padmavana Rasa (xvi) Thula Sunya Rasa (xvii)Gupta Tika or yantra Tika (xviii) Dhama chhatra (xix) Vaishnaba Purana and (xx) Sisu Mantra Vichara.

The titles suggest that Ananta also wrote similar theological books and had to resort for legitimizing to some "grand scholastic narratives about knowledge of Brahman". His 'magnum opus', Hetu Bhagabata was a narrative of human liberation and enlightenment through knowledge, a Hegelian attempt to narrativize the dialectical self-realization of spirit. Written in nine-lettered meter, Hetu Bhagabata enunciates the difficult ways of opening the doors of knowledge. The discourse is conducted through dialogues between a preceptor and a disciple. The easiest way is

"To transform the inner mind
Imagine yourself as a woman
Deck it up as a teenager girl.
You can touch the space where the jiva (Being)
merges in the Parama (Supreme)".

Sisu Ananta also believed in the concept of love as detailed in Yashovanta's Prema bhakti Gita. In Ananta's milieu the idea gained ground that all theoretical works constitute a genre of sublimated narrative. The author, it seems, gained the gratification by writing such narratives of virtual knowledge. Sisu Ananta's works characterize his ethical paradigm that mixes worldly weariness and cleverness. He accepts disorder both in the body as well as in the society and endeavors to master it up through rigorous discipline.

Ananta Das, like his elderly peers, was intelligent enough to discern the intense crisis of faith in his milieu that was passing through Muslim and Afgan invasions, demolition of temples and burning of sacred texts of Sanskrit written in volumes of palm leaf sheets. It was his responsibility to restore the faith of the common folks and get them empowered by practicing occult and Mahayana Tantra. After the introduction of the Pancharatra practices in Jagannatha temple, tantric power was considered essential for anyone who chose the path of divinity. On the other hand, the decadence and the inefficacious Brahminical orthodoxy needed a thorough demolition.

Ananta had to acquire some miraculous tantric power to attack on Brahminical ignorance. He believed in St. Sandilya, the promulgator of Pancharatra, and Kaularnava Tantra who had also declared that only Agama Sastra (Tantra) would rescue the world in Kaliyuga. Pancharatra did not admit the casteist discriminations and invested the common folks with humble origin with occult power. However, one had to undergo its course of rigorous sadhana. Ananta Das, it seems, was highly influenced by Yashovanta and Achyutananda and devoted more time to a godhead which was void, shapeless and beyond all mantras. It was nearer to the Madhyamika philosophy of the Buddhists. This affiliation was reasonable since the Brahmins hated him and did not allow him to touch the texts of Vedanta. Ahirbudhnya Samhita has shown how the Vedic texts were inferior to Pancharatra agamas and Sisu Ananta included these principles in his quasi-literary theological texts.

The Sisu sect of Vaishanvism as propounded by Ananta Dasa distinguished itself for its emphasis on divine love, exuberance of feeling and nurturing of fervent emotions. The Vedic school gives its due place to devotion, but it was neither exaggerated nor made emotional. While Sri Chitanya intended to emphasize emotion in Raganuga bhakti, Ananta built up his own cult of "Sisu–ism" by mixing up the tenets of Pancharatra. Bhakti is an emotional force in Sisu sect and it needs to be exercised and cultivated. It is even made an end in itself to achieve Panchama Purushartha (the fifth goal of life; beyond dharma, artha, kama and moksha) for Ananta's disciples.

Ananta's Thula Sunya Rasa, Gupta Tika /Yantra Tika and Anakara Sabada are three important books in addition to his magnum opus Hetu Udaya Bhagavata. These three books connect him to the philosophy of Yashovanta, Achyutananda & Balarama Dasa. In Thula Sunya Rasa Ananta conceived Shoonya as the highest truth and insisted on the annihilation of subjective imagination that weaves the dualistic conception of the world. It is called Shoonyata because it transcends all forms of divisive taxonomy. Sisu–ism and his teachings in Gupta Tika and Anakara Sabada admit two levels of truth: empirical and transcendental .The empirical truth is nearer to nescience since it superimposes a form on a non-existent one and thus creates an obstacle in having a correct view of reality. The form should not, therefore, be supposed to really exist. If all that is perceived by the senses is to be accepted as truth, then a fool's knowledge which is acquired by the senses would also be true. Ananta holds for the disciples that the body of a woman, though naturally impure is regarded as pure by a man. The mind here is swayed by attachment.

One of the essential characteristics of Shoonya is that no enunciation can be made about it. One is to realize it within him. Those with an obscured vision cannot realize how the objects which they perceive directly by sense organs can ever be conceived as unreal.The village folks refuse to understand those abstruse arguments without the help of illustrations, which they are familiar with.

Similarly, Bramhan is eternal and in it there is a total extinction of empirical life along with the relative distinctions of subject and object. What the Shoonyata doctrine positively insists on is the annihilation of the imagination that weaves the dualistic conceptions of the world. Mahayana sutralamkara (11.13.P.58) justifies the doctrine. We do not know whether Ananta Das was well conversant with the Madhyamika philosophy as Balarama and Achyuta were. But the essence of Anakara sabada and bakhara poems (Thika bakhara, Ude bakhara and Chhata bakhara) boils down to an identical philosophy. It is that by abnegating all phenomenal existences we can reach that state which is the highest. But Madhyamika does not define that state arrived at by such abnegation. Ananta does not enter into the mystic area in which Shankara's Brahman and the void (shoonyata) of Madhyamika appear as supplementary and complementary doctrines. His disciples were village folks.

Ananta, therefore, used folk language to caption his books: Thika bakhara, Ude bakhara and Chhata bakhara. His message is simple and communicable. His poems intend to impress that the world we see about is supposed to be existent, but in reality it is not so. The only reality is other than this, which supposes this to be existent. We attribute existence to this world, but this attribution is false. Those which exist in other than these false attributions are true. Hence what we see as sensory reality is void, Shoonya. The three Bakhara poems mentioned above are attempts at enunciating this concept of Void.

Ananta's spiritual poetry also seems to be a convergence of the Buddhist concepts of Tathagata garbha and the Vedantic conception of Brahman or Paramatman. The Buddhist Dharmakaya and Vedantic Brahman are non-dual, absolute pure and are identical with all beings. The only difference is that Brahman, when individualized is given the special functions while Tathagata garbha remains the same. It can never be individualized and given the special appellation "Jivatman" and to it is attributed certain special functions. Tathagata garbha in Buddhism remains the same and can never be individualized and has no special function. It is like a space within and outside a jar. (p.27) (43)

As the beginner of Sisu-ism, Ananta used a special folk dialectic to dislodge nescient views about the world and to establish the correct ones. His poetry appealed to the common folks.

His other texts appear more theological than literary. However, his devotional songs are popular and these songs are still sung in villages to prove him a popular poet:

Mind Lunatic!
Why do you ride this broken boat on?
It's fake.
You've kept the nectar away
And dip yourself in stray
dirty water. Pull the oars quick
Muttering his name: Chintamoni
Look at your preceptor's feet
They are like oars
Pull yourself up to cross
The river in spate.
Desire and anger
Engulfing greed
Are the waves that pull and sway
Toward a cyclone
Of sin
You are overpowered
and destroyed.

Surendra Mohanty did not admit such songs into the category of literature. But at times, like the poetry of the Sufis and those of Kabir, Ananta also wrote esoteric poems:

Meditate on those shapeless alphabets
Utter his name
One without vowels
Sins of million years would vanish.
Measure the Immeasurable
In your heart Utter the silent.
The phonetics of his name
Not fricative, labial or dental
Neither through tongue
Nor in alveolar ridge.
Nither mantra, nor a Yantra
Yet you won't miss
The form of the formless.

It seems Ananta Das was highly influenced by Achyutananda in such prescriptive bhajanas that impressed the village folk at Balipatna, because of their anti-Brahmanic thrust.

Pancha-Sakha Poetry: A General Estimation

The theosophical poems written by the five different poets and clubbed together under the rubric of Pancha sakha poetry constitute a part of the trends in medieval Indian poetry. The whole of India was swept by Vaishnavite thoughts and we find kabir writing exactly like the Pancha sakhas. It is a well known fact that persons worshipping the same God, believing in the same religion, have stood by each other, with much greater strength and constancy, than people of merely the same descent. The Panchasakhas have struggled to transcend the limitation of the senses. All religions of the world, thus, have made a strong statement that the human mind, at certain moments, transcends not only the limitation of the senses, but also the power of reasoning. The "miracles" concerning each of these prophet poets become crucial to the readers of the twenty first century. Are they fantasies, legends believed by blind and illiterate followers? If they think so, they can check it for themselves even today. There are ordinary looking Sadhakas (persevering men) in Orissa who can fly sitting on a grinding stone or a large burning log of wood. So, the phenomenon of Achyutananda and Ananta flying on the broken walls does not seem to be folk–tale magic. There are true powers acquired by consistent inner discipline and perseverance that can make such flights possible, A clinging to sensations, a grappling with them, a harking back on them may generate what the ancient psychologists called neurasthenia. When neurasthenic self adjustments and scrutinizes cease, awareness becomes unusually and preternaturally keen and sharp in which such flights are possible. Moreover, the tantric yogic focus gave them the power to actualize will power that helped those envisioning poems as well as flights. The Panchasakha poets of the Odia Bhakti movement combined in themselves metaphysical experience and artistic expression.

Knowledge and devotion are the two attributes common to all the Pancha sakhas. The Bhagabat Gita also prescribes both the personal and the impersonal aspects of God for attaining liberation. The path of devotion and the path of knowledge are synthecized in Odisan form of Vaishnavism, although a higher place is assigned to devotion in Bhagabat Gita.

Ramanuja, in his commentaries on Brahmasutra defines devotion as perpetual memory of God, an attachment to divinity that is never disconnected, Patanjali defines devotion as a state of mind in which the desire for material gains is relinquished and the ego is totally merged into cosmic consciousness. Narada's Bhakti Sutra (Principles of devotion) classifies devotion into two categories: transcendental devotion and the devotion to worldly attachments. The second category is further divided into three sub-categories: Sattviki, Rajasi and Tamasi.

The Structural pattern of devotion in Chaitanya's Sect of Vaishnavism can be understood from the following table:

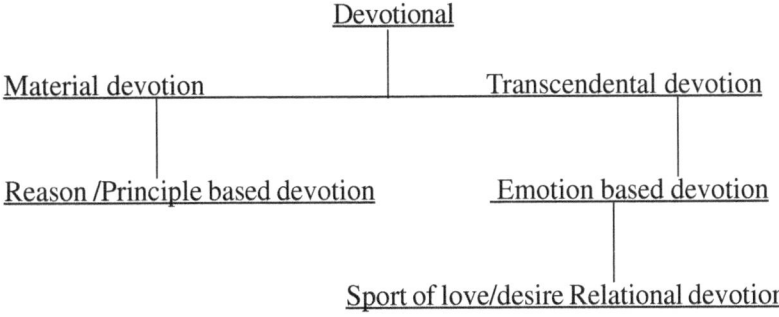

(feeling of Gopis for Krishna)   (like a friend, servant, surrendering self, affection for the child etc.)

The Panchasakhas of Odissa appear to be the devotees under the category of 'principle /reason' for whom Sadhana was primary and composing poetry was secondary. In their perseverance they encounter the supreme consciousness with or without variations of form and their poems document their reactions. The quest, at times, grew transgenderic in which the devotee imagined himself as a unique, chaste woman devoted to her husband. Achyutannada and Ananta adhered to a path of devotion as steadily as a fighting hero in the battle. Such a mindset refers to steadfast, heroic devotion. Poetry was not their goal; it was a mode of their expression of the super-conscious realizations. Thus, their poetry turns into their discursive religion.

There were two clear paths before them: the way of knowledge and the way of devotion. A higher place is given to devotion because it suited to the generality of mankind, while the path of knowledge was difficult; it was accessible only to a few who had exceptional spiritual caliber. In Gita the lord dissuades Arjuna to follow the path of knowledge since the senses offer them the only experience of reality. The Panchasakhas had devoted their lives to the path of selfless action that combines itself with knowledge. The main aim of the path of knowledge (followed, for example, by Yashovanta, Balarama, Jagannatha and Achuyuta) was to discriminate between 'self' and 'not-self'. One has to discriminate and give up the idea that matter is real. The self alone is real and all else is illusory.

The prophet poets of PanchaSakha literature, therefore, constantly harp back to their true nature; the true nature of self, once understood, they believed, would definitely help in separating the self from the not-self. As Bhagabat Gita has revealed, unswerving devotion to Lord is a means to this attainment of knowledge, and therefore has to be adopted. Thus, with knowledge are combined meditation, action and devotion though knowledge is the main note in this symphony. In one of the Panchasakhas' lores, Balaram Dasa desired to visit Lanka to render an actual poetic description of the place in Jagamohan Ramyana. The wise lore records that Lord Jagannatha appeared in his vision transported him to Lanka and Balarama wrote what he envisioned. This virtual reality cannot be refuted as untrue and hoax.

Western rationalism offers too narrow a vision to fathom this description. Any empiricist, who believes the impressions of his eyes, ears, nose, tongue and skin to be real, would discard such an experience. Jayadayal Goyandka in his book 'The Secret of Prema yoga' has devoted a chapter on "Dialogue with the Lord during meditation." Goyandka records some findings of the Prem Yogis:

"Let him then withdraw his senses from their respective objects and renouncing all worldly thoughts makes the mind totally void of impressions. Thereafter, let him invoke the Lord, the Deity of his heart, in a pure state of mind, free of sloth and full of dispassion. He would know that when the Lord will appear before him during meditation, the mind will be full of joy, peace and light and though his eyes may remain closed, he will, as if, see the whole universe lighted up by a supernatural light. Where there is peace, there will be no sleep or sloth. He should firmly believe that when God is invoked and prayers are offered to, the Lord appears before the devotee during meditation. There should be no difficulty in meditating on the form of one's own deity" (Goyandka, 43) (44)

Most of the Panchasakha poets have superimposed the methods of Shakta Agama on Vaishanava Agama. But a Vaishnavite phrase called "Nitya Rasa" (perpetual frolicking and indulgence in the act of physical union) has either eluded or misguided the readers. Ramanujacharya had introduced a consort with Srikrishna and their eternal union is captioned Rasa kreeda (the game of perpetual love making) in a book of poems by Jagannatha Dasa. Actually they refer to the ideas of Prakriti (nature) and Purusha (The masculine principle). In Bhagabata Gita both are said to be without beginning (Gita13/19). Though both of them are beginningless, they are distinct in nature. Prakriti is perpetually active whereas Purusha lies dormant without any activity. Activity continues in all states of wakefulness, dream, sleep, unconscious, trance and creation. Activity goes on every moment in all the evolutes of nature such as minds, intellect, senses, bodies, stars, planets, sun, moon and ocean. There is a continuous process in them, from birth to death, even though they appear steady.

The Panchasakhas admit three kinds of activity during the state of slumber: (i) the light sleep gradually develops into sound sleep. (ii) Our tiredness vanishes and one is refreshed (iii) the body decays and paces toward extinction. Nature (prakriti) continues its activity of decay from the time of creation to its state of dissolution. The Panchasakhas as the spiritual guides of sixteenth century Odissa, therefore, have emphasized on the union with the self, which is equivalent to the union with God.

A larger portion of Panchasakha literature, therefore, hinges on Yoga and instructions about Yoga. Lord Krishna, in Bhagabata Gita defines "Equanimity is called Yoga" (2/48) and "disconnection from contact with pain is known as yoga (6/23). Both the definitions mean the same thing: equanimity would lead to disconnection with worldly contacts: while discarding relationship with the world would lead to equanimity. Panchasakha literature establishes this throughout; calling it the total extinction of the world, along with root ignorance and attainment of the supreme bliss.

Whether the Panchasakha have followed the Saptanga Yoga of the Nathist literature or not is a different issue. But most of the Panchasakha poets have dealt with such applicative issues. Yashovanta's Siva Svarodaya and Atma Parche Gita, Balarama Dasa's "Brahmanda Bhoogola" Sareera Bhoogola and Kundalini Yoga, Jagannatha's

Padmakalpa Tika and Anameya Kundali, Achyutananda's Anakara Samhita, Sunya Samhita, Sisu Veda, Tattva bodhini, Chaurasi Yantra and Amara – Jumara –Samhita, Ananta's Gupta Tika, Hetu Bhagabata and Thula Sunya Rasa etc. embody different precipitous about Yoga.

The number of texts written on Yoga is so large that one understands its centrality to the Panchasakhas' literature. Yoga takes place when there is stilling (in the sense of continual and vigilant watchfulness) of the movement of thought, without expression or suppression – in the indivisible intelligence in which there is no movement. A popular phrase from Patanjali- "Yogas chitta vritti nirodhah" is crucial to the Panchsakha mendicants. Chitta (mind) is undivided consciousness and the Vrittis are the apparent modifications of the mind: thoughts emotions feelings memories etc. which change all the time. Vrittis in terms of psychology are 'learned knowledge' mixed with untutored knowledge or the instincts. It is very difficult for the common man to refrain from memory, imagination and learned knowledge. The Saint, Vasistha in Yoga Vasistha describes this gathering of the mind as "The indivisibility of the Chitta which is realized as water mixing with water" (the cocept of samarasa in Buddhism). The vritti and the Chitta being made of the same stuff, become one –as water becomes one with water.

In the state of yoga, intelligence functions naturally in its own natural form or formlessness. It may be 'nirodha', a restraint or suppression. But how does one suppress the thoughts? The Panchasakhas, almost every one of them, explained the theory of the functioning of the body which includes a mind. It is possible that the mind is nothing but pure intelligence. The pure intelligence somehow confuses this small, temporary, insignificant fragment called a passing thought (or experience) with the whole of the mind. When this confusion somehow arises in the mind there is trouble; but when the totality of the mind-which is intelligence-observes this fragment called anxiety, what happens within is called "nirodha". It is controlled, but not controlled in the ordinary sense of the word. A mysterious 'something' takes place within you which Patanjali calls understanding, knowledge or self knowledge. (45)

The saint poets of the devotional movement of Panchasakha literature have, no doubt, borrowed the ideas from Patanjali, but it was a social requirement in a time when the Afgans and the Moghals were destroying all the palm leaf texts containing our ancient knowledge. Like Kabir in North India, the Panchasakhas did also explain the root forces of Sahaja sadhana, not in the way the Buddhist practices of Sahaja Yana degraded it to the Sexo-yogic esoteric, but through controlling in sense organs and deploying the mode of "chitta-vritti-nirodhah". A detailed understanding of this body of literature leads us to a conclusion. The Panchasakhas were Vaishnavites, yet as poets they were in search of a creative delight, which also admitted impressions of beauty. They had realized that beauty in also a concentrated form of delight. Thus, the Panchasakha poets were able to create that fine many-sided poetry which still remains the fountain head of all our evolving literature. They could be able to make a fusion of 'delight' and 'beauty' in epiphanic moments and proved that they had an instinct for beauty even when they wrote about yoga and void and Brahman. The earliest surviving poetry of this country, (the Vedas and the Upanishadas), was religious and philosophical. The modernists of today, however, tend to create a divide between the aesthetic and the philosophical, a separation between the spiritual and the aesthetic. We might have failed to discover the aesthetics of the void and to make a fusion of beauty, power and truth. Perhaps we do not know that the profound truth is derived from and lived by bliss of the eternal spirit, in the powers of a universal delight. Similarly, the idea of beauty, the spontaneous satisfaction in it, the worship of it as in itself is divine, religious and philosophical. The Panchasakhas attempted at a syncretic religion amalgamating all the vital features from different religions.

They were not sectarians. Achyutananda, the most radical of them also believed the formless God of the Turks (Turukhas). In fact, all the five prophets have emphasized the concept of Void (Shoonya), the void as the formless Supreme consciousness. We may examine their verses:

i. Formless and beyond logos He's without a beginning without an end. Achyutananda (Anakara Samhita)
ii. Void self is steady, indifferent But throws a net
iii. The great Void has Effulgence, from which Forms were born. Jagannatha Dasa (Tulabhina)
iv. What you call gross void Is formless, luminous No feet, no hands Exists, anonymous -Sisu Ananta, Bhajana-
v. Beyond the void is a luminous zone And above it: Grand void again There exists a space called consciousness, I've found there my right niche. Yashovanta Dasa (Prema Bhaki Gita)

Either the prophet poets believed in the great Odissan tradition of Buddhist concept of 'void' or they tried to propagate a synergetic religion of tolerance instead of confusing their disciples by the multiple forms and shapes of the deities of Hinduism. The Vaishnavas of the time have recurrently referred to the concepts of Nitya-goloka and Nitya rasa-leela continuing within the psychic interior, which they equated with the concept of void. Achyutananda, in the VII chapter of Sunya Samhita proceeds a step further to include the Muslims, Afgans and Turks into his fold of worship.

He's Alekh, Turukh and Alif
All in one, no difference, but if
I am a Hindu, must find relief
To meditate on Alekh.

Achyuta's Mani-varana Gita provides an interesting account of how Yashovanta, Balarama, Jagannatha, Achyutananda, and Ananta had visited Dakhina Kalika at Kolkata. After staying there for some time, the Panchasakhas proceeded toward Guwahati to visit Kamakshya. But before they reached the temple, they felt as if they were drained out of their life spirit. Balarama felt as if some terrestrial power sucked in his blood. Achyuta intuited some kind of spiritual disorder and sat in deep meditation to identify a Tantrik who deployed his powers to invalidate the five associates. Achyuta counter deployed the Tantrik, who sent the force of goddess Kamakshya. Mani varana Gita closes the account by depicting how the goddess blessed the five associates and fulfilled their mission.

One more common theme in Panchasakhas' literature is cosmogenesis. The Panchasakhas had a common motif in translating all theosophical ideas and doctrines into consciousness. They had their monasteries and disciples in Puri, Nemla, Ranpur and Adhanga etc. Achyuta counted the number of his female disciples to be 300 and there were thousands of them for every preceptor. They needed their theosophical doctrines to become living knowledge to be used as gateways to direct experience and the devotees of the Odia country of the 16th century considered this direct experience to be their supreme prize.

As such, we notice the first chapter of Prema-Bhakti Gita is devoted completely to cosmogenesis and the ontology of knowledge. Balarama's Brahmanda bhoogola, Jagannatha Dasa's Tula-bhina (ginning cotton), Achyutananda' Sunya Samhita and Achyuta's Hetu Bhagabata deal with cosmogenesis, partially or entirely.

Cosmogenesis has always been a favorite subject of theosophical literature all over the world. Every religion feels the necessity of knowing its Supreme creative Deity and the process of the emanation of the universe.Connoisseurs of theosophical literature turn towards the function of our existence and contemplate the purpose of our life and the laws which govern the harmonious and happy fulfillment of that purpose. In the process the readers would also be seeking the way of power, of its attainment, and of peace. The lines of Tulabhina (cotton ginning) envisioned by Jagannatha Dasa would be of great help to us:

> And ultimately, the void manifested
> Scintillating; it had its immanent glitter.
> The luminosity produced a gross sound
> Then was visible
> A half– circular alphabetical mark
> A dot on its head;
> Faded in, then an omkara
> the sound of Transcendence.
> Listen to me, oh, Parvati!
> This cosmic world, the boundless space
> Had nothing, but this sound:
> The Omkara,
> In which all shapes dissolved;
> But a world there was
> full of smoke, bleary, engulfed
> In darkness

The 'boundless space' mentioned here is not a created thing, since this is not mentioned in any of the Upanishadas. The Vrihadaranyaka Upanishada mentions, "verily this universe is made up of three things: name, colour (form) and action". (Mantra: 1/6.1.)

Jagannatha Dasa has negotiated one of the major questions of advaita philosophy: how has the infinite, the Absolute become the finite? The 'absolute' has become the universe. By this the material world is not only meant; the universe includes the psychic universe, and its spiritual manifestations too, heavens and earths and the abyss. Mind is the other name for change; and ever-changing transitoriness of the universe.

Jagannatha Dasa's cosmogenetic vision in Tulabhina explores four foundation concepts of physics: space, time, matter, and number; and their relationship to human consciousness. Space is treated also as a metaphor. A metaphor suggests more than an analogy. Metaphor (here 'space') implies the creation of an idea (be it 'omkara' or, 'brahman', the supreme consciousness) or a symbol, which not only stands for something else, but, in fact, stands alone as a new evocation of meaning.

Today, in a world of advance sciences, when we use a concept like space, we tend to construct an image. The image, despite its abstract character and quantitative description, evokes and summarises what our being and existence feel like to us. The spatial metaphor (boundless space) signifies what it is like to exist as an entity that is separate from, and related to, other things. Our experiences of location, notions of distance, connection of the self with the Other, gain meaning and coherence through this Cosmo-genetic poem. We see ourselves located at a point in space, separated from other things by the distances of space, connected to them through light (luminosity and sound (omkara) which travels across space. What might otherwise be some kind of meaningless, inchoate experience of our own undifferentiated existence is transformed through the metaphor of space into awareness. It is an awareness of differentiation, diversity and separateness. Space organizes and gives meaning to our tangled experiences through its attributes of place and distance.

About five hundred years after Jagannatha Dasa wrote Tulabhina, the boundless primeval space becomes synonymous with all these experiences. But we cannot see it as a representation of them, nor can we see clearly what is standing for what. Tulabhina and for that matter, the other works of cosmogenesis sproject the evolving human consciousness in medieval Odissa.

The second question that disturbs the empirical mind is the probability of the space generating luminosity and luminosity engendering omakara sound and so on. For physicists probability does not exist in and occupy space. Nor can probability be measured by such doubting scientists. They cannot, fundamentally, be configured in the spatio-temporal terms we apply to gross matter. The notion of configuring the Void Self in the icon or the non representational (non-mimetic) eyes of Lord Jagannatha ultimately rests on a generalized hypothesis of the idea that two things cannot occupy the same space at the same time. Hence two meanings cannot occupy that space. Probably; an idea of extension or occupancy of space is concealed within the creative imagination of Jagannatha's poetry.

Jagannatha's cosmogenesis, the concept of the boundless space and the concept of "void" in Achyuta, Balaram, Ananta and Yashovanta appear to be interrelated. The boundless psychic space is filled here with a feeling of perpetual union (Nitya rasa mostly in the Raganuga school of Sri Chaitanya. The idea has been directly borrowed from the 'Yuganaddha' principle of Buddhism. In Sri-chakra-sambhara-Tantra the "void" is Prajna, the female deity with attributes like tranquility and bliss. All men are Upaya, whereas all ladies are Prajna.

"In the Pancha-karma of Nagarjunapada we find four grades or stages in shoonyata, of which the first is Shoonyata and the second is Ati-shoonyata. Shoonyata has been described as Prajna and it is also called the woman. Atishoonyata is called Upaya and the sex analogy is imbedded there. In some places Prajna is described as the female organ and Upaya as the male organ. Prajna denotes the female genital because it is the abode of all pleasure, which is bliss (mahasukha). It can also be inferred that the female organ is called the prajna because all the beings have their birth from there. All the 'beings' have their origin from the Prajna or the Shoonyata. (Dasgupta, p.117)(46)

These two aspects of reality in Vaishnavism are represented by (Krishna=Upaya=nivritti) the static principle and the dynamic principle (Radha=Prajna=Pravritti).But the ultimate goal of both the schools is the perfect state of union, –the union between the two aspects of the reality and the realization of the non-dual nature of self and the not-self. The principle of Tantricism being fundamentally the same everywhere, The superficial differences, whatever these may be, supply only different tones and colours. (p.3) (47)

The purpose of this eclectic juxtaposition of the theories of space (Akasa/void) is to prove that the Panchsakha theosophy was synchronic in nature. It can be envisioned in an enlightened state of awareness. Such awareness, states Patanjali, is "Keen" intense and operative even in the field of the first seven of the eight states or limbs of yoga practice."(P.179)(48)

The eighth limb of Yoga is Samadhi, which is enlightenment itself. This awareness shines resplendent with the light of intelligence when the inner psychic impurities that befoul the vision of truth, are eliminated by the intelligent practice of the "limbs" of yoga. Discipline, observances, posture, exercise of the life force, introversion of attention, concentration, meditation and illumination (atonement) are the eight limbs of yoga or the direct realization of oneness (Patanjali-II.29,P.131)(49) Jagannatha Dasa had undergone these Astangas (eight limbs) in the course of his sadhana. When the light of intelligence or the awareness of the truth illumines his mind-stuff, psychological order comes to prevail and perception of the Cosmogenesis is possible. The process of this envisioning entails a higher consciousness, a consciousness which Sri Aurobindo alludes to in his Savitri;

> Since God has made earth
> Earth must make in her God;
> What hides within her breast?
> She must reveal;
> If man lives bound by his humanity
> If he is tied for ever to his pain
> Let a greater being then arise from man,
> The super human with the eternal mate
> Through earthly forms. (Book XI,Canto.1 p.693) (50)

In this supra conscious state Jagannatha envisions the Godhead as sky and then as the sound of Omkara. In Bhagabat Gita Lord Sri Krishna defines Himself: "I am, O son of Kunti, sapidity in water, lusture in the moon and the sun, the syllable Om in all the Vedas, sound in ether and enterprise in man."(p217)(51).The sound Omakara,and the meaning behind it (which is present in the mind at the time)are present together in a confused state. By performing samyama on the sound, the confusion is resolved and the meaning of the cosmogenetic sound becomes comprehensible.

Balaram Dasa's Kundalini Yoga, in addition to its total explication of Kundalini, the sushumna (the gross spinal cord) which is also called brahma Nadi depicts its functionalities. By contemplating on the chakras (plexus) that exist in this Nadi (column) the yogi destroys all sins and attains the Highest Bliss.

Nada (sound) that is heard through the ears is of ten kinds. The first is the sound 'chini' (like that of the pronunciation of the word), The second is chinichini, the third is the sound of the bell, the fourth is that of a conch, the fifth is that of a lute, the sixth is the sound of cymbals and the seventh is the tune of a flute, the eighth is the voice of a drumu (bheri), the ninth is the sound of a double-drum (Mridanga) and the tenth is the sound of thunder. Balaram explains that in the case of one whose chitta-vrittis have been almost stunted and he does not hear the stratas of sounds, a fusion is to be brought about. Such an absorption in one another of the knower, the knowledge and the known is brought about in the Kundalini yoga.

The Panchasakhas or the five devotional poets leading the life of mendicants had known each other, had an epistemological relationship amongst them, had traveled together to Dakhinkalika and Kamakshya and were potent practitioners of different Tantras, Buddhist, Shakta, Saiva and Vaishnava. Hence, they should not be considered only as the disciples of Sri Chaitanya. They were pals on the psychic and spiritual levels also.

Finally, they would be remembered in the history of Odia literature as the first group of active neo-Buddhists who demystified the truths of Brahminic hierarchy and demonstrated an ethical mode of salvation through mainstream religion. The Brahmins had committed the greatest blunder by rejecting the common man as unfit for studying the books of theology. Yashovanta from Adhanga, Balaram from a minister's family in Puri, Achyutananda and Ananta from the periphery taught the orthodox Brahmins of the capital city (Puri) a great lesson. They revised their world view in general and their attitude to the mass when they were ostracized from the pedestals of religion. Achyuta rejected the Puri Brahmins and people from the sudra communities from Nemala and Ranapur built monasteries for him.

In the Vedic world also Viswamitra and Raikva were the only two non-Brahmin sages. The cultural structures of the Brahmins,on the other hand, was hedonistic and their literary aesthetics was also one that embodied the principles of pleasure. If asceticism and ethical conducts were the codes of Panchasakha culture, the orthodox counterpart of the hedonistic Brahmin group was to assure the commoners that salvation was also possible through delightful art experience. They alluded to Bharata's Natya sastra, and his theories about rasa. The Brahmins like Bharata were tactical and they offered audio visual medium in which the higher and lower castes of audience could sit and enjoy without any caste-centric prejudice in mind. What was needed was Sahridaya feeling, the feeling of "like-heartedness", called otherwise as brahmanada sahodaras (connoisseurs of literary pleasure).

In other words, the theological world view of the Panchsakhas was taken over by Brahminical aesthetics that was originated and established as mass culture. The Brahmins attempted for enlightenment through emotional purification instead of achieving ethical purity, which necessitated a transcendental order, not understood by the common men. Immediately after the Panchasakhas, their junior contemporaries wrote therefore, mythologies, Puranas
and romances that blended the ethics of the Upanishadas with the erotics of the romances. "Rati –Sukha-sara" (the essence of mundane sexual union or the Sahaja Yana notions) taken from one of the songs of Jayadeva's Gita Govinda, began to percolate into these Puranas and the romances.Let us cast a quick glance over this immediate post-

Panchasakha literature. Even there were contemporaries who wrote and yet they did not lead the life of mendicants. The poetry of the Age of Panchasakhas, did not, however, stay confined only to the theological poetry of the saintly poets. There were other poets, who lived with their own families and yet they were faithful to Vaishnavite philosophy, and yet were also committed to Lord Jagannatha . Deba Durlabh Das, the poet of Rahasya Manjari needs a mention here. The book deals with the mysterious relation between Sri Radha and Sri Krishna, which is depicted as love. Love, the lover and the beloved, though they appear to be three, are actually one. The poet invokes Lord Jagannatha as Krishna and tries to preach the message of love. The Lord himself is the divine lover and in his vision the world appears as full of the luminous light of transcendent, divine Love. Rahasya Manjari depicts the unalloyed love of the Gopies (the cowherdesses of Krishna's place) for Lord Sri Krishna. Sri Radha, as the Hladini Sakti (potency for engendering the feeling of ecstasy) of the Lord occupies the central place among these entwined mystic creepers that rest on Krishna. Some Minor Poets of the Panchasakha Era Sisu Sankar Dasa's Ushabhilasa (c 1555) is not a Purnaic Kavya in epic form. It is the first attempt in Odia literature that combines epic and romance successfully, comparable to Beowulf, Faerie Queene Camoes'Lusiadus(French) (1571) or Tasso's Gerusalemme Liberata (1575). As we compare these Italian, Portuguese and Odia epic romances historically, we find so much similarity, but there is no logic to connect them together. Like Arthurian romances, we have in Ushavilasa giants and enchanters and super natural events in which the medieval renaissance meet along with the modern and the classical.

The theme of Ushabhilasa has been collected and combined from various sources: Sarala's Mahabharata, Bhagvata, Harivamsa Purana. Written in XVChhandas (cantos). this epic of a romance has a unified story with the chivalric account of Usha, the daughter of the demon called Bana. Bana Asura kept his daughter isolated from the rest of the world. One day, she gets united with the hero, Aniruddha, the son of Kamadeva (Cupid) in a dream. The song, in which Usha weeps importunately after the dream, is accepted as a marvelous example of literary composition that is in a transit toward Riti poetry:

> Ill fate! You showed me a jewel
> and then looted it, leaving me to wail.
> What do I know about sex?

Uninitiated, a young lass, I'm
just a novice.

The cantos of Ushabhilasa are written in different chhandas. The Chhaanda is a typical poem for songs, tuned to different indigenous Odissi ragas. Sisu Sankar has composed different chhandas in ragas like Malwa, Nandini gowda, Dhanasree, Mangala-gujjari, chokhi, Kedara, Bangala sree, Ashadha Sukla vani, Vichitra Desaksha and Chinta Bhairav etc, some of which are typically Odia and others imitated from Jayadeva's Sanskrit songs which were sung in the temple regularly during the three hundred and twenty five years of Ganga rule. However, the lyricists after the Pancha Sakhas have taken the lead in making the Odia verse form. The nine-syllabic verse of Sarala Dasa and Balaram Dasa now got complicated with the introduction of classical ragas.

The poetry written toward the end of the age of the Pancha Sakhas bifurcated into two roads: one through the simplest folk lines and the other through the highly Sanskritized elitist verses. Since the latter would be dealt with in a separate chapter, let us take up the folk stream first.

Markanda Dasa

Markanda Dasa is famous in every Odia house for his poem Kesaba Koili, a genre of Vaishnavite folk poetry written as an 'address' to the Koili, the Cukoo. It is not a messenger poem as Kali Das worked out in Meghdutam. The author's creative persona makes an inroad into Yasoda's psyche and Yasoda downloads her Vatsalya (filial love for the child Srikrishna) through the Koili. Like a drama within a drama, Markanda Dasa deploys a voice within a voice to communicate the intensely internalized filial love:

Cuckoo, my dear! Listen,
In the nights when the moon shines
My child, Hari, demands, "Fetch me the moon!
Bring it down!"
His father, helpless Nanda looks up blank
While Hari, the naughty one
Laughs aloud, sitting on his lap.
Cuckoo, my dear!
His father would swing Hari and he'd feign a fall
To the shock of his father, poor Nanda
too small a mortal.

The memory of the naughty child Srikrishna is neither important here, nor the use of onomatopoeic sound (in Odia) for folk lyrical effect. Yashoda was thoroughly convinced by this time, in the absence of the child Srikrishna though, that their naughty child swinging, laughing and pining for the moon was none other than Sri Hari, the Lord himself, incarnated as a child in their house.

Damodar Dasa

has written Rasakulya Chautisa in various ragas during the first part of the 16th century. The text depicts Krishna and Radha's love, separation and reunion etc. The language includes a mixture of words from Assamese, Vrajaboli, Awadhi and Bengali.

Brundaban Dasa

He is one of our senior poets of the era of Pancha Sakhas and one of the ancient translators of Jayadeva's Gita Gobinda. Late Prof. Artaballav Mohanty of Utkal University had retrieved the text of his Rasa Varidhi from the palm-leaf version and published it by Prachi Samiti. Prof. Mohanty speculates that Brundaban had written Rasa Varidhi before Chaitanya's arrival, i.e. before 1510A.D.

Arjuna Dasa

His Rama Bibha and Kalpalata were two important lyrical kavyas that have been frequently alluded to by the later poets like Kartik Das and Dhnajay Bhanja, who have followed the classical musical ragas deployed in the chhandas of Arjun Das. Ramabibha is identified today as the first musically metered kavya of our literature. Arjuna Dasa had accepted Sisu Ananta Das as his preceptor. Thereafter, he was known as Sisu Arjuna Dasa. His lyrical poems embodied the concepts of the Sisu sect of Vaishnavism. Arjuna's poetry attracts the connoisseurs for evocation of the rasas and the aesthetic descriptions. Similarly, Kalpalata is accepted as the first poetic romance of our literature. The book depicts the story of a dancer named Surekha who falls in love with a gandharva (ranked above the human beings in the 'Chain of Being') named Vasantaka. Milana Chautisa is one more kavya based on the romance of Sri Krishna and Chandravali.

Dharanidhar Mishra

Some ancient critics believed Dharnidhar to be the first translator of Gita Govinda. But the author of Rasa Varidhi takes this credit for that. Dharanidhara would, however be remembered as the second translator of Gita Govinda.

Kartik Dasa

Kartik Das, who belonged to the first part of the 17th century has earned a name for his Kavya, Rukmini Bibha. The title, itself, suggests that Kartik Das emphasized the folk language (bibha for vibah=marriage) and believed in producing a kind of pop literature. He brushed aside the literary modes of the High-cult and Mid-cult literatures and instead, attempted to appeal to the mass minds directly. Rukmini Bibha has a dimension, a thrust, and most important, a reality that has very little to do with aesthetic accomplishment". Perhaps, Rukmini bibah has more merit than is often given to it.

Danai Dasa

If clarity is given preference to metaphysics in literature, Danai's Gopi Bhasa would be remembered with priority. When Odia text books were not available, the beginners used to read Danai's Gopibhasa during the 1930 and 1940s.Pandit Suryanarayan Das places him between the last part of the 15th century and the first part of the 16th century, as a junior contemporary of the Panchsakhas.

Raya Ramanada

Born in Bentapur village near Puri, and son of Bhavananda Pattanik, Ramananda was a military officer and King Prataprudra's representative in South Kalinga. He had profound knowledge in Sanskrit and has written Jagannatha Ballava Natakam before he met Sri Chaitanya. As a resident of Puri, he learnt and wrote in Brajaboli and had also contributed immensely for the development of Bengali literature. Ramananda's Odia was as perfect as his Brajaboli.

Odia:Jaya Gokula Narendra hrudaya chandana
Brajabasi hrudaya bhramara padma -vana
Bhubana mohana jaya arata bhanjana
Ramani mani rasika ananda varshana
Brajaboli:Pahalihi raga naryana bhanga bhela
Anudina badhila awadhi na gela
Na So ramana na ham ramani
Duhun mana manobhava peshala jani

It is unfortunate that most of the Vaishnavite poets wrote in Bengali and Brajaboli after Sri Caitanya's stay in Puri. The Vaisnava raganuga emotion, they thought, needed to be expressed either in Brajaboli or in Bengali.

Madhabi Dasi

Madhabi Dasi, the sister of Sikhi Mohanty, was a startling feminine voice in the era of Vaishnvite poetry. She would not have found a place in the history of Odia literature had there been no frequent references to her name in Chaitanya Charitamrita written in Bengali .Madhabi's oeuvre does not include a kavya. Her poems in Odia, Bengali and Brajaboli have not yet been collected into a compendium .Yet, we notice her poems published in Mukura, part-II, No.4. 1314 (p.95) and her reference in Pathachakra Prabandhavali, Utkal University –part-III (1971-72) p.56-57.

Damodar Champati Ray

An employee in Prataprudra Deva's court, Champatiray wrote Vaishnavite verses in Odia and Brajaboli languages. Dr Artaballav Mohanty, in his book, Prachina Gadya Padyadarsha has compiled some of his Vaishnavite poems. But the kind of Odia he wrote has plenty of Brajaboli influences.

Dibasa tapai tapana kharara
Rajani tapai tiaia
Chandana raja chuta mandira kintu nahin
Sakhi Sukhaia.

(This quote in Brajaboli is reproduced to give the feel of the language). It seems, Vaishnavism had a multicultural and multilingual dimension. Prema bhakti or the concept of devotion through love perhaps does not have a language. This intermingling of cultures and idioms has generated a cluster of poets, who hardly cared for linguistic boundaries.

They lapse into a new subgenre called Poi literature, perhaps a folk version of "padia" (stanza) The poi literature is identified by the number of stanzas they write: as they call chatuspadi, shatpadi and ashtapdi in Sanskrit , the poi-writers also denote their poems by calling them sathie padia (sixty stanza), Sahe padia (hundred stanzas) and so on. Nilakantha Khadenga's Sahe padia is colourful description of a heroine. Bamdeva Pattanayak, who is almost unknown to Odia literature, has written a chhapana padia (56-stanzas) describing the female protagonist from the top to the tips.

More of these padia poets would merge in the post–Bhanja era, and they would be enlisted in the next chapter. The narrative count shows that at a particular age, in which saintly poets ponder about the soul and the creative process, a host of folk writers concentrate only on female anatomy. Perhaps Vaishnavite poetry ended up ultimately in Vaishnava Tantra in which the binary oppositions of the body and the soul were no more seen as contraries. They were resolved and synthesized. However, the next course of evolution did not come through concealment and restraint, but through an ornate exposure. Language is a thin piece of decorated cloth to hide the translucent nudity imaged in the mental space of the Riti poets.

Kanhei Khuntia
This poet was a major figure in Chaitanya Charitamrita, as a prominent figure in Sri Chaitanya's Odissan associates. A resident of Harachandi street of Puri, he was a servitor in the temple. In Nandotsava (a festival of the temple) he used to don the role of king Nanda and Sri Chaitanya used to honor him as a father figure. Kanhei's Mahabhava Prakasa expounded the concept of emotional / empathetic Vaishanvism (Raganuga).

Madhav Pattanayaka's Chaitanya Bilasa, written around 1516 AD, is constituted of ten chhanda's. Vaishnaba Lilamrita (1535) can be treated as a book of 16th century history that embodied events about Chaitanya and Jagannatha Dasa and some political events of Prataparudra Deva's time. Moksha Purana was another book on the Vaishavite mode of attaining salvation.

Partha Srichandana, the king of Ranapur had written a romance captioned Kalavati .Late Kedarnath Mohapatra has argued that a poet named Bishnu Das was the actual author and it was published in the eponym of the king. Kedarnath's observations have not been authenticated by evidences.

Bishnu Dasa was the court poet of King Partha Srichandan of Ranapur. Then he went to Banapur and stayed there as a court poet of Raghunathraj Harichandan. Savitri charita, Prema Lochana and Lilavati are Bishnu Dasa's works. He has also written some Chautisa poems. Prabasa Bahuda chautisa, Mandakini chautisa, Malyavanta Chautisa and Raghubira Chautisa are some of his important song poems. But Bishnu Das shall be remembered for his Premalochana, a significant romance written in Panchasakha era. Princess Premalochana of Padmakara state gets introduced to a handsome prince named Sudhkar from Madhuvatipur through a duck that acted as a go-between. They fell in love with each other and were united in marriage. But unfortunately due to adverse circumstances they had to be separated from each other for fourteen months. They were finally reunited by the grace of Lord Sri Ramachandra .This romance embodies some prayer songs in Sanskrit language, but the language of the romance, as such, included lots of folk words current in those days –vinoi, ,Chitoi, ghatana, lahudi etc.

Banamali Dasa

This poet wrote towards the end of the sixteenth century and Chata Ichhavati is one of his major works. Dibakar Dasa's (18th century) Jagannatha Charitamirta mentions the name of one Banamali Dasa who was a disciple of Jagannatha Dasa. The Odia historians presume the poet of Chata Ichhavati to be the same Banamali. The text of Chata Ichhavati is constituted of six chhandas. Prince Charubrahma from Darpaka Desa, studied with Ichhavati, the princess of Bhoja nagara. As they grow up they were attracted to each other and one day they were physically united in a flower garden. This brings an end to their education. After giving up the studies, Ichhavati goes back to her place in Bhoja nagara But her friend Ambuvati arranges their union in Ichhavati's chamber. One day Charubrahma was caught by the palace employees and he was taken to the king. The king was delighted to know Charubrahma's identity and finally offered his daughter in marriage.

It is interesting to note that these pastoral tales of fantasy with their nature of adaptability to the popular taste gradually occupied the literary space. The serious subjects of theology and cosmogenesis etc. could not be written at all. It was hard for the ordinary court poets to envision a Tulabhina or Brahmanda Bhoogola. The lovers of these imaginary pastoral tales and romances were mechanically driven by cupid in palace bed-rooms. They were probably found languishing in amorous pallor and tossing on the palace beds in sleepless nights.

Raghunath Raj Harichandan

Ragunatha Harichandan was the king of Banapur during the mid-seventeenth century. Basically he was a poet and was in the company of reputed poets of his time. Bishnu Das was his mentor and preceptor for some time. He taught him some techniques of writing poetry in the course of editing his poems. His Lilavati was so thoroughly revised by Bishnu Das that some of our historians have designated Bishnu as its writer. Lilavati embodies the elements of romances and pastoral tales. The First chhanda describes the importance of Nilagiri kshetra (Puri) in Panchasakha style and the subsequent chhandas are devoted to the physical description of the heroine. The visual and virtual scenes of her erotic play in the honeymoon night are enthusiastically depicted. Whether the Kavya belongs to Bishnu Dasa or to Raghunath's oeuvre, we need not negotiate the controversy, but, Lilavati as a romance attracted the secular readers of the time for its picturesque, charming descriptions and its 'rhyme royal' in deference to the princely poet.

Devadurlava Dasa

Devadurlava's Rahasya Manjari is considered to be a major work of Vaishnavite era, the literature of the Sixteenth century. The kavya chapterised in chhandas is based on the importance of the character of Radha in Vaishnavism. Jagannatha is Sri Krishna and the author probes into the mysteries of Krishna's life while Radha's 'premabhakti' is considered to be the best amongst all.

Committed love is the best devotion
the one found in gopi-women:
Total surrender, I-ness dissolved
The women are to be adored.
Surrender in love and love in devotion
Otherwise, how can one merge in him?
A male devotee turns women
Love obeys no gender, no distinction.
(Rahasya Manjari)

Although the kavya limits itself to the standards of Sri Chaitanya's Vaishnavism and the tenets of Vedanta, its literary qualities, at times, transcends those of the Panchasakha poetry. The dry reasoning, the Vedantic hermeneutics overloaded in their literature, kept the ordinary mortals away from them. Devadurlava's Rahasyamanjari, its esoteric, yet provoking endless disquisions, alliterative rhythm and lyrical euphuisms invite a new age, a new brand of literature that would cater to the aesthetics needs of the common man.

Rahasya Manjari makes its esoteric experiences as well as its metaphysical realities easier for communication and enjoyable because of the poet's lyrical sense. The moral and ethical profundity was gradually dissolving into entertaining literary aesthetics. The repeated invasions of the Moghal soldiers, their atrocities felt on public life changed the cultural attitude to Jagannatha temple. It was no more a centre of Odissan cultural identity. Literature had also changed its rules and conduct. The later medieval literature, thus, was prone to spend upon the subtleties of sentiment. The minor poets, therefore, stepped away from theological discourse and concentrated on writing imaginary romances.

Chanda Dasa was also a poet of the last part of sixteenth century and he is famous for his small kavya captioned Gopichandana. It seems to have been influenced by Devadurlava's Rahasya Manjari. The subject follows the pattern of the imaginary romances and pastoral tales.

One day, Sri Krishna narrated his experience with the gopika lasses in front of his eight patavamsi queens. They felt jealous and wanted to check up for themselves in which way the gopi women excelled the queens. Sri Krishna sent them to Gopapura on a Puspaka Vimana (Vedic aero plane) escorted by Uddhava and they witnessed the Rasa Lila (the circular movements in dance) with Srikrishna, who multiplied his figure into many so that he was present with each gopi and each one of them felt his physical touch.

The text, thus, extols the (raganuga bhakti) emotive devotion of the gopika women with Srikrishna. Chanda Dasa had also written Gopa jivana –Chautisa, a lyrical text in which Srikrishna sets out for Mathura. The gopi women weep sentimentally imagining the pains of separation and Srikrishna promises them to return soon.

Uddhava Dasa

A disciple of Jagannatha Dasa, Uddhava, and a blacksmith by profession had translated Jayadeva's Gita Govinda in nine-syllabled rhyme. Like Dharanidhara Mishra. He is also the author of Kaligamana chautisa.

Sal Beigh

This Muslim poet is famous though out Orissa even today. His devotional songs are popular in Radio and television. He was born in seventeenth century. He writes "my mother was a Brahmin lady and my father, a Muslim." Sal Beigh was a great devotee of Lord Jagannatha. He had been to Vrindaban and spent his last years at Puri. "Kene gheni jauchha Jagnathanku" (where are you taking away my Jagannatha /who shall I offer my prayers to?) and Ahe Nilla Saila (Thou art my Blue Hills) are famous lyrics even today.

Dibakara Dasa

This mid-17th century poet is famous for his Jagannatha Charitamrita which is now treated as the only exhaustive, socio-spiritual history based on the Jagannatha temple, the cultural as well as religious centre of fifteenth and sixteenth century Odissa. It also embodies the life of his preceptor Jagannatha Dasa and some of the incidents concerning Sri Chaitanya. It may be compared with Madhavi Dasi's Vaishava Leela Mrita written much later. Dibakara Dasa is the first biographer in Odia literature and is, thus, alluded to as an authority on Panchasakha era.

Sridhara Dasa's Kanchanalata, Dasarathi Dasa's Vraja vihara and Leelamrita, Bhupati Pandit's Prema panchamrita and devotional songs, Kapileswara Dasa's kapatakeli and Narasimha Sena's Parimala are famous texts of this era. These poets of the transitional era bridged the gap between the theological poems and the erotic poetry of the Riti era. Narasimha Sena was a palace physican (Raja Vaidya) in Prataprudra Deva's time (1496-1535) and he belonged to a Brahmin family in which the members used Sanskrit as the language of common conversation. Yet he confesses in the 7th chhanda of Parimala: "I composed verses in desi' language for communicating my feeling to the commoners".

The 19th chhanda captioned Parimala provides us with a synchronic description of Indra performing an erotic worship with his wife Sachi and one lakh naked women in Malaya vana, the forest of Spring-gale. In a society mostly controlled by the Brahmins in 17th century Orissa, this quasi –tantric festival of erotic practices refers to the Madana Utsava held in different kingdoms of India The king and the common women used to meet each other under an Asoka-tree and copulate with each other without any barrier of caste or socio economic status. Such worship of cupid (Madana) and sexual indulgences mirror such practices in Tantric societies and they preach a concept of classes sexual; practice as has been advocated by Herbert Mercuse in America during the 1960s.

Sisu Shankar Dasa belonged to the Sisu sect of Vaishanvism of Sisu Ananta Dasa. He seems to be a major poet of the period of transition with a kavya captioned, Ushavilasa, to his credit. The epic-romance is called from Jagannatha's Bhagavata and Achyutananda's Harivamsa, which embodied some imaginary episodes that were not there in the original. The Ushavilasa offers a unique model of a combination of epic and romance successfully, comparable to Beowulf, Faerie queen, Cameon's Lusiadus (1571) and Tasso's Gerusalemme Liberata (1575). It is quite striking that creative writers of Odissa and those of Italy and Portuguese literature attempted a similar genre of poetry. We find no logic to connect them, though one may also search for a similarity in Arthurian romances. Strangely enough, the plot of Ushavilasa embodies giants, enchanters and events that belong to another level of reality which the mundane people are prone to define as supernatural. It should be remembered that the Panchasakha tantrics performed many such supernatural magic starting from change of gender to commanding sepulchral. Brahma Rakshasa to lead the way to Puri.

Ushavilasha was written in a time of political instability. Prataprudra Deva was killed and his military general Gobinda Vidyadhar killed his two minor sons and usurped the throne. This Karana usurper spread a rumour that Prataprudra had ruined the kingdom because of Sri Chaitanya and the patronage he gave to the Vaishnvites. Sisu

Shankar's Puri was no more a centre of culture. The Moguls and Afghans had started attacking Odisha from the south as well as from Bengal side. Gobinda Vidhyadhara's son Chakrapratap's rule (1549-1557) was also memorable to the people because he compelled the Brahmins to cut grass and feed the horses in the stable. Ushavilasha, written by this time, could not return back to the themethe metaphysics of creation. Literature was there to narrate an imaginary story to entertain the king and the courtiers.

The poetry written toward the fag end of the age of the Panchasakha, bifurcates into two roads: one through the simplest folk lines, and the through highly sanskritised elitist verses. Since the latter would be dealt with in a separate chapter, let us take up the folk stream first.

The folk themes included the stories of the Puranas. Balarama's Jagamohana Ramyana and Jagannatha's Bhagabata had already become a part of folk literature Sisu Shankara's Ushavilasa is typical to us in the sense it was an amalgamation of the folk tradition, the puranic tradition and also it stands out as one of the earliest precursors of t Riti poetry.

The theme of Ushabhilasa has been collected and combined from various sources: Sarala's Mahabahrat, Bhagabat, Harivamsa and Brahma vaivarta Purana. Written in XV chhandas (cantos), this epic of romance (Ushavilasa) has a unified story with the chivalric accounts of Usha, the daughter of the demon called Bana. Bana kept his daughter isolated for, rest of the world. One day, she gets united with the hero, Aniruddha the son of Kamadeva (Cupid) in a dream. The song in which Usha weeps after the erotic dream is accepted as a marvelous example of literary composition that is in a transit toward Riti poetry:

Ill fate! You showed me a jewel,
And before long did despoil. leaving me to wail.
What do I know about sex?
Uninitiated, young lass I am
I'm just a novice.

The aesthetic culture that was emerging on the terminal point of the era of theological poetry may be identified with the aesthetic culture, cultivation of arts and their experience with the fundamentals of social praxis. What these unsophisticated power crazy Bhoi kings preferred was a sound culture of emotions not a quest for the meaning of self and its relation to the Supreme self. What was primarily needed was a sense of appreciation of each other's emotions.

Sisu Shankar's Ushavilasa is based on the love of Bana Asura's beautiful daughter Usha and Sri Kirishna's son Aniruddha. The erotic emotion of Usha is considered archetypal by our historian critics. The aesthetics of the emergent era was to treat erotic emotion as a primary idea that was in practice much before the beginning of the Christian era. Vatsayana, the author of Axioms on Erotics (Kama sutra) who belonged to the second and the third century observed that the poetic art and the aesthetic sensibility of sex (Sringara) are entwined archetypally. The trend of "knowledge literature" that began with the Buddhist poetry continued through the Nathists to the Panchasakhas' poetry. There was an implicit hostility towards visual primacy in literature. Thus, the ground was prepared for the reception of hermeneutics. No less a literary philosopher than Hans-Georg Gadamer has reiterated all through "The primacy of hearing is the basis of the hermeneutical phenomannon." 50True issues of soul probing and self knowledge could be easier when literature was aural during the Panchsakhas. Perhaps the scene began to change now.

Notes

1. Qtd.Pathani Pattanyak's — Odia Sahityare Itihasa Nalanda, Cuttack.1997.P.233
2. Basant Kumar Mallick, — "Patronage, legitimacy and cultural Assimilation in Medieval Oidssa", in Exploring Orissan History, Ed. Nihar Ranjan Pattanayak, Kitab Mohal, 2005.PP.198-212
3. K.C.Panigrahi — History of Orissa, Kitab Mahal, Cuttack, 1981, p.216. We do not know whether it is a fact or a legend .How ever, this finds a place in Pangrahis history.
4. Hemant ku. Parija — "Vaishnavism in Orissa" The Religious History of Orissa Ed. Nihar Ranjan Pattanayak, Indian Publishers Distributors, New Delhi. 2004
5. Mayadhar Mansingh — Land marks in Oriya Literature
6. Herman Kulke — "Early Royal Patronage of

7. Ranjan Gurukkal

8. Kailash Chandra Dash

9. Ajit Kumar Tripathy,

10. Eschman, Herman Kulke

&G. C. Tripathy

11. Qtd. Pradip Ku. Panda

12. Kunjbehary Mohanty

13. Jaeques Derrida

14. Lavanya Nayak

15. Regina Bendix

Jagannatha cult in Cult of Jagannatha and Regional Tradition of Orissa, Ch. VIII. Vol XXX, 1978 PP.150-155.
"The socio–economic milieu of the Kerala Temples: A functional Analysis, Studies in History, Journal of the centre for Historical studies, J.N.U, New Delhi,1980
"Patitapbana Jagannatha", The Orissa Historical Research Journal, Vol XXXIX. No1.4, 1994
Sri Jayadeva-O-Sri Chaitanya (Odia), books India International, Bhubaneswar, 2002
The cult of Jagannatha and the regional
                    Tradition. 1st Edn.1978
"Introduction" to Prema bhakti Gita, Ed. P. K. Panda, Directorate of Distance and continuing Education, Bhubaneswar 1997.P.6
Achyutananda Das, Orissa Sahitya Academy, Bhubaneswar, 2004, P.19
"Economimesis", qtd. In Martha Woodmansee, The Author, Art and Market, Columbia University Press, 1994.P.II
Yasovanta Das, Odisa Sahitya Akademi, Bhubaneswar-1993
Marmot, Memet and Marmosit:Further research on the folklore of Dyads, Western Folklore: 46PP 171-191

16. Ibid
17. Rolland Barthes "The death of the Author", in Untying the Text: A Post Structuralist Reader, 1981.
18. Michel Foucault 'What is an Author' in M o d e r n Criticism and Theory, David Lodge Ed. PP196-210" Introduction"
19. Bidhu bhusan Panigrahi "Sakti Upasana-o- Tantra", Sakta Svara, Ed. Bhavani Sankar Panda, District council of Culture, Suvarnapur, 2009
20. Gokul Behari Mahanti: "Introduction" to Adrusya Nata and Nindita Gajapati (Two plays by Harihar Mishra) Sathi Mahal, Cuttack, 1990, P.6.
21. Bidhubhusan Panigrahi "Sakti Upasana–O-Tantra", Sakta Svara, Ed. Bhuvani Shankar Panda, 2009 District Council of Culture, Subarnapur, pp.8-10
22. Lavanya Nayak,(Dr) Yashovanta Dasa (Oriya) Orissa Sahitya Akademi, Bhubaneswar, 1993 Pp6-13
23. Bijoy Chandra Majumdar, "Introduction" to A Typical Selection from Oriya Literature, Vol.1. as quoted in Pathani Pathnayak's Odia Sahityara Itihasa Nalanda, Cuttack, VII Edition,1997,P.265
24. 'Introduction' C.Rajagopalchari Kuraal: The Great book of Tiruvaluvar, Bhavan's Book University edition, Bharatiya Vidya Bhavan, Bombay, Ed. R.R. Diwakar and S. Ramakrishnan, VIIth Edn. 1993
25. Bijoy Chandra Majumdar Typical Selctions from Oriya Literature, vol.1. as quoted in

26. Elemire Zolla — Archetypes, George Allen & Unwin, London, 1981.P.1.
27. Patanjali — Yoga Sutra: Sutra 1/17.
28. Hemant Kumar Parija, — "Vaishnavism in Orissa" Religious History of Orissa, Nihar Ranjan Pattanayak, Ed. Indian Publishers and Distributors, Delhi, 2004
29. Swami Gambhirananda, — Tr. Kena Upanishad Advaita Ashrama, Calcutta, 1998, P.41.
30. Sitakant Mahapatra — Jagannatha Dasa (Makers of Indian Literature series) Sahitya Akademi New Delhi, 1989 Pp.35
31. Ibid P.59
32. Ibid
33. — Quoted in "Introduction", Five Approaches to Literary Criticism, Wilbur Scott, Collier Books, New York, 1962. P. 26
34. Sitakant Mahapatra — Jagannatha Dasa (Makers of Indian Literature series) Sahitya Akademi New Delhi, 1989
35. — Karanas were of four types in the 15th century Khurda: (a) Kotha-karana (b) Sista–karana (c) Chhamu Karana and (d) Aho-karana
36. Kunja bihary Mohanty, — Achyutananda Das, Odisa Sahitya Akademi, Bhubaneswar, 2004, P.15. 37 Ibid. P.105
38. — One may refer to Ch. II of Vedantasara, Ed. Commentary by Swamy Nikhilananda, Advaita Ashrama, Kolkata, (Xth Edn) 1997, Pp 20-68

Pathani Pattanayak, Nalanda, Cuttack, VIIIth Edn, 1997, P.268 — History of Oriya Literature,

39. Ibid
40. Vedanta Paribhasa Nyayapanchana'a Edition
41. A.R.Bhattacharya "Brahaman of Sankara and Sunyata of Madhyamikas", Indian Historiacal Quarterly, XXXII, Nos. 2& 3, June – Sept,1956.Pp 270-285
42. Tanaya Das Goswamy Mahapurusha Sisu Ananta (Pancha Sakhanka Kahani-1), Tanaya Das Goswamy, 101, Priya Apartment, Lewis Road, Bhubaneswar-14, 2000
43. N. Dutt "Tathagatagarbha", Indian Historical Quarterly, Vol. XXXiii No.1.1957 Pp 26-39
44. Jayadayal Goyandka The secret of Premyoga, Govinda Bhavan Karyalaya, Gita Press Gorakhpur, 4th Edn.1999
45. Swami Venkatesananda (Tr) Yoga sutras of Patanjali Ch.1.Divine life Society, Shivananda Nagar, Uttaranchal, 2001. Pp3-10
46. S.B. Das Gupta Tantric Buddhism, University of Calcutta, Culcutta, 1950 P.117
47. Ibid. P.3
48. Ibid. p.179
49. Ibid p.131.
50. Sri Aurabindo Savitri, Book IX, Canto 1.P.693
51. Swami Vireswarananda Srimad Bhagavad-Gita, Sri Ramakrishna Math, Madras, 1972. P. 217
52. Hans Georg Gadamer Truth and Method, Newyork, 1975. P. 420

CHAPTER-IV

TRAFFICKING IN SOUL: COLLUSION BETWEEN THE COSMIC SOUL AND THE SOUL OF POETRY

(i) Vamana's dictum in Kavyalamkara Sutra that "Riti (Visista pada racana)-ratma kavyasya"or, Riti (deployment of appropriate words) is the "soul" of poetry kicks our memory back to the quest for "soul" through the observations given in Achyutananda's Sunya Samhita or Jagannatha Dasa's metaphor of ginning cotton (Tulabhina). For that matter, the Panchasakhas' investigative hermeneutics make attempts to wade through the dark waters of Nasadeeya Sutra to figure out and define the contours of some "cosmic soul". Language was used here to further the interests of religion. The Odia poets were matured enough by now to realize that morality was external to art and "art" should begin at a point in the space where morality ends. Others claimed that didacticism, being an integral part cannot be fully done away with. So, they should display a delicate balance between aesthetics and morality. The "words" were at the centre, however, but the poet needed to struggle for the right choice. Otherwise, aesthetic contemplation lends to the same kind of exalted experience as required in meditation on the cosmic soul. Such aesthetic contemplation also necessitated an arduous discipline, moral as well as intellectual with an additional search for a wholesome, integral beauty of poetry in which the gross form was constituted of words.

The difference was found in consequences of both- the "meditation" and the literary "creation. If the experience of creating poerty does not bring the bliss of "moksha", it definitely beings an aesthetic bliss incomparable in its capacity for evoking inner gratification. Our Sanskrit Masters have laid down that art generates "Sahridayas", percolates the aesthetic pleasure to them and both conjoined together lead to another level of bliss which the saints and the yogins are deprived of. But at their centre was also the "soul", the "soul of poetry".

The creative artist, therefore, meditated on the problems of aesthetics, its conceptual requisites, qualities and blemishes, and probably searched for the ways of artistic experience which would be identifiable with the ultimate goal of life. However, they were not sure whether to insist on spontaneity and selfless detachment or to enter into the labyrinths of mundane illusions through writing poetry.

The classical Sanskrit works conveyed them that while the "words" and their "meanings" (Sabdartha) formed the body of poetry (kavya sarira) eight kinds of concepts like Rasa (emotions) alankara (ornaments), guna (positive qualities), dhvani (sounds) Anumiti (intuition), Vakrokti (oblique language) and auchitya (appropriateness) may help formation of the soul of poetry. Their search for the "soul" of poetry, thus, branched off into eight schools.

The aim was, however, to attain a level of transcendence as the key to open up a new vista of aesthetic delight and here, the poetry is raised to the level of man's "Supreme benefactor" in so far as it is capable of communicating art experience to the mass. It is called the process of "Sadharanikarana" (general affectivity) of rasa.(Ref.Ch-VI, Natya Sastra) The circulation of the concept of beauty as a value needed to be striven for and achieved by constant perseverance. It is like the attitude of the devotee towards their god; nothing less, in its profundity, to a spiritual quest. A sympathetic/empathetic insight was to be executed signifying "complete disinterestedness". It was equal to what M. Hiriyana termed as emancipation from the entanglements of life (jivanmkukta state). The aesthetic pursuit was a quest for perfection (1) Thus, the new generation princely poets emphasized "rhetorics" or the art of using language effectively. It involved three audience appeals: logos, pathos and ethos, as well as the five canons of rhetoric: invention or discovery, arrangement, style, memory and delivery.

However, the westerns were/are on the opposite pole. "Language speaks" says Heidegger, not "man". "Man acts as though he were the shaper and master of language, while in fact, language dominates as the master of man". (2) The Odia aesthetes would consider Heidegger as a glaring example of manifested nescience. They were confident that the choice of a word, even a 'phoneme' in their new poetry of "Riti era" might lead to Jivanmukti. Our readers would meet accomplished literary yogis like Dinakrishna and Upendra Bhanja who would play with "the same phoneme" within our language (e.g Dekhare nalini, nalini, nalinire purita in which the word nalini is thrice repeated with three different meanigs) Saussure proposed the principle that what we identify as "the same, phoneme" within a language is not determined by the physical features of the speech sound itself, but by its difference from all other phonemes in our language. Sassure's important claim is that the principle of difference, rather than any "positive" property, functions to establish identity, not only for the phonemes, but also for units on all levels of linguistic organization, including signs and the concepts that the signs signify. Then Upendra Bhanja would try the next level of linguistic experiment; after phonology, it is morphology - the combination of phonemes into morphemes and into words. The vision of these riti poets entails a fascination for obscurity to substitute what the Panchasakhas in Orissa, and Kabir and the Sufi poets in North India aimed toward achieving a level of hermeneutic mysticism.

We are sorry to inform Heidegger that "language speaks" but it can not sustain as the "Master of Man". The Odia poet, it is clear now, can engage himself in a masculine game with language, since he mastered it (not was mastered by it). The Odia poet, as Heidegger writes in Being in Time,3 is a part of that historicity which he explained in terms of the "heritage" the "fate" and the "destiny" of "Dasein" (=being there).

As we transit from the Panchasakhas to the Riti Era, we understand the differences and yet, at the same time, feel that there is a subtle continuity between them that underlies the differences. History is the event of the destiny of Being (here, the Creative Being), not just any happening as one witnesses in a TV soap. The happenings of history occur essentially in the destiny of the truth of being and from it.

(ii) This historical report will show a new turn toward a major accomplishment in Odia literature – its nourishment through Sanskrit poetics. The shades of alamkara in Pancha Sakha poetry got washed away and inundated over by the flow of their robust theosophical themes. But gradually, as we cross around five decades after Sisu Sankar's epic romance Ushabhilasa, the Odia poets are found to be impelled by the call of the ancient classics to write a kind of poetry that was in vogue in the other vernacular literatures of India, mostly in Telugu and Tamil. This was an attempt to image an identity for the Odias in the national map of literature. For the first time, the Odias seemed to stop looking at themselves as different Vratya entities; and perhaps others stopped looking at the Odias as curiosities in a literary zoo. The Odias began to share a common cultural heritage, a common empyrean dream and a common plight at the same time with other vernacular writers.

The plight began with the invasion of the Afgans and the Mugals. The blown-up bubble of a national ego manipulated by Kapilendra Deva with his flair for justifying usurpations as ideals of monarchical expansionism was punctured no sooner the Chalukyas and the caste centered Bhois took over the throne of the king.. Mukunda Harichandan, also a southerner, occupied the throne for about eight years and he began to commit diplomatic blunders in his foreign policy. By providing shelter to one Ibrahim Khan Sur in 1559 A.D. he incurred the irritation and displeasure of Suleiman Karrani, the Afgan ruler of Bengal. Karani destroyed Orissa in 1568.

Odissa was an Afgan colony for some days, and thereafter, hostilities between the Afgans and Mughals broke out for a competitive supremacy. Akbar sent Todarmal to subdue one Daud and finally Odissa was annexed to Akbar's empire and was controlled by the Mugal province of Bengal for administrative purposes. We need not enter into the intricacies of this power-struggle. Both the Afgans and the Mugals targeted at the demolition of our culture and they were our enemies.

They targeted the temple of Jagannatha, and with it, the edifice of Odia culture and literature. In July 1621, Ahmed Beig Khan, a nephew of Empress Nurjahan, became the Governor of Odisa. Purushottam Deva took shelter in Manitri Fort and died there same year. The capital was shifted after that from Puri to Cuttack.

The Odia culture and literature suffered atrocities during Aurengzeb and after his death, one Shujauddin (Murshid Quli Khan's son-in-law), became the Naib-Bazim. Thereafter, Odisa was controlled by the Nawabs of Bengal.

At this cultural juncture, the Five Saint-Poets (the Panchasakhas) and the immensity of their achievement suffered undeserved neglect. Their Mantric poetry, that took us back to the Vedas and placed us in the national tradition with an unprecedented leap, appeared to wither away and get dissipated under alien attitudes toward poetry. The Five Stalwarts were like the poet-seers of the Rig-Vedic hymns, those who had "seen" and "showed" as well – "drastas" and "darsanikas," those who showed the "riti" of life, the "marga" for an aesthetic and moral living. Like Mircea Eliade they differentiated between the "sacred" and the 'profane', like Malinowski, they endeavoured to deal with the emotional stress of the people working toward social stability and like Talcot Parson deployed religion to make sense of everyday experiences. The purpose of bringing these modern sociologists into context is to adumbrate the Pancha Sakha as practiners of an applicative literature, as deployers of the sociological ideas through literature, as religious reformers.

What happened to Odissa with the Mugal block-busters of culture can be traced back to the ramnants of the broken temples, battered idols and the moth-eaten bundles of Jagannatha temple records called Madala Panji. Destroyed were our epitomes of cultural pride.

One Ramachandra Deva-II, a Bhoi-Karana-King of Khurda (1580-1609), who married a Muslim girl was ostracized from the temple of Jagannatha and later, he avenged the orthodox Brahmin priesthood by ordering them to "cut grass for the royal stables".

(Panigrahi, 240)4. After that, Odissa came under the invading wheels of the Maratha chariots. Some of their Subahdars were Mugals, though. Fortunately, all these cultural subversions could hardly damage our literature. It was just relegated to the collective unconscious.

A grandson of Kanhei Khuntia or Sivanand Sen (associates of Sri Chaitanya at Puri and Vaishnavite poets) after hundred years, now, while tramping over the half-dark bylanes of Puri, on some full-moon-night, may be on the eve of Dola Purnima, must have heard the sepulchural Samkeertana sound of a dead Chaitanya and his Odia Pancha Sakhas sanctifying the sky. Half enchanted, these young men must have glanced toward the gigantic, fluttering flag of the Jagannatha temple, now moistened by the hitherto "unheard melody" of the Samkeertana. And then, must have been born a line of poetry in the glossopoeic Shoonya (void) of Achyutananda that sprawled beyond the temple flag. The pollutant dust emitted by the Mugal-Maratha horses would have miserably failed to stain those lines of Kavya written on the prestine sheets of paper spread across the silver sky. A half-dazed bird on the coconut tree of Sakhigopal must have awakened with the confusion of an unwarranted morning. The bird, might, then, have winged across with oceanic feelings across the windows of Arjun Das, Deba Durlav and Bishnu Das, may be toward the distant mansions of Pratap Rai or Dhananjaya Bhanja. They heralded a new symphony of embellished poetry later recognized as belonging to the Riti-Guna School. The other scholars preferred to categorize them under the 'alamkara school'. The arguments for the classification of this post-Pancha Sakha poetry are taken from Bhamaha's Kavyalamkara, a treatise on poetry written th. around 6th-7century. Vamaha defines "Riti "as the soul of poetry" and working out this figurative description, he finds the body in the combination of Sabda (word) and Artha (meaning) and Riti was its soul.

The Gunas are defined by Vamaha as factors that produce poetic charm. Gunas bring poetic charm while alamkars enhance it. Hence Gunas are essential and invariable (nitya) but poetic figures of speech are optional (anitya). Gunas being in direct relation to Riti, pertain to the soul of poetry, while poetic figures relate to Sareera (body) i.e words and their meanings (Sabdartha) Vamana was able to point out a convincing distinction between the gunas and the alamkaras (earlier writers considered both as factors contributing to poetic charm, but could not show how one differed from the other, which resulted in a confusion between the two concepts), and to some extent anticipated the later and more authoritative differentiation found in Anandavardhana's Dhwannyaloka.

Defining the features of Riti Vamaha states that Riti is visistapada rachana or a special arrangement of words. However, this arrangement does not allow the poet to take liberties and write in "spontaneous overflows" which ultimately leads to a surrealistic subgenre called "automatic writing" that was popular in America around 1960s. The visista (particular) arrangement of words rests upon certain definite combinations of the different Gunas, or, fixed excellences of composition (Dey.42).5 It should be observed that the term Riti is hardly an equivalent of the English word "style". Although artha (meaning) is admitted as a major element in Sanskrit poetics, the Riti consists essentially of the objective beauty of representation. It is not, like the "style" the expression of poetic individuality, as it is generally understood by western critics.

Vamana enumerates ten Gunas and divides them into two categories: qualities of the words (sabda-guna) and qualities of the meanings (Artha Guna). We would tabulate Vamana's scheme of Gunas.

Sabda-Guna (Qualities of the words)	Artha Guna (Qualities of the meaning)
1. Compactness of word-structure (Ojas or gadha-bandhata), where "bandhata" means pada-rachana)	1a. Maturity of conception (Ojas means artha-praudhi)
2. Laxity of structure ("Pr asada" means here Saithilya)	2a. Clarity in meaning (artha-vaimalya) by avoidance of superfluity.
3. Coalescence of words resulting in smoothness (masrunatvam)	3a. Coalescence or commingling of many ideas (ghatana)
4. Homogenity of manner of construction (Samata)	4a. Non-relinquishment of proper sequence of ideas (Samata in Prakramaveda)
5. Symetry due to orderly ascent and descent, i.e when the heightening effect is toned down by softening effect, and vice-versa (Samadhi)	5a. Grasping of the original meaning arising from concentration of the mind (Samadhi Karanatvat)
6. Absence of long-compounds and distinctness of words (Madhurya)	6a. Striking utterances.
7. Freedom from harshness (Saukumarya)	7a. Freedom from disagreeable ideas.
8. Liveliness in which the words seem as if they are dancing (Udarata)	8a. Delicacy and absence of vulgarity.

9.	Explicitness of words whereby the meaning is easily apprehended (artha-vyakti)	9a.	Explicit ideas that make the nature of things clear (artha vyakti)
10.	Richness of words, brilliance (Kanti)	10a.	Rasas or the emotions depicted prominently (Dipta-rasatva=kanti)

The "guna-dosha" (Excellences and defects) concept of Riti leads to another branch of poetics called the School of Alamkara. It is an accepted fact that the Mahakavya tradition was nourished with the prescriptions of the Alamkara School. Our enlisted Mahakavyas in Sanskrit, as those of Asvaghosa seem to have followed some of the dicta incorporated in the teachings of the Alamkara theorists. Some of the Odia critics discover only alamkaras in Riti poetry and are inclined to caption this age as the Age of Alamkara. In Telugu history of literature, this phase is called Medieval and post Medieval and lots of Mangala Kavyas have been written in Bengali literature during this phase. The Assamese call their literature of this period as Neo Vaishnavite literature (1500-1650) and later Vaishnavite poetry (1650- 1826 AD). Thus, it seems the historians have borrowed the term from Hindi.

The three hundred years of Riti poetry spanning from 1550 to 1850 not only make it clear that there is a distinction between the ordinary speech and poetic speech, but also it prescribes norms of writing good poetry. Riti poetry assimlates the Vratya mindset of the Odias into the traditions of RigVeda, in which the words kavya and 'gatha' (a verse that is sung) occur several times showing how poems with sweet words were highly valued in those initial days of Odia Vratya civilization.

It would be convenient for us to divide the Riti era of poetry into three parts:-
(i) The Precursors of Riti school (1550-1680)
(ii) Riti Era (1680-1790)
(iii) The Contemporaries and the Successors (1790-1850)

The Precursors of Riti School

The period from Mid-15 th century to the end of 17 th. century has been identified as the Pre-Riti period. This period overlaps with the age of Pancha Sakha. Some serious historians of Odia literature do not admit the Pancha Sakhas as pure poets since they indulged too much in metaphysics. Tolstoy's What is art? reports that art is to be known by its power of wholesome emotive "infection" and at the end of Chapter V he says that art transmits religious emotion. There are several other chapters (VI, IX, XI, XX) where he seems to say that art always transmits the genuine, the fresh religious emotion of any age.

The Panchasakhas were aware of the highest life-conception accessible to their age and were associated with a religious cult called Vaishnavism that centered on the temple of Lord Jagannatha. They declared positively the necessity of an alliance between morality and literature. No one, for example, extricates the Christian Humanists from literature. But the common connoisseurs, perhaps, were tired of metaphysical themes; their austere Methodism must have induced an aching seriousness into their mindsets. Hence by the middle and last part of the fifteenth century, a new sensation for poetry was created by the younger generation who depicted stories of romance, poetry of mundane imagination, a fusion of passion and psychology since they felt that art emanated out of an easy liberated mind.

Literature of Passion and Psychology: Odia Romances

The literature that conjoins the Panchasakha search for the "Cosmic Soul" and the new elitist search for the "Soul of poetry" is the poetry of passion and psychology, otherwise called the Romances. Our conservative canonists have dismissed this popular genre (they were modernists believing in scientism-a trend outdated now) as playful frivolity and therefore have attempted to ignore any serious generic discussion. But despite the modernists' apathy for romances and support for realism, the Odias could never write realistic literature either following the French Emile Zola or, the Russian Belinsky.

Bharata classified the mimetic tradition as Visual mimesis (drishyanukriti) and Emotional mimesis (bhavanukriti) in his Natya Sastra. Religious scholasticism, however, encouraged the non-real, but did not sharpen its critical awareness in terms of fantasy and supernaturalism although they used them as magical probabilities. For the kings and the Brahminic coteries of the court all supernatural fantasies were accepted as "true" (something like 'magic Realism') and therefore ethically distinct from the lies of the "Fables". The active and operative antagonists of Hinduism also circulated Bauddha Jataka Tales.

The Afgans and the Muslims, who invaded us, refused to accept chimeras and pegashses. Our contemporary critics who believed in realism deflected inquiry away from the relationship between fantasy and the unconscious, thus discouraging systemic analysis in that direction till they accepted it in terms of psychoanalytical genres. Now as we focus on the psychological validity and artistic effectiveness of these romances, we need to struggle to correct our present indifferences.

We have discussed some of the Odia romance writers like Sisusankar Das, Markanda Das, Danei Das and a cluster of their contemporaries under the subheading: "Minor poets of the Age of Pancha Sakhas". We admire their blending of the description of female bodies as pieces of living architecture and their psychic terrains that engendered gothic designs of feelings. These poets had the insight to locate the beautiful, be it in nature, in female body or in poetic diction. Imitation included inner human actions too. Figures and colours in these verse narratives were not imitations, but signs of moral habits, indications which the body signalled of various states of feelings.

By this time, the plot (muthos) was considered as the soul and the first principle of poetry. A shift in interest to character can be traced back to Sarala Das, Jagamohan Ramayana and the Bhagavata of Jagannatha Das. Plot without a character might have been a puzzle and character without a plot would have been reduced to poetic soliloquies. The heroes embodied larger-than-life qualities. The protagonist's sufferings, mostly unpredictable and without measure, were ascribed to hands of Gods and the heroes had nothing to do except demonstrating an illustration of stoic endurance. They committed errors under the influence of passion, for outbursts of anger and strong sexual appetite. Chance is given a priority since these are capable of bringing good fortune and thought, A protagonist may commit a blunder by defying the actions of the Supernatural. The result, then, would be boundless in its import and consequences...

These later mediaeval poems were written with a stylus on palm leaves and they were read out / mostly recited to elite as well as uneducated congregations of listeners. These Odias were not beasts "Puccha vishana heena" (without tails and horns). The farmers and the plebians had an ear for comprehending the sweetness of poetry. The poets, on the other hand, intended to keep their listeners mesmerised by adding supernatural and sensual descriptions.

We have mentioned Sisu Sankar's nayika (heroine) Usha, who, after an erotic dream-coitus, wakes up at dawn and searches through her body to find out the hero who she thought, was within her body. Fifty years later, Upendra Bhanja's nayika gets up and searches for the hero in between her breasts. The tactile pleasure continued to persist as a sepultural presence and the young heroine wept in the absence of the divya taruna (handsome Youngman). The action of putting her hand between her breasts to locate the hero demonstrates a pursuit of an elusive reality in the lyrical romances. The more she pursues this, the more she finds it filled with the things of the mind.

Sisu Shankar uses the alamkara in Bhamaha's sense. There is no Sabdalamkara (verbal rhetorics). Bhamaha used the word alamkara (a device of embellishment) in a broad sense, meaning not mere external embellishment superimposed on a work, but rather meaning the inherent beauty of the work in a wholistic manner. Sisu Sankar generates a kind of rasa with the deployment of alamkara. Besides, he was equating 'rasa' with 'alamkara' like Upama-alamkara (metaphoric rhetorics). Sisu Sankara's aim was to evoke Saundarya (perfect beauty) in a broad sense. Wherever there was Saundarya, there was rasa and whenever there was 'rasa', there was alamkara. The ornateness was not only limited to the avidha (denotation), but it could also be traced in vyangya (satires) or in vakrata (a quality of deviation in expression, at times oblique, at times hyperbolic and all intonations employed due to paronomasia (slesha). Thus Sisusankar's Ushavilasha marks the initiation of our Riti-Kavya tradition.

Pratap Ray's Sasi Sena is important for two reasons ":a) the Kavya was not written in the vicinity of Kalinga or by the Pundits of Puri. The author, Pratap Ray belonged to Suvarnapur and the story is woven round Oddiyana. The Somavamsi kings had their capital at Suvarnapur and the different innovative tentras of the Charya period were initiated from Oddiyana region.

Dr. P. M. Nayak presents the story of this Kavya:"Sasisena, princess of Amaravati, marries Ahimanikya,a minister's son and both of them elope to distant Kamantapur (the ancient name for Subarnapur), where, fascinated by the winsomeness of Ahimanikya, Jnanadei Maluni (one of the seven famous tantric ladies of the Buddhist tantra era) takes him home and through her esoteric practices transforms him into a sheep by day and a young robust prince by night. Sasi Sena in the guise of Sasadhara serves in the army of Raja Madhav Chandra and marries his daughter by killing a terrible rhinceros. But Sasadhara re-

History of Ancient Odia Literature | 227

fuses to touch the bride until his year-long vrata (vow) is performed. A temple is built and a big fair was arranged. One night Ahimanikya comes with Jnana Dei and leaves his address on the temple wall. Next day Sasadhara calls the sheep of the town brought for sacrifice and forces Jnana Dei to convert Ahimanikya back into a prince. Ahimanikya, reunited with Sasi Sena, accepts the daughter of Madhab Chandra". (Nayak 73-74).6

The Kavya makes use of the tantric supernaturalism as those were part of the Shakta culture of Suvarnapur. It should be noted that the Panchasakha poetry was full of such magic because of the Vajrayana Tantric practices of the prophet poets which were kept in a recondite level. This feature of Sasisena alludes to the relationship between fantasy and the psychological desires of both the author and the listening audience- another feature of Riti poetry.

The tendencies noticed in Ushavilasha and SasiSena indicate a loss of faith in religion. Jagannath Puri no more remained a cultural centre. The new poets therefore, had to choose either of the two ways left for them: they could view poetry as a human triumph made out of our darkness, as the creation of verbal meaning in a blank universe to serve as a visionary substitute for a religion, or, they could, in a negative way, extend their faithlessness to the realm of new poetry (romances) that comes with Riti Era.

Throughout the span of Odia civilization literature has served different functions in keeping with the shifting cultural patterns. Conceding the over simplification, this historian would like to suggest that within these one thousand years (from Charya to the present) there have been three fundamental kinds of literature, though the main stream is woven around religious and allied metaphical feelings. The first category offers a kind of literature by our traditional society, a society with a unifying religion; the second develops with religious myths, either by accepting them blindly or by questioning them; the third category discovered after the discursive mode of the Panchasakhas-yielding definitely a new kind of poetry with an implicit function of linking the experiences to everyday reality.

The kings as patrons of literature could afford to patronise erudite Sanskrit scholars who acted as their tutors and guides, and the Brahmin gurus found the kings hedonistic and incapable of internalizing metaphysics. So, they combined literary aesthetics with delightful experience and indoctrinated them into a brand of literature that would erase the boundaries between the bourgeois and the proletariat and formulate like-hearted connoisseurs (brahmananda sahodaras) through affecting Sringara and other Rasas.

The kings being the poets now, their creations took the shape of wild fantasies. Their fantasies existed in the basic myths; they asserted values that could not be validated scientifically, and the stories they told were most decidedly not verifiable. The deeds of th the semi-divine beings and the 16th century culture heroes were magical. Displaced from the mythic level we find tales of heroines and heroes, many of whom still dealt with the marvelous adversaries since such enemies were necessary to define their capacities as the heroes of Romances.

With the emergence of these court writers, the emphasis shifted to the verbal medium, rhetorics and a marked concern for metaphor. As words are imitations and the voice also, which of all our parts is best enough for singing verses the poets became rhapsodists and actors, whose first love was to use ornate words.

Dhananjaya Bhanja (1611-1701)

Impractical and undiplomatic as a king, Dhananjaya was an obsessive poet with six romances, four chautisas, a book of translation and a number of Chhandas. His uninterrupted sixty five regnant years (1636-1701) with a number of queens and 12 sons waiting for enthronement geared off some unhappy incidents inside the palace, and finally he was poisoned. Dhananjaya's court in Ghumusar was filled with creative Sanskrit poets and scholars who kept the climate of literary fecundity conducive and activated. Dhananjaya's erudition in Sanskrit and his feudal hegemony acted as impelling forces to build up new strategies of literature. He reinvented the 'sacred' (of the Panchasakha tradition), scanned into its components of magicality and reforged them in ornate language.

The five romances of Dhananjaya are Ichhavati Ananga Rekha, Tripurasundari, Madanamanjari and the unpublished Ratnamanjari discovered and interpreted by Prof. Sarat Chandra Rath. Dhananjaya searched for a secular equivalent of Devadurlava's Rahasyamanjari, Narasimha Sena's Gopakeli and Parimala, Banamali Dasa's Chata Ichchavati, Kapileswar Dasa's Kapatakeli and Raghunath Harichandana's Lilavati. However, Dhananjaya sought to convey the sacred, not as a presence as in Arjuna Dasa's Milana Chautisa, but rather as a determinate, marked absence at the heart of the secular Ghumusar. Dhananjaya's Icchavati, Tripura Sundari, Madanamanjari and Ratnamanjari shrewdly slip past the sacred signified of the post Panchasakha poetry. It is safer therefore to compartmentalize them within Pre-Riti period. A new genre of Kavya was produced during this phase, spread tentatively between 1550 and 1680 A.D. Magical narratives occasionally touching the tangents of mythology, tender descriptions of nature, a fusion of the angelic world with the mundane ones, deferred gratification of sex presented in graceful musical narrations- all these put together constituted the body of this new poetic genre. These poets also showed interest in the portrayal of the psychology of two incommensurable and irreconcilable inner dispositions on the one hand, and a realm of spontaneity and sensibility, of the erotic as well as the political passion, on the other. The first phase (precursors of Riti poetry, written between 1550 and 1680) would include into its fold all those poets from Arjun Dasa to Dhananjaya Bhanja. We would discuss Dhananjaya's romances as worthy attempt of Riti poetry.

The conceptual form in Ichchavati, Tripura Sundari and Ratnamanjari seems to have been taken from the 'liminal fantasy' of magic and the works are gradually formulated in terms of providence. The central god of the Panchasakahs is absent here. Te religious sense of destiny is secularized until Dhanjaya wrote Raghunatha Vilasa. A close inspection of these texts of Romance also suggests the incorporation of psychological analysis. Prof. Sarat Chandra Rath's research has helped us to trace these details about Dhananjaya Bhanja, hitherto not available to us.7

Dhananjaya has culled the story of I c h c h a v a t i from Banamali'Das's Chata Ichchavati, but he has also reformulated the sequence of episodes that it looked new. Madhukara and Ichchavati are fallen angles and they carry over the passionate desire for each other from their previous angelic life. Thus, as small child students in the hermitage they pined for a union. The passion grew fiercer as they grew up in age and one day, they gratified their desire in the bucolic setting of the flower garden. But soon after that Ichchavati went back home after the completion of her education. Madhukara, while making clandestine, nocturnal trips into her palace was caught and Ichchavati's father ordered the young hero to be beheaded. At this moment of crisis the divine saint, Narada emerged, revealed the secret of their passionate attachment to each other in this life, and the king arranged their marriage.

Dhananjaya does not treat love in a light and fanciful way, never more than half in earnest, it was grounded on practicality and therefore, usually frank and trivial, gross and sensual. Love ceases to be mere sentiment to be played with and jested over; it becomes an intense passion, a Sambhoga Sringara (the act of coitus) leading to tragic tensions of life and death.

Dhananjaya, however, rarely retreated to spend upon the subtelities of sentiment. He manifested his enthusiasm for translating portions of Bilhana's Chaurapanchasika to include in the last five Chhandas of Ichachavati. Long sixty five years of uninterrupted regnal supremacy helped him to approach the zenith of his artistic energy and in the full spendour of that illumination, he wrote Ratnamanjari, composed in seventeen Chhandas. The last poet of the romance, reports Prof. Sarat Chandra Rath, is irretrievable since the manuscript is destroyed.

The Kavya begins with an invocation to Lord Jagannatha and the main protagonist, Kusumaketu is introduced. Like a young love-god. Kusumaketu, clad in silk-embroidered apparel is found languishing under the bower of romance, and at times his wings of imagination spread in angel-like splendour. He frolicked in a flower garden in his villa of romance. A pond with tamed swans lay adjacent to him and Ratnamanjari on the otherside of the pond gazed at the hero intently. The swans acted as go between, or as emissaries between Kusumaketu and Ratnamanjari.

The pair also had a supernatural past. They were fairies in heaven and have taken birth on this earth after Indra (The lord of heaven) cursed them. Kusumaketu who, at times, appears to be the authorial prototype hovers between a marvelous primary world and a mundane secondary world. The secondary world acts as a space that perpetuates a passionate desire in the absence of Ratnamanjari. Dhananjaya Bhanja has devoted quite some chhandas of erotic and exotic depiction of sexual fantasy.

One of the most striking features of Ratnamanjari is the deployment of a talking swan. Dhananjaya's concept of establishing Kusumaketu's relationship with the swan strikes a deep chord of imagi-

History of Ancient Odia Literature | 231

native recognition in the human consciousness. Kusumaketu and Ratnamanjari's instincts are exteriorized through the swans' behaviour, and they manifest parellally althrough marks of kinship with the lower animals. The poet chooses the swan as the instinctual representative of the passion-ridden pair.

The talking bird (the swan) enters Dhanjaya's verse romance also as a folk-tale motif. To the earliest composers of folk tales, the parrots and the mynas were interesting both for their symbolic values, and for the magical qualities with which they had been endowed in tribal religion and rituals. The use of the cunning swan that advises Ratnamanjari how to meet the hero during the summer festival reminds us of the qualities of the archetypal hero and W.B.Yeats' Leda and the Swan. Kusumaketu's bewildered entreaties to the swan to convey Ratnamanjari about the genuine pinings of his heart and the swan's prescriptions for materializing their marriage acts as a powerful tool for allegorizing a socio-political criticism on one hand and an attempt to justify the mode of fantasy on the other. The most curious blend of naturalism and the marvellous generates the listener's interest.

One can identify any of the following possibilities within the swan-fantasy:

i. wans are the equals or even the superiors of men.
ii. The swan may be an expressive symbol for human character and behaviour.
iii. The community of swans in Dhananjaya Bhanja's palace pond provided a frame work for a satire on princely passion.
iv. Dhananjaya presents an accurate and faithful picture of animal life.
v. The swan-tale acts upon as a unique (Chamatkara) illulstration of the genre called fantasy.

Dhananjaya's literary work was almost faultless and as he progressed in skill, his music became varied and flexible. This literary artist, as a pre-Riti oral poet, was highly effective with his listeners. He wrote with a metrical accuracy, fluency and variety that have rarely been surpassed and his capacity for lending a delicate heed to the niceties of poetic rhythm tone and colour inspired his grandson, Upendra Bhanja.

The four chautisas (Bangalasree Chautisa, Keli Kalpadruma chautisa, Panditabadha Chautisa and Anuchinta Chautisa), based on

Krishna-Radha themes are densed with motif of physical union (Sambhoga Sringara), Bangalasree Chautisa provides an example. In Keli Kalpadruma Chautisa Sri Krishna has accepted Sri Radha as the boon-tree of erotic fulfillment. The gopies, too, are restless in the absence of Gopinatha. They contemplate fancifully their past intimacy with Krishna and deplore his absence.

Panditabodha Chautisa delivers a piquant verbosity of the hero to coax a heroine. Finally, the hero wins through his power of words and the Chautisa ends in a happy union. Anuchinta Chautisa is a depiction of the painful memories of a loving pair while they are separated.

Dhananjaya has also written some Mangala Giti (Songs for auspicious occasions) meant for singing during marriage ceremonies. An auspicious song, on the occasion of Balarama's (Sri Krishna's elder brother) marriage, is very often discussed in Nanda's (Their father, Nanda was the king of a small estate) family. The poet, it seems, was conscious about the heavy religious literature of his predecessors and has attempted to release poetry from the bondage of religion and axiology, and to give it a secular color. Writing 'Mangala giti' and reciting them in auspecious occasions is still a living custom in Ghumusar area.

The literature of the Pre-Riti period does not end here. Narasimha Sena and Dinakrishna Das could have comfortably be positioned in the pre-Riti phase, but our historians, for reasons best known to them, have accommodated these two poets in the pure Riti phase. The generic traits of the pre-Riti romances are, however, more important to us, than the placement of the poets in pre-Riti or Riti phase of poetry.

It would not also be possible to investigate into the details of all these Kavyas for want of space. Further, we cannot limit the Pre-Riti Kavyas only to the imaginary romances which present a mélange of the 'fairytale'-'folktale' models without any allegorical import. Considered on the basis of their themes, these verses can be divided into the following categories:

(a) Mythological Romances: We may include Arjun Dasa's Rama Bibaha, Narasimha Sena's Parimala, Kartik Dasa's Rukmini Bibaha, Vrindabana Dasa's RasaVaridhi, Bhima Dhibara's Kapatapasa, Lakshmana Mahanty's Urmila Vilasa, Harihara Dasa's Chandravati Vilasa and Dhananjaya Bhanja's Raghunath Vilasa. The stories of these romances are culled from Mahabharata, Odia Bhagavata and Odia Ramayana.

(a) Myth as topos:
The older term for recurrent poetic concepts or formulas is the "topos". (Greek, for "a commonplace"). Passionate love, belated gratification, sufferings of separation and the celebration of the union occur as a pattern very frequently, rather repeatedly in the pre-Riti romances. Mythical characters entering into the social happenings and performing acts of miraculous transformation etc. constitute the 'topos' and the medieval verse narratives of the Pre-Riti era treat many such ancient literary topoi. The uninhibited scenes of physical union become the leitmotif (a guiding motif) in these kavya fantasies. Mythology is used in some romances as a structural element, not as a theme. While Banamali Dasa's Chaata Icchavati is an original fantasy, Dhananjaya Bhanja's Ichchavati, after the character of Narada is introduced, leans on toward the probability of a mythological make-belief. Bhupati Pandit's Prema Panchamrita Kapileswara Dasa's Kapata Keli may also be positioned under the rubric of 'structural mythology'.

(b) Erotic Fantasies: Generating an occasion for the individual heroine's sensual arousal and providing the logic for such auto-eroticism gradually became the focus for this new genre. Sasisena, Kalavati, Parimala, Ratnamanjari and Ichchavati were exceptionally well realized heroines of our Pre-Riti Kavyas. We watch them passing through romantic reveries, about imagining physical union with their angelic heroes, princes who were Gandharvas (half-divine-beings) in past life and had fallen from celestial grace. They do also sing mawkish songs of erotic obsession.

These enthralled mediaeval princesses moistened with erotic monologues replace their emotional instincts by object-s- a flower, a bower, a bird and so on. The author describes how falling in love becomes a drinking of potion. The metaphysical "nitya-raasa" of Radha-Krishna narratives of the Pancha-Sakha era is translated now into erotic engagements in flower gardens. Ichchavati and Ratnamanjari are examples.

Our first erotic fantasy was Arjun Dasa's Kalpalata. Its linear verse narrative begins when the heavenly dancer Surekha (She is from Karnataka) faltered her steps in a dance recital. The king of heaven investigated into this artistic failure and discovered that a handsome angel (a gandharva) named Vasantaka had fired the Cupid's arrow at her. Both of them were sent to the earth to be reborn as lovers. Surekha was born as a princess in Karnata desa and Vasantaka as Prince Amarsikhara in Mallala desa. Then they were married, separated and reunited. The A-B-A (love-separation-reunion/love) formula was set for the erotic narrative and then a host of other poets had followed Arjuna Dasa's steps. Narasimha Sena's Parimala composed in 24 Chhandas in which the heroine's young body is provokingly painted and her erotic wishes are narrated without inhibition. It has inspired Upendra Bhanja to compose stories like Koti-brahmanda-Sundari and Lavanyavati.

In an age of mass production of "a-b-a" formula romances the authors had no other option than forging some novelty into their stories. If the function of this post Panchasakha poetry would have been to repeat mythic patterns (as it was done in Jagamohan Ramayana and Harivamsa etc.) readers would neither have expected nor wanted novelty, since the myths did not change. Erotic fantasies needed detailed exploration and illumination of human behaviour.

As these fantasies were recited, the listeners looked into their expressive function. Others searched for rhetoric, significant as they were in so far as it had the power to affect an audience. If swaying the audience is what it matters, then any technique which succeeds validates itself. As these fantasies belong to the literature of sentimentality, the rhetorical end was focused to persuade the audience to respond to the finer things of the extant world of the gandharvas and the heavenly entities.

The erotic fantasies could not have succeeded by imaging a world free of connection to our experimental world. They could not therefore afford to create characters and situations that can not be seen as mere inversions or distortions of that all too recognizable cosmos. Thus, if we must acknowledge that reality of eroticism, it inevitably would elude to our human languages. We must admit as well that the language of these erotic narratives can never conduct the human imagination to a point beyond this reality. If the poets could not reach it, neither could they escape it. And for the same reason they were bound to be in it. Fantasy to them was an impulse behind their creation of no less importance than mimesis. Ultimately they could escape neither one entirely. Both together constituted their literature.

Padmanabha Srichandan's Sasirekha and Partha Srichandana's Kalavati can also be analysed within the parameters of mimesis and fantasy.

Although the entire gamut of Riti poetry was constituted of verbal adornment, it was primarily meant to be read out to an etilist courtly audience. The poem-audience relationship, thus, necessarily brought in some issues of mass communication, social psychology and public sentiments. Most of the Riti poems had been written as lyrics that used to deploy classical ragas. The poets had to have thorough knowledge of music and words. The moral issues and those of sociological commitment were not counted as merits. Such stunts were just tangential to the understanding of the poems. The Mugal and Afgan Badshahs nurtured poets and musicians as professional entertainers and generators of high voltage eroticism (the uddipana vibhaba). The so called purity in the Sthayi Bhavas was just relative. Thus, the Riti poets had to harp repeatedly on the prak-vasana of the listeners through verbal stimuli.

The business of Riti-poetry was not to treat of things as they were, but as they appeared, not as they existed in themselves, but as they seemed to exist to the senses. The poets, by and large, trafficked in appearances, and in diversities. Thus, they were compelled to suggest through metaphors and by analogy (rupaka and upama alamakaras). Let us pick up an extremely erotic stanza from one of the major pioneers of Riti poetry: Upendra Bhanja's Keli-Kalanidhi (The Wealth of the Erotic art). This epoch maker of Riti poetry follows Vatsayana's Kama sutra and narrates the erotic act of the hero. As the hero advances sexually toward an uninitiated girl he wrote.

Gupta sthana chalante balai 'Nahin'
'Nahin' Sabada prakatai
Pade Kandarapa Rajah Ghare huri Uru duari
jauchhanti thari".
--Keli Kalanidhi: Upendra Bhanja

[Then (the hero) forced his way into the "gupta sthana" (=secret site, here, alluding to the female genital) and she (the nayika) repeatedly uttered 'no'. Yet a commotion broke out in the bastion of Kandarpa (cupid). The two thighs, like the two gate keepers, began to tremble and gave way].

The lines have been chosen, not to represent Upndrabhanja as a poet of pornographic writings, in early eighteenth century, but to illustrate the need for using metaphors for public performace. The adeherents of the Alamkara School thought of poetry as a living body (Kavyasarira), which required adornment. This body on the one hand, and the set of poetic figures on the other, were two main entities of poetry. The body consisted of a group of words which was not devoid of an agreeable idea. Hence, the body is constituted of two basic elements (a) sabda or sound and 'artha' or sense. According to Bhamaha, kavya was constituted of the combination of these two elements. But this body of poetry never shines without proper adornment of the form.

The stanza quoted denotes to a physical body and simultaneously to kavya sarira with ornaments. Thus, the stanza leads to a field of aesthetic perception also. The Pancha Sakha school of poets had dislodged beauty of the body (and sex) from its erstwhile primacy among the value categories. Upendra Bhanja, as a radical reactionary to their statements of sexual repression, calls for a drastic reassessment of the relation of fine art to morality and other nonaesthetic concerns.

The stanza, describing, a sexual intercourse in a highly orthodox and repressive patriarchal society, calls for a psychoanalytical discussion either with Freudian principles of pure pleasure, or with Herbert Marcuse's concept of sexual-Marxism, in which the notion of the 'sexual-haves' and 'have-nots' would be eliminated leading toward the desxualisation of the society through over-use as it happened in America during the period of counter culture (1960s). Thirdly, the lines may also be considered from libertarian Freudianism as it is advanced by Wilheim Reich.

As we are forced to explicate Upendra Bhanja at a wrong place because the context is eroticism (he would be discussed in the next sub-chapter in detail), it should be kept in mind that he was the grandson of Dhananjaya Bhanja. The Bhanja dynasty, at Khinjili Mandala, ruled for more than one thousand years by the time the later Gangas invaded Kalinga through South. The first Sanskritized Odia kavya had been written by one of his great distant grand fathers, Balabhadra Bhanja (1026-1057).

Narasingha Sena

This famous Riti poet relates Parimala to Rasa Sastra through Alamkara. This alamkaravadin considered embellished speech alone as 'poetic speech' and he believed that the alamkaras (the embellishing factors) were of prime importance in the evocation of poetic appeal.

Narasingha Sena, at one self-reflexive point of Parimala, declared himself as Rasika Bandhu (a sahodara of the Brahmananda called Rasa). If the listeners were inclined to recognize rasa as a factor contributing to aesthetic delight, there was no alternative but to consider Parimala as a kavya with alamkras, though these are of auxiliary and secondary importance here. Parimala as a kavya emphasizes parakeeya prema (extramarital love), the melancholic lamentations made by Parimala in the absence of her paramour. She loved one Gandharba (an intermediary between a man and a god, mostly an artist) but married to Makaraketu. He is in tune with the trend.

Dinakrishna Das (1650-1710)

No writer in Odia literature ever gathered with a fuller hand the accolades of literary calling along with the vicissitudes of imprisonment and starvation by the same king. No poet in an era of monarchy surrounded by sycophants and corrupt literary practioners could dare to revolt against the orders of the Gajapat king of Pur to write poems under his eponym. Bhakta Ram Das records the king's statement.

"If you compose verses in my name
I shall gift you land and fame,
Powers more than you deserve"
This is my order; and if you don't
Forget, that you will survive henceforth
I would, surely, ruin you unto death.

This poet from a village called Matunia near Jaleswar on the bank of river Suvarnarekha had already led an impecunious life in his village under the despotic rule of Aurengzeb who deployed Ihtishan Khan and subsequently Khan-i-Duran as the Subahdar of Odissa. These Moghal Subahdars looted Dinakrishna's village and his family was ruined. Dinakrishna was a rare scholar of Sanskrit in that area and had no occupation for a survival other than writing poetry and succumb to beggary and humiliation. The chaotic Muslim rule followed by religious fanaticism and bigotry on one side and poverty alongwith an attack of leprosy compelled Dinakrishna to leave his village and walk around five hundred miles to take shelter under his tutelary god, Lord Jagannatha.

The hateful and loathsome behavour meted out to him in the houses of the feudal Lords in Jaleswar engendered equal loathing in Dinakrishna's heart for establishment. The replied the king:

Hardly does this poet
Care for your threat.
Mightier than you is my Lord
This world may ruin

Under your unjust fume, O King!
Never shall I write a poem in your eponym.

A rebel born in a wrong time, Dinakrishna believed in writing pure rhetorical poems on Vaishnavite themes and offering them to Lord Jagannatha, treated by him as Lord Srikrishna. He postulated the Lord's grace would redeem him from tortures, social and fiscal; and his devotional offerings through poetry would bestow him with divine joy.

Dinakrishna's poems were different from the erotic fantasies of Dhanjaya Bhanja and the other Kavya-fantasies of the contemporaries like Sasisena, Kalavati, Parimala, Ratnamanjari and Ichhavati etc. written in his time. Dinakrishna did not write either about the prince-angel heroes or about the fallen Gandharba-Princes who come down into palaces to get engaged in erotic play with the betwitching princess heroines. He could not discontinue tradition, and chase his protagonists from religion. He believed that Radha and Krishna who "after inundating the pair of lovers would also engulf the entire universe enflaming the reader's intelligence" (The lines are from the partial translation of Gopala Champu)

He exercised remarkable restraint and perfect economy over his language. This rare talent must have incited the envy of many scholars in Divya Singha Deva's court at Puri. He must have discoursed on metaphysics explicating the subtle nuances of the erotic self and the soul, or, extolling aesthetic experience in comparison to Yogic states of mind, but his style is concise, terse and taut. He postulated that poetic art must endeavour to remove violence perpetrated on the Hindu temples of Odissa by Aurengzeb and his deployed Subahdars.

The pursuit of truth may be an insufficient point to accord poetry a touch of immortality unless its soul and form of delight impact the perception of truth. After the death of the Panchasakha poets, Odia literature lapsed into depictions of physical erotics and Freudian obssessions. The kings in Odissa consider it a tactis to lure people into sensuality. Literature, to Dinakrishna, on the contrary, was poetry in music that was capable of affecting the society with rhapsodic didacticism.

Dinakrishna migrated from Jaleswar and established himself in Puri. This was not a small job. He could become the towering creative intellectual of his time because his words combined visual painting, music and a bit of maverick quality that suited the listeners of Puri. The power which this Pre-Riti bard exercised over their auditors seems now to our post modern generation of listeners as almost miraculous.

It was not, however, an enlightened milieu. The crude authoritarian power demanded to offer the highest order of perfection in the poetical works. Probably this forced pursuit and communion with perfection invested Dinakrishna with a bit of cynicism that impelled him to answer the king's corrupting suggestions: "Hardly does this poet/Care for your threat/Mightier than you is my Lord./ This world may ruin (me) / under your unjust fume, Oh, King!/ Never shall I write a poem in your eponym". Dinakrishna's meta-ethical concepts worked and gradually engendered a new philosophy of consciousness. His philosophy lived dangerously, but also fruitfully, in proximity to an ascetic, puritanical moral rage. Finally, this radical thinker succumbed to the cosmic forces of religion and a firm faith on his tutelary gods-Sri Radha and Sri Krishna, whom he realized in the nonanthropomorphic shape of Lord Jagannatha. It was a cool and sublime acceptance of the cosmic side of Radha and Krishna's love.

Dinakrishna attempted the integration of the high art with the plebian art. High art of his time was deprived of its seriousness because it was programmed; low art was put in chains and deprived of the unruly resistance inherent in it when social control was not yet total. Dinakrishna had already realized that we see nothing by direct vision; but only by reflection, and probably in anatomical dismemberment. The acute attack of leprosy, probably, generated its own stoic logic He revolted against the supremacy of Sanskrit, proved that Odia as a language was capable of standing in par with its affluence and capacity of rich courtely rhetorical showmanship. It could take a still subtler shape by the inclusion of folk words and colloquialism.

Dinakrishnas' Rasakaiola (The waves of delight) ultimately could be able to give the honour to our posterity. John Beams, who later became the commissioner of Odissa, was highly impressed by Rasakallola's language and feelings, translated some portions into English and got published in Indian Antiquary (1872) in two consecutive issues of the magazine. He had also enlisted Dinakrishna as Odissa's most popular poet and the ordinary folks enjoyed the public rendering of his poems. Later, Rasakaiola has been published in more than fifty printed editions.

He had composed Jagamohana Chhanda describing the festive rituals of Puri. By the time he composed Rasa Vinoda (the author of this book was not another Dinakrishna as some of our old scholars speculate. Kindly refer to the monograph by Prof. Nagendranath Pradhan published by Odia Sahitya Akademi) He was excommunicated from Puri by the Gajapati king and was living in a village called "Eka gharia" on the bank of river Brahmani.

"He would settle at Srikshetra"
Dinakrishna thought singing
the glories of the Lord.
"I've chosen a noble profession
Sheltered at this feet
How can I offer my prayers now
To a damned rogue?
Isn't it like to hit
a scalpel on your own chest ?

Dinakrishna realized his creative force that exercised and expanded his own latent capacity for empathizing with the infinite, where every pulse and each separate influx is a step upwards. By the time he composed Rasa Vinoda on the bank of river Brahmani, he had written the following books: Gunasagara, Bhava Samudra, Bhuta-keli, Samsara, Boli, Amrita Sagara (Boli), Muktisagara, Kaliyuga, Prastava Sindhu, Tattvasagara, Jagamohana Chhanda, Jambavati Bibha Vrundabana Rasanka Bibha, Jnana Sagara, Kamsa bibha, Dharna Sagara, Panchapata vamsi bibha, Daridra Damodar Dvija, Nama Ratnagita, Jnana Chudamani, Rasa Vinoda, Narakasura Badha Bhakti Sagara and the Chautisas Like "Artatrana Chautisa" and Kamala- Kanta Chautisa etc.

The rest of the works are published after Rasa Vinoda : (a) Rasa kallola (b) Nava keli (ghata-boli) (c) Alamkara Boli (d) Sarira bheda Bhajana and other songs (e) Subhadra Harana (kavya) (f) Bauda Brahma Gita and (g) Namabrahma Gita. The Sagaras, Gitas the Bolis and the Chautisas remind us of his predecessors of Panchasakha poets and Dinakrishna seems to have emulated them avidly.

The literary trends set by Sarala's Mahabharata and the philosophical, scholastic poems of Panchasakha were kept aside by the profligate kings, who, probably with the help of the court Pundits began writing the decadent literature of erotics and fantasies so far. Dinakrishna takes the Odia literature back to the traditional axiological base and uses the bolis (bolis are vachanas of the rural Odisha and they evidence how poetry flourished in the apophthegms and the adages of our rural folks). Dinakrishna, never a sycophant in the court, blended the Sanskritic rhetorics with bolis and vachanas and the outcome was amazing. His poetry was placing both the elites and the plebians.

Lokanatha Vidyadhara, (one of his senior contemporaries), while writing a serious spiritual discourse like NiladriMahodaya, has included an episode describing the erotic play between Lord Jagannatha and Mahalakshmi. Such liberties evidence how Dinakrishna's contemporaries were succumbing to the demands of the profligate Brahmins and the libertarian listeners, or, to the demand of the brawny kings. He was, on the otherhand, evidently concerned with interplay between various sorts of attention. But that does not mean that he was not as capable as Lokanatha, Dhananjaya, Arjun Dasa or Narasingha Sena. If one listens to his lines with dissective attention to the consonants, he would find that they begin and end with the same consonant. In Rasa Kallola it is 'Ka'. Dinakrishna's firm belief in Krishna stories gave him an impelling and ebullient kick-back to repeat them in all Kavyas. In Rasa Vinoda he prefaces about Guna Sagara.

> My beginning word would count 'ere
> it's a' boli': signals Gunasagara.
> An ocean of jewels and virtues
> Noble readers'd harvest peace
> It's a work in eight hundred fourteen verses.
> Devotion it'd arouse, knowledge of truth
> A rare text it is, a road map
> to the ways of sinners.

Guna Sagara synopsizes how the gopis felt desolate and frustrated after Krishna set out for Mathura. One day, Sage Markandeya arrived and narrated how Krishna, whom they thought to be a human child, was himself the supreme Lord. Then the sage described his virtues (the gunas) and supernatural powers. The milkmaids listened to the sage intently and their sorrow was alleviated.

Bhuta-Keli (Krishna's impish games) is based on Krishna-Jagannathas' naughty games played on the milk-maids. One dark night Krishna entered into Radha's bed room in the absence of Chandasena to play his erotic games. Chandrasena came back and knocked at the door but they did not open. The husband eavesdroped and discovered the truth. Radha, flabbergasted, took shelter in Srikrishna's lap. He transformed himself into a horrendous black ghost and Chandrasena was frightened. Presuming that his wife Radha would be killed by the ghost, he ran to their leader, Nanda and when the army of cowherds arrived with their sticks, Krishna's terrible ghostly shape turned more ghastly and began to howl in thunderous voice. The Cowherds were frightened.

The cowherds, then prayed all gods and godesses and promised to feed them with cakes and sweatmeats and finally the ghost Srikrishna disappeared by late midnight. Dinakrishna's Bhutakeli (Impish games) is a very popular book through out Odissa and rural womenfolk used to read the story till mid sixties in leisure hours until the outbreak of feminism.

Naba Keli (Mischief in the boat), alternatively captioned Ghata Boli is one more imaginary Krishna-story based on the all pervading presence of Krishna who emerged at the beck and call of the milkmaids. The ladies of Gopa had been to the market place of Mathura to sell curd and on their way, back home, they discovered that river Yamuna was in sudden, untimely spate. There was neither a boat nor a boatman to save them from this accidental flood. The evening was drawing fast and darkness cast all around. Radha discovered a boatman coming toward them; and they found him to be a haggardly fisherman. All of them almost fell at the old man's feet and requested him to help them cross Yamuna to reach their homes. The reluctant old man finally acceded to their request.

The old fisherman rowed them to the middle of the river when a thick evening mist shrouded the river and the path ahead was concealed. The old boatman was floundered and lost control over the boat. The gopika women were bewildered and they looked helplessly at the old fisherman. Radha was the most timid amongst them. She bemoaned for the costly jewellery she would lose once the boat is drowned. They turned to each other to ask the boatman to be steady, but the old haggard had disappeared. The gopika women prayed the Lord and all the goddesses they knew. At this point of juncture, the old man informed Radha to throw all her jewellery into to the water so that the water god would be appeased and rescue them from the clutches of the water demon. Radha felt reluctant and suggested instead that the oldman, should rather, take all her jewellery instead of throwing them into the river.

The old fisherman answered:

"Jewellery I don't need, wealth I'd fling

All that I need is your well being
Redeemed if you are, I'd feel prized
A drop of compassion from you
Keeps my life going.
The dirty old Sailor's witty words amazed Sri Radha.
She retorted:
"How dare you speak such words profane?
Mind your language, you dirty fisherman.
Should I quit my kith and kin
Sleep with you and commit a sin?"
Radha scolded the old boat man,
rude words she pelted
The old man did, then, show his actual form:
He was the dazzling blue-saphire, SriKrishna!
Thrilled in amazement
Radha fell at his lotus feet:
"Save me my lord, save me out
of this spated river of lust".

Such boat songs were written by Rupa Goswami, Jagadananda Ray, Surya Das, Mukunda Bhattacharya and other Bengali Vaishnavite poets. Dinakrishna replicates the scene of flood in Yamuna from the actual floods of Odissan Rivers. The union of Sri Radha and Srikrishna shown on the bank of Yamuna do not look vulgar; rather the incident depicted arouses interest.

Dinakrishna's Alamkara Boli is also a folk narrative written in pure folk style. A "boli" poem generally narrates a story or episode. A predecessor named Madhua has written a "Khosha-kata Boli" (An episode of cutting the knot of hair) Sri Krishna transformed himself into a rat to graw the hair of gopi women. Poets have imagined Sri Krishna as a cat, a flower seller, a jewellery seller etc. Dinakrishna's Alamkara Boli is one of such "Boli" poem that represents Krishna as a goldsmith who vends jewellery on the road from Vrindavan to Yamuna.

Dinakrishna's Prastava Sindhu is a dialogic poem in which the Sanskrit slokas on ethics are given in folk forms. Dharma Sagara, also known as Dharma Purana is a collection of ethical adages useful for the villagers. But each ethical poem narrates an imaginary poem from Mahabharata. The imaginary episodes related to Karna, Duryodhana and Krishna are purely works of fiction. Yudhistira attempts to perform a Yajna(a fire sacrifice) and Duryodhana out of jealously generates impediments. He donates the valuables from the treasury so that the yajna could not be performed. Bhima came to Kubera to take a loan of some paddy. Kubera agreed but on the condition that Krishna-Jagannatha would settle the terms of interest. Namaratna Gita is reported to have been written in two thousand five verses in Rasa Vinoda and it is also a dialogic poem that includes questions and answers between Sri Krishna and Arjuna. The book embodies the usefulness of the name of Hari, the relation between a merchant and a loanee, about the methods of Yoga, the birth of Vedavyasa the story of the crocodile and the monkey etc. Dinakrishna's attempt to educate the villagers through these poems is transparent in such books of everyday poetry of parables.It is solely the power which stands behind this everyday poetry today and impress us with its colourfast and lavish presentation that can still deceive the adults about the extended childhood that is only prepared for them so that they might function in all the more 'adult' a fashion.

Rasa Vinoda is also a didactic work written in forty two chapters. This long didactic poem includes episodes from Deva Durlava Dasa's Rahasya Manjori, Braja Dasa's Jnana Sagara, Siva Dasa's Radha-rasamrita and the episode of Rani Ratnavati in his own Prastava Sindhu etc. This mythopoeic poem spins imaginary stories regarding the previous life of some Mahabharata heroes.. The episode of Bhusanda Kaka from Mahabharata, the fighting between Bali and Sugreeva in Ramayana etc are purely imaginary.. This collage of imaginary stories embodies a chapter on the values of poetic work, a poem on the effects of reading the book as well as one historical poem on the legends related to the kings of Khurda from Ramachandra Deva to Divya Singha Deva.

A slender book captioned Bauddha Brahma Lekhana narrates a story about Jagannatha, how the Lord turned into a shapeless void. The book, in a nut shell, explicates Achyutananda's concept of Shoonya (the void) as Brahma. The void-self (the Shoonya) is conceived here as the Supreme Godhead. The entire interpretation is original and Dinakrishna deploys an allegorical mode of narration to justify the difficult epistems of neo-Buddhist metaphysics. In such poems Dinakrishna emulated Panchasakha poetry.

Rasakaiola is Dinakrishna's magnum opus and it is a model for his successors. Upendra Bhanja before his self-reflexive boastings that he was the "emperor of the alamkara", admits only one predecessor and he was Dinakrishna. He revered Dinakrishna as his Guru and his only preceptor. Critics are also of the opinion that Upendra was inspired by Rasakollola and accepted it as his model for writing Baidehisa Bilasa (1722), a Rama Kavya of early eighteenth century (1722). Dinakrishna was a close follower of the Panchasakha poets. Jagannatha Dasa's Shola Chaupadi, Gopala Dasa's Padmapada Sudhanidhi, Balarama Dasa's Vendantasara Gupta Gita, Virata gita, Achyuananda's Parama Rahasa, Yasovanta Dasa's Premabhakti Brahmagita, Ananta Dasa's Kalki Bhagvbata. Siba Dasa's Radha rasamruta Gita Dibakara Dasa's Jagannatha Charimutra had inspired Dinakrishna Das to write one more Krishna story, instead of erotic fantasies. Besides, Jayadeva's Gita Govinda had exercised a great influence on Rasakaiola.

The Kavya depicts the story of Krishna from his birth to death. Although the story is known to every Hindu in India, this author feels it necessary to synopsize it for the posterity who would never get a chance to study Bhagavata.

After an invocatory chapter on Jagannatha, Dinakrishna traces the story from Kamsa's abusive behaviour to his sister Devaki and brother-in-law Vasudeva, how he kicked both of them out of the pedestal of marriage and put them behind the bars. Kamsa could have beheaded Vasudeva on the marriage pedestal, but they were released because the couple promised to give all of their newborn children to him. Vasudeva had, in fact, offered seven of his male children to Kamsa and he killed them mercilessly, without any compunction, rather rejoicing at his own monstrosity.

Finally, Devaki was pregnant for the eighth time in the prison cell and Krishna was born. Vasudev wanted to save the life of this eighth child. He decided to leave the baby in his friend's house, in a neighbouring village, on the other side of Yamuna. Providential super powers left the prison doors open, a spated river gave way to Vasudeva and he could carry the new born Sri Krishna to his friend, Nanda's house. He did so, and replaced the baby by a girl child born to his friend in Devaki's lap in the prison.

The child Krishna grew up despite the hazards caused by Kamsa; most of them were monoeuvred as threatenings to his life. The story, culled from the Bhagavata of Jagannatha Dasa, runs through Yasoda's fostered love for Krishna, his frolicksome games with his cowherd friends, playing of his hypnotising flute, love games with the gopies and Radha and finally the arrival of Kamsa's messenger-diplomat Akrura to invite his nephews Krishna and Balarama to the festival of Mathura.

Vasudeva and the Gopikas including Sri Radha could sense an impending danger for Krishna's life. Akrura reminded Nanda how Kamsa would be vengeful if he disregarded his invitation. Finally, Krishna and Balarama set off with Akrura on the chariot he brought with him. Vasudeva had to concede lest his children would be avenged.

Dinakrishna has depicted the sequence of departure as an emotional and a touchy event. Krishna, the darling of the gopies and the love of Vasudeva's town was parting and an apprehension as to whether he would come back with his life was the question:

Some gopies wailed aloud
Others' heart throbbed
in trepidation; some one sighed
The rest kept mum, like the cuckoos in monsoon.
The other said, "Why should we live a loveless life
Here; let's all go to Mathura with him."

But Krishna, after reaching Gokula (Mathura) had to perform multiple duties. A rider with a violent elephant was posted at the gate of Kamsa to trample over and crush the two children. But both were dead. Next came two wrestler killers to combat with them and both of them were killed. Kamsa was trying frantically to destroy the eighth issue of Devaki (Krishna) since he was growing in Gopa as his killer. The demon king, now, felt more insecure as to his security and life. He was contriving all mean methods to deal with hiowns anxieties. Kamsa's exhibition of power through prepatrating misrule and inflicting physical torture on the naïve and innocent cowherds was a manifestation of his own ontological insecurity.

His desire to kill his powerful rephews on one side, and his diplomatic invitation to call them to the annual festival of Mathura illustrated the workings of a schitzophrenic self. The silent onlookers of Mathura characterised their own alienation from the cosmic forces.

Dinakrishna's Krishna story does not narrate the events straight. He details different psychological states of his major characters. Mathura, devoid of social and financial security, crushed under the demonic misrule, encounters for the first time some undefinable, unidentifiable presence of a guardian spirit. The moral aridness of Mathura vanishes. Kamsa is killed and Ugrasena is enthroned by Krishna as the new king.

Krishna's stay in Mathura is not of a prank-loving mischevious darling boy of the village Gopapura, but an individuating boy stepping on to the threshold of youth. The old women Kubuja availed a chance to play with Krishna a sexual game. Krishna offered his body for the appeasement of her hunger. The affair was divulged and the gopies fumed with physical hunger.

The process continues in this Krishna story also as it has been depicted in other Champus, Chautisas and Chhandas written by his successors. The trend does hardly differ from that of Sri Jayadeva's Songs of Dark Lord (Gitagovinda). Even in his musical play, Harilila staged in the Natamandira of Jagannatha temple during the coronation festival of Kamaranava Deva in 1168 A.D. But Dinakrishna's idiom and deployment of language brings a specialty to his Rasakaiola, Rasakallola is composed of 34 cantos in melodious chautisas. Each line of the cantos begins with the initial alphabet 'Ka', the first consonant of Odia language. The rhetorical device proves Dinakrishna's poetic ingenuity. The cantos, further, are musically conditioned to Odia indigenous ragas.

Rasakaiola provides us with unique illustrations that prove the ability of Odia language to depict mythopoeic verses with alliteration, ending a line with same consonant sound and a diction that blends spicy Sanskrit and folk Odia.

Writing in a milieu of pre-Riti poetic fantasies and spinning of 'Romances', Dinakrishna takes an alternative path. He borrows profusely from the Panchasakhas, but treats Krishna and Radha as purely mundane characters so that enough, space can be created for their erotic Lila.

The Vaishnavite Krishna-Jagannatha of Odisa was parama Brahma to Dinakrishna, invested with cosmic forces. But Krishna Das (Dinakrishna ends many of his poems calling himself Krishna Das) creates a mundane Krishna in yellow silk and wild flower garlands, his dark skin annointed either in sandal oil or paste, jewelled earrings dangling in play,- an imaginary romantic hero moving in a fictional Vrindavan situated somewhere in Odissa. Dinakrishna's cowhered women and Radha are nearer to Jagannatha Dasa's gopikas in Bhagavata and Rasakreeda.

Later he was jailed and driven out from Puri for not obeying the orders of Divyasingh Dev to write poems with the King's eponym.

Lokanatha Vidyadhara

There are confusing statements with regard to the preiodization of this pre-Bhanja poet. The historians have either evaded the dates or have placed him in the 18th century. Most of his writings are preserved in palm-leaf manuscripts at Jayadeva State Museum, Bhubaneswar. Lokanatha is known as Vldyadhara and Lokanath Das in his palm-leaf writings. His published works are two Kavyas: Chitrakala and Sarvanga sundarii. Among the unpublished works, the historians have mentioned Padmavati Parinaya, Brundavana Vihara, Rasakala and Neeladri Mahotsava.

The publication of a poetic treatise captioned Premalamkara in Eshana -Vol XXV. Dec. 1992 (Pp. 34-48) opens up a vista of new information that to some extent, clarifies the earlier misconstructions about this poet. Late Gobinda Ratha, Aparna Panda, Tarini Charana Ratha, Pt Binayak Mishra, Dr Sudarsan Acharya and Dr. Brundabana Acharya have proved Lokanatha to be a poet from Banpur. But Pt Suryanarayan Das and Bhagaban Panda have placed him as a poet from Rodhanga (in the district of Khurda). He was born between 1640 and 1715. The present historiographer prefers to place Lokanatha as a Pre-Riti poet as well as a Pre-Bhanja poet. His father, Jagannatha Vidyadhara, was the Mahapatra or the Chief Minister of Raja Divya Singh Dev (till 1716 AD.) Lokanatha has mentioned his name as Vidyadhara in his manuscripts titled Premalamkara, Abhoga Chitau, Chautisa Raga Chautisa and Gopaleela Saptaraga Chautisa. In some of the songs of the last two chautisas, however, he has mentioned his full name.

What is worthiest of mentioning about Lokanath Vidyadhar is that his Premalamkara is a theory on Alamkara School of poetry. The Alamkara School, in Indian poetics, presents a confusing array of epistemes. Bhoja's Sringara Prakasa, Hemachandra's Kavyanusasana, Kesava Misra's Alankara Sekhara along with Mammata's Kavya Prakasa are some of the Indian texts that enumerate alamkaras. But the most authentic and elaborate treatise on Alamkara has been written by an Odia - Viswanatha Kaviraja's Sahitya Darpana (15th Century). He has also written a commentary on Mammata's Kavya Prakasa. The manuscript of Sahitya Darpana was discovered by Stein from

History of Ancient Odia Literature | 249

Jammu which was dated Vs. (Vikram Year) 1440 equivalent to 1384 AD. But reputed Indologists like M.M. Chakravarti, H.P. Sastri, P.V.Kane, and S.K.De have placed Viswanatha in the 14th century since he refers to Allavadina (Allauddin Khilji) who died in 1315 AD. This shows that Odisa was famous for the Alamkaravadins(the practitioners of almkara/rhetorics) and Lokanath Vidyadhar's attempt at another theoretical text after 200 years does not seem out of place. The Odisan adherents of the Alamkara school of thought conceived of a Kavya sarira (the body of poetry) which required adornment. "Just as the face of a damsel, though beautiful, lacks lusture if unadorned, so is poetry (Vijaya Vardhana, 27-28).9 Thus, through out the history of the concept of the alamkaras, their number is ever on the increase. Bharata mentioned only four: Upama, rupaka, dipaka and yamaka. By the time Appayya Dixit's Kuvalayananda was written, the number of arthalamkaras had reached one hundred and twenty five.

Lokanatha, in his Premalamkara, has taken a female body and has elucidated 25 alamkaras of love-making. Sahitya Darpana (Ch.lll) has mentioned about 28 gestural ornaments for the Nayikas. In Premalamkara, a sex-ridden Nayaka, away from his Nayika, reminisces about these twenty five alamkaras. Lokanatha has composed verses for each alamkara and explicates the sexual gestures of the Nayika.

The first three hava, bhava and Hela are called angaja alamkaras (alamkaras born from the body). Bhava is the initial mood or the spring board for Prema (love) and it leads toward hava (gesture of erotic mannerisms) and hela (absent mindedness). The next seven alamkaras i.e. Sobha (beauty), Kanti (brilliance), Dipti (floridity and brightness), Madhurya (sweetness), Pragalvata (eloquent naughtiness), audarya (loftiness) and dhairya (patience) are generated within the personality of the Nayika effortlessly. These are called ajatanaja alamkaras. The remaining 18 alamkaras e.g. Leela (illusive play), vilasa (enjoyment), vichhiti (strangeness), vivwoka, kilakinchita, mottayitta, kuttamita, bibhrama, latita, mada, bihruta, tapana, mauradhya, vikshepa, kutuhala, hasita, chakita and keli are called Svabhavika (natural) alamkaras. Thus, Premalamkara describes only 25 alamkaras of love-making and just refers to and suggests about the other three.

Lokanatha, in the IInd chapter mentions about the asta sattvika lakshanas copied from the Sanskrit poetics of Rasa: Stambha (paralysis), sveda (sweating), ronmancha (horripilation), swarabhanga (change of voice), vepathu (trembling), vaivarnya (change of colour), asrupata (weeping) and pralaya (fainting). The nature of these sattvika bhavas fall into the category of anubhavas, i.e. physical effects that result from the emotion.

The IIIrd chapter describes the seven states of Prema (bisrambha pranaya, anuraga, premavaichitrya, anubhava, ruddha-bhava, adhiruddha- bhava and bibhava.

Lokanatha proceeds further to delineate the characteristics of the generation of the feeling of love that seem to have followed the text of Kamasastra more than that of the alamkaras.

Harihara Narendra

It would be unjust to omit the name of Harihara Narendra who has written a number of Chautisas and Mangala giti, but the scripts are not available to this author. However, his mythological romance Madalasa stands out with an identity. The theme of Madalasa is culled from Markandaya Purana (Ch XVIII-XXII). Madalasa, written in XIII chapters confirms to the standards of Guna-Riti school of poetics.

Upendra Bhanja (c.1675-c.1753)

Upendra Bhanja is as much important to Odia literature as Shakespeare is to English and Rabindranath to Bengali literature. When around 1870, the Bengalis raised a jingoistic furore that "Odia is not a separate language'" and its archaic alphabets should be replaced by the Bengali ones, for all educational and official purposes. John Beams, the-then District Magistrate of Balasore defended the position of Odia language citing examples from Upendra Bhanja. He proved the richness in Bhanja's poetry equating it with the foundation of Odia literary culture that was totally absent in Bengali language. Banga, as one of the ancient Vratya countries was distantiated from the Vedic traditions and thus, from the Sanskrit traditions and the Aryan poetic modes. As a contrast, Kalinga was sanskritised since the invasion of the Early Gangas around 3rd /4th century AD and had already produced great Sanskrit short fiction writers like Vishnu Sharma th around 5/6th century and followed by lots of Sanskrit playwrights (post Bhavabhuti era). The Principal of the Sanskrit College at Srikurmam (The other name for this ancient city was Mukhalingam and it was the southern capital of Parlakhemundi state) was Jayadeva himself, who was a master in classical music and dance and directed his own Sangitakas (Theatre with songs and dance only, a form th special to Orissa) in and around Kalinga during the 12th century.

History of Ancient Odia Literature | 251

This Kalingan Brahmin migrated to Kenduvilwa later, when he came to Puri with his Mukhalingam Troupe to perform in the king's coronation ceremony. He came to Puri with his troupe of dancers from the college at Srikurmam to perform the dance drama (Harilila) on the eve of the coronation ceremony of King Kamarnava Deva in 1168 A.D. The king (old Choda Ganga Deva, Kamarnava's father) was overwhelmed by the performance, recognized the talent of Jayadeva and granted him some land at Kenduvilwa. Srikurmam, now in Andhra, was in Kalinga and the king of Puri was considered to be the only Gajapati king. Puri was the cultural capital for the recognition of all Kalingan artists. Jayadeva wrote lots of Oriya poems also in his own sanskritised lyrical style.

What we intend to establish here was that a rich tradition of riti-alamkara-musical poetry of the Sanskrit breed was already in practice in Kalinga, and the Rili era that was initiated and nurtured in Kalinga was not even a neo-classical style; it was rather a kind of post colonial attempt in those days when the Mughals. Afgans and the Marathi (Burgi dacoits) captured large tracts of Orissa, destroyed its books of wisdom: of Ayurveda, Astronomy, Astrology and literature and left the Odia nation culturally bankrupt.

The leftist poets and the so called chimney-smoke realists of the Calcutta jute-mills-culture argued that the literature of Upendra Bhanja was rhetorically manouevred, artificial and feudalistic. These prejudiced and jealous critics with colonial mindsets worked hard to promote pro-Bengali colonialism. They boosted Brahmo homosexuals and villified Bhima Bhoi (1850-1895) as a seducer of women, relegating him to the last phase of Riti era instead of recognizing him as one of the pioneers of Oda literary renaissance.

John Beams, one of the most objective cultural historians of Orissa, was the District Magistrate and he understood the entire phenomenon and saved the Odia language from an impending cultural debacle. The attack launched by Kantilal Bhattacharya and other cultural fundamentalists of Bengal could not have been resisted without a learned Britisher like Mr.John Beams. The Bengali administrators came here from the Imperialist capital, looted the state economically and finally, the diasporas attacked the Odias to impose cultural imperialism. Unfortunately, the jute-mill culture guardians of Utkal also considered it unwise to protest against such cultural invasions. They did not like to read what was written In Kalinga since it was in Madras Presidency and the two regions generated a cultural as well as attitudinal polarity.

John Beams argued that Bengali as a language was incapable of producing as rich and sophisticated a literature as Upendra Bhanja has. He is believed to be a contemporary of Joseph Addison (1672) and Steele (1672) Upendra Bhanja's exact year of birth has been lost to us during the invasion of the British Moghal and Marathas. They have burnt all the culture records of Orissa stored in the poems of palm-leaf scripts.

Our Upendra bhanja Scholars differ in their opinion about the exact year of Upendra's birth. We may examine the following table: Scholars on Upendra's birth and creative period

Pt. Vinayak Mishra	1780/1782
Dr. Harekrishna Mahatab	Between 1693-1720
BichhandaCharan Pattnayak	1685 AD
AnantaPadmanabha Pattnayak	1670
Pt. Sridhar Satpathy	1675 (Magha Sri Panchami)
Gauri Kumar Brahma	1675/76
Dr. Artaballav Mohanty	between 1670 and-1720.
Pt. Suryanarayana Da	between 1688 and 1751.
Sachidananda Mishra	1675-1753 A.D

We have arrived at a decision basing on the latest essay of Dr. Sachidananda Mishra written during 2003. 10

Out of the forty Kavyas he has written the scholars could only retrieve, edit and publish twenty five texts Kalakautuka, Rasamaniari and Chitra-Kavya Bandhodaya are incomplete amongst those that are reprinted from the palm leaf scripts. Rasamaniari written around C.1734 is a treatise on Alamkara Sastra (A theoretical work on Alamkara). Rasa Panchaka is another theoretical text and the third one about which the poet mentions in Chaupadi Bhusana is lost to us. Thus Upendra is the author of three theoretical prabandhas on rasa and alamkara.

To provide an easy and simple reading about this "Kavi Samrat" (Emperor among the poets) we would trace the development of his poetic art through three distinct periods. Upendra Bhanja the grandson of King Dhananjaya Bhanja has been nurtured and educated under this king's direct supervision. In Chitra Kavya Bandhodaya he mentions that he has deployed his knowledge of Sanskrit, Bengali Tailanga (Telugu), Khoratha and desi bhasas of India. Thus, he was a polyglot of his time.

In Ganjam Manual, based on the Imperial government's papers of 1882, W. W. Hunter mentions about this poet: "xxx one of the best known and most celebrated authors in the language was Upendra Bhanja, one of the rajas of Ghumusor" (P.124).11 Although the dates of Upendra's accession on to the throne remains controversial, it is probable that he was crowned in C 1705 and was dethroned by a cousin named Ghana Bhanja in C. 1708. Upendra's first period of creativity began after his dethronement.

First Period (C.1708-C.1718)

Upendra's first Kavya is Chandrarekha (C.1708), in which he confesses:

A deep trouble corrodes me
I'm undone, it baffles my being.
I'm a victim, I bow down
My head on His divine feet.

The Lord here refers to his tutelary deity, Rama. But no ritual was yet ceremonised in the palace. (He turns into a pure devotee of Rama around 1722 when he wrote Baideheesa Bilasa in the second phase of his creative career.

He has devoted his time to mythological themes and occasionally turns to romance during this gloomy early phase of dethronement. Chandra Rekha (1708) is the first Kavya he ever wrote, but only two of the Chhandas (yrical poems) deployed as chapters) could be retrieved so far. Rasalekha (1710) is a romance. Chhandabhusana, written during this period is his maiden venture in mythological Kavya writing. Upendra valued mythologies as the store house of the finest of themes to be selected for the Kavya narratives. Gitavidhana (1717) Subhadra Parinaya and Sholo Poi (1718) are the three Kavyas of this period in which the poet ends the poem with his name inscribed as "Bhane Upa-Indra Bhanja Nrupati" (Thus concludes Upa-indra. the king of Bhanja dynasty).

Some critics, therefore, conclude that Upendra continued as a king after he wrote Sholo Poi (1718) at the age of 43. One of these kavyas is written with words constituted without vowels emitting a different dhvani (sound) while being recited. Poetry was in recitative stage in those days since there was no printing press and the palm-leaf scripts were not being circulated beyond the court. Upendra was used to the customs of court poetry and he wrote his Kavyas following Vamana's Reetiratma Kavyasa" (Riti is the soul of poetry) theory. He was trained fully in Sanskrit poetics both by his grandfather and the court pundits of Ghumusor as a young man.

Dhananjaya Bhanja used to hold literary group discussions everyday neglecting his administration and other imperial duties. Upendra was growing matured as a poet by this time. Literature was a game to be played with words as tools of play. The poet had learned the art of using language in different modes of communication. He knew that the language of rhetorics involves three components of audience appeal: logos, pathos and ethos and the five canons of rhetorics: Invention, arrangement, style, memory and delivery. With Sholo Poi (1718) the poet experiments with proper diction, a diction which emphasizes softness and sweetness in stead of the "glorious" or the "imposing" (it is the Panchali riti and the diction is vested with "Madhurya" and "Saukumarya").

Rasa Arnava, Rasa Taranga and Ramalilamrita may be bracketed within one stylistic category since in all these three poetic works abana akshara (words constituted without vowels) is used. But Rasa Arnaba is an incomplete work and the other two books are based on the story of Rama. It may be mentioned here that Dhananjaya Bhanja's Raghunatha Bilasa, was the source book that inspired Upendra to attempt Rama-Kavyas. These two are mythical narratives with touches of symptoms that extend toward romance.

Kalinga, prior to Upendra Bhanja, had three great narrative writers, who built up the tradition for Upendra: Vishnu Sharma, the famous Sanskrit writer of Panchatantra, Balaram Das the author of Jagamohan Ramayana and the third, Jagannath Das, the famous translator of the Sanskrit Bhagavata in nine syllabled couplets.

The novelty in Upendra Bhanja is his self-reflexive style. Self-reflexivity, otherwise called 'metapoetry' is a postmodern feature In European literary genre. Metapoetry is a term given to poetical writing which self consciously and systematically draws attention to its status as an artifact in order to pose questions about the relationship between poetry and reality. Upendra Bhanja's increased level of Meta levels of poetic discourse and experience is partly a consequence of an increased social and cultural self-consciousness. Beyond this, however, it also reflects a greater awareness within contemporary culture of the function of language in constructing and maintaining our sense of everyday reality. The simple notion that language passively reflects a coherent, meaningful and objective world was no longer tenable in Upendra Bhanja's world of experience which was full of usurpations, invasions by the Mogals and Marathas including his own dethronement and exile. Upendra had followed the footsteps of Dinakrishna, and to some extent Loknath Vidyadhara as far as his self reflexive style of writing about his own art of writing is concerned. He had rejected the wealth and power and lived in destitution amid his tribal subjects, but was never unhappy.

He lived with his muse. Poetry sustained him through the period of dethronement:

What pleasure does pelf impart?
What charm does Indra's fulsome wealth bestow?
With your wife you return
To a resting place, you call it home
You celebrate the delights of this universe
Contented, you feel like a sparrow in springtime.
The Pandavas ravaged and
thrown out of the throne
Lived with no remorse
Draupadi was there to make a home;
And Rama never felt dispossessioned
Sita was his resting site, may be with leaves for a roof
Or a sky over his head, he was never rueful.
The spouse makes a home
Extinguishes the fire of rage in you
makes you feel content.

Upendra's poetry, here, is metapoetic and confessional. He reflects, constructs and mediates his experiences of the world through language. Language sustains his poetry and poetry sustains his life of deprivations. Poetic language is an independent, self-constrained system which generates its own meanings. Its relation to the phenomenal world is highly complex, problematic and regulated by convention. 'Meta' terms, therefore, are required in order to explore the relationship between this arbitrary linguistic system and the world to which it refers. In poetry they are required in order to explore the relationship between the world of poetry and the world ouside poetry. Peter Hutchinson, in a book captioned, Games Authors Play (1983) describes what a self-conscious narrator does in his experimental narratives: "The natural successor to the self-conscious narrator is to be found in the twentieth century modernists' concern with the novel of self-analysis, which is concerned with its own structure, its methods..." (P.33) Upendra, probably was our would-be postmodernist, who still stays with us as a contemporary, playful in deployment of language, initiating a game of words and living a life of the flower children of the 1960s.

The Orissan leftist critics who attempt to transform literature into a play ground of the 'have-nots' and the industrial labour-class people do have a point, but their logic of argument is inapplicable to Upendra's ouevre. It would sound stupid to measure the immeasurable with a silly western yard stick. The plebians should note that Upendra Bhanja was not a courtly writer showcasing feudal motifs. What one is astounded to observe here is that he has initiated these experimental strategies of self-analysis in Oriya poetry four hundred years ago. The poet also discusses how the mythological themes and especially the Rama-themes are perpetual and superior to other themes.

Chhandabhusana, his first mythological kavya may be cited as an example. Besides, Rasa Arnava and Rasa Taranga, too, refer occasionally to verses wherein Upendra advocates about his poetic structure and stylistics. The most emphatic feature of his first period of writing is his experiment with dhvani (how the "uttered sound" manifest "sense", speech-act theories). In early 18th century, when Upendra wrote, there was neither print medium nor its readership. Literature was basically oral and meant to be sung. Upendra had a keen sense of music and histrionic affectivity. He was an accomplished singer. He learnt the art from his grand father's music tutor.

The grammarians of his time in Kalinga believed that individual sound units in a word are not competent to convey any meaning. The sounds manifest an external and imperceptible sphota that really conveys the idea that srikes the mind of a listener. In the process, Upendra simultaneously theorises and deploys them in his experimental works. "Words" according to Upendra function in three-fold application and consequently are used in three different manners: abhidha (denotation), lakshana (indication) and Vyanjana (Suggestion). He deploys them in his poetry in which suggested senses prevail. The suggestive word conveys suggested ideas and imparts suggestivity. As a result his poetic content acquires the quality of chamatkara (uniqueness as a rhetorical mode) or charu (poetic appeal)

Subhadra Parinaya (1718) has Iines that imbed varna-dhvani, upasarga dhvani and samghatana dhvani. In his second Kavya (Rasalekha, 1710) we notice the use of padamsa dhvani (morphological sound) and vakya-dhvani (syntactical sound). It seems in the first phase of his poetic career only Upendra has asserted that kavyasyatma dhvanih (dhvani is the soul of poetry) Hemamanjari, Premalata and Kalakautuka were the other kavyas of this period in which the dhvani component finds a focus.

Second Period (C.1722-C.1729)

The works of the second phase include Baideheesa Bi!asa (1722) Purushottama Mahatmya (1725) Suvarnarekha and Rasika Hararavali (written between C.1725 and C.1729). While retaining the interests in mythologies, Bhanja switches back to pure romances. These are not exclusive choices of the author. Literary Genres of his time were, and perhaps in the present era, too, are tacit contracts between a writer and his readers. No ideology or personal idiosyncracy even needs to be injected. Eversince the pressure from above has ceased to tolerate any longer the tension between the individual and the universal, then, what is individual can no longer express the universal and art becomes a form of justification, or, at least a means of eliminating the period of fruitless expectations.

The popularity of romances was an obvious factor in the early eighteenth century milieu and the signals were furnished by the context of their utterance, their recitative factor that attracted listeners. The physical presence of the dethroned handsome king (Upendra Bhanja) with his gesturativity and intonations, his affective performance also provided the impetus for enriching the mimetic appeal of the 'speech act' of the romances performed by the author.

Further, in the process of Upendra's self-conscious theorization about the properties of an ideal Kavya, he has already mentionedin Subhadra Parinaya: "Saptatirisa pade poorita veera-karunya-hasya-adbhuta vivatsa, bhayanaka susanta raudra-Srinagara/ Suvyakta puni chhanda chhandake prateeta heba alamarike suni trupati Hebe rasike pandite nare je". (In thirty seven stanzas shall this kavya be composed, It would embody rasas like veera, karunya, hasya, adbhuta, beevatsa. bhayanaka, susanta raudra and sringara.) The self-reflexive Meta element is clear in these lines. Upendra states that in every poem it should be properly communicated so that the aesthetically accomplished listeners would be entertained properly). Prema Sudhanidhi, Ramalilamrita, Gitavidhana, Bhavabati, Kalavati Rasa panchaka and chitrarekha etc. belong to the second phase of Upendra's writings.

One of the major features of Upendra's second phase of writing is its maturity and rendering of a "rasa-dhvani" kavya called Prema Sudhanidhi. As a riti-kavya, Premasudhanidhi is pregnant with emotion (rasa), sonorous sound of the words (dhvani), alamkara, vakrokti, auchitya and mythic nuances. The riti and its constituent gunas come in as a sine qua non (essential condition) in the production of its beauty. The poetic figures do also contribute immensely to heighten its effect.

Upendra was a great scholar of Sanskrit poetics. He understood the distinction between the Guna and the Alamkara as to their respective position in a formal scheme of poetics, which is adumbrated by Dandin and developed by Vamana.

Premasudhanidhi embodies figures of thought or tropes of Naishadha, the style of Kalidasa in deploying the dialogical mode and ornate verbosity to create the typical riti charm of poetry. Premasudhanidhi is constituted of sixteen Chhandas embodying both Sabdalankara and Arthalankara. The kavya was published in 1866 by Gourisankar Ray, editor of Utkala deepika, and the medieval kavya generated positive criticism from the elite critics of the state. Pt. Nilakantha Das has written, "The poet would have excelled the Sanskrit scholars had he not departed from the standard usage of commonplace and easily communicable Odia. He has alluded his kavya to a coconut that has a hard exterior and very soft, life-sustaining water within".12 Prof. Benimadhav Padhi praises the startling Sabdalankaras more than its arthalankara.13

Upendra's ouevre includes erotic fantasies like Lavanyavati, Rasika Haravali, Koti-Brahmanda Sundari, Prabhavati, Rasalekha and Chitralekha. But in Premasudhanidhi he has chosen a typical Odia story.

The king of Koshala in the course of his earnest search for a daughter-in-law for his handsome son of lofty qualities finally selects a teenager girl Premasudhanidhi. A child marriage takes place, Premasudhanidhi goes to Koshala and attains her puberty. The erotic fantasies of the young prince get realized in the physical union that takes place in the honeymoon night. Then the prince is deputed to Malava by the king and a space is created for the lively depiction of Prema Sudhanidhi's vipralambha Sringara. As an expert in deployment of alamkaras, Upendra considers Vipralambha Srinagar and Karuna akin to one another, embodying very many similar properties. Thus the poet invests this portion of the kavya with sweetness unique to Vipralambha Srinagara. The experience of the rasa is marked by the melting of the "Sahridaya's" mind.

The other characters like the king of Kerala, the astrologer, the servants and others have been portrayed realistically; Premasudhanidhi is saturated with emotions of Sringara achieving a synthesis of speech and height of sound and sense.

Thus, by the time he wrote Baidehisa Bilasa, a poem based on the "husband of Vaidehee" (Sita), Upendra could generate space to create occasions to revert back to Sringara, or the play of the erotic sentiment. Sage Viswamitra at one point narrates the beauty of Vaidehee (the daughter of the king of Videha country, Sita) to Rama, in this story of Ramayana. Upendra's narrative is intended to evoke the Purvanuraga (precondition) for vipralamhha Sringara (a motivation for eroticism evoked either through visual/ painted pictures or, through encounters, dream or magic/occult.) Baideheesa Bilasa is a Kavya in which each line begins with the consonant•'B". Upendra has confessed that he has borrowed the style from Kuntaka's vichitra marga.

After Vamana, Kuntaka in Vakroktijivita made the most substantial contribtion to the Guna-Riti Theory, remedying some of the defects of Vamana. Following Dandin, he too used the term 'Marga' for Reeti. They are taken as three in number: "Sukumara-Marga, Vicitra marga and Madhyama Marga, thus dispensing with the geographical terminologies like Panchali and Gaudi. Sukumara corresponds to Dandin's Vaidarbhi and Vichitra to Gaudi."Madhyama is standing midway"14 .Vichitra marga springs from learning and practice in figurative devices and art of ornamentation. Thus, Baideheesa Bilasa is a Sastra Kavya wherein the scholarly properties of the Kavi-Samrat are displayed.

Upendra's second phase is devoted to his engagement in scholarly stylistics. It is a gifted combination of pratibha (talent) and Vyutpatti (Spheres of Knowledge). But he also possessed a surplus energy to stay obsessed in Sringara (eroticism). The maid servants in romances play the role of sex-educators for the young princes and princesses of the palace. ln Rasika Haravali pure verse-romance, Biprakamini (an old woman and a Brahmin go-between who works in the palace as an expert in evoking erotic interests) describes the physical contours of a Princess of extraordinary beauty and advises the Prince to go to Puri during Chandan Jatra (A Summer Festival in which people make profuse use of Sandalwood paste) and enjoy a glimpse of her beauty. The first Chhanda (a musical composition very special to Odissi style of singing) of Rasika Harabali narrates the poet's "Kavya adarsa" (poetic ideal/ norms) in a self reflexive style and gradually the verse romance proceeds to depict the psychological conditions of eroticism. Upendrabhanja metaphorises erotic feeling as "Biraha-Anala"/ "Kama-Agni" (erotic fire produced in the body during the period of physical separation) and links it up with feminine psychology. The heroine contemplates with an extended metaphor - which her body would be burnt in erotic fire and a waft of wind would carry her ashes to her lover. Then out of the ashes she would resurrect again with flesh and blood. This is how the poet generates the effects of Sringara Upendra's (c) "quest-romances",15 thus, become an intense search for the libido or the desiring self for a fulfillment that delivers it from the anxieties of reality, but still retains it. (Frye,Northrop Anatomy of criticism.. (1957), p193).16 The mixing of religious-mythological themes with romances is also a creative game and an invention, and that serves the purpose of a secular substitute for religion. Sringara, for example,is the religion he practices.It is a stunning meditation on erotics:

Sringara. It's without parallels
Nothing like that.How can
the mundane man would know?
May take six months to comprehend
For the fools, it needs a full year!

By this time Upendra Bhanja was already honoured with the title of "veerabara" (A valiant hero of the literary wars). His literary adventures have already ferried into the fairy lands of imagination; but they unfold, beneath the sign of destiny, either benevolent or malign motifs...

His romances, however, imbed instances of metaphysical transcendence. The difference between the motifs and the transcendental effects he scored is ultimately conveyed by the quality of the wish fulfillment involved in his ouerve. It is an autonomous formal development in which the Bhanja model of narrative can only be compared with the Italian and Spenserian poems or, a similarity may be sought in

History of Ancient Odia Literature | 261

the twilight of a Shakespaeran spectacle, in the verses of Abhijnana Shakuntalam, or in the guise of novels that are called art-romances of Stendhal, Balzac and Emily Bronte.

Third Period (C1730-1753)

If we make a third stage of tentative timing according to the growth of Upendra Bhanja's poetic career, we encounter a mature phase of fecund poetic romances like Lavanyavati (C.1730). Koti Brahmanda Sundari (C.1732) and a Prabandha (theory written in verse) named Rasa Manjari (1734) available to us in fragments. The third phase signifies a transition from the poet's obsession with embellished language and his attempt toward a theoretical justification of his style:

I'd deck them with jewels;
I'd also wish to deploy
Simplest of the dictions
Yet its music should hook
The rasikas,

In 1735, Upendra was honoured with the title of "Mangaraja" and then followed Ya m a k a C h a u t i s a, Kunjabihara, Bhavabati, Chaupahara, Chaupadichandra and C h a u p a d i b h u s a n a modelled on Dhanjaya Bhanja's Chaupadis (quartrains), Yamakaraja Chautisa and Rasa Panchaka. All these books are concluded with eponyms like Mangaraja and "Veera Mangaraja Lavanyavati and Koti Brahmanda Sundari are pure romances written on the model of Sriharsha's Naishadha Charita (famous Sanskrti Kavya). In Lavanyavati (I, ii, iii), and Koti Brahamanda Sundari (xxxxxii and xxxxxvi). Upendra admits this influence:

Words are to be imaged
They would incarnate shapes
I'd deck them with jewels;
I wish to deploy
Simplest of the dictions
Yet its music should
hook The rasikas,
Entertain the seekers of meaning.
That's what my 'dream genre' of poetry would be.
(Lavanyavati, i: 2.8)

This justifies Upendra's intentions of experimenting with language as an Artha-Kavi at this point in addition to using his talents as an Alamara kavi.

The categories of the creative poets are mentioned in Rajasekhara's Kavyamimansa. Panchaka is an extension of his Sastra-Kavya (theoretical poetry: Prabandha) written earlier in Rasamanjari (1734). The poet expects that this would definitely be appreciated by the fans of Sahitya Darpana (Sahitya Darpana is a Sanskrit poetics written by Viswanatha Kaviraja of Orissa in 15th. Century, a predecessor of Upendra Bhanja). This evidences that the Sanskrit Kavyas and the theories related to poetry were discussed very often in the court symposiums conducted by his grand father Dhananjaya Bhanja. Upendra was raised and nourished by words and idioms: avidhas, lakshanas and vyanjanas of the classical tradition.

Odia poetry, by this time, was severing its ties with its tribal-Buddhist-folk roots and was emerging as an assertive literature in par with other sanskritised vernacular literatures of India. Our court pundits attempted to trace the affinities between aesthetics and philosophy. The classical theorists of Indian aesthetics and philosophy were invoked to illustrate how philosophy percolated to every department of life in ancient India. The tribal mindsets of the Odias were well acquainted with the Buddhist and Jainist aesthetics and philosophy. Now, in a time when the Moghal and Afgan block busters were demolishing our ancient knowledge, the Bhanja kings of Ghumusar attempted to emulate them through debates on why and how the Indian Poetics came into being. The court debates rested on concepts like prama and bhrama (right knowledge and illusions), the nescessities of stirring of an awakened conscience to pursue one's svadharma.

Fabular modes and dream-packed imagination were also thematic/narrative embellishments (alamkaras). The plebians understood the idioms and the barriers to communication were cast dowm, emotion poured itself forth unrestrained and undisguised. The Mughal-Maratha pillages left the common man to their sufferings; 'they were men, condemned alike to groan' in a bleak atmosphere of frustration. Upendra himself dethroned and exiled did perhaps lie down like a tired child of Saraswati and weeping away a life of cares. May be, words solaced him and he made his petty princely provisions to solace them through poetry.

Upendra's Koti-brahmanda Sundari is modelled on his grandfather and guru Dhananjaya Bhanja's Anangarekha, Ratnamanjari and Ichchavati. Thus, Lavanyabati and Kotibrahmanda sundari combine a happy amalgamation of poetry of creative imagination and scholasticism. At the same time his literature bears an inescapable resemblance to reality. None the less, these two Kavyas are astonishing tributes to the eloquence and rigour of Upendra's endowments, a mélange of intellect and emotion.

The text of Kotibrahmanda Sundari offers compound alamkaras (misralankara) by combining rupaka, anuprasa and yamaka. In western terminology, Upendra deploys loaded figures of speech that at once combines similes (comparison between two different things): metaphors (expression that denotes one kind of thing, is applied to distinctly different kind of thing) yamaka alliteration (repetition of the speech sound in a sequence of nearby words) with tropes or "figures of thought" (meaning 'turns' and 'conversions'). As an effect, Upendra's Kotibrahmandasundari and Lavanyavati embody idioms that are used in a way that effects a conspicuous change in what we have taken to be their standard meaning. These "rhetorical figures" or, "schemes" are unique. The departure from standard usage is not primarily in the meaning of the words, but in the order or syntactical pattern of the words.

We are sorry that for the convenience of exposition we are not able to cite the figures of speech treated in the above two Kavyas. The speciality can be deciphered the moment we probe into the linguistic genesis of the words. He uses Sanskrit words and juxtaposes them with words culled from folk registers. These would be unfamiliar to the aliens. However, at the end, we are forced to realize that visista pada racana is riti.

To brief our discussion on this great poet, we may skip over to Chaupadibhusana, a compilation of erotic verses engineered in the classical Odissi musical tunes. The themes of these chaupadis hinge mainly on the protagonist's erotic fantasies about the paramour, the female protagonist's body consciousness, the process of sexual celebration and alienation that occurs between herself and her lover:

The most glamorous of them
hooked me, I was enthralled;
She packaged my mind
with live images of inverted sex
while she surveyed them reflected on a mirror:
it was a game of auto-erotics

she played it riding on me like a man
playing the game of sex.

Upendra's Chaupadi (tetra-stanzaic poems) are structured like Chautisas and tuned in Chhanda-Vritta (a musical metre typical and indigenous to Odissi style of singing). Chaupahara is another collection of Chaupadis. The total number of Chaupadis is 34+4=38 but if we add the 16 Chaupadis of Chaupadi Chandra, the 49 Chaupadis of Rasa panchaka and 21 separate ones, the total number comes to 38+ 16+49+21 = 124 songs. This evidences that Upendra's poetic iourney begins as a sastra-kavi. Sabda-kavi. artha-kavi and alamkara-kavi, proceeds through rasa-kavi and Sabdartha-kavi and ends In musicality and lyricism, a mellowed state of Prayojana (utility) which the singing poet realized toward the end of his career (The Sanskrit terms are culled from Rajasekhara's Kavyamimasa).

Upendra proved that in the boundless realm of poetic poverty, he alone was the creator and his creative world revolved through its self gratificatory process,. He preferred to dwell upon the erotic sentiment in his poetry and the entire world around him was suffused with sringara. Like the resources of primordial Nature herself, the infinite possibilities of poetic themes could never be drained off Upendra's creative reservoir even after his incessant evacuation through varied literary compositions.

The Kavi Samrat proved that there can be no impoverishment of themes as long as they are dealt with a genuine feeling and mature mind. His maturity rested on his style of representation, in the deployment of words and imaginative syntax. Anandavardhana's modes of embellishment of Vastu, Rasa and dhwani impressed him and he experimented by producing the musicality in consonance with various kinds of dhvanies (alphabetical sounds). Upendra Bhanja's art was a quest after perfection and his oeuvre is bound up with a technique of pursuit. Music to him was a means of breaking the cycle of birth and he efforted to prepare his listeners to realm of God. However, his art was secular and yet he distinguished poetry of mere amusement from the intellectual arts.

The chaupadis represent subjects categorized by Rajasekhara in Kavyamimansa as Loka-vidya-prakirnaka. Upendra, as a dethroned king and a lovable singing poet with his handsome physique lived as a common man, interacted with common folks and intimately shared with their lives. Upendra liberated himself from the fetters of mundane dailiness of the palace life that denied pleasure, joy, a sense of self and an honest experience of being. Dethroned and ousted from the palace he moved alone, and as a gifted and talented prince he enjoyed the love of the best of the early eighteenth century Odia women. He used the female body as a text and treated elaborately on its texture. For him the body was an open space, an open text with neither a beginning nor an ending. The hermeneutic body uncovers its secrets and hidden nuances.

However, poetic projections of sexuality in Upendra's kavyas do have deeper connections with very remote layers of unconscious, both personal and collective. It must also have been a part of the historical developments of the Bhanja zeitgeist. Upendra's psycho- kinetic leap from eroticism to Sriram centered poetry indicates that the germs of his spiritual development also lie as unseen and as unrecognized as his obsession with physicality. They lie in the collective unconscious where they continue to grow until the time of their flowering arrives. Probably sex was his religion.

The Moghal and Afgan invasions left the Odia psyche demented. It was an ugly reality and sex was primarily objectionable to some because of the support it gave to the sterile materialism and uncivilized style of life (treating male/female bodies as cullinaries on the kitchens of life. The Maratha invaders were mean and despicable decoits (pindaries) and hooligans who looted the temples and raped women. The material prosperity they enjoy today is a harvest of the crimes and unscrupulous hooliganism committed in the past.

In such a milieu Upendra Bhanja realized that life in Odisha would remain sterile until the Odia folk experienced a conversion which should lead them to spiritual rebirth and harmony. He, therefore, devoted his very inner potencies to attacking the forces that he believed were corrupting and destroying man and to setting forth the way to a more harmonious and creative kind of life. He held that man would achieve harmony only if he came to terms with his deepest instincts and brought those instincts and his intelligence into adjustment with each other.

Upendra Bhanja's art experience consummated during the recital performances of poetry. Such events also signalled his quest for the sublime. The Ghumusar folks enjoyed, responded and participated in the aesthetic process. Such ecstatic participation generated a space that highlighted the polarities of his unconscious contents. It is for this reason that eroticism and spirituality have blended dexterously in Baideheesa Vilasa. Perhaps, the oppositions were reconciled in the poet's mind as he was aging and maturing. The projection of these polarities into people, or into the milieu, through participatory situations illustrates how these contradictory elements (sex and spirituality) are emanated from the same undifferentiated deep layer of the poet's mind. When a large part of his psyche is projected, the individual poet is hardly separated at all from the environment. All that happened happened in him as well as outside. In these moments of intermerger and erosion of the inside and the outside, he had very little sense of personal identity and no clear differentiation of the poetic - 'I' from the 'Not-I', either of the inner world of the collective unconscious or of the external world represented by the people.

The kavi-samrat balanced the opposition between eroticism and spiritualism on the interface of music and melody. The poet himself was a trained singer in classical music and has composed chhandas that have contributed to the development of Odissi music as well as to the lyrical poetry of our literature, now recognized as a separate technical subgenre of verses. The Chhandas written by Upendra Bhanja are also modelled on the popular tunes of Odissa. The record simultaneously shows the development of Odissi music from Charyapada through Nathist songs through .Iayadeva to the recitable romantic ballads of the Pre-Riti and Riri Chhandas.

The progression on the thematic level shows the Dombi of Charya developing into a ferocious goddesses of Nathist poetry, then leaps into Vaishnavite tantra in which Radha and Laxmi were given importance along with Parvati (though our literature is scanty on Saiva Tantra). The Prema-bhakti (devotion through love) as a concept of Vaishnavite literature is reduced to only Sringara in Riti era. Blended with Krishna and Jagannatha themes, Sringara in Vaishnavite aesthetics is not a total release of the instinctual desire. But heroines like Usha, Parimala. Princess Sasi Sena, Kotibrahmanda Sundari and Lavanyavati constitute a different species altogether.

The sonorosity and the choice of vocabulary in Upendra literature appears romantic to some critics, but it was pure imagination and imagination is one of the great human powers. The romantics belittle it. The imagination is the liberty of the mind. The romantics are failures to make use of that liberty. It is to the imagination what sentimentality is to

feeling. It is a failure of the imagination precisely as sentimentality is a failure of feeling. Let us take one of the erotic descriptions as an example from Keli Kalanidhi. The book is a treatise on the craft of sex:
He proceeded toward her secret site
A little aggressive he was, and she muttered
"No, and no, and No!
A commotion broke out, a shout
Her thighs, posited as gatekeepers for the secret site
Shuddered, they cleared the way in trepidation.
There is absolutely no sentiment in these lines. It is pure imaginative description. Critics speak of the romantic as the French commonly call in a prejorative sense. Otherwise, poetry is essentially romantic, only the romantic of poetry must be something constantly new, and, therefore, just the opposite of what is spoken of as the conventional romantic. Without this new romantic, one gets nowhere; with it, the most casual things take on transcendence, and the poet rushes brightly, and so on. Upendra Bhanja did hardly have any evasive nostalgia for romanticism. Perhaps the critics designate him so because of his bold descriptions of the female body, which was nothing but verbal aesthetic strokes of a painter. If that is romantic every modern work is romantic.

In Upendra's oeuvre, as much as in Riti literature we find two distinct kinds of women (a) woman as commodity in male-produced literature and (b) women as consumer (as listeners of Bhanja poetry, the handsome singing prince was only a consumer item to those women) of oral tradition. But in Riti poetry the unspeakable sexual desires of women are articulated for the first time and Upendra Bhanja takes a leading role to discover the libidinal fire in the vital organs, aillowing the fire to burn inwardly, flameless. The Bhanja heroines hardly utter a cry of protest even when the imprisoned flame consumes them. Bhanja's poetry signifies the return of the repressed women, their repressed, anarchic and unacted desires resurrected in verse. Lavanyavati and Koti Brahmanda Sundari are the Pandora's boxes of unleashed female libido.

One of the most untapped resources of Bhanja literature is its gothic mode of composition. The landscapes in his poetry are the sources of its energies. The description of the seasons, the Keli Udyana (gardens for erotic fulfillment), emergence of supernatural characters in the bed room dream sequences, inclusion of folk and uncanny elements and the half-lit psychic terrains of the heroins constitute the texts of these verse romances. The main protagonists encounter the powers of darkness in nature and in self. At times he incorporates mythic elements into this gothic mould.

The gothic element gets further intensified in the presence of the female go-betweens who work for the heroines. Premasila and Susila of R a s a l e k h a and Saibya of K a l a k a u t u k a are memorable women messengers (Patraharini) who carry letters from the lover to the beloved and vice versa. Sometimes they communicate messages in gestural or symbolic languages (Amitartha) and others help in communicating the exact feeling of one to the other (Nisrutartha). Some of these female go-betweens are the contemporaries of the heroines, some are very old, and others younger.

The elderly go-betweens were florist women, Brahmin widows, and Vaishnavite nuns. Now let us take the case of Lavanyavati. She is the princess of Sri Lanka. Once the Ceylonese King agreed to give her in marriage to Chandrabhanu, the Odia hero comes back and Lavanyavati went thin and lanky day by day pining deeply for the absent Chandrabhanu. Lavanyavati's mother knew the cause and brought an old servant from her mother's place. Her name was Kautuki and she was a lady with a bright sense of humour. Besides, she knew the Vasikarana Mantra (a mantra for casting the magic spell) and had a fair knowledge of herbs - herbs for fattening her body, making the breasts harder and bigger, for the growth of strong and long hair, for reducing the body odour and perspiration and for training her in rati-ranga (the of sex making). (Chhanda No.29).

In Prema Sudhanidhi, a nameless old maid servant comes to the prince to inform that the princess had attained puberty.

Then she gives the prince some tips about Smara-sastra (textual knowledge of Kandarpa-Vidya or the art of sex-making). The prince gifted her one lakh gold coins. (Chhanda No.4) These verse romances depict the life of the Princes and palaces in alliterative lines, word games and Chhanda lyricism, typical to Odissi songs. Bhanja's poems appear like Anglo-Saxon poems and his plot parallels the stories of pagan life of the Germanic tribes written prior to Chaucer. These old go-betweens seem to have sold their expertise and experience in mundane matters for the living. They used to have a lovable status in the palaces.

Viswanatha Kaviraja (15th century). the famous Sanskrit critic of Kapinjala Dasa family of Bira Harekrishnapur Sasana, near Puri and author of Kavyas, natikas and a commentary on Mammata's Kavva Prakasa writes about one such situation in his Sahitya Darpana (Chapter III): "Nachameva gachhati yatha laghutam / karuna yathacha kurute samayi/ Nipuna tathaninamabhigamya vede Ravi dooti Kachiditi Sandidise". The heroine says to the female go-between: "Dear maid, you tell him in such a style that your words would not prove me an inferior one. He should be totally mesmerized and must come to me. You would tell him everything in a lonely place so that a sense of pity for me would be evoked in his mind". (qtd. In Tripathy, 168)17

Obviously, these female go-betweens were very cunning and they knew the art of conversation. They knew the strategies of customer management. The art of conversation rendered by the Purohit of Simhala in Lavanyavati is also remarkable. Brahmachari, a messenger in Lavanyavati finding no other way to hand over Chandrabhanu's letter to Lavanyavati, deploys Champu-vandhana-vidya (a tantric mode) and transforms himself into a female being and enters into the palace of Simhala. Elsewhere they transform into parrots and mynas.

There were also some Nasta dutikas (fallen go-betweens) who, instead of communicating the emotional pangs of the heroine, indulge themselves with the princes. One such Nasta dootika is described in Rasa Panchaka. They come from a wide range of locales. The cultural geography available to us in the verse romance illustrate the poet's wide range of travelling. His romances had an added excitement of revealing stories about countries which his listeners had never been able to visit. He gave an authenticity to these adventures and captured the taste of his generation following Naishadha. Landscapes, towns, gardens and human character are all conjured up before the reader, along with his princely interpolations. Everything is arranged ultimately to be the background of his exotic verse romances.

The target listeners/readers of Upendra Bhanja literature may be divided into four categories: Kovida, Rasika, Bhabuka and Kalpajana. The first two belong to the group of elitist society. But it seems, towards the first and second decades of 18th century, Upendra Bhanja made extensive use of palm-leafs or Bhurja leafs. Dinakrishna and a later later kavi, Abhimanyu (yet to be discussed) had probably used palm leafs since all these poets had taken a keen interest to give a visual turn to their poems. These are called Chitralamkara, the alamkara of painting, which the Riti poets have deployed.

The western counterparl for such an experiment is concrete poetry. The Riti critics denote this phenomenon as Bandha-kavya. Upendra Bhanja has deployed Padma-Bandha (A poem written in a lotus design, a concrete poem), Naga Bandha (as a cobra), Ratha Bandha (as a chariot), Teera Bandha (as an arrow), Dambaru Bandha (as the percussion instrument played by Lord Siva), Bahitra Bandha (as a boat) and many other concrete shapes. Dinakrishna has worked out poems with Chakra Bandha (circular lay-out), Teera Bandha (within the design of an arrow) and Padma bandha (lotus lay-out).

Taking advantage of the extra impact which can be given to words by visual lay-out is, of course, a common device in journalism and advertising. This is one of the skills of the graphic designer and the newspaper compositor. It has been used by various modern poets in Europe. Lewis Carroll in the mouse-tail poem from Alice in Wonderland, Appollinaire in his Calligrammes and George Herbert in Eastern Wings have used such structural configurations that stand somewhere between poetry and painting, but with an extra addition of visual wit, that is in addition to the poem qua poem, and a stanzaic outline which controls the contraction and expansion of the line lengths to match the meaning.

C h itr a k a v y a - B a n d h o d a y a (1740) of Upendra Bhanja constitutes a Chamatkara genre of alamkara in which meaning arises out of the associative conjunctions that the patterns bring about. The constellation of words is a system, a playground with definite boundaries. Bhanja, Abhimanyu and Dinakrishna have designed their playgrounds as fields of force and have suggested their possible workings. The new group of readers had to accept them in the spirit of the play and then probably they played with the bandhas, worked out on palm leaves. They must have occupied themselves in decoding the common Bandha/constellations and some thing new has definitely come into the Odia literary world. They are challenges and provocative invitations too. These concrete and structural poems of Riti era generate new spatial elements and establish poetry as a means of producing economically and arrestingly certain effects which would not otherwise have been possible.

Upendra was not only a musician, but a visual artist, too. His last work, Chitrakavya Bandhodya (C.1740) is a precious document of his calligraphic acrobatics as well as of visual imagination.

History of Ancient Odia Literature | 271

Chitrakavya Bandhodaya is a creation of verbal artifacts which exploit the possibilities not only of sound, sense and rhythm, but also of space. His skill as a graphic designer is a culmination of his artistic playfulness, another quest of ananda. A close observation of the 'Chitrakavya' (concrete poetry) reveals that Upendra Bhanja exploited the possibilities, not only of sound, sense and rhythm-in the traditional fields of poetry, but also of space, though it is the flat, two-dimensional space of graphics on the palm leaf with a stylus.

The first concrete poem, written in Raga Bangalasree (a typical ethnic meter) is the 5th Chhanda (Canto) of Chitrakavya Bandhodaya and it is called 'Attali-bandha', a poem structured like a building. The Odia alphabets are quizzically arranged within the boxes and the reader has to trace the alphabets through the building design carefully. The first four stanzas of the Chhanda are arranged in Ataii bandha (i) While stanza 5, 6, 7, 8, 9 and 10 are spaced within the design called Surya-ratha (the chariot of the sun) bandha. Stanzas 11, 12, 13, 14, 15 are structured within the space called Prasada bandha (Prasada is also a building, but a smaller one; not as elaborate and gothic as the Attalii or Attalika. Stanzas 16, 17 and 18 are spaced within the Peedha Prasada Bandha that is like a ground plan of the edifice. The fifth is Vimana-bandha (Vimana is a wooden arch likel structure to carry the idol of Lord from the temple to a festival) and the sixth is Mandapa (the pedestal) bandha that contains 4 stanzas- 22, 23, 24 and 25. The eighth structure is in the shape of a Grand Chariot (Maha Ratha B a n d h a) contains only one stanza/couplet) and the 9th Chitrakavya (stanzas 28 and 29) is termed as Puspaka Vimana Bandha (One that Ravana used to kidnap Sita to Lanka).

The XIth chitra is a simple Ratha (Chariot) Bandha while the XIth Chitra is shaped the Pracheena Ratha (the chariot of the olden days) containing stanzas 34, 35, and 36. The next four chhandas in couplet form is spaced within Chakra bandha 12th chitra, or picture) and the 13th chitra denotes five fishes entwined into a compounded configuration - Pancha Matsya Bandha. The next one is called Yugala Nagabandha and the 15th Chitra is one big fish devowing a smaller one (Gita Matsya bandha). As per the list goes:
16. Shula bandha :(the picture of a shuli (guillotine) (Used here for the speech of a female go-between)
17. Khadga-bandha: (the structure of a sword)

18. Muraja-bandha: (these designs are drawn in rice-paste or chalk powder, some time used in coloured chalk powder called "Pancha-Muraja" in Odia, denoting basic colours).
19. Muraja-bandha: One more design.
20. Parasu-bandha: The shape of the weapon used by the legendary Parasurama of Ramayana.
21. Puchha bandha: The structural shape of the tail of a bird.
22. Matsya bandha: The shape of a fish.
23. Shankha bandha: The shape of a conchshell.
24. Shodasadala Padma Bandha: A 16-petalled lotus
25. Siva Bandha: Like the Lingam of Shiva.
26. Kabata Bandha: Shape of a door.
27. Astadala padma bandha: 8 petalled lotus
28. Abruta Padma bandha: Close petalled louts.
29. Chaturanga bandha: Horse's steps
30. Aswagati bandha: The galloping horse.
31. Kabata bandha: Another type of door
32. Guchcha bandha: A bunch of flowers.
33. Gada bandha: Shape of a club.
34. Simhavalokana: Veering back and forth like a lion
35. Dambaru bandha: Shiva's dambaru percussion
36. Sakat bandha: Shape of a bullock cart
37. Vajra Bandha: Shape of a bullock cart
38. Vajra bandha: Shape of the thunder
39. Karma Bandha: Shape of a tortoise.
40. Veena bandha: Shape of a veena
41. Rava Bandha: Shape of a musical instrument. We could be able only to provide a sample of the shapes used by Upendra Bhanja depending on the technical possibilities of scanning the pictures clearly. We do have no

ଶଙ୍ଖାଳୀ ଛନ୍ଦ (୧)
ରଚନ ଭିତ୍ତି
ରୂପ — ବଜ୍ରଖଣ୍ଡୀ

ବହୁବର୍ଣ୍ଣ ଅରେ ଅଙ୍ଗୀକରଣୀ ପୋଡ଼ଶେ ୩ ପଦାନ୍ତ
ଦ୍ୱାଦଶାକ୍ଷରେ ବକ୍ର ବକ୍ରରେ ବକ୍ରା ବଳ ଉତ୍ପନ ।।

(ଚିତ୍ର ଓଡ଼ିଆରେ)

ଶୁଣରେ (୧) ମହାନଦରେ କଥା କେତେ କହି ପ୍ରିୟ ପ୍ରିୟାକୁ ପୋଢ଼େ ।
ଥାଇ ମାଆ ରୁଆଣ ଏ ଗତି ଉଦୟ ରାକେନ୍ଦୁ ଦେଖେ ।।୧।।
କୁ କୁହୁ କୁହୁସ୍ୱରରେ ଶିକ୍ଷୁନ୍ତୁରୁ ରାତ୍ର ରେଞ୍ଜରେକ ମନ ।
ଟଣାଟୁ ଜଟି ତଂପାତ ମହଣ୍ଟରେ ଠରର ରାତ୍ର ଠରର ରୁମ୍ୟ ।।୨।।
ଭୋଗ ରଜରେ ଭଟ ଟଟରେ ରାମେମ୍ୟ ଭଣ୍ଟାରେ କହ୍ୟରେ ।
ଶୋଗ ରାଣ ଇଣ ଉରରରେ ଆପତାପ କୁପ୍ରଶ୍ରୟେ ।।୩।।

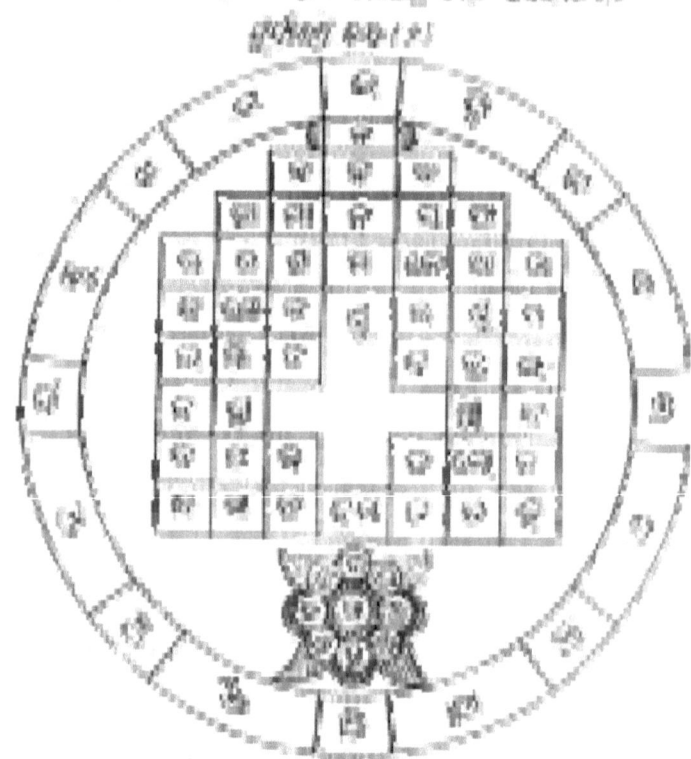

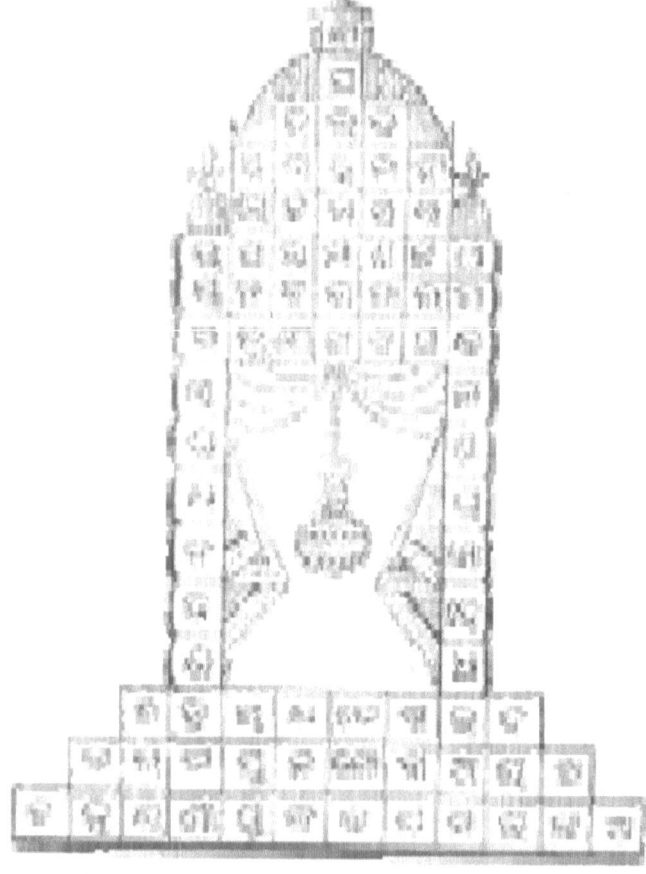

ଏହି କାର୍ତ୍ତିକ ମାସ ବଣ୍ଡୁ, ଦୀପଦାନ ହୁଇଥିବ କୀର୍ତ୍ତନ ସାର୍ଥେ ।
କ୍ଷେତ୍ର କର୍ପୂରରେ ଆସିବ ପ୍ରଭୁ ପାଖିକି ଦେଖି ଭୂଲସାଇଁ କହୁ ॥ ୨୭ ॥
ବ୍ରମ୍ଭଣ ବୋଲାଇ ହୁଆ ଆଗରେ ଅକ୍ଷର ଅଛି ଦେଖିଲେ ମନ କରଇ ସନ୍ଦେହ ।
ଅକ୍ଷରକୁ ଯେ ନ ଜାଣେ ସୁନାବନ୍ଧରେ ତାର ଅର୍ଥକୁ ଭୁଲେ ॥ ୨୮ ॥

ଶ୍ରୀମନ୍ଦିରେ ଚନ୍ତ୍ରଯନ୍ତ୍ର (ଚକ୍ର)

ଶ୍ରୀକ୍ଷେତ୍ରରେ ଚନ୍ତ୍ରଯନ୍ତ୍ରକ ହୁଏ ଥାଇ ସୁଯନ୍ତ୍ରରେ ଥାଏ ।
କେତେ ଯେଉଁମାନେ ପାଖ ମନ୍ଦିରେ ରାହି ହୁଆଇଁ ମନ୍ତ ଜାଣନ୍ତ ॥ ୨୯ ॥
ଦେଖୁଁ ସେଥୁରେ ଅକ୍ଷରମାନେ ରହେରେଣୁ ବୋଲାଇ ଚାହୁଁ ମାନୁ ମାତ୍ର ଜାଣୁ ।
ଅକ୍ଷରକ ଯିଏଁ ନ ଜାଣେ ଜନ୍ମସଫଳ ଅଚ୍ଛଇ କେଉ କଲଇ ॥ ୩୦ ॥

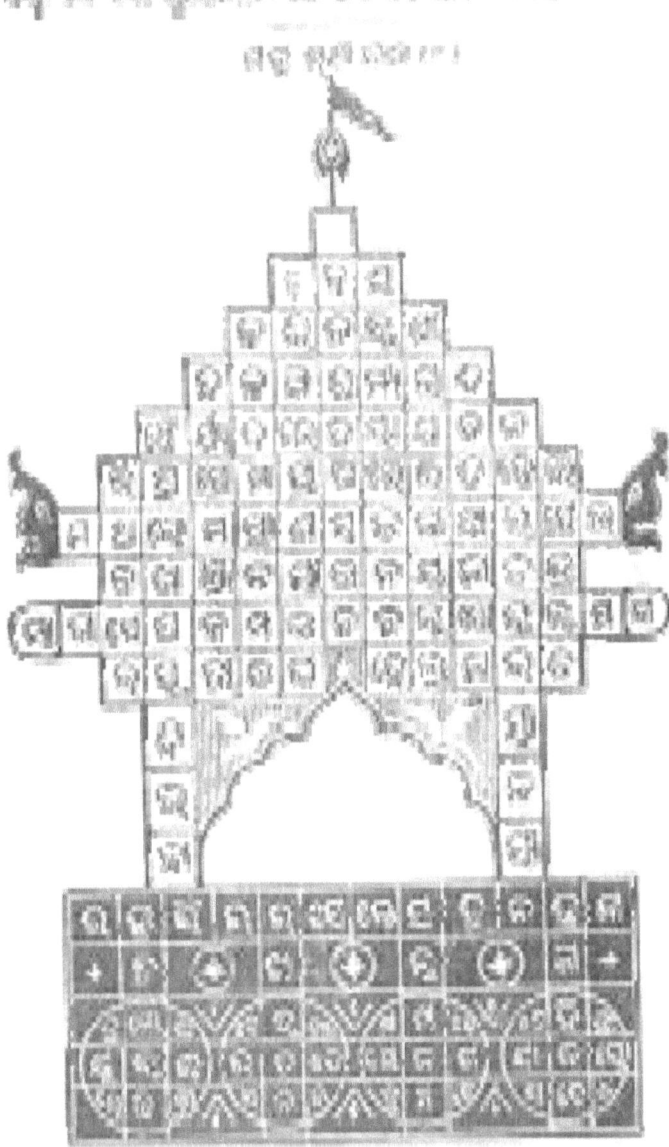

ତୁମ୍ଭ ସଦୃଶ୍ୟଗୁଣ ଭଲୋକେ ଦେଖି ରହି ସୁନ୍ଦରୀ ॥
ଲୋକନି ଣ ଦେଖ ଭଲୁସିଣ ସୋତଲ ନୟନ ଯୁଗ ॥
ସହସ୍ର ଗ୍ରାମ ଦେଖିଲି ସହସ୍ର ଦେଶ ବୁଲୁଛି ॥
ତାଳୁ ଆକାଶମୁ ପୁଣି ବହୁ ଭୂଇରୁ ଖୋଜୁଅଛି କିଣ ।
ଲୋକାଲୋକ ଗିରି ଉତୁ ତ ବେଢି ବୁଲିଲି ॥
ତୁମ୍ଭ ସମାନ କାହୁ ନା ଦେଖିଲି ହୁ ତୋ ଜିଣ ତୋଷୀ ହୁଁ ତୁ ॥
ବାମନୁ କରି ଯାଏ ଦକ୍ଷିଣ୍ୟ ନା ।ଲୋକିଲି ॥ କେତେବ୍ରମ୍ୟ କୋତେ ରୁଦ୍ରଣ୍ଡି ॥
ଭଳ ଅକ୍ଷର ପାଇଁ ଗଲ ହେଲ ଏଡେ ଯାହା ଖୋଜିଲି ଦୁମ୍ୱ ॥

ଦୁଃଖ ମୁଖପଟ(ା)

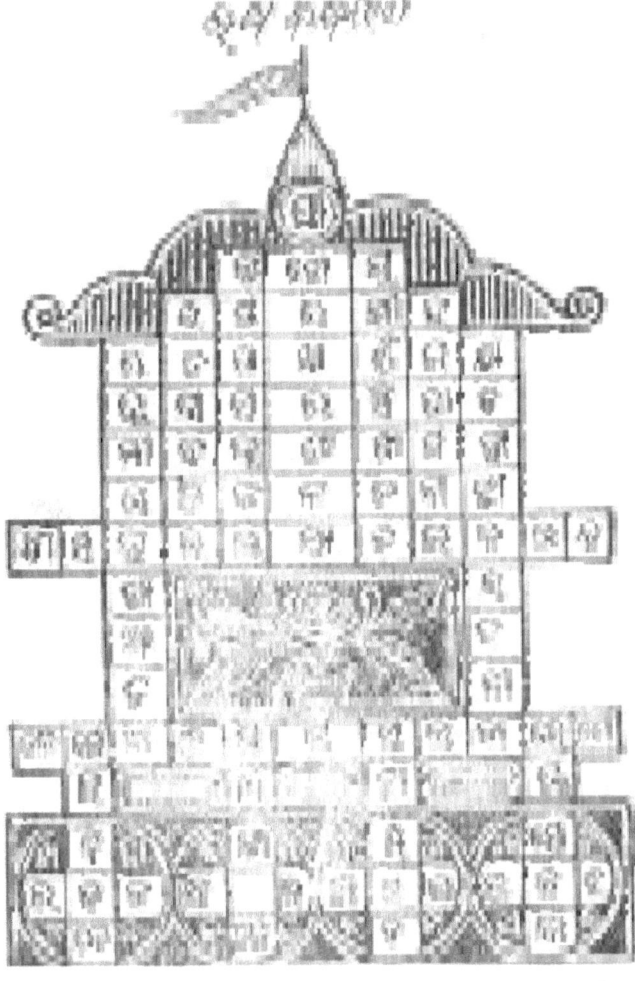

ମୂଳ ପୋଥି ସୂତ୍ର [ପୃଷ୍ଠା......] ଆଧାରରେ ପ୍ରସ୍ତୁତ
କରାଯାଇଥିବା ବିଭିନ୍ନ ଯନ୍ତ୍ରର କେତେକ ନିଦର୍ଶନ :

ଚିତ୍ର ନଂ ୧ (କ) : [ପୃଷ୍ଠା.....] ଅନୁସାରେ ପ୍ରସ୍ତୁତ
ବିଭିନ୍ନ ଯନ୍ତ୍ର ମଧ୍ୟରୁ କେତେକ ଯନ୍ତ୍ରର
ଚିତ୍ର ନିଦର୍ଶନ, ଯଥା ଏ ଯନ୍ତ୍ର ନଂ ୧

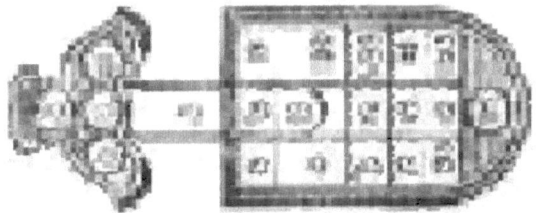

ଅର୍ଥାତ୍ ନାରୀର ଗର୍ଭଧାରଣ ପ୍ରତି ଆଲୋକପାତ
କରାଯାଇ ଏହାର ବିଭିନ୍ନ ଗର୍ଭ-ସଞ୍ଚାର ଲକ୍ଷଣ

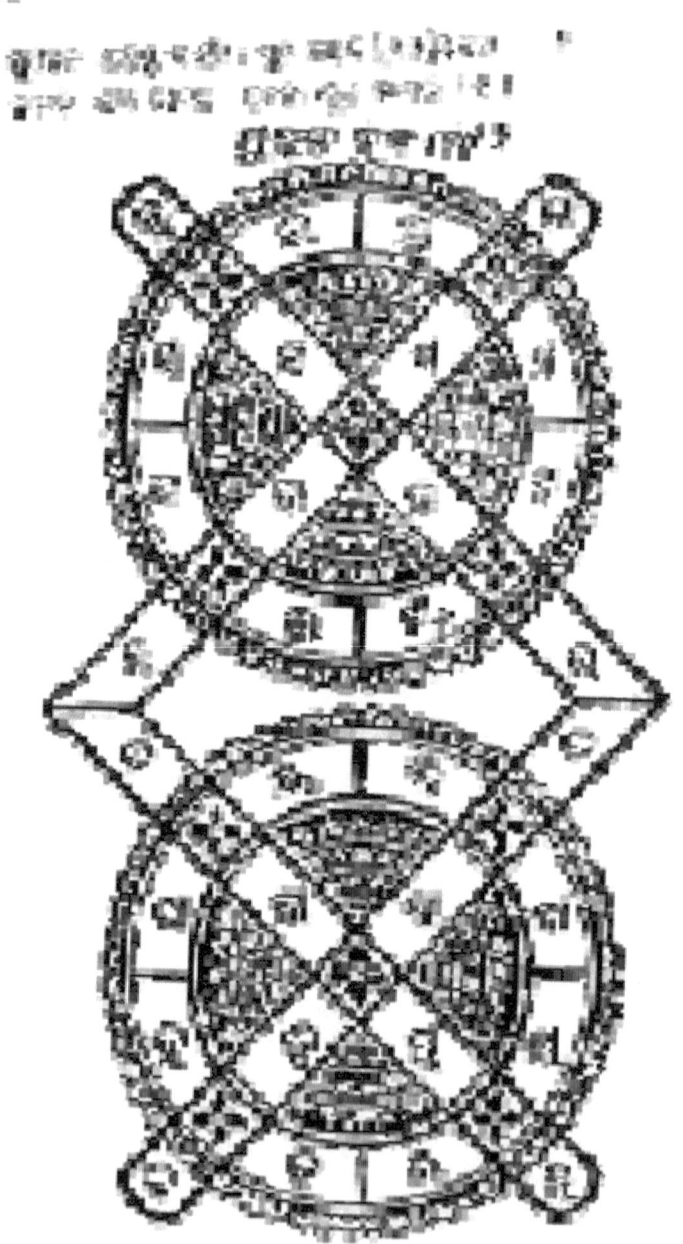

ସଦାଶି ବୁ ଶୁଭେ ଶୁ । ଶୁ ଶୁର ଶୁଭ ଶୁଭ ।୧୭।
ଶାରଦା-ଶ୍ରୀ ଶରୀ । [ଶ୍ରୀମତ୍ ଶ୍ରୀ ଶ୍ରୀ ଶ୍ରୀ ଶ୍ରୀ]୧୮।
ସୁହି ରାଧା । ଶୁଭ ଶୁଭ ଶୁଭ ଶୁଭ ।୧୯।
ଶୁ ଶୁ । ଶୁଭାରୁ । ଏକ ଏକ ହରି ମୁରି ହରି
— ସ୍ରୀକୃଷ୍ଣ ଜଳକେଳି (ଅଂଶ) —

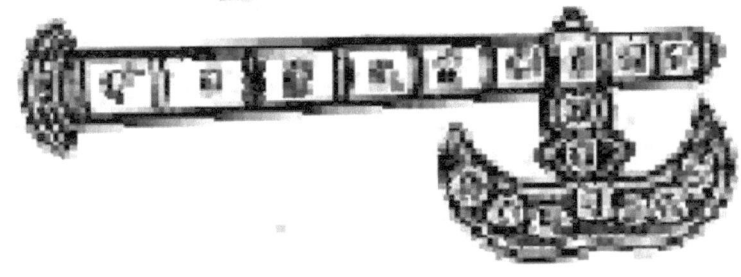

— ଅ୦ ୨ ୩୦ —

ବୁ ଶୁଭୁ ଶୁର୍ଣ୍ଣ୍ଣ । ଶ୍ରୀଶୁଭ ଶୁଭ ଶୁଭ ହରି ।୧୭।
ଶ୍ରୀଶୁ ଓଡ଼ଶରର । ଓଡ଼ଶର ଶୁଭ ଶୁଭ ଶିଖ
ଓଡ଼ଶ ଶୁ ଶୁ ଶର । ଶ୍ରୀଶର ଶୁଭ ଶୁଭ ।୧୮।
— ଶୁଭ ଶୁଭ ହରି —

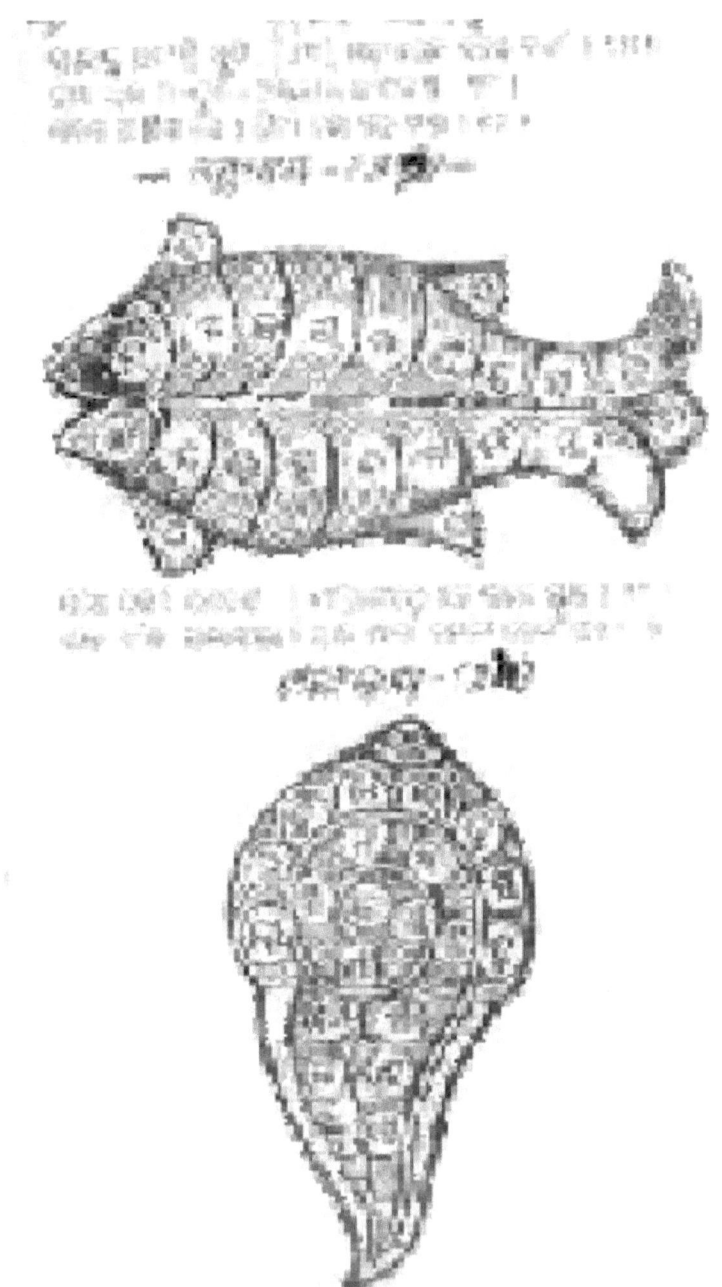

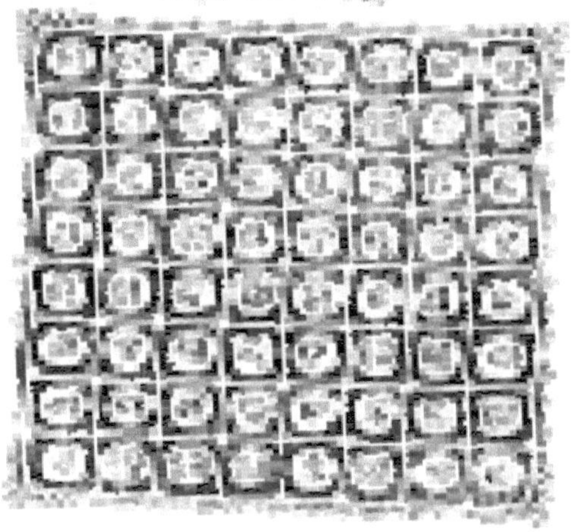

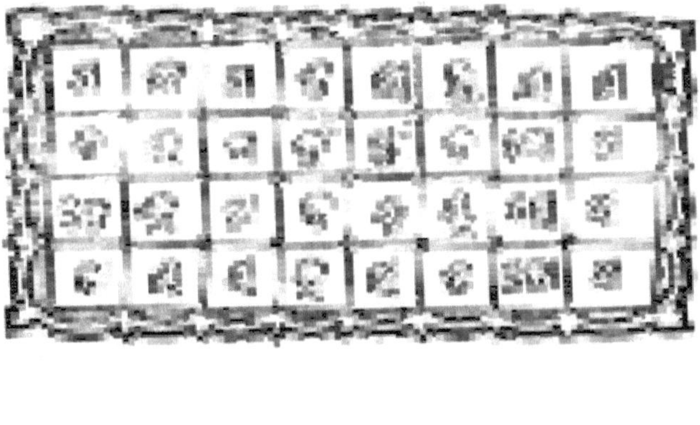

History of Ancient Odia Literature

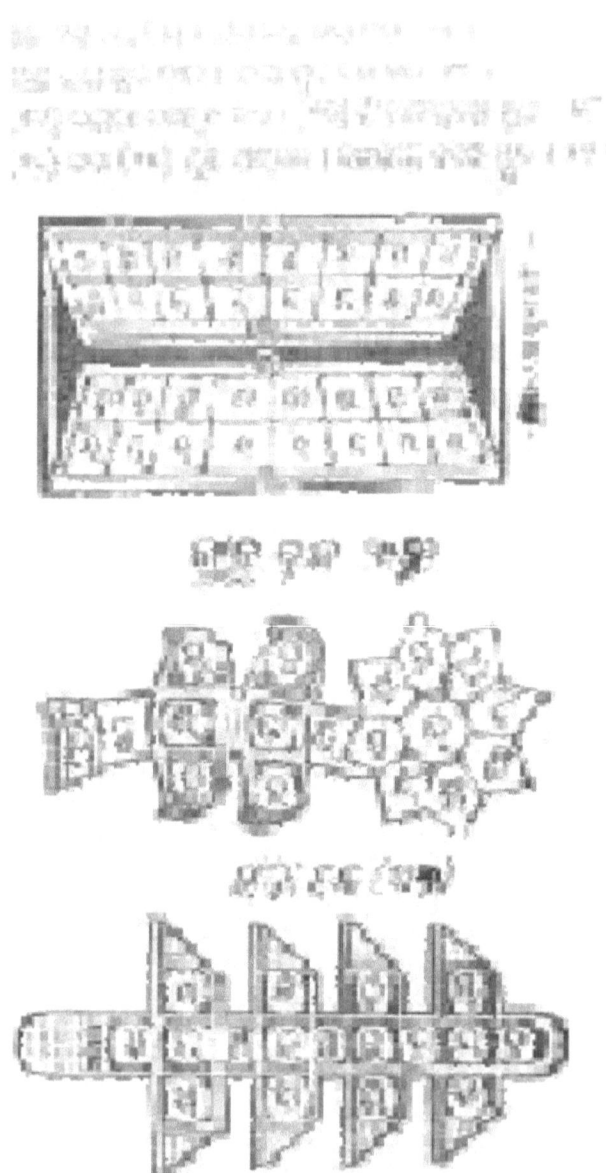

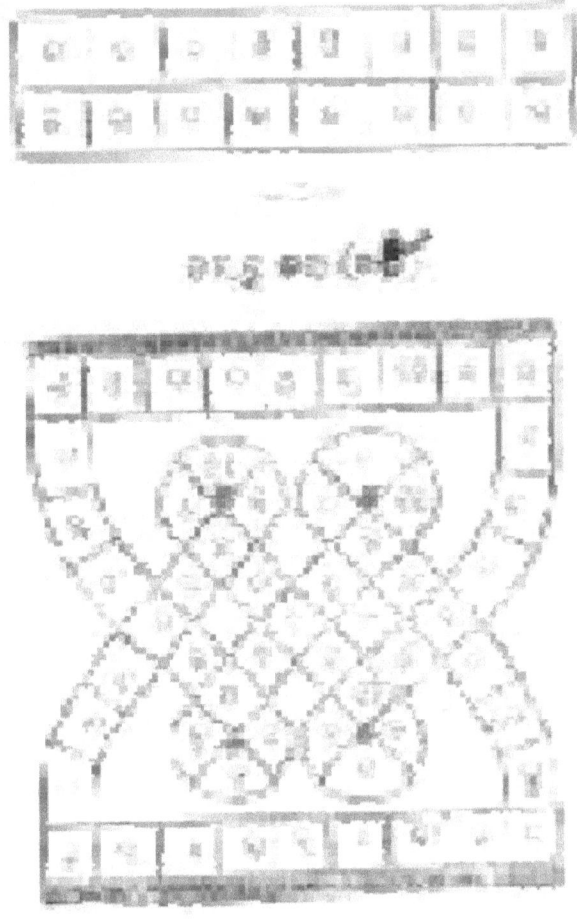

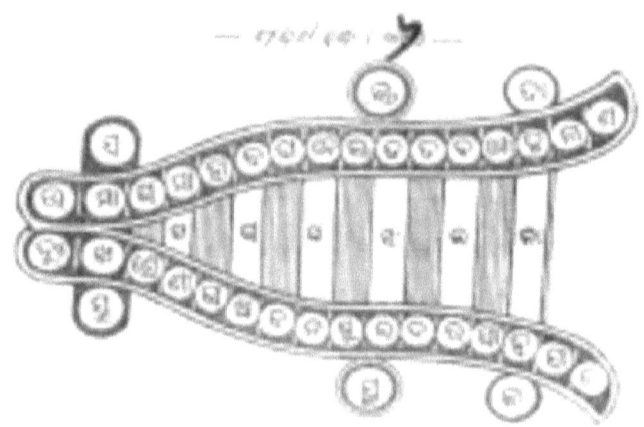

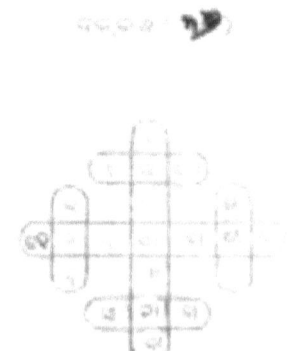

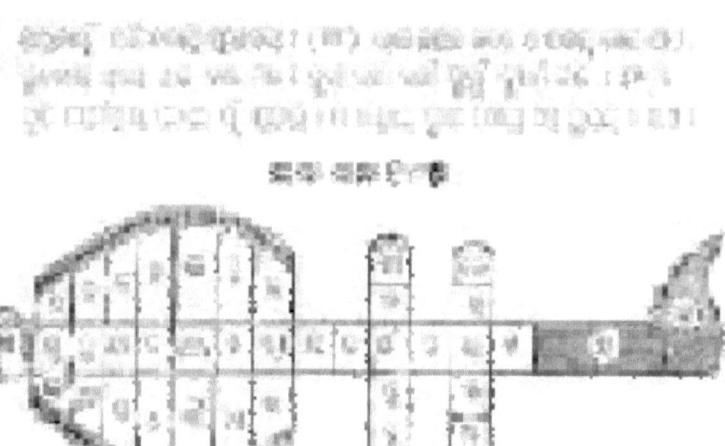

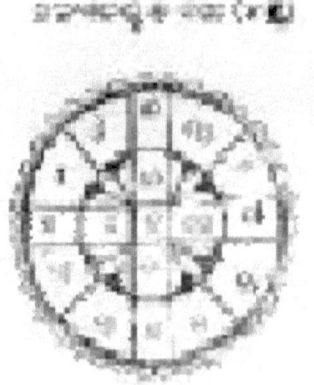

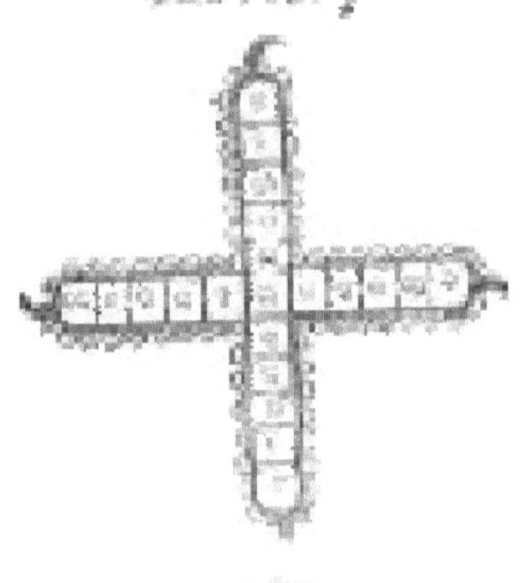

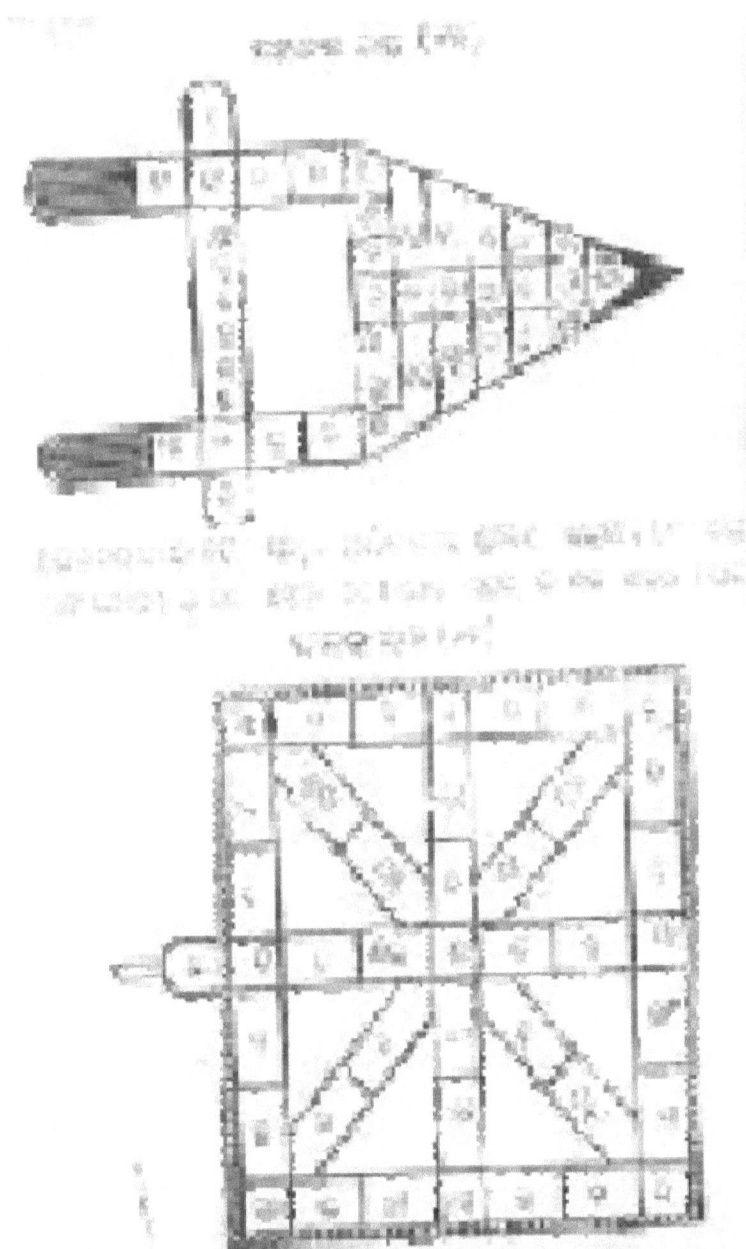

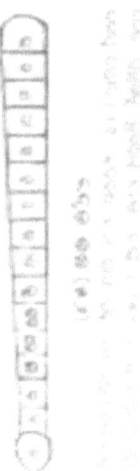

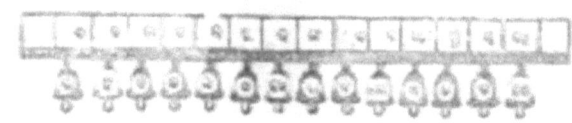

ଚେଣ୍ଡା ହାର (୫୧)

ମୀ ଗୋବୁର୍ଜ୍ଜ ହାର (୫୩)

History of Ancient Odia Literature | 303

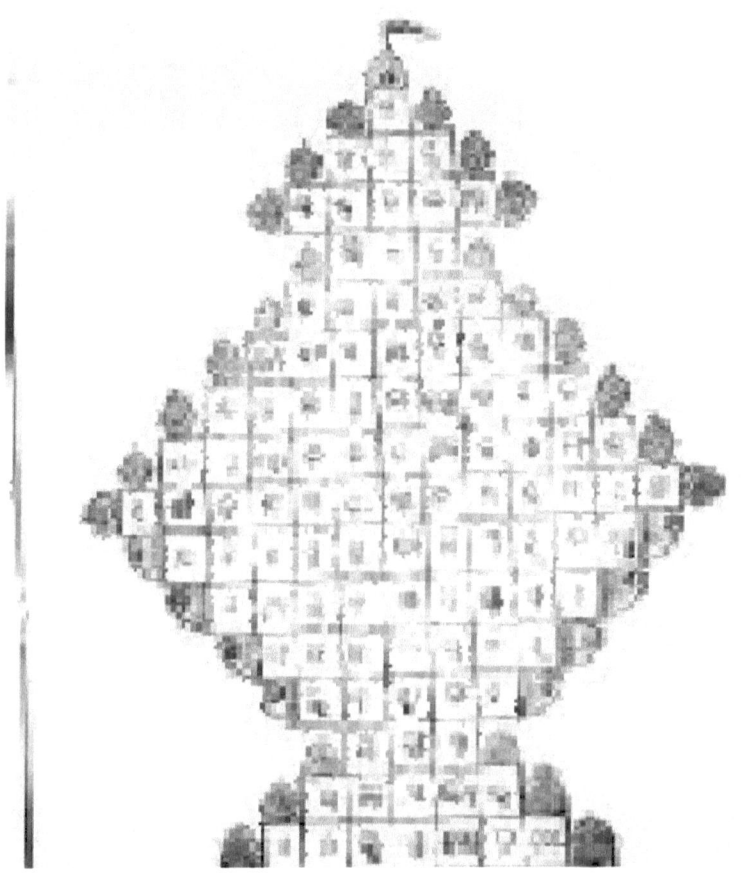

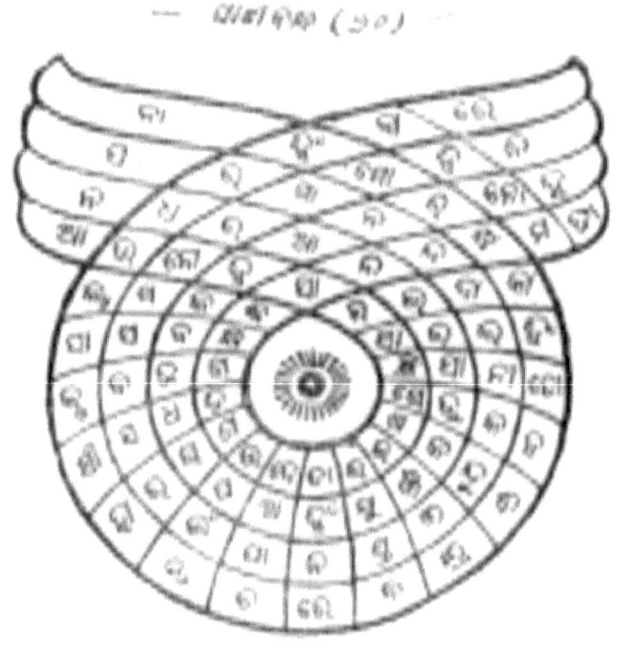

History of Ancient Odia Literature | 305

such tradition in the English poetry except what they call calligrams and concrete poetry. Such visual lay-outs may be discerned in advertising, graphic design of a newspaper, Lewis Carroll's mouse tail poem in Alice in wonder-land and in Apollinaires Calligrammes. A concrete poetry movement lasted for about less than a decade in 1960s in America. Such picture poems are but an indication of the poet's comprehensive view of culture which touched every aspect of life. For such a man art was a profoundly meaningful way of life.

Upendra Bhanja, probably, has used these spatial structures as an essential element to his own aesthetic realizations since "aesthetic experience" as says Sri Auribindo, in his The Harmony of Virtue: Early cultural writings, "is of the skin you love to touch, or the fruit you love to taste".

B u t e v e r y t i m e h e s e e k s f o r t h e n e w. What Rabindranath said in 20th century, Upendra Bhanja proved it a century or more ago; and as a seeker he was not a prince but an ascetic, indulgent though. A poet today is like a trade union leader, who demands an award, seeking it through the the thrown away crumbs from the dining table of the Power. One is reminded of Ananda Coomaraswamy's prescription quoted by Sri Aurobindo in The Foundations of Indian Culture (P.266) in which he "demands more opportunities to be an artist".

Upendra has engaged himself in word play, which includes games with repetition of words of same sounds and different meaning assonantal and consonantal echoings and other verbal acrobatics. One of the best examples of such a c r o b a t i c u s e o f w o r d s c a n b e i l l u s t r a t e d f r o m t h e chyutakshara principle deployed in Kotibrahmanda sundari.

The rainy season is described in a couplet. If the reader deletes the first alphabet of the couplet, the raga would change and alongwith it, the seasonal description would change to denote the winter. This is Chyutakshara (deletion of alphabets) alphabetical game inscribed in Kotibrahmanda Sundari. We would illustrate this with an example without distorting the structure through translation.

Asara Saghana Kala hoi udaya
Asita parabola - ru darasamaya
(25/1, Koti Brahmanda Sundari)
This chhanda is written in chinta-desakhya raga and the couplet gives the description of the rainy season.

In Chyutakshara principle, the first letter of the couplet shall be deleted. Now it reads like this after the deletion of the first letter "A".

Sara Saghana kala hoi udaya
Sita parabola - ru dara samaya

With the deletion, the change brings a semantic transformation along with a shift in the musical raga. This becomes a description of winter and the raga transforms into Kafi - Kamodi.

Now let us delete its first alphabet according to Chutakshyara principle. The first alphabets here are Sa and Si. After deletion the couplet would become

Rasaghana kala hoi udaya
Tapara bolaru dara samaya

The raga of the Chhanda now, is Mala Baradi and the couplet with first two alphabets deleted, describes the summer season.

The poet must have sung the couplet in three ragas (Chintadesakhya, Kafi-kamodi and Malabaradi ragas) to the listeners to establish the Chamatakara in Koti Brahmanda Sundari. But as we examine the continuity of the Sanskrit tradition of Odia literature, we would also cast a side glance at the Sanskrit literature generated in Odisa as a parallel to the Odia writings.

Before the first kavya of the Sanskritized School was written by Balabhadra Bhanja (1026-1057) Murari Mishra (c. 9th century) had written Anargha Raghava, the play.

The famous historian of the state, Kedarnath Mahapatra, after having read two inscriptions at Niali, on the Prachi valley has confirmed the poet's place birth in Orissa. He lived around 9th century. Murari is positioned after Bhavabhuti. Winternitz places him in between 1050 and1135 (M.Winternitz, History of Indian Literature-Vol-III, P.271). A.B.Keith accepts the reference of Murari made by Ratnakara (a Kashmiri playwright) in his Haravijaya (855-884).

However, this author does not have any information about any 'Chitrakavya' written in Sanskrit. In Upendra Bhanja's concrete poetry meaning arises out of the associative conjunctions that the patterns bring about. The 'constellations' viewed randomly would appear meaningless. These lotus, cobra or fish-patterned poems are not directly articulated through sentences, but poised in spatially, operating in suggestive relationship to one another.

Each pattern appears as a play ground and its constellation system has a defined boundary. The poet has designed the playground as a field of forces and the reader accepting the spirit of the play ventures to decode the meaning. At the end, the impenetrable constellation makes a meaningful inroad to poetry. However the patterns of the poems are mentioned (in Odia), of course since they are untranslatables.

The Contemporaries and the Successors:

In the preceding pages we focused on Upendra Bhanja exclusively in order that by isolating his works we might better see its absolute qualities. We must now turn to those poets who worked at the same time and in many cases side by side with him, and try to get some notion of the wonderful variety of the Riti poetry during its period of full bloom. And we must trace briefly how the long verse narratives declined both by the over use of pastiches and simulacrums and by hostile politico-cultural tensions.

The trend of Riti poetry started around two hundred years ago and Upendra Bhanja died in 1675. Yet our literary historians have put the practicing poets under the sub-heading of "Later Riti Poets", as if their poetry had been a product of historical nomenclature. But most poetry seems to function at a level remote from history, where a dissociated mind confronts a landscape innocent of social meaning. Most of the riti poets were kings and princes and such an illusion is one of the most powerful enchantments poetry weaves. But there is no such thing as an innocent poem. All poetry, at its deepest levels, is structured by the precise historical experience from which it emerged, those conjuctures in which its author was formed, came to consciousness, and found a voice.

But we doubt whether the cluster of around more than twenty 'poets had similar poetic selves, and mindsets.The Riti style may not be a creed and if it was, the practitioners were not their ownselves. "their own selves" but the replications of their previous progenitors. We may pickup a female poet named Vrindavati Devi, as an example, who stayed in a Vaishnavite family in Malipara village near Khurda. She wrote a Vaishnavite devotional Kavya captioned Poornatama Chandrodaya, which was completed in 1699. Her husband Chandrasekhar Mahapatra wrote "Srikrishna Tattva Chandrodaya" and her son Bhima Das wrote Bhakti Ratnavali. Vrindabati's grandson Krupasindhu Das also had written Upasana Chandrodoya.

Our historical records, however, show one more Krupasindhu Das (1700-1720) from the village Dalijoda (Cuttack) who wrote a Kavya captioned Vraja Vihar, completed in 1745. One more Krupasindhu Das of Mangalpur village of Dharakote (Ganjam) wrote Krupasindhu Ramayana.

Raja Rama Chandra Singh (1701-1732). This king of Dharakote ruling between 1701 and 1732 had written Kshetra Mahatmya basing on the Jaganatha temple and the twelve monasteries (Matha) of Dharakote that preached the Raganuga Vaishnavism of the Bengal School and Sri Chaitanya.

Dasarathi Das of Ranapur wrote another Kavya with the caption Vraja Vihar and completed it in 1731. The contents of this poem had been culled from Bhagavata and Brahma Vaivarta Purana. Bhima Dhivara's (Other details not known) Kapatapasa was also a long quasi-epical poem on Krishna-consciousness.

Sadananda Kavisurya Brahma (C.1720), born in Bhikaripada near Sarankul had written a long Kavya Prema Tarangini. His actual name was Sadhu Charana Ota and he was honoured with the title "kavisurya Brahma" by Gajapati Maharaja Bira Kishore Deva. This poet has mentioned the names of his 23 Kavyas in a verse romance captioned Mohanalata. His major works, to name a few, are Prema Kalpalata, Prema Tarangini, Lalita Lochana, Yugala Rasamrita Lahari, Biswambhar Vihara and Tattva Tarangini etc.

Bhakta Charana Dasa (C.1722–1813)

Keeping aside the usual controversies regarding his year of birth, we have assigned Bhakta Charana, the earliest year (Others place him between 1729-40, 1740-50, and 1750-60 which do not have any significance for us. Neither do we have a space to fight for a temporal controversy). Named as Bairagi Charan in his childhood, this dark, slim and short man, born either in Sanapadara of Khurda, or in Sunakhala, had studied Bhagavata Amarakosha, Agamas on Nyaya and medicine, later he was indoctrinated into the Bengal School of Vaishnavism and changed his name to Bhakta Charana. Bhakta Charana is known to us as the author of Mathura Mangala, based on Srikrishna's exodus to Mathura. The episodes, in which King Nanda and mother Yasoda weep and the gopies feel abandoned, are depicted poignantly. The most striking feature in Mathuramangala is the poet's migration into the feelings of the gopies.

This authorial entry into the emotional terrains leads to a total and transformed surrender in Krishna consciousness impersonating as a female lover. To brief his intention, one may classify him under the school of Raganuga Bhakti (emotional Vaishnavism) and find continuation of the Vaishnavite thoughts of the Panchasakha Poetry. Born in the year in which Upendra Bhanja wrote his Baideheesa Bilasa, Bhakta Charana was not much affected by the erotic imagination of the Princely poets of Riti.

As a successor of the orthodox Vaishnava poet, his writings reflect the ephemerality of mundane pleasures and attempt to detract the readers from the pleasures they seek through physicality. His Manabodha Chautisa is a monologic poem, in which the conscious ego addresses the Id and the instinctual self to dissociate from the evil desires and the follies of the libido. He insists on necessity of a preceptor, who is equivalent to Govinda. His Manasikha (Education to the Mind) is a persuation to the psychic being to stay away from the mundane search for wealth and power. He seems to be an ardent moral teacher who extols the prophets and the saints of the time. A common man's inner self is depicted here to be in a schizoid condition since there is a persistent scission between the self and the body. What the Odia commoner regards as his true self is experienced as more or less dismembered, and bodily experience and actions are in turn felt to be part of the false self system.(Laing, P.78) 18

Bhakta Charanas' literature, however, is remarkable as far as he moulds his language according to the changing practices of rhetorics. While reviving the theme of the axiological literature of the prophet poets, Bhakta Charana deploys the fashionable alamkaras' and the rhetorics of comparison. His sensibility reacted so violently to the problems of the age that intelligence and reason was not always able to control them. The artistic outcome was a strong abhorrence toward the growing destruction of balance between feeling and intellect, toward this destruction of reality through the cravings of unruly emotions and the desperate vagaries of imagination. The theme of the conflict between the spirit and the senses was not a new one, but obviously it stands as a resistance to the erotic laxity depicted by the princely poets of the time. Thus, he endeavoured to achieve a quality of "elevation" in writing, a verse that would be entrenched in intensity or eloquence, touching the sublime horizons of the sky. With all these attempts, however, Bhakta

Charana has minimized the possibility of talking about the poem rather than about its objects, about what it may be rather than what it may say. Bhakta Charana's Vaishnavite invectives against the ocular-centric sensualities have a lasting effect.

Bhakta Charana had witnessed serious socio-religious devastations in Orissa. Upendra Bhanja had witnessed the fall of the Mogal administration in Orissa in 1751. The Marathas took over the northern part of Orissa whereas the Southerners were exasperated by the exploitation of both the Muslims and the Marathas. Bhakta Charan witnessed Mogal, Maratha and British occupation of Orissa before his death in 1813.

Chandra Sekhar Dev, the king of Boudh who ruled between 1725 and 1760 belonged to a family of poet-kings. Govinda Bhanja's son Narayana Bhanja wrote Rukmini Parinaya in six Sargas (Chapters) Yugma Bhanja had written Dasa Poi and Bara Poi and Juga Bhanja's son Nilambara Bhanja had written Krishnalilamrita.

Chandrasekhar Deva's Premamanjari was a trendy verse romance modeled on the post Panchasakha (Pre-Riti) fantasies. The female protagomist was a princess from Kerala who fell in love with Viswaketu, the Prince of Mallar (we do not know the geographical details of the place). Chandrasekhar, it seems, had a profound knowledge in the rhetorics of alamkara (embellished language) and he uses his embellished language in the primary source of beauty and charm.

Sri Dinabandhu Hota, one of the authorities on Chandrasekhara's art of embellishment reports that the XVIIth Chhanda of Premamanjari is narrated in Chautisa style and the following alamkaras are deployed : Trirangi, Chakra- Simhalokana, Upama, Adbhuta, Virodhabhasa, Adya Yamaka, Pranta yamaka, Madhya-Yamaka, Avana, Vana, Chchekanuprasa, Asaya, dhvani, chhala, Adya-pranta yamaka, Adya-Madhya-Pranta Yamaka, Mala-Yamaka, Chyutakshara and slesha etc.19

Chandrasekhar's Sangita Sataka is a collection of his lyrics in which he concludes as "Kanjamitra" (Kanja = Padma; mitra= Padma's friend, Chandra).

As it appears, Chandrasekhar was adept in Sanskrit poetics and he believed that poetic speech is marked by a round about turn of expression (Vakrokti). There were one hundred and twenty five varieties of "alamkaras" (embellishing devices) by the time of Kuvalayananda. Chandrasekhar Dev mastered some of the extant varieties and deployed them so that his Premamanjari presents a very tough and playful exterior with unique modes of deployment of words and meters with strange arthalankara (which adorned the sense aspect of the words) that helped enhancing the "Kavyasobha" Braja Sundar Pattnayak (1728-1778) later changed his name to Braja Sundar Das. Born in Digapahandi, Braja Sundar wrote Sulochana Madhav, a quasi-epical fardasy that blended the bold strokes of verse romance with a mythic secondary world as it happens in "immersive fantasies"(Ref.Mendlesohn's Rhetorics of Fantasy A Chhapana Padia, a musical poem or a long lyric of 56 stanzas was written by Brajasundar Das, popular in the court of Digapahandi Raghunatha Bhanja was the king of Mayurbhanja between 1728 and-1750 and he had attempted a verse romance captioned Rasalahari in thirteen chhandas, Rasalahari is the princess of Kanchi and Pushpatilaka, the prince of Nishadha were in love and the entire Kavya focuses only on the erotic transaction between them.

Banamali Das (1729-1780) born in Dolamandapa Street of Puri was a lyric poet and the writer of Suchitra Ramayana. However, there are controversies about this author since there were two Banamalis. Banamali later changed his surname to Das. Earlier, he was Banamali Pattnayak.

Raja Krishna Singha (1729-1789) This great king of Dharakote was the translator of the 100,000 slokas of The Mahabharata. He introduces himself in his Mahabharata as:
Great grandson of King Purushottama
I am; the grandson of Ramachandra
My uncle is Jaya Singha
He composed Dronaparva of Mahabharata. One of the grandsons of Krishna Singha engaged Kavi Sekhara Chintamani Mohanty in 1906 to retrieve the Manuscript and it was slightly delayed because of Kavisekhar's illness. Finally, it was retrieved and published at Boudh. Madanmohan Singhdeo, his grandson published it later by Cuttack Trading Company in 1925.

Krishna Singha, the king of Dharakote is still remembered by "Krishna Kanan", a park-like open air space that still exists at Dharakote on the college Road. The king had taken liberty to improvise the Mahabharat in this Kanan (garden) to suit the Orissan milieu. Draupadi, for example, is described as an Odissi Woman. The description of the seasons and the nature bear the imprint of his Dharakote estate.

Raja Krishna Singh had also translated Harivamsa from Sanskrit. His only original work was Radha Biraha Chautisa, which can be classified under the Bengal school of Vaishnavite literature.

Brajanatha Badajena (1730-1799). Born in the family of the legendary devotee named Raghu Arakhita of Puri, Brajanatha's family migrated to Dhenkanal and settled there. A junior contemporary of Upendra Bhanja, Brajanath has authored Kavyas like Kelikalanidhi, Bidesa Anuchinta, Dasapoi, Gopi Bilapa, Shymarasotsava, Bichakshana, Ambika Bilasa and Samara Taranga. Besides Brajanath has written devotional songs and Chandi-malasree. Brajanath wrote a long poem captioned Gundicha Bije in Bhojpuri, His Chatura Binoda is a compilation of prose romances. These excellent stories have been telecast as TV serials.

What Dhananjaya Bhanja and Banamali Das wrote in embellished poetry, Brajanath attempted in prose. The heroes can be sharply discriminated by their adventurous nature and their quest for an ideal. Chatura Binoda is divided into four parts: Rasa Binoda, embodies erotic romances in which one Chanchalakshi, a beautiful girl from a Vaisya family would be eyed by a Prince while she was bathing in river Surekha and then affairs proceeded. It seems the Odia society, repressed sexually was entertained by such stories. In most of such verse romances the princess was either from Kanchi or from Karnataka, Kerala or Ceylone, but Brajanath's female protagonists are from Orissa. The second category of comic stories is given under the rubric of Hasa Binoda. The humorous stories suggest a kind of release from restraint and discharge of tension. Such humorous narratives offer a pleasant sensation for the reader. Niti Vinoda (didactic stories) and Preeti Vinoda (love stories) are the other two categories of stories written by Badajena. Poems written in the praise of the kings lack the personal eccentricities though he attempts, rather, with his almost unparalleled fund of ingenuity and caustic wit, to laugh his opponents off the stage.

Raja Jaya Singh (1732-1758) ruling between these regnant years translated the 'Drona Parva' from Vyasadevas's Sanskrit Mahabharata, then he translated Bhagavat Gita. Jaya Singh's Subalaya Kavya and Hayagreeva Sataka are original works.

Padmanabha Srichandan (1735-1757) : He was the king of Banki and he ruled between 1735 and 1757. This author of the verse romance called Sasirekha was a contemporary of Upendra Bhanja,

Sasirekha and Padmadhuaja were Kanjanana and Chandrakanta in their previous life. Everything that happens to them can be filled into the usual archetype of the other verse romances.

Pitambar Das (1735-1815) : Born in a village called Tahanra, situated on the bank of river Rushikulya. He wrote Nrusimha Purana, Pitambar stayed immune to the erotics of language and feeling in Riti literature and concentrated on the powers of the Man-Lion God. He was blessed by goddess Sharada. Nrusimha Purana is composed in seven Ratnakaras (Chapters) and the myth presents a philosophical vision.

Bipra Rama Das (1736-1793) : Bhakta Kabi Bipra Ram Das, born in Dura, near Berhampur, needs a special place in the history for his Dardhyata Bhakti Rasamrita in two volumes. The verses written in Navakshari Chhanda (nine lettered metre) narrate the lives of twenty five saints known to him: King Bali, Harischandra, Karma, Dinabandhu Das, Damodara Das, Biswambhar Das, Ram Das, Raghu Arkhita, Nilambara Das, Raghu Behera, Gangadhar Das, Bandhu Mahanty, Balaram Das, Jagannatha Das, Madhvacharya, kabir, Mani Das, Krishna Das, Tilachha Mahapatra, Ankana and Madha Na', Kirtichandra, Ganapati Bhatta, Ananta Sabara and Mlechha. Most of these saints, it is interesting to observe, are also poets (or Saint Poets) belonging to Pancha Sakha and Riti Age. This compendium of biographies provides us information about the miracles occurred in the lives of these poet-saints, mostly in their devotional relation to Lord Jagannatha. The depiction of the lives of Raghu Behera and the tribal Sabara called Ananta and the untouchable Raghu Arkhita (Sri) Chaitanya's great companion) proves that the Saints were not born in Vedic times in Brahmin families only, but any biped belonging to any caste might elevate himself to the throne of God and partake in the perennial blessings of Almighty, even in a Vratya land like Odissa. A complete translation of Dardhyata Bhakti would have illustrated how in every nook and corner of Odisa a saint emerged to illumine himself along with his society evidencing superb moments of epiphany. Bipra Ram Das received the patronage of the king of Mahuri. His other works are Shakti Rasamruta, Baisakha Mahatmya, Gundichabasanta, Sivaratri Mahatmya and Janmastami Mahatmya. He was conscious about the loss of faith that excoriated all values of the society under Mogal rule. Thus he felt the necessity of recording the lives of the saints. The Mahatmyas are meant for reawakening a faith in religion.

Prophet Arakhita Das (1757-1837):

The prophets never aspired to undertake literary projects as poets and creative authors do. They do, however, wish to share their spiritual experiences with the common people as sheer revealations that stand with in- compareable strength and clarity, and a fascinating life story of struggles. The account of the 'Panchasakhas' was a veritable treasure house of learning and wisdom. At times they were so stunning that ordinary mortals either disbelieved them or accepted them as miracles.

The literary historians are rather impelled to include them into their chronicles of creative dreamers. Since at times prophetic meditation and literary dreams appear as cognates and they tend to strew sparklers in the mind's eye.

We are not sure whether to introduce Arakshita Das primarily as a prophet or to evaluate him as the poet of a different pantheon. It would be proper for us to zoom into his personal chronicles – how Prince Balabhadra Dev was transformed to Arakshita (meaning the abandoned and the unprotected0, rather than to engage in the wild surmises of the literary historians related to the exact year of his birth. His year of birth remains unsettled between 1743 and 1788 A.D.

Prince Balabhadra Deva (also fondly called Birabara) as a child was an incubator of endless questions that neither his father (King Padmanabha Deva of Badakhemundi ruling from 1774 to 1805)20 nor his grandfather Purushottama Anangabhima Deva (1726-1773) could answer. He asked questions that a child prince in histories never asked:

"Who made the sun that rises behind the hills everyday?"-"God"
"And who made the God?"
-"May be a super God"- they answered. "And where does He live?" –"Beyond those hills, beyond that Kerandimala mountain that overlooked the place of Badakhemundi" asnswered his granny He asked the questions to the wandering mendicants who visited the palace.What they said was also baffling and the adolescent prince stared at them in silent amazement till the life-breath of the mendicant's music faded behind the mysterious jungle route of the Kerandimala woods that girdled around Digapahandi. Not yet an adult, and not entirely a child, Prince Balabhadra seemed to have been encased in a bubble never being able to comprehend what made prince Gobinda Chandra (the mendicants sang about him) to renounce his palace. Was the quest a sheer illusion? or, was the God a reality?'

Balabhadra asked the same questions to the palace deity (Stambhesvari) never verifying whether Her infinite Gifts came to him or not. He sighed and murmured to himself, his head over loaded with unanswered questions. The horizon of his thoughts began to extend toward the infinite searching for the abode of Almighty. And oneday, he felt the Lord stood at his window like a lonely moonlit summer night, mysterious. He felt someone beckoned him from the woods to sit quiet and face to face with him.

The prince crossed the portals of the palace that midnight and entered into the chiaroscuro, the labyrinthine play of light and shade in the moonlit woods. The palace groaned behind. Balabhadra crossed past the wild animals and hurried through the meadows and hills. Never did for even once he looked back, till at one point the tired prince stretched his limbs on the grass. The night was nearly spent waiting for the Lord, in vain.

Days passed and weather tattered his princely robes. "It was good" he thought, "let the robes tear, a loincloth would do". A bonding knot that shut him off was unfastened. Hunger excoriated his stomach as he passed through a grove of ripe mangoes. The prince stood in hunger looking at the Mangoes to fall. People thought him to be a thief. Balabhadra was beaten until he was black and blue. The prince describes in his spiritual autobiography: Mahimandalara Gita".

Unable to bear this pain
My Lord ! no one
Offers me a morsel of grain
when I beg. Yet I keep
This soul for you alive, in hunger
for ten days, I drink only water.

The Prince, now in a loin cloth on his body, moved alone through Khallikote and Banapur till some one, in a village called Sorana, gave him a humble meal. Thus he moved, eating when someone offered and hungry most of the time.

And one day, he stood in a coconut farmyard and gazed at the horizon, where he discoverd the flag of the temple of Jagannath fluttering above. But the watchman of the farm took him to be a thief and an unsocial. He thought he intended to steal coconuts from his orchard. He was slapped and kicked till the 19 year old fell on the ground bleeding from nose and mouth. He writes in his spiritual autobiography:

"Didn't know,
Never knew my Lord!
One who trusts You
Has to bear with such torture."

This 19 year old prince sat quietly near the Aruna Stambha for five days desperately. He sat in hunger, but the Infinite did not appear. Uninitiated, this young boy felt that he, who is sprawled all over the cosmos could never be confined to a temple. However, his importunities continued during the entire night. The boy's spiritual anguish did never diminish: "I consoled my self/ there's no point sitting 'ere/ His presence is filled all over / In the void, and in the skies / Every where".

What this prophet wrote was candid and clear, with no conceits and metaphysical rhetoric. He stayed for somedays in Khandagiri and met the Buddhists. Then he proceeded through the bank of the river Mahanadi, from Kantilo to Banki, from Haripur to Jhankad Sarala's temple and then to Kendrapara and finally to a cave in Olasuni hills. That was his permanent seat. Here he was known as Arakshita Dasa, a metaphor he invented and identified himself with.

In the Chapter XI of Mahimandalara Gita prophet Arakshita wrote:

Not in wooden icons, nor in rudraksha
Not in images of stone
Nor in the chanting of the Mantras
He is present; You can't meet him
In a pilgrimage, nor realize him
In the yantras, too
How can he find you
When you are absent? Hidden
In the caves of the world
Shrouded in illusion?
Hence I wander naked
In the hills, voiceless
Never uttering a word

These lines do only express, they do neither suppress nor attempt to impress. It is important to note that impressions are often formed either by suppression, or through suggestion. His senior contemporaries in literature deployed vyanjana, the principle of suggestion.

What seems peculiar in the words of the 19/20 year old quester is a point of distinction he makes between the outer and the inner. He reads an interior on the exterior. The young Saint identified amazement in the banal, the unreal in the real, the new in the old, the fresh in the stale and the archetype in the stereotype.

After two hundred years of his death in 1837 when civilized people are seen fighting for temples without God, one feels to look intently into the anguish and the inner struggles of Arakshita.

In Olashuni cave near Kendrapara, Arakhita used to offer his God, the "Non-attributable, shapeless Void" dried fish and fermented rice water with boiled vegetables. When Radhesyam Narendra, the King of Kendrapara shirked to accept such dirty food as offerings to God, Arakhita explained:

Listen to me, O Mind:
This body is non-vegetarian food
The semen and the ovum
Also this creation (Part IV. M.M.Gita)

This "nondual Abadhuta", through his deceptive simplicity, professes the concept of non-attributes (Nirguna). He believed that every being of the world has the potency to become God. Every ordinary man, irrespective of his class status, and food habits has a god within him. It matters little whether he consumes the ghee-soaked fresh rice, or, the stale fermented rice water with dried fish and burnt cakes. There exist within him all possibilities of becoming a Samyak-Sambuddha i.e. the perfectly enlightened Buddha. Food habits and the external rituals of worship do not carry much meaning except creating just a psychological ambience for worship. The simple poetic depictions of Arakhita Das breathe the spirit of universal compassion, and if at all one reads a metaphysical discourse in them, they are produced avowedly with the intention of redeeming the suffering ordinary folks. Arakshita in his twenties could realize that religion should not be captivated either by the world of desire or be an instrument of the material world. This Neo-Buddhist Saint did not repose too much faith on the supernatural sphere of existence either.

The young renunciant's experiences during the course of his journey from the palace to the caves of Olasuni revealed the illusory nature of the religions. The essence of all religions is inscribed in the sky itself. The sky pervades all space and it mixes up with nothing; but, it hardly remains unmixed; it is indescribable, invisible and cannot be substantiated phenomenally; so is to be understood the nature of mystery in all religions.

Arakhita, whether aware or unaware, was almost thinking like the exponents of Sriguhya- Samaja- Tantra, which is included within the school of Vajrayana. He believed in the utterance of 'nama' (the name of God) which is equivalent to mantra. He talks of "Ekakara" (that which is folded into a unitary single shape) and "Ekakshara" (a seed mantra) but not of "Prajna" or the presence of any female partner in the process of perseverance. From the very beginning his experiences taught him how to do away with the illusory appearance of things and perceive their ultimate nature as infinite, non-dual pure consciousness. In Mahimandala Gita, these concepts are explained through a dialogic discourse between 'Mana (Psyche) and Chaitanya (consciousness). The Mana (surface mind or the psyche) asks (as Arjuna asked in Gita) and the Chaitanya (conciousness) (like Srikrishna (in Bhagavat Gita) explains.

Arakshita's other works include Bhakti Tika, Gupta Tika, Balyabodha, Abadhoota Samhita, Sakabda Samhita, Padma-Kalpa Gita and Bhajanavali. Arakshita's philosophy is to be compared with Mahadeva Dasa's Brahma Gita and Dharma gita, Kabir's poems and the devotional songs of Bhima Bhoi, who wrote after Arkhita Das. He who realizes Brahma undergoes certain conceptual changes within. In quasi-poetic prose Arakshita states that binary opposites in the mind generate complications that alienate one from the realization of the Brahma because of inner division

One who realizes and internalizes Him Never cares for food and sleep

For the scorching sun, monsoon
And biting winter
Non-evolute is the primal nature.
He who knows Brahma
Is in a state of equipoise of attributes
Like virtue, passion and dark instincts.
He supercedes the five sense organs
and the twentyfive evolvents.
The true realization of Brahma
Is to rise above

The polarities, of good and bad
Health and maladies, truth and falsehood
The saint and the devil.
He comprehends the ultimate, the immutable
And the unchangeable One, never cares
for the four Vedas.
The spirit is neither an evolute
Nor an evolvent.

This young prophet who did not pay much attention to the studies and who spent a large portion of life in starvation and walking through the roads and meadows, talks about the philosophy of Samkhya without knowing it, talks like a neo-Buddhist Mahayani Saint without knowing much about their philosophy. In him there is absence of origination and destruction of the three worlds, his literature is a unification of the knowledge and the knowable; god with form and without form is embraced by him, he reaches a stage in which he is the immutable bliss bereft of all lower pleasures. His literature professes the attainment of perfect enlightenment, not only for the self, but for all the beings, to be the final aim.

Ramachandra Pattnayak (1757/63-) Born in Badamba gada in the family of Bebarta Bhagirathi Pattnayak and imprisoned in the fort of Barabati, Cuttack, this long forgotten poet, Ramachandra Pattnayak wrote two folk romances in the mythopoeic mode-Haravati and Anuragavati. Haravati is the daughter of a Sweetmeat dealer and the hero is from a farmer's family of the countryside. The earlier princes and angels of the "portal-quest fantasies" are deconstructed and the language is purely folk without any attempt for embellishment.

Abhimanyu Samantasinghar (1757/60–1807)

The entire edifice of Riti poetry rested on the linguistic quicksand. Not only is the entire possibility of thinking founded on language, but language was also at the centre of reason's misunderstanding with it. Hence there was an undercurrent of conflict and vacillation between the Sanskrit and the Prakrit languages. While the royal coteries of Kalinga and Kangoda had a common impulse for Romantic imagination and a structural fixation with the concrete, the common practitioners of poetry in Utkal had a great fascination for Prakrit since the days of Sarala Das. The Sanskrit-Prakrit opposition finds a synthesis in Abhimanyu Samanta Singhar.

The formalist notion of poetry, in other words, is an imaginative order slightly divorced from linguistic references and social contexts. Relations between the imagination and the words or figurative events through which the imagination realized itself were no longer perceived as reciprocal. Abhimanyu, as the unfortunate son of a feudal Lord in Balia, Jajpur (He lost his father at the age of 17 and his wife was dead in the midspring of his life) was aware of this problematic vitality of language.

Abhimanyu, nurtured in a zamindar's family must have been acquainted with the works of Upendra Bhanja (1675-1753) and he must have understood the norms of literary aesthetics in vogue- that the formalist model is a game rather than an icon. The formalist set of aesthetic values favoured those works that can be seen and read, and simultaneously listened to its aural music at a glance. But Abhimanyu, who began writing "Bagha Gita", "Chadhei gita" and "Bole hum ti-Gita" in his childhood, had realized later that the shapes of poetry should be ludic rather than iconic. His Tiger Song (Baghagita) written in his childhood, opens with a description of his native place and palace.

The death of his wife at the prime of his youth led him towards renunciation. He sublimated his feelings of separation by writing Prema Chintamani (1788-89) at the age of 28/29 years. Immediately followed by Prema Kala (1789-90), Rasavati (1791-92) and Sulakshana (1796) Prema Chintamani is a mythic romance composed in 68 chhandas. The romance centres around Sri Radha's erotic attachment with Srikrishna through candid description of the techniques of sex-making with sixty fourr exercises, sixteen varieties of sringar mingled with madhurya bhakti (Striking qualities in utterances of devotion, an impressive periphrasis for special charm). However, this entire package of repressed eroticism is metamorphosed into Gaudiya Raganuga Vaishnavism (He is from Jajpur and is garbed in saffron Vaishnavism), and therefore, more exposed to the Gaudiya =Bengal mode of literary as well as Vaishnavite expressions).

Premakala in 64 chhandas embodies occult, Shaktism and magic realities. The heroine, for example, is bestowed with the powers of the goodess and gets married to shyamasundar (The name alludes to Srikrishna) and then they are separated. The story mirrors the subjective feelings of Abhimanyu though he garbs it within a mytho-romantic format. Abhimanyu asserts that mythopoeic fantasy is an advantageous genre for the complete literary expression of a world view based on the existence of supernatural or spiritual power. This unique genre also opens up a space to transform personal and social consciousness. Sri Radha in Premachintamani accommodates the obsessive memories of the poet's dead wife. This mythopoeic allusion to articulate through the mythic figures opens up a secondary vista of meaning. Beyond the exterior of a Gaudiya Vaishnavism the libidinal forces of the inner poet overpower this 28/29 years old widower.

It is reported by the historians that his father Indrajit Samanta Singhar had appointed Sadananda Kabisurya Brahma as Abhimanyu's home tutor and hence Brahma's Vaishnavite world view and Vamana's poetic figures are found reflected in Premachintamani.

Sulakshana (1796) the daughter of Duryodhana and Srikrishna's son Samba are in love and the poet fantasizes their erotic thoughts and actions as one finds depicted in the sixteen chhandas meant for singing in different ragas.

Abhimanyu's fourth fantasy, Rasavati (1791-92) may be categorized under "Intrusion fantasy"21 in which one may notice the play of formats that generates a kind of post hoc heuristic frisson. This may be frolicksome, but it strews sparklers in the listener's psyche. The element of fantasy enters the fictional world as the feelings of Rasavati evolve.

Thus, Abhimanyu creates a fictional mythology basing on the fact that all fantasies have their roots in myth and his work creates a closely bonded sub-genre. One of the peculiarities of these fantasies is that this Jajpur poet's heroines are ethnically chosen from Assam whereas Lavanyavati, Kalavati, Haravati, Premalata, and Premamanjari etc hailed from South India.

Abhimanyu's magnum opus is Mathura Mangala, a "mangala Kavya" written in "Gaudia Riti tradition and at times in "Panchali Riti". Composed of 96 "Chhandas", The book seems to be incomplete. The poet wanted to complete the "Kavya" in 108 chhandas, but the poet breathed his last on the way to Vrindaban in 1807.

Mathuramangala is a Krishna-Kavya that embodies Yasoda's filial love and Krishna's mischief, love episodes with Chandravali and Sri Radha, jealousy and separation, etc. Pournasi, a cowherd woman working as a go-between interferes and Krishna is reunited with Radha. Critics interpret that the book is about transcendental eroticism in

Vaishnavite order (this is a mystificated configuration which no one understands now. What is transcendental about erotics?). The young generation of readers of 21st century would interpret 'Aprakrita Prema' as sexual perversion.

Nilambara Vidyadhara (1760- ?) Dr. Satyanarayana Rajguru discovered the palm leaf text of this author belonging to Khalikote Royal family and the text, he read, was written in 1786 A.D. The name of the text is Prastava Chintamani and it documents the commercial transactions of 18th century Orissa in poetry.

Nilambara Das (1760 -?) Though details about this author are not known, this Brahmin poet has composed Padma Purana, Jaimini Bharata and Purushottama Deulatola in addition to Ramlila, Krishnalila, Harivamsa and Kriya Yoga Sara etc. Rasika Manjari is built around a small fantasy of erotic adventures. This author is also known as Bipra Nilambara.

Hadi Das (1772-1837) A younger contemporary of Abhimanyu and born in champapur of Jajpur subdivision, Hadi Ojha became a disciple of Mast Ram Das at Puri and thereafter he was known as Hadi Das.A prolific poet of late eighteenth and the first half of nineteenth century, he hailed from a blacksmith's family, wrote Sankha Navi, Lakshmidhara Bilasa, Hanumanta Gita, Ananta Gupta Tika, Ananta Goi, Kshetra Mahatmya, Nilamadhab Gita Bhairaba stuti and lots of folk songs. Hadi Das wrote about the importance of Puri as a pilgrimage, the philosophy of Jagannath and his realizations with regard to the understanding of supreme consciousness. His prayers to god are at times satires and abuses. It seems he was little out dated since in a time Riti verse fantasies; he emulated the footprints of the Panchasakhas.

Tribikram Bhanja (1773-1782) This despot king of Bhanja dynasty who ruled between 1773 and 1782 was condemned for his imperial injustice and misrule. Other details are not available. However, he would be remembered as the author of Kanakalata It is a famous verse romance of his time. This Kavya, written in 29 chhandas is replete with figures of speech, playful rhetorical devices and alliterative techniques, but violent erotic descriptions abound the text.

Suryamani Chyau Patnayak (1773-1838) Born in Dengapadara (Ganjam) in 1773 and died in 1838 at Chadheyapalli, Suryamani was a minister in Srikara Bhanja's court. Srikara Bhanja, father of Dhananjaya Bhanja ruled in Ghumusar for two terms: from 1789 to1799 and between 1819 and 1832. During the first phase of Srikara Bhanja's rule, Suryamani Chyau Pattnayak translated Adhyatma Ramayana into Odia and during the second phase (1819-1832) he wrote Bhanja Vamsavali.

Krishna charana Srikarana Pattnayak (1774-1870) Gangadhara Srikarana Pattnayak's son Krishna Charana has translated Valmiki's Ramayana and Srimad Bhagavata into Odia. Krishna Charana belonged to Dharakote and his mythological works are still popular. His Kalki Purana and Vamana Purana are still waiting for government's help for publication.

Vakravak Chakrapani Pattnayak (1776-1836) Born in Badakhemundi, this very popular and fashionable personality had composed Gundicha Champu in Sanskrit. Stava Pushpanjali and Krishna Vilasa Kavya are still unpublished. Son of a famous poet Braja Sundar Pattnayak (1728-1778), Vakravak Chakrapani inherited the art of writing poetry from his father. He was patronised by Purushottama Ananga Bhima Deva (1726-1773) for some time as a court poet and after his death went to Manjusha and was honoured there by the scholastic circle of the court. Chakrapani was, it is said, a very stylish pundit and people reminisce about his spotless dhoti and kurta, and imagine him with a walking stick in his hand. His Guru Vasu Praharaj of Athagarh was a great Tantric of his time and Chakrapani got the Vakratunda Mantra from him for practice and he performed the 'Purascharana' (a tantric ritual of the final stage of mantric practice). so that he was endowed with the power of using "periphrasis" in his daily conversation.Chakrapani's speech sounded witty and interesting). One of the characterizing feature of this late eighteenth century scholar is a play on words where the listener understands from an expression more than one idea, due to intonation employed (Kaku) or due to paronomasia (slesha) present in the signified. If some one introduced himself to chakrapani by saying,"I am Hari", Chakrapani used to retort "what are you? Are you a monkey, then?" Hari also means "Monkey" in Sanskrit. Chakrapani had a profound knowledge in Sanskrit and he used Sanskrit in daily conversations. One day Pandit Bhagaban Kaviraja commented Chakrapani about "Kim Vasasa Chikkana Kunchitena" and Vakravak immediately retorted "Vasah pradhanam Khalu Yogyatayah".

Kabisurya Baladeva Ratha (1779-1845) Son of the poet Ujjwal Ratha, Baladeva was born in Badakhemundi and lived for about four decades under British colony. His father, Ujjwal Ratha was the author of Sajjanananda Champu and Rama Champu in Sanskrit and was conferred with the title Kaviraj Brahma by the King of Badakhemundi. He was Baladeva's first Sanskrit teacher till he was ten years old and lost his mother. The motherless boy was, then, sent to Athagarh, his maternal grandfather's house (now the place is called Kavisurya Nagar). Tripurari Ota, his grand father was a great Tantric whose tutelary deity was goddess Chhinnamasta (A goddess who severed her own head and drank her own blood). Tripurari's tantrik powers were transmitted to Baladeva and he soon grew up as a scholar in Sanskrit, Odia and Telugu with the blessings of the goddess.

Ujjwal Rath got his son married to Ramakrishna Mishra's daughter, Ratnamani of Puri when Baladava was only a 15 years old teenager. But soon after the marriage, Ujjwala passed away leaving Baladeva an orphan teenager. He then moved to the king of Jalantar (now in Andhra Pradesh) with his wife for sustenance. King Ramachandra Chhotray was a scholar with profound interest in histrionic arts and he had written the Prahallada Nataka. He loved young Baladeva since he was a classical singer. King Chhotray encouraged Baladeva to exercise his creative imagination and write poems. Baladeva tried his hand in poetry, and his poetic art was further sharpened and polished in the court of Jalantar. The company of the Telugu and Odia pundits of Kalinga must have given him an exposure to their rich literature.

The milieu inspired him and Baladeva composed his first verse romance, Chandrakala. Baladeva's verse romance registers the name of his own beloved (Chandrakala) and he weaves an excellent narrative fantasy adding some imaginary magical elements. While the primary level of Chandrakala is quasi-autobiographical, the secondary world of imagination is built with the elements of "magic", the "marvelous", and the 'uncanny'.

Chandrakala was the foster daughter of the King of Athagarh and was a paragon of beauty. She loved Baladeva, but died a prematured death. That is how the verse romance was left incomplete. Besides, the time was no more conducive for long romances like Lavanyavati and Ichhavati. The connoisseurs of literature in the court circles were more interested to listen to the lyric forms- the chaupadis, plenipotentiaries and at best, to the "Sankhyatmika" chautisa Poems. Kavisurya wrote Chandrakala under the eponym of Ramakrishna Chhotray and then, found it comfortable to compose such slender lyrics only. The Moghal emperors of Delhi wanted the slender poems to be sung and that changed the trend of the regional literatures. It was easy for Baladeva to be with the trend of the time.

Chandrakala begins with invocations to the gods of the smaller shrines that cluster around the temple of Lord Jagannatha, the second chhanda narrates the previous life of Anangasundara and the city called Manimanjula. The Chhandas captioned, "Mahagajaghosa Stava" and 'Kumara bibhava' introduce the capital city of Kamarupa and the birth of Ananga Sundara. The fifth Chhanda decribes a State named, Kavibibhava wherein the city named Manimanjula was located. The Vth chhanda also narrates the story of Chandrakala's birth. The sixth Chhanda (Kumari Vinoda Ranjana) is a description of Chandrakala's Childhood.

The Seventh and the eight Chhandas carry Chandrakala through her teens toward puberty and hereafter the chapters are subtitled as K u m a r i - K a u t u k a and K u s u m o d g a m a. The ninth Chhanda captioned Nepathyapathya is a description of Chandrakala as a young woman, but it also continues through the 10th and 11th Chhandas with the description of Chandrakala's picnic in the forest with her friends and swimming frolicks.

The king orders the Minister to find a groom for Chandrakala in the 12th Chapter (Chhanda Parinaya Mantrinandana) and the Minister, in turn, deploys a magician to move along the length and breadth of the country to search for a groom. The magician fixes Anangasundara, whom Chandrakala encounters in a dream and falls in love with him in Kumara Mohana (Chhanda No.13). Ananga sends Hamsa as the emissary to Chandrakala, who after the dream-meet with the hero bemoans for the parted hero and Kundalata consoles her. The 15th Chhanda, Captioned Svapna Sambhoga is about the restless Chandrakala craving for Ananga and in the 16th Chapter Kundalata advises Chandrakala to write him a letter asking him to come to Kamakalanagri to witness the Madhaba festival. Ananga sends Hamsa with a letter (17th Chapter) and in the 18th Chapter Ananga sets out for Kamakalanagari.

Here ends the incomplete Chandrakala. Kabisurya, following the footprint of Upendra Bhanja, has also acknowledged that he has followed "Naishadha" while writing this verse romance. However,

Chandrakala has lots of Similarities with Lavanyavati. The protagonists in both the romances had their previous births in divine origin and they were preordained to be united in this life. Dreams and magic play a vital role in both the stories. Upendra Bhanja has a Chhanda, specially devoted to the female protagonist's 'rajodarsana' (the attainment of puberty). Kavisurya's 'Kusumodgama' is composed as an imitation. Both the Chhandas are composed in Kedara Chakrakeli Vani. The treatment of the heroine's frolicsome forest games during the spring, swimming games; make up and the style of ornamentation are rendered the raga Rasakulya in both the romances. As an important poet of the post-Riti era, Baladeva Ratha's lyrics deserve a special consideration. We do not know about his total oeuvre since most of them were lost to us. Late Damodar Pattnayak, a 19th Century poet was the first compiler of Kavisurya's lyrics, and he published six slender volumes embodying 38 songs only. Pundit Kulamani Das had published Kavisurya Granthavali in 1928 and the volume embodied Chandrakala, Kishora Chandrananda Champu, Ratnakara Champu and 160 small poems. But prior to him Gobinda Ratha had published Chandrakala in 1898. He had also published two of his chautisas: Mohana Chautisa and Pakala Chautisa (Dutta Press, Cuttack) in 1915. Hasya Kallola, Jagadamba Malasree and Malasree Malika were published in 1910.

Kalicharan Pattnayak edited a volume of Kavisurya Granthavali (1968) that contained Premodaya Champu, Five Chautisas (kamalavasini Prana, Virahi Chautisa, Manjula chautisa, Mohana Chautisa and Sakhi Chautisa), and three quizzical Manasa poems, or poems of desire (Thes poems are mathematical quizzes. You wish for a fruit, flower or jewel out of a list and the poem would guide you locate the desired fruit, flower or the jewel)). The Granthavali edited by Kalicharana also embodied eight chhandas. Kalicharana's Sangita Sagara excludes three songs. He has included the songs of 'Sangita Kalpalata (a chapter) of Kavisurya Granthavali. A volume captioned Kavisurya Kavita-Sita (1954) was followed by two more volumes later. One Mr. Abhinna Nayak had published his Kishori Champu in 1873 which was later published as Kishora Chandrananda Champu, Mr. Nayak had also published his Ratnakar Champu in 1880.

Odia Giti-kavya Samkalana (1964) embodied Kavisurya's Manasa Poems (Poems of desire), three epistolary poems (two by the male protagonist and one by thefemale protagonist) two "Padia" poems (Two numerical poems, one consisting of 54 stanzas and another in 35 stanzas).

Bhubaneswara Mishra (Kavi-ballava) of Ramachandrapur (an agrahara village under Dharakote estate) had published Kavi-Ravi-Gita-Gangambha in 1961 and his introduction stated that his grand father Padmanabha Mishra was a close friend of Kavisurya and he had a collection of about one thousand poems written by Kavisurya. Kavi-ballav Bhubaneswara Mishra wrote, "My grand father was the custodian of the literary property of more than one thousand unpublished songs of his close friend, Kavisurya. He'd very often show me the palm leaf scripts kept in our home. He is dead and his friend Kavisurya is no more. The palm-leaf scripts were stored in a wooden box. But my indifference and negligence resulted in the destruction of the scripts. Termites entered into the wooden box and destroyed them. Exasperation and remorse ate into my soul the day I discovered the ravage done by the insects." ("The Remorseful confession of the compiler", Kavi Ravi Gita Gangambha, 1961). The compendium published embodied 76 Sanskrit and Odia songs only.

Kavisurya's entire oeuvre (what ever is available to us through the Kavisurya Granthavali,22 Ed. Prof Krishna Chandra Behera, 1998, Friends Publishers, Cuttack) falls under four major taxonomical divisions: (i) Kavyas ii) Lyrical Kavyas iii) Gadya-Kavyas and iv) Chautisa and miscellany.

The Kavyas: We have synopsized Chandrakala as a Kavya and discovered how the elements of fantasy, magic and supernaturalism shroud the text in consonance with the imaginary epic style of verse fiction typical to the trend of post Panchasakha Odia poetry. Kavisurya's deployment of fantasy in Chandrakala may be classified under "Immersive Fantasy" (See Rhetoric of Fantasy for details. The authors move from one category to the other with in the text and they invariably assume new techniques like cadence-shifts and metaphorical changes). Kavisurya follows the classical principles of deploying rhetorics evoking three typical audience appeal mediums (media): logos, pathos and ethos.

The Lyrical Kavyas: Lyric writing was Kavisurya's major forte as the Mogal durbar culture demanded smaller, witty lyrics only as practiced in Urdu literature. Baladeva Ratha was appointed as the diwan of the state of Jalantara at a very young age and he was conversant with the diplomatic strategies that were followed in the late 18th Century palaces. Besides, the state of Jalantara, situated on the Northern extreme of Kalinga, had a larger Telugu speaking population and was controlled by the culture of the Nizams of Hyderabad. Baladeva's cultural alienation and his instinct for survival must have increased his level of assimilation in cultural practices. He was not yet twenty years old and was already orphaned. On one side, the training he got from his father Ujjwal Ratha and the Tantric powers invested on him by his grand father, Tripurari Ota impelled him to build tremendous self-confidence within him. His casteist and traditional roots were very strong. Ramakrishna Mishra of Puri, Baladeva's father-in-law, gave him additional moral support. On the otherside, was the administration of the Marathas and the Mogals who were bent upon inflicting a state of cultural dementia, and an unscrupulous destruction of Odia cultural values.

The poetic art of Baladeva Ratha was, therefore, deeply influenced by the social and political forces of Late 18th Century India. One index of the artist's helplessness is his more and more frequent resorting to the grotesque, to the "humour noir", the desperate grin, angry laughter and vain outcry in poetry. Being the youngest artist dewan of Jalantara, Chhotray must have given him ample opportunities to share the rich rhetorical poetry of Prahallad Nataka.

Kavisurya's, Sarpa Janana (Prayers to Lord Jagannatha envisioned as a Snake) and "Jagate Kevala" (It would happen in this world only) are famous satires written in such moods of cultural alienation. "Jagate kevala, Jane Hasibe ehi tahun phala" (The world would laugh at him if a rapacious one camouflages and impersonates a pious one etc) introduces satire also as a rhetorical meditation, to show the difference between appearance and Truth. "If a country swine / sprinkles holy water on its body and impersonates a sacred cow/ the society would rather laugh at it!" The lines appear to reflect clear-headed sanity Of Baladeva Ratha's poetic observations. The poem is a reflection of the society under Moghal and Maratha rule in Orissa.

Alienation, solitude and isolation in the middle of society are expressed by the artist (Baladeva was a singer-poet) in such poems in which wickedness and folly is censured. But the poet administrator was never a negative character. He was fecund with original and constructive ideas and as an administrator he understood the king and the plebians with equal sanity. On the positive side, his literary output may be characterized by a feverish quest for the new and the striking, and hatred for everything that was outdated, retrograde, fossilized or conservative. Kavisurya's cynicism is edged with contempt. At times he is sardonic and his laughter is blunted with chagrin and mortification. Upendra Bhanja was the only model present before him. But the riti-guna-school of rhetorical poetry was an overused, fossilized style. People needed something new. Baladeva Ratha, the 'dewan' and scholastic young poet could feel the pulse of his listeners. Probably a creative artist is sometimes a utopian, unreal personality, when he individuates as a freely developing member of a society transiting toward a change-new values he is not able to cope with, a new world order into which his classical norms and values do not fit in.

The poet wishes to overcome alienation that formulates this image of axiological man: with the ideals of a value-based, happy and complete personality. This whole may well be more than the sum of the parts, but to appreciate the whole, we need to look at the parts also. Kavisurya's modes of disposition and conduct of satire has to be judged wholistically from such a socio-cultural perspective. His literary products of the later years, moved toward a neo-rhetorical brand of poetry that made a mélange of the classical and the folk, an undifferentiable idiom that would be appreciated simultaneously by the stale, decadent court pundits and an emegent society of disinterested listeners.

It was an insecure society in which their wives and children were raped by the Marathi brigands, their culture demolished by the Moghal invaders, the temple of Lord Jagannatha looted by the Maratha decoits, their palm-leaf scripts on astrology and ayurveda, on Vastu technology and art of building temples (Silpa Sastra), a precious book of dramaturgy called Udra Gandharva Veda (Pre Natya-Sastra) were burnt. The Marathi hooligans were deployed by a Mafia King operating from Nagpur who ordered them to loot the temples and destroy the libraries and the museums of Odissa. The Odia people met the English men, fell at their feet, and invited them to invade Odissa. Kavisurya Baladeva Ratha, the poet-administrator, experienced the whole gamut of these socio-political cataclysms, and probably there was no occasion for him to dream about a hero named Anangasundara or a beatiful princess like Chandrakala any more.

The state which Kavisurya described in Hasya-Kallola had lots of "Mahabahadurs" (brave heroes): Kanji Bairiganjana, Todi Bharoi

Malla, Kunda Satru Sala, Madaranga Medini Ray and Kalamba Baliar Singh etc. He had to sing something for these good-for-nothing sardars (Chieftains/Knights miserably vanquished by the invaders) of Odia society. The elderly traditionalists were nostalgic about Gitagovinda and Krishna-conscious poems. Baladeva found "Champu" as a suitable genre and introduced it with great success in Odia literature. We have Kishore chandrananda Champu, Ratnakar Champu and Premodaya Champu in addition to more than 500 lyrics collected so for, we may put his lyric-Kavyas under four thematic categaries : (i) based on Krishna consciousness (ii)On Social heroes (iii) Devotional Lyrics and (iv) Satires.

The climate of creativity in which Kavisurya operated was most fecund, a period in which Jadumani, Gopalakrishna, Chakrapani Pattnayak, Damodar Pattnayak, Gourahari Paricha and Ramakrishna Chhotray etc. wrote as contemporaries. The advantage with Kavisurya was that he was a "dewan" to the king of Jalantara and thus, he was an administrator capable of mastering power for him. What he needed was a niche to be carved for his poetic career. It did not necessitate a movement; there was no need for a cultural synthesis. He wanted to recreate the unity of art and public, and bring about a radical change. But times were different; with British administrators on one side and the Marathas and Mogals on the other side pulling one backwards. The legacy of Upendra Bhanja did not fade into amnesia. His models were there to inspire a beginner in literary practices. Despite the presence of these electrifying poets, the public discourse took on certain characteristics that people seemed to agree upon. For example, when people talked about the advent of Christianity the Mogals and the Hindus wanted to maintain a status quo. People shared, without much thinking about it, values of religion, family and literary taste that included public recitation or, the musical performability of poems written in rhetorical style. Baladeva Ratha was a classical vocalist and an instrumentalist too. His stay in Jalantara and his association with the South Kalingan Sanskrit Pundits added one more feather to his administrative cap. He could attract crowd even at Puri whenever he visited his father-in-law's place. The Gajapati king of Puri admired him and conferred titles on him. He had to invent new styles, new forms and a new diction to distinguish him from the other bright geniuses. Thus, Kavisurya's poems imbibe a new sensibility, an experimental form that was intended to emancipate the literary practitioners from the shackles of rigid classicism that began with Dhananjaya Bhanja (1611-1701). It is precisely because of this aim that Baladeva was bent upon Champu, Chautisa, Chaupadi and humour, new genres for those days. Champu Kavyas were also not totally new. Chakrapani Pattnayaka's Gundicha Champu, and Chandan Yatra Champu, Bhagan Brahma's Mrugaya Champu had already become popular in Puri by that time. The Chandan Yatra Champu also appealed to the plebian taste. Subsequently, a few champus were written in Sanskrit and were then appended with Odia lyrics written in alphabetical sequence pertaining to the context of the Sanskrit portion. Kavisurya's Kishorechandrananda Champu may be taken as an example. This is basically a work in Sanskrit, but it has 34 Odia lyrics in its appendix written in alphabetical sequence in which the first letter of each line was a consonant. The champu genre was deployed in Telugu, Tamil, Kannad and Malayalam literatures since long. It was most popular in Kannad literature from 9th century onwards. They used Saptapadi (Seven-line verse) ashtaka (eight line verse) and Shatakas (hundred line verse). Tripadis (in use since 7th century) were also written in South Indian literatures. Kabisurya's exposure to the Champus of Telugu literature (called akkara) might have inspired to write 'Champu' in Odia. Romances, fictions, erotica, satires, fables and parables were written in South Indian literatures. Nagachandra (1100-1126) was a great name in Kannad Champu literature whose Mallinatha Purana (the biography of the 9th Tirthankara of the Jains) was very popular.

A Sanskrit scholar like Baladeva Ratha might also have read the Champu Ramayana of Bhoja and Lakshmanasuri. The Charita Puranas of the South Indian literatures are also followed in Odia literature, but the genre was most profusely used in post- Kavisurya period. Many poets who composed Odia songs in the alphabetical sequence named their poems as "Champu".Gobinda Rajguru's (1861-1902) Vrindabanachandra Champu, Damodara Pattnayaka's Jivan Champu (1888), Shyamabandhu Dasa's Jatiya Champu (1908), Harihara Mishra's Premalahari (1904), Nityananda's Mohanananda Champu (1927), Nabakishora Mohanta's Kishori Bilasa Champu (1933), Ananta Chandra's Bahma Jnana Champu and Mahima Bhajana Champu justify the popularity of the genere till the 3rd-4th decades of Twentieth century Odia literatue. Kabisurya in a way lays the foundation for the literature of modern Odia literature, though our literary critics with a colonial mindset extol Radhanath as the harbinger of modernity for his unscrupulous deployment of pro-western form to the level of cultural subversion. The purpose of listing these minor writers of Post-Kavisurya Champu literature is to impress that Kabisurya had introduced new forms in Odia poetry and made a mélange of the Sanskritic and South Orissan folk dialects in his writings.

Krishora Chandrananda Champu depicts the age old story of Krishna and Radha, but Kabisurya's treatment of the Radha Krishna theme was mytho-sociological in nature. Krishna and Radha are viewed only as two love-lorn souls and they are engaged in wooing each other through deceptive threats, scoldings, false acusation as well as wrong statements/lies for sheer fun. Love acquires a new definition in Kishore chandrananda Champu. The love games between Radha and Krishna are programmed and monitored by Lalita, an intimate partner of Sri Radha's libido, in the process of acting as a go-between. Baladeva stayed for 12 years in Jalantara and Ramakrisha Chhotray conferred him with the title of 'Kavisurya". After executing lots of developmental works at Jalantara, "Kavisurya" came back to Athagarh and took shelter under King Balunkeswar Harichandan Jagaddeva from 1795 to 1817. He was a Vaishnava and Kavisurya had written Kishorachandrananda Champu with the eponym of Balunkeswara to express his gratitude. The Champu ends with the line "Kshamadhipa Jagaddeva Samapana Kare he" (The Monarch of the Pardoners thus, completes the champu here) Kavisurya was invited to the court of the Gajapati King Mukunda Deva-II as his fame spread in Puri. The Gajapati tested his powers by arranging a scholastic encounter in the presence of the famous court-poets of Orissa. Mukunda Deva-II was ultimately impressed by his talents and issued a copper grant (a notification) conferring on him the tile of "Kavisurya Rayguru Mahapatra" in 1815. Kavisurya dedicated some devotional lyrics to the eponym of Mukunda Deva-II. After his retirement from Althagarh estate, the Madras Presidency appointed him as the Manager of Mahuri Kingdom for some time. Then he acted as the guardian and teacher of Prince Jagannatha Narayana Deva of Parlakhemundi. The landed property and fiscal grants received from the kings of Jalantara, Althagarh, Mohuri and Parlakhemundi was sufficient for the smooth running of his last life at Berhampur till around 1845 when he died of small pox. Pundit Kulamani Das, one of our earliest biographer commentators on this great poet reports that Baladeva

Ratha was a handsome man with a gifted voice. His sweet and suave behaviour attracted men and women, young and old equally. Never did he boast of his scholastic excellence and as an administrator he was benevolent and helpful to the Ganjam people.23 The Text and Design in Kavisurya's Literature : Our reference to Kishorachandrananda Champu remained tangential since it demanded a separate literary discourse after an awareness of its textual origins. Systemic symmetry and archetectonic fullness as its real virtue; but before that Kishorechandrananda Champu should be foregrounded as a text centered on Krishna- (Radha) – consciousness. Such texts were written in plenty and poets from Madhab Pattnayak and Kanhei Khuntia to Jagannatha Dasa (Rasakrida) had written on the frolicsome love-games in addition to the Lilas and Rasas enacted through out Odisha. Should this text, then, be treated as a simulacrum or a pastiche? Did kavisurya attempt this Kavya only to repeat the same Lila? How does one distinguish Kishore Chandrananda Champu from the poems in Gopalakrishna Granthavali since they were contemporaries?

The Krishna-Radha love games depicted by the Panchasakha poets and their successors were the only outlets of erotic expression under the mask of divinity, though the Vaishnavites interpreted them as achintyavedaveda bhava of the Bhakti theology. The 16th century culture of repression allowed erotics only at a higher level, a level of trating the union as a metaphor for the meeting of the body with the soul, the soul with the supreme soul and an imaginary state of 'nitya-rasa' perpetual erotic play). That was the notion of Vaishnavism. Jayadeva's Gita Govinda treated such erotics and it had a tremendous influence on Odia literature after 12th century.

The Gopala champu perceived such erotic play with an overwhelming emotion. A translation of a relevant portion of Gopala champu would explain:
    This love, which after inundating
    The pair of lovers, Radha and Krishna
    With its own bliss
    And their girl friends, too
    Constantly engulfs the entire universe as is well-known
    May that love enflame
    our intelligence.
    (Gopala Champu 15.4)

Love inundates with joy. The essence of Vaishnavism is the recognition that love and joy are intimately connected. The object of love is a source of joy. At the same time, one seeks to give joy while in love. The concept of achintya-Vedaveda has been explained with so many ways that it becomes esoteric, an impersonal force.

By the time Kavisurya wrote, the Maratha "Bargies" looted the faith from Odia hearts through inhuman rapes and pillage. People no longer had a mindset to accept anything spiritual and transcendental. Hence Baladeva Ratha has treated Radha and Krishna as ordinary, rational people of flesh and blood with loving hearts. Let us examine the "Champu" and its design of representation.

It begins with an invocation called Mangalacharana written in Sanskrit and praying for the Supreme Savior (He who provides clothes to Draupadi when she was forcibly stripteased on the court, he who saved the life of the elephant from the enemy crocodile etc.) to bless him to complete the poetic enterprise. The Mangalacharana ends in a self-reflexive style and the poet initiates a game with the readers: "Where do I have a space to excercize my faculty of imagination? Where does stand this dull-headed poet? Where could this bold literary venture dawn from? How could I dare to depict a divine story like this?"

The speech act is dramatic, and it signifies how a serious subject is narrativised in a formal and elevated style, viewed from another angle, Kavisurya's language is self-reflexive and he initiates a game (playful) with the reader-listeners. An interaction between the reader and the text has started from the invocatory song. The Sanskrit sloka is followed by a "Churnika" (Prose, here used for paraphrasing in Sanskrit) and then begins its first song in Odia in raga Saberi. The song depicts Radha's confession of the frission she experienced the other day:

My worlds fail to speculate, O dear;
how the sound of his flute could implode me within,
ruptured my inner being.
I could cast a far-away look. It was
a lotus in meditation: deep, closed
in itself, yet to foliate, A peacock
feather on his head. The glint of a
blue sapphire pierced, my vision
goading me all through.
(Verse one: Letter 'Ka', Raga Saberi)

The language would differ and the representations vary, but all compositions in all languages would boil down to the same story, same beginning, middle and end that began with Gitagovinda. Though Radha and Krishna are manifestations of the divine syzygy, with all the implications inherent in this Jungian archetype, they are more than simply the external projection of repressed ideas of romantic love, and the theological and philosophical superstructures around them contribute to their depth, richness and endurance as symbols. Never the less, they cannot completely be comprehended without an analysis of the idealized love in general and erotic love in particular. If a married woman like Radha feels so deeply infatuated with the "blue lotus" and the "glint of the blue sapphire piercing" into her psychic perception, it would signify a protest against the conventional system of marriage. If Radha didn't gather the courage to demonstrate an open protest, she would confide Lalita and find out some other outlet. That is how the Radha and the gopies of Jagannath Dasa's Rasakrida (16th Century) are found to have changed in Kishorachandrananda Champu.

It is not possible to discuss all the works of Kavisurya in detail. Kabisurya can not, however, be disposed of as a writer of Champu and chautisa poems. A new genre (Champu poems) begins during his time. He has followed the foot prints of a senior court poet of this period, Brajanath Badajena, one of the pioneer prose writers of the era of rhetorical poetry. Kabisurya's Hasya Killola depicts the story of a country of fools, called Rahasya Ghosa. But it also begins with a Sanskrit sloka and the rhyme pattern is maintained. The ending word of the first sentence rhymes with the ending word of the second sentence in the narrative. The country called Rahasya ghosa is described like this:

"It happened like this, Ho, it happened like that. There was a great country called Rahasyaghosa, a country's territory counted as five hundred less miles from fifty miles in total. All follies are treated there as virtues. People frown at intelligent men. The Brahmins are only cooks. People quench their thirst by munching nuts. They derive great pleasure by castigating prophets and saints. A pig is called an elephant and castes and races are not identified in that country. The Brahmins carry knives with them and out of great devotion they butcher the "Vaishnavas" only. Kavisurya was an administrator and he knew the royal families of Jalantara, Athagarh, Mahuri and Paralakhemundi. He must have observed such neighbouring estates where such crudity and brutality persisted. The author exposed the follies of the nineteenth century gadjat estates and castigates their vices. At times Kavisurya narrates the completely trivial and juxtaposes them with the heavily didactic. Impotent soldiers, cowardly commanders, ugly and deformed prostitutes, malevolent priests and foolish astrologers crowded the milieu. The court poets of the king Keertipratap recite poems distorting the words from Telugu and Marathi and that was considered to be the standard of literature.

Hasya Kallola is splintered with limericks in Sanskrit and Odia. One may discover at least four ways by which the satiric meaning emerges : by what a man does, (or fails to do), by what others do to and say of him, what he reveals about himself and finally what the author says about them. Kavisurya the administrator understood that satire is about people and there must therefore be some form of characterization. The simplest form is that of description by the author. One can find such portraits in Chaucer or Dryden. Rahasyaghosa is a country comparable to Pope's Dunciad. One may meet the rogues of Rahasyaghosa in Chaucer's Canterburry Tales. A different side of the poet is revealed in Hasya Kollola.

Kavisurya was an administrator poet and stands at the opposite pole of his predecessor Dinakrishna Das. His entire life was spent in feudal courts either as an entertainer singer or as a diplomat sycophant.

He catered to the entertaining needs of the feudal court circles in Jalantara, Manjusha, Athagarh or Mahuri. Thus, Kabisurya as a poet stands at the terminal point of a tradition established and pioneered by Dinakrishna Das of Jaleswar.Our contemporary generation of students does not know about Manjusha and Jalantara since they are a part of Andhra Pradesh now, since the new political Odissa was formed in 1936. But the Kingdoms the Kabisurya's time were in Southern Ganjam and North Kalinga.

Gajapati Divyasingh Dev-I (1688-1716) had invited the King of Manjusha (Harihara Burma) and crowned him with the title of Rajamani". His son Harisaran Rajmani was enthroned after him and by this time the Southern Utkal was under the Moghals. In 1724, this Northern "Sarkar" was under Nizam-ul-Mulk and he declared himself independent. The Northern Sarkar, including Manjusha and Jalantara were occupied by the French invaders. In 1757 the French commander, Count. D. Bussey killed the king of Bobbili (Gopala Krishna Ranga

Rao) and entered into Ganjam. The Zamindars had surrendered voluntarily to the French. By that time the British had already entered and in 1768 Edward Cutsford defeated the French and brought Ganjam to their fold of power. It was a trying time for Harisara Rajamani. But his son Laxman Rajmani (1779-1823) stayed loyal to the British government and continued to gain the favour of the Madras Presidency. So, he could be able to contribute sufficiently for taking up developmental projects for Manjusha.

Kavisurya had been to Manjusha during Laxman Rajmani's time. He was an ardent Vaishnava and he performed a gorgeous nine-day Brahmotsava at Manjusha. This Vaishnav festival, the legends reveal, was first performed by Brahma in Tirupati temple and this nine-day festival was also performed by different Southern gadjats. The Ramaswamy matha was also established during his time. Kavisurya was very popular in Manjusha and Jalantara because, he was a young, scholarly Vaishava and wrote poetry based on Krishna's leela and over above knew Telugu and had a fair aquintance with the literary trends. The king used to construct a wooden chariot and Mahavishnu alongwith Sudarsana toured over the estate. Swamy Ramanuja called this Mahavishnu as Venkatesha and had offered one consecrated Sudarsana to accompany Lord Venkatesha. There was a severe famine in Ganjam during 1790-1793 and 60% of the farmers were dead. The famine was called Panchamania Kantara and the surviving farmers left their landed property and fled away to other places. In 1800 AD one William Brown was appointed as the collector. Brown invited the landless farmers of Vijayanagar and the nearby Telugu villages and offered the lands free of cost for cultivation. The Odia population was almost rooted out from Bahuda to Nagavali- a vast tract of the Odia country.

Kavisurya Baladeva Ratha was in Jalantara in those days writing poems on Vaishnavite faith. He was also in Jalantara by that time when the king of Budharsingh invaded Manjusha and devastated around 30-40 villages. The same year around four hundered paikas of Manjusha counter-attacked Budharsingh and defeated its king Gaurachandra Nisanka who after getting severe injury on his arms and chest, had escaped into the mountains. His queen Nisanka Rayrani returned to her father's palace at Jarada and wrote there Padmavati Abhilasha.

Padmavati Abhilasha of Nisanka Rayrani is still considered as one of the most famous Kavyas of Post Riti era of Odia literature.

However, the quarrel between Jalantara (Budharsingh) and Manjusha was settled by Kavisurya when this young poet was deputed to Manjusha as an emissary. King Lakshman Rajmani, almost old by that time treated Baladeva most affectionately and gave him a very warm reception. After Laxman's death in 1823, his son Srinivas Rajmani occupied the throne and Manjusha had gained popularity as a Vaishnavite place of pilgrimage. Srinivasa Rajamani had written a number of numerical Chautisa poems and had translated Amarusataka and Mitakshara and had written a Kavya captioned Muktalatavali in which Krishna Lila is depicted in Chautisa poems. Srinivasa had also composed a Vishnu Sahasranama Bhasya and Lakshmi Ashtottara Sata namastrotra.Srinivasa's daughter Harivallava had married the Durgamadhava Singh, the King of Badagada. This king of Nala dynasty was influenced by his wife and changed himself into an ardent Vaishnavite. He composed Krishnalila as well as Radhaprema Lila and they were pioneering works in the lila genre of performance.

Kavisurya's posting as 'Dewan'(an officer looking after Revenue matters) and as court poet of different Southern estates not only gave him an exposure to the scholarly ornate poetic tradition of Telugu and Tamil literatures but also had provided scope to encounter Moghal, Maratha, French and English cultures. Srinivas Rajamani was treated as one of the finest Kings of the North Sarkar of Golkonda and was treated by Governor Hon'ble Mount Stuart Elphinstone Granduff (1881-1886) as a friend. Both of them were in habit of writing personal letters. Kavisurya was quite aware of the changes that were taking place in the society, though he was not quite sure that those were the footsteps of modernity. His official position as dewan demanded him to be aware of some functional English, and he learnt the language to correspond with Madras Presidency in workable English. Phakirmohan Senapati was only a two years old child when Kavisurya breathed his last in Berhampur after a short spell of suffering from small pox.

Jadumani Mahapatra (1781-1866)

A contemporary of Gopalakrishna, Kavisurya, Abhimanyu, Brajanath Badjena, Arakshita Das and a host of post- Riti, lyric age poets, Jadumani was Born at Athagarh (Ganjam on 8, January 1781) and married and settled at Itamati under the patronage of the king of Nayagarh in 1791. In Prabandha Purna-Chandra, Jadumani writes:

This book is a product
Of a poet from sudra caste
Never treat this rudely, I entreat
Don't vent your anger on the text. (1st Kala, 7th stanza) The caste prejudice was so violent in the 18th-19th century society that Jadumani, son of a carpenter suffered from an inferiority complex in the courts of Khandapara, Nayagarh and Ranapur, though they could not cast him away as a poet. Jadumani, in addition to being an expert carpenter was also a painter, a singer and an instrumentalist who played different percussion and string instruments. As an obstinate and truant boy in early childhood he did hardly concentrate on studies, but learnt music and painting. His father, widely known as "Nabajia Mukunda", was very writly and his gift of the gab made him popular among the folks. Jadumani inherited music, painting and the art of chattering from his father. Then he was sent to Pundit Bhagaban Kaviraj Bahinipati of Bishnuchakra village (Ghumusar) after he completed his primary education with Pundit Vidyakar Mahapatra. The 18th Century Odia Society was in a vortex of caste prejudices and Jadumoni had doubts whether he would be allowed to learn Sanskrit. But Kaviraj Bahinipati argued "Sudram Kriyavidam" (One who performs the rituals succinctly, yet perfectly, can be admitted into Sanskrit academia even if he has a lower birth). Jadumani as a boy was an expert in slokanta competitions (One would recite a sloka and the competitor has to compose another, to deploying the end alphabet as the starting alphabet of the sloka) and his knowledge in Sanskrit impressed Pundit Bahinipati. Pundit Bahinipati also read the inherent art of comedy in the boy's Sanskrit sloka composition. The Pundit Knew that the quintessence of pedantry in 18th century Odissa was nothing else than the art of pretending to outdo nature. The pundit therefore attempted to protect what was latent and spontaneous in Jadumani from what was automatic and mechanical in Sanskrit learning. Jadumani expressed his desire that he had come to him only for getting a clue to creative excellence and to honest honour, not for any material gains. Pundit Bahinipati, then, indoctrinated him with Hayagriva (The Lord of education/vidya) mantra. This tall, black, handsome artist came back from Ghumusar at the age of eighteen and had been on a short sojourn to Daspalla, to his grand father's place where he met a Sanskrit scholar named Pindika Mahapatra. He polished his knowledge of Sanskrit. A very rich carpenter named Raghunath Sutar

lived next door and Pindika arranged the marriage of Jadumani with Raghunath's daughter, Khanjana.

Raja Vinayak Singh of Nayagarh ordered Jadumani to prepare some Pata Paintings and in the process he became the favourite artist of the palace. The queen and the other members of the palace loved his art. Vakravak Chakrapani Pattnayak (1776-1838) of the Khalikote Court visited Nayagarh in 1810 and invited the Sanskrit scholars of the Court for a contest of wits. In those days wit and repartee were considered as significant faculties of human intelligence, inventiveness and mental acquity. The congregation was full of half-wits. Such contests were designed in 18th century to amuse or to excite mirth in the audience. But the court scholars of Nayagarh somehow, dodged the event, may be because of inadequacy. The King could realize that the situation was taking an ignominious turn. But some court officials brought in Jadumani for the encounter with Vakravak Chakrapani.

Vakravak Chakrapani used a kind of aggressive verbal expression which was brief, deft and intentionally contrived to produce a shock of comic surprise in a typical form almost equivalent to an epigram. The surprise was usually the result of a connection or distinction between words or concepts which frustrated the contestant's expectations.Jadumani's practice of "Hayagriva Mantra" worked that day and he defeated the giant of a scholar. Vakravak Chakrapani, elderly and experienced, submitted candidly, "I declare myself vanquished by this young poet-Jadumani." He then embraced this 19 year old young poet and blessed, "I bless you to come up one day as a jewel of Utkala Desa and people would feel honoured to utter your name. The king, highly, impressed, appointed him as the court jester of Nayagarh.

Vayasya (the jester) in Indian context, however, may not be an equivalent of the works of a 'court jester'. Jadumani's wit, repartee and humour controlled the central part of his brain now. As a jester he developed a new intimacy with the inmates of the palace. His literary works as well as everyday repartees were strewn with humour, satire wit, irony, fun, sarcasm, mock, parody and lampoons. As court jester he did not develop sycophancy, rather deployed satire as a polished razor, an instrument of amending the follies and vices. A large part of Jadumani's literature was, thus, devoted to polish the manners of men, to promote attention to the proper decorum of social behaviour and above all, to render vice ridiculous.

Medieval Odia literature, especially the writings of Jadumani, Brajanath Badajena and Kavisurya Baladev Ratha embody plentiful illustrations of satire, irony and humour. All the three poets generated a trend, a subgenre of embellished satire that also enjoyed the popularity of the connoisseurs. Books like "Jadumani Rahasya" have gained immense popularity in the Orissan countryside till the 70s of twentieth century and the village folk still quote Jadumani's witty epigrams as an evidence of their own intellectual achievement.

But Jadumani's oeuvre can not be surveyed only with emphasis on his wit and humour. His poems, especially written on his wife Khanjana unfold the innate humane quality of his literature. Jadumani Gitavali, edited by Dr. Janaki Ballav Mahanty (Bharadwaj) embodies 74 lyrics out of which theirteen are addressed to Khanjana. His marital relations with Khanjana and his extra marital relations with Devadasi Tillottama, Manorama Jhalakamani, Parvati, Vasi, Lavanya and a number of sister-in-laws (Bhavi) he was related with, are alluded to in these lyrics. The Indian classical literature embodies such female inspirers with reputed poets like Kali Das, Vishnu Das, Vilva Mangala, Bilhana and Kavisurya, Vishnu Das- Lakshahira, Kali Das-Manjarika, Vilva Mangala-Chintamani, Bilhana- Mandaramala and Kavisurya-Chandrakala are enthralling erotic- pairs known to classical literary circles of the courts.

Jadumani's first kavya, Raghava Vilasa was written on the model of Upendra Bhanja's Baideheesa Vilasa. Upendra had practiced the famous "Ramataraka Mantra" at the Raghunath temple of Odagaon, a famous village of Oda country or the ancient Oddiyana. Jadumani had been to Odagaon with the king of Nayagarh and remembered the Sadhana (meditative excercises) practiced by Upendra Bhanja in that temple. He, too, took a vow there to compose one Raghava Vilasa. The Kavya alludes to the early sepoy Mutiny of 1817. Written in 39 Chhandas, the epic poem begins with the origin of Kavya literature in Raga Ramakeri. The second chhanda in Sankaravarana depicts the family of Ravana, the birth of his two brothers and a sister, Ravana's marriage, his victory over the gods and ascendance to power. The third chhanda in Raga Kalasa depicts the famine in Champavati state and the story of Jarata and Rishysringa. The language is decked with Yamaka alamkara. The fourth chhanda in Ashadha Sukla raga narrates how Jarata deployed her techniques of magic eroticism on Rishyasringa, Saint

Bibhandaka's advice, the performance of the fire sacrifice, and King Dasaratha's invitation to the Young Saint to come to Ayodhya. The 39th chhanda ends after Indrajit's death. Ravana takes a vow to kill Sita and Trijata advises Ravana that he should refrain and retreat from such a vow since Sita is beyond death and indestructible. The deployment of adyanuprasa, prantanuprasa, puns and homonyms provide a typical riti structure to Raghava Vilasa. The plays on words that are identical in sound (or very similar) but are sharply diverse in meaning generate various "Yamakas". A special type of pun called "equivoque" that refers to the use of words having two/three disparate meanings are also deployed by Jadumani. These scholarly touches evidence his merit as a scholar of etymobgy.

Prabandha Purnachandra, the second long poem is dedicated to Jagannatha who is conceived of as Srikrishna. Jadumani began writing the Kavya in 1840 (at the age of 59) and intended to replenish the poem with the sixteen digits (Kala), but it was left unfinished with eight kalas when his only daughter Rama was dead in 1850 AD.

The story of Prabandha Poornachandra narrates the episodes related to Rukmini. The subject has been culled from Magha's Sisupala Badham, kartik Das's Rukmini Bibaha and Jagannatha Dasa's Bhagavata. The story line proceeds in strict accordance with the classical five Sandhis related to : Prarambha (the beginning), Prayatna (the endeavour), Pratyasa (expectations), Niyatapti (Probabilities) and Phalagama (Achievement). The dominating Rasa in Prabandha Poornachandra is Sringara. It is "Sringara-ranga-ratnakara-taranga" (P.P.4.1) (Waves of the ocean of colourful erotics)

But the most striking feature of Prabandha Poornachandra is its "hasyarasa"(comic element) deployed as "double entendres". Vritiyanuprasa, Chhekanuprasa and Adbhootalamkara, Jadumani's expertise in music and Knowledge in medicine, astrology and grammar generate the purple patches of his poetry. He possessed knack for writing in a variety of metres. The metaphors, rhythm, diction, repetitions and figurative language illustrate his skill in making his lines march to the measure of his thought. Jadumani acknowledged Upendra Bhanja as his model and his close interaction with Kabisurya generated identical thinking in style and depiction. Both were musicians and had tantric realizations of literary efflorescence. Dr. Sudha Mishra, a profound musician and Music scholar of contemporary Odisha (Presently the Director of All India Radio, Cuttack) writes in Sangita Sudha that "the epistemes of music has a very subtle base that becomes opaque for literary critics. They are outside its impact, but a life that is bereft of the capacity to appreciate its affective powers is futile"24. Jadumani has deployed music as "a toy for the children, as an accompaniment to youth, a walking stick for the old, a salvation for the mendicants, an enjoyable commodity for the consumer kings and as therapy for the sick people".25 His association and exchange of letters with Kavisurya Baladeva Ratha had an affect of enjoyable repartee in poetry, but the reasons for this attraction was music. Kavisurya was also a musical performer and an actor director of a champunataka which was staged at Athagarh. Jadumani's exchange of letters with Tilottama Devadasi of Chudanga Street, Puri and their meetings semioticize hardcore perfermative elements. Prabandha Poornachandra is basically a dramatic narrative.

Jadumani's Bhakti Gitika is a compendium of his lyric poems. It signifies his personal involvement in the musical arts. Lyrics dedicated to the authorship of his patron kings of (Nayagarh and Khandapara) are also to be included in the list of his lyrics. He has donated / published a lyric in Chandan Hajuri's name. These lyrics are directed to be performed in the following Ragas : Ramakeri, Sankarabharana, Kalasa, Kalahamsa Kedara, Ahari, Rasakulya, Dhanasree, Kumdhakamodi, Asavari, Bibhasa gujjari, Malava, Kali, Mangala Gujjari, Lalita Kamodi, Chinta Bhairava, Vasanta Ahari, Ashadha Sukla, Sindhuda, Khanda kamodi, Soka Kamati, Chokhi, Bangalasree, Panchama Varadi Kannada and Vasanta etc. Music experts would identify that some of these ragas are purely indigenous Odissi Ragas, i.e. neither do they belong to the Carnatic nor to the Hindustani Schools.26 Chakradhara Mahapatra, to quote only one of the stalwart critics of our language, evaluates Jadumani as a pursuant of the hard core truth of life, a full size icon of Odia nationalism and a strong, pillar-like, steady presence to assert the identity of the Odias. It is regretted that his merit is still shrouded by a darkness of nescience. It is amazing to discover that he plied the chariot of his life for eighty five years trampling over this ignoramus, inertia-filled cultural space. We do not know when this hibernated race would wake up to identify this undaunted practitioner of a vibrant and juicy life." (Translated from Mahapatra, P.5-6)27.

Late Chakradhara Mahapatra was a respectable cultural critic and historian from Cuttack who devoted his entire life in unearthing the buried pages of Orissan history and rearticulating the silenced voices of the repressed Odias. Thus, what he represents here as the politics of downplaying Jadumani demands our attention. Jadumani stands at the tail end of the post- riti poetry. The Sociocultural as well as the political background of Odissa undergoes quick changes at this point, and with that, the taste of the people and their aesthetic notions. Jadumani for the first time identifies the real and the material, as distinguished from the verse-remances and the fantasies of the poet kings. Thus, while speculating the reasons for laying under emphasis on his literature, we may survey the changes of the literary scenario, and examine whether the rhetorical and aesthetic feudalism was losing its ground in Orissa.

Transitions toward a Vaishnavite Revival: This longlist of poets recorded here under the rubric of the quest for the "soul" of poetry seems to be encouraging and the three hundred years (1550-1850) we have demarcated for a particular verbal rhetoricism is undoubtedly the most fecund period in the history of Odia poetry. Why should then the literary historians underplay Jadumani Mahapatra's merits and shirk to pay "a piece of the pie"28 he deserved? Is it because Jadumani was a painter, musician poet par excellence breeding jealousy in the hearts of his contemporaries? Is it because he belonged to the caste of the carpenters and was discriminated against? We have noticed since the fifteenth century how the temple-based Brahmins of Puri under-estimated great literary works like Balarama's Jagamohan Ramayana and Jagannatha's Bhagavata. We have seen how a great prophet lile Achyutananda was denied a seat at Puri. He had to settle at Nemala in an Ashram built by his disciples. The casteist wars were so ugly that Jadumani entreated in the first "Kala" of Prabandha Purnachandra": "This book is the product / of a poet from sudra caste/ Never treat this rudely, I entreat/ Don't vent your anger on the text."

But the Brahminic supremacy was suppressed by the Kshatriya kings since last hundred years. The Pattnayaks had mastered Sanskrit and Chakrapani had blessed the young Jadumani after he was defeated. If it was not a casteist prejudice, why was then Jadumani marginalized in the texts of literary history? The politics of representation entailed a critique of cultural representation and probably the ruling feuds promoted prejudices of domination and oppression. Liberal truth-speakers like Jadumani were taken to be the representations of the opposition and they were negatively valorized, Jadumani's humour and occasional satires were intended for the correction of faults and amendment of certain practices. Jealous courtiers might have prejudiced the kings that Jadumani Mahapatra by attitude was counterhegemonic. His cultural representation could have been negatively represented in the court circles.

Though Jadumani's world view intended to promote egalitarian social justice and a signaling toward emancipation, the hegemonic power might have viewed it negatively. In a corrupted feudal society ethics tended to be subordinated to politics and the moral dimensions of culture tended to be under-focussed and downplayed. Despite dire poverty and the death of his son and daughter, Jadumani held his head high with the pride of a fullfledged artist and continued writing his moral critiques of society and culture. He was more than usually consciousof the follies and the vices of his fellows and he could not stop himself from showing that he was.

It was unfortunate that Riti poetry could not be accepted as the expression of poetic subjectivity, as it is generally understood in Western criticism. It was merely an outward presentation of beauty called forth by a harmonious combination of more or less fixed literary excellence. Jadumani, despite, his treatment of "Sringara", was identified only for his deployment of hasya (humour) and the Odia critics did not accept humour as a respectable emotion. It is for this reason that while his listeners savoured the humour and satire, the courtly circle undervalued them. The urban kings and their court pundits were foregrounded as centres of culture and ethnocentrism pushed this artist from Itamati-Khandapara-Daspalla-Nayagarh-Ranpur area to the margins of Odia poetry.

Ethnocentrism engenders the idea of cultural relativism. They view how individual beliefs and value systems are culturally relative. Painting, carpentry, vocal, instrumental music and poesy make an enviable multiplex of arts and the contempory poets might not have been as much grifted as Jadumani was. As we take an over view of the interplay of representations and ideologies of class, gender, race, ethnicity and aesthetic norms of the cultural texts, we realize that Jadumani had the right kind of nerves to articulate the potentials for resistance in oppositional subcultures of the courts. The courts had always been seats of corruption. Dinakrishna Das wrote hundred years ago:

Adulation to an idiot
(Be he a king or despot!)
Pushes the poet into a dangerous pit, that
Tantamounts a self-stabbing
On your chest
With a knife.

We do not know whether the kings with whom Jadumani was affiliated were idiots or not. But Jadumani was obviously safe under their patronage in the "gadjats". There was great trouble outside in the "Mughalbandi" area, and more in Khurda, Puri, Balasore and Cuttack. Orissa suffered a large-scale pillage and plunder during the Maratha rule. It was a "Segmentary State" with dual power-the Marathas at Nagpur as the political centre and the Zamindars/ feudal lords as immediate tax collectors. The Nazim of Bengal appointed Naib-Nazims for Orissa and according to the treaty made between Alivardi Khan of Bihar, Bengal and Orissa and Raghuji Bhonsle of Nagpur, the Choudhuries/ Talukdars/ kanungoes (revenue collectors) were appointed for the collection of different taxes and for sending the money to Nagpur. The Marathas imposed pilgrim taxes from the Jagannath Pilgrims; the artisans, merchants and traders had to pay taxes. The peasantry and the traders were virtually fleeced in the Moghalbundi (the plain and coastal lands of Orissa). The Gadjats (where the kings ruled and paid some annual tax to the Marathas) on the other hand, were safer. The Martha rule continued for 52 years (1751-1803) and Jadumani's patrons-the kings of Nayagarh, Khandapara, Daspalla, Ranpur and Boudh were away from the trouble centres.

Jadumani as a young man of 22 could witness British activism and their cool and peaceful acquisition of Orissa when Sadasiva Rao, the last Maratha governor of Cuttack was defeated in 1803. Orissa passed on to the hands of English Administrators. W.W. Hunter reports, "Wretched as the state of Orissa had been under the Moghals, a half century of deeper misery for it under the Marathas."[29]

This transition from the Moghals to the Marathas to the English administration forced the society into radical cultural changes. We would therefore briefly trace how this change engendered new distinctions between the world of value, the world of fact and the world of literary aesthetics. More than two hundred years of engagement in word play, rhetorical excercises and embellishment of the body of poetry probably,

History of Ancient Odia Literature | 347

was reaching a terminal point of fatuity, in which the "soul" of poetry was missing. The listeners could discover only dense clusters of metaphorical description in alliterative puns and homonyms and allusions introducing a game of literary hide-and-seek. Ultimately, by the time Jadumani played with etymology and Amarakosha literature had already become a game with tacit conventions and to violate them partially or totally was one of the many joys of the game.

Jadumani's artistic production was constituted of a rhapsodic multiplex of picture, poetry and songs. He allowed some latitude for innovations which appeared unproductive. The new generation of kings and listeners questioned whether there were any rules in such poetic games. There were certainly traditions which were commonly adhered to. When the economically fleeced peasantry and the guilds of traders observed the production of art, they discovered that the poem-making work stood quite consciously outside the boundaries of ordinary life. It was a pleasure seeking activity through words and songs. But, it was a fruitless activity, the matured Jadumani observed, connected with no material interest. Even after the death of his children, there was no dividend for the sacrifice either in cash or in kind. The awareness of this transparent fatuity and unreality of literature was rather against the hardcore realities of life.

The life outside (after 1803) was a greedy and gross quest for materiality. The new generation emulated the life style of Marathas and the English men. They were seen getting attracted toward the perversions of western culture. Jadumani's hyper-masculine world view and the ludic exercises of wit failed to bear with the changes. The art of rhetorical games in composing poems was turning into a sado-masochistic exercise breeding nothing but an empty pride within. No amount of embellished erotica could exculpate him from the guilt he suffered from after the death of his son and daughter.

"Sringara", hereafter, was a drab, mechanical pursuit. The younger generation of connoisseurs/listeners understood sringara only as a strenuous physical exercise. Vibhavas and anubhavas did not lead them to any immediate or deferred realization. They inherited stunted mindsets, and, therefore, the evocation of rasa was hindered. The younger generation of the kings had no inclination to emulate their fathers' literary pursuits. Kangoda, the earlier citadel of riti romances and mythopoeic fantasies, passed over to the French Lords by a new treaty signed by Nizam Salabat Jung and General De Bussey. The latter joined the Northern Sarkar (Ganjam area) as the overlord in 1753 A.D. This political change engendered small revolts with regard to the payment of taxes. Before the French could fully assert themselves in Ganjam feudal states, the battle of Plassey (1757) started. It made the East India Company the Master of Bengal and whetted Lord Clive's imperial teeth. Instead of selling goods the British decided to rule the country Odissa was the only patch of land that stood between British presidencies at Madras and Bengal. So, they wanted to annex this patch quietly. Sir William Jones founded the Bengal Asiatic Society in 1784 to rediscover India's past. Hastings established the Calcutta Madrassa in 1781 for pursuing the studies in Arabic and Persian. The Northern Sarkar was given to the British by a notification made in 1776 and the new generation kings, instead of engaging their leisure in amorous verbosity, stood on their toes apprehending danger to their fiscal securities.

The Gadjat kings lived under "non-modern" cultures and the Englishmen targeted them. General Cotesford found that the kings of Mahuri, Ghumusor and Parlakhemundi were in a mood of revolt. But before that the mutiny at Khurda (1817) was initiated. It was followed by the Ghumusar Revolution of Chakra Bishoyi (1836-1856) and the Kondh rebellion of Parlakhemundi. The Zamindars were trapped within the vortex of politico-economical problems as well as civil rebellions. Khurda was brought under the direct control of the British Government in 1809-10 it was let out as a farm for 10 years to a Bengali speculator named Shamanand Raee and the rapid deterioration of Khurda territories began from that year, till the burgeoning of a revolt in 1817. "The extension of the salt monopoly in 1814 to the southern division of the district must, of course, have increased the misery of the unhappy people by trenching materially upon their consumption of an article of almost indispensable necessity."30

The enjoyment of rasa in the Gadjat kitchens and literary romances was immediately affected. The king of Mahuri had surrendered before the British already in 1782 and the king's widow (Krishnapriya) took shelter in her brother's place at Chikati. The Majhia Deo was put in Mussalipatnam jail till 1818. These disturbances impelled the kings to envisage a new danger to their culture and religion.The Odissan world view was totally polarized. The "fully homogenized, technologically controlled and absolutely hierarchized world defined by polarities like the modern and the primitive,the secular and the nonsecular,the scientific and the un-scientific, the expert and the layman,the normal and the adnormal, the developed and the undeveloped, the vanguard and the led, the liberated and the savable" 31 was emerging as a new generation experience. The British divisive policy triggered off such internal schisms. The Odias under the British colony were found dividing themselves into multiple antinomies. Where was a space left for literary pursuits? The traditional poets and the status-quo seekers suggested that the spiritual bankcruptsy caused by their disparagement of Vaishnavite belief-system in literature tolled the bells of death. The tradition-conscious poets, thus, switched back to writing Vaishnava Padavali (Psalms on Vaishnavism). Occasionally, a Krishna-kavya was attempted in champu form moulding it into a performative narrative. The form, however, was introduced by Kavi surya in Kishore Chandrananda Champu and Jadumani in Prabandha Poornachandra earlier. These were 'ramya-kavyas' in true sense of 'kavyeshu nataka ramyam' The traditional Odia Society in Mughalbandi (Coastal and plain lands of Odissa) was almost pulverized. They were probably trying the idea of a "brave new world" of adjustments and compromising strategies of survival. The South Orissans reminisced in their glories of ancient multicultural Kalinga and stood firmly against all new fangled literatteurs. At such a juncture we find two stalwarts emerging from Ganjam: Gopala Krishan Pattnayak in Parlakhemundi and Kavisurya Baladeva Ratha in Athagarh. Both of them, as contemporaries of Jadumani, were connected with administration and both of them had knowledge in music. They also had some flair for performing arts. Both were Sanskrit scholars capable of deploying grandiloquent styles that could mix with the homely idioms and colloquialism. These new changes rendered their padavali songs communicable as well as popular. Gopala Krishna Pattnayak (1784-1862) "As the notorious low-caste woman of pratistha (honour and recognition) has captured my mind, you (O, my mind!) Should be determined to drive out that low-caste woman by serving the higher caste devotees"

-Gopala Krisha in 'Mana Siksha' A modern reader would immediately discern two distinct selves in Gopala Krishna: the imaginary ideal self with its desire for Vaishnavite spiritual ascendance and the real poetic self whose inner feelings are overflowed spontaneously on the poems he wrote on the walls of his house. He did not have the time to search for the stylus and the palm-leaf. He would write a poem on the wall, leave it for some time to be read by a visiter, and may be, before that he would wipe it out to write another. Gopala wrote on stone-paved floors and slates also.

A contemporary poet of 21st century, who joins the award races would write, arrange money for publication, arrange translators and prepare an imposing biodata for lobbying with the award mafia, finally would win a central akademi prize to waste a life in solipcistic glory. Gopalakrishna would appear to him as an unpragmatic imaginative masochist, and yet a person with violent axiological determination. Every moment his ideal Vaishnavite self gets pulverized and disappears at contact with the reality of writing he would renew himself into a normal Gopala and consider writing evanescent poems as vak-seva for his tutelary god Rasikaraja who still gets worshipped at Parlakhemundi. A poetic tension continued inceassantly within him to cause this subtle schitzophrenic rift between the renunciating Vaishnava on one side and the passionate poet on the other.

Had there been no Haribandhu Bebarta, the musician son of his friend, the erasable transient poems from the wall could not have been retrieved (thirty percent of them, though) in palm-leaf bundles. Poems were Vak-Seva (word-offerings) to his tutelary Lord (Rasikaraja), like flowers one offered while doing the Puja rituals, never to be preserved thereafter. We are amazed to find his junior contemporary Radhanath Ray, on the other side of the moral pole, writing an elegy on the death of Queen Victoria to get knighthood (K.C.I.E. title) from the British government. The dead queen was a "Mother" to Radhanath, biologically not though. Pursuing an illusion called 'honour' was, on the other end, a sin for this poet. One remembers Kabir's lines, "I know Maya, a great betrayer she is/ thus speaks Kabir, an inexpressible secret of life".

Kavi Kalahamsa Gopala Krishna is so inadequately focused in our literary histories (despite his athletic body and assertive mustaches) that one suspects whether ethnic ideologues operate in valorizing the potentials of this senior contemporary of Radhanath Ray. Does Odissa anticipate a civil war on this ethnic marginalization? This has already been hatched and manifested in cold wars of cultural fields.

Let us, then, summarise Gopalakrishna with two interesting vignettes culled from his biographical accounts:

(i) A dark, naked lad of five years comparable to a "jumping frog" enters into a meeting place; in front of his house, on Bebarta

History of Ancient Odia Literature | 351

Pattnayak's platform at Parlakhemundi. His father, Banabasi Pattnayak, a learned executive in Gajapati's court was conferencing over Vaishnavite metaphysics. The year was 1789 tentatively. The unassuming charm of the naked lad who had painted prominently the sect mark of Vaishnavism on his forehead attracts the attention of the scholastic friends of Banabasi. They asked whether the boy had started reading Bhagavata and Banabasi frowned: The boy never read (all the way through) a single palm-leaf script. The pundits objurgated the boy, and it turned him into a serious-minded lad.

Two years later, the Karana Street of Parlakhemundi found a disciplined boy named Gopalkrishna Pattnayak who studied Amarakosha and after that mastered Yumara Vyakarana, in classical Sanskrit. He was a regular visitor to the palace and the company of learned men evoked a keen interest in him to learn the rules of maintaining revenue records. He got a job in Gajapati's court and Gopal Krishna got married at the age of twenty. The vignette No.2 discovers him as a young man of twenty, now married, and leading a disciplined life of an athlete. The daily chores of Parlakhemundi life around 1804 demanded a strict regimen- getting up at 4 A.M, finishing the ablution etc. by 5.30 AM that was preceded by vigorous desi health keep-ups and excercizes. At 6.00 AM Gopala used to drink 1 1/2 sers (around 2 1/2 litres) of unboiled milk. The rest of the day was spent in studying Sanskrit classics. Kafi-Kamodi. Gopalkrishna's carefully raised mustaches gave him the look of a robust wrestler and a brahmachari of a hyper-masculine vigour.

No one knew that this young man's warrior visage did hide within it a soul, soaked deep in the tender feelings of mother Yasoda for child Srikrishna who she thought played truancy. Gopalkrishna was later indoctrinated into Vaishnavism by Vinayak Dasa Goswamy known as Loknath Dasa Goswamy in Parlakhemundi. Gopala Krishna's Sanskrit composition captioned Sri Radha Nakshatramala is dedicated to Sri Lokanatha Dasa Goswamy. He had one more composition in Sanskrit: Sri Vrishabhanuja Prema Namavali in 30 stanzas. Rasikaraja was his tutelary deity at home.

Gopalkrishna's father (Banabasi) had actually migrated from Kansakabati, Jajpur to keep away from the Maratha desperados. He was sheltered by the Maharajah, given the job of a record keeper and then, he grew into a land lord. Later, after some palace intrigue, the Gajapati King was given some cooked-up information about a fiscal scam about him and the king suspected this Jajpuri-Karana (that was the ethnic prejudice). All those Karana and Brahmin employs were expelled (around fifty families) from Paralakhemundi. The Gajapatis are the direct descendents of the royal families of Puri and Khurda.

Banabasi had to flee from Paralakhemundi to Ganjam for some days. Ganjam around 1803-04 was a confluence of South Orissan court poets. Krishna Charana Srikarana Pattnayak (1774-1850) and Vakravak Chakrapani Pattnayak (1776-1836) were the local ones in those days as poet rhetoricians.The twenty years old Gopalakrishna raised on the north bank of river Mahendratanaya found himself now on the sands of river Rishikulya at Ganjam. He met Chakapani and Krishna charana on the bank of river Rishikulya in some lovely afternoons; when one day, they encountered an extremely charming Vaisya girl carrying water on her head. The two elderly rasikas and young Gopalakrishna were immediately captivated unawares. Srikarana Pattnayak, the older one, suggested, "Let each one of us compose a poem to commemorate this ecstatic moment. But Gopala did not know how to compose a poem. He fidgeted at first and then attempted a poem.

"Don't go away striking
the cupid's arrow, my dear !
stay for a while
And steal my soul away.

Next evening the seniors extolled the young man's lines. Chakrapani, always in search of young talents, advised: "Never digress from writing poetry, Youngman! It would fetch you lots of honour." Thus was born one of the most loved Vaishnavite lyricists of Odia literature, the favourite lyricist of the singers of HMV Record Company, (in early 1940s), of the singers of All India Radio and the Rasalilas of late 1940s and 1950s. Gopalkrishna is still a favourite of the Odissi maestros in cultural performances. He was known in every house-hold of South Orissa when the HMV Company brought out "Mohana Madhuri", rendered by Apanna, the blind poet from Parlakhemundi estate.

Thanks to his friend's son Haribandhu Bebarta who collected Gopala's lyrics from the walls and the slates and the stoney floors where he used to write poems every day and wiped them to write another. Otherwise Gopalakrishna's poems could not have been published. However, he never aspired to be a poet of repute and inscribe his honour on

History of Ancient Odia Literature | 353

a slate of eternity. Occasionally when he wrote a poem on the palm-leaf sheet, he would gift it to a friend. Otherwise, most of his lyrics were spontaneous overflows and he wrote them with a stone chalk on the ground or on the walls. His Dolagita (Songs on the festival of colours) was published in 1898 in Padmanabha Narayana Deva's press and two of his numerical poems (Chautisa poems, also known as Sankhyatmika" poetry) captioned Jaiphula Chautisa and Jalada Chautisa were published in Gopalakrishna Sangita and Gopalakrishna Padyavali (1913). Damodara Pattnayak had published Gopalakrishna's poems in Sangita Sagara. The poet's great grand son Ramakrishna Pattnayak published his biography (1924) and some more poems in 1935. Ramakrishna was a head clerk in the office of the Superintendent of Police, Cuttack and he had resigned from his job in 1919 to engage himself in bringing out his grand father's poems to light.

However, the 291 lyrics anthologized in Gopalakrishna Padavali32 have stood the test of time. An overview of Gopalakrishna's lyrics reveals the intense process of his creative mind that undergoes transformations while writing. His soul, it seems, grows tenderer. Each lyric embodies a state of mind, single and focused. The poet muses in solitude and most of the time his songs bring on to surface the archetypes of Sri Radha, Yashoda and Radha-Gobinda. A true Vaishnava as he was, the mythopoeic figures are visible looming vaguely behind the background of the poets' pastoral Parlakhemundi, where the river Mahendratanaya engulfs his mind, unawares, mysteriously.

Gopalakrishna's writings on Astrology and Ayurveda are lost to us. As Babaji Vaishnav Ch. Das Goswamy informs, his other unpublished writings are Priti Chintamani, Nama Chintamani, Prema Kalpalata, Radha Govinda Lilamrita, Braja bhavanavrita, Sri Vrindavana Parikrama, Prema-bhakti Chandrika and Svapna Bilasa.

Scholars report us that only 619 poems of Gopalakrishna have, so far, been published out of which 99 are folk songs. His epynomous poems are dedicated in the name of Gajapati Jagannatha Narayana Deva, Gaura Chandra Gajapati, Prataparudra Deva, Padmanabha Deva and Purushottama Anangabhima Deva. The list shows Gopala Krishna's popularity and intimacy with different kings of Orissa.

Gopalakrishna had also written "boli" poems called also as Dayika and Vachanika form of dialogic poems, Navanuraga Boli may be positioned under this category. Suka-Sari dvanda is also a Vachanika poem in which a dialogic discourse takes place between a male and a female parrot. These fabular and dialogic poems appear more post modern and avantgardeist than those written by his junior contemporary Radhanath Ray. Beyond being a traditional rhetorician, Gopalakrishna had a concern for deploying voices in addition to the mythopoeic ones that speak through the lyrics. He, too, had a concern for the persona behind the dramatis persona, and even behind the first person narrator. As the poet laureate of Parlakhemundi state, Gopalakrishna had dedicated 17 poems to Prataparudra Gajapati Narayana Deva. The king, himself was an avowed devotee of Srimad Radha Gobinda and he patronized Rasikaraja Mahaprabhu. The broad concept of Vaishnavite brotherhood impelled Gopalakrishna to adapt these seventeen slokas from Sanskrit in the name of Gajapati Prataparudra. 33

Veering back to our study of voices in Gopalakrishna's lyrics we discover a larger number of lyrics composed in which Sri Radha is posited as the first person narrator. These poems embody a pervasive authorial presence. The most powerful Vaishnavite emotions (filial love as devotion), however, are articulated through Yashoda as the speaker. The subjective author is personally involved with the poignant emotions of the conventional period- figures: Sri Radha, Yashoda and Srikrishna. These poems characterize an impersonal or objective quality in which the author maintains an aesthetic distance, as opposed to a subjective writer like Dinakrishna. The tone of his poetic utterances reflects his sense of how he stands toward these divine characters. The narrate remains here an implied auditor.

Gopal Krishna's lyrics may also be considered from the point of "Voice", a term used currently, to identify the use of the tone in such speeches of persuasive rhetoric. Such uses do also suggest this traditional rhetorician's concern with the importance of the physical voice in poetic orations. The Dola-gita songs articulate Yashoda's filial anxiety when Krishna, as a shepherd boy delays to come home in evening hours. Such an implied author is also discernible in the dialogic parrot-poems in which a male and a female parrot are engaged in a metaphysical discourse. The "Koili" poems are addressed to a cuckoo, who figures as a real listener to lonely Gopalas's lyrical inner voice. These are "true voices" since they are the expressions of genuine authorial feelings. These empathic lyrics not only signify the involuntary projection of the genuine poetic voice, but also identification with the

Vaishnavite godheads with physical sensations, finally resulting of an "inner mimicry game". Some of these lyrics are also written in the form of dramatic monologues that designate a component in a play. The organizing principle and focus of interest is not necessarily the revealation of the speaker's distinctive temperament, but also the evolution of his observations, memories and thoughts toward the resolution of inner tension. Jadumoni Mahapatra introduced such dramatic techniques in his Prabandha Poornachanra.

The Navanuraga Poems (Pp.42, 52, 55), the Purvanuraga song (p.55) and Vanamaligita (p.87) are in pure dialogic form. Similarly, Vilapa-I (p.63) is in chautisa form and Vilapa-2 (p.69) in a poi-vani. These (Koili, Poi-vani, doligita, chautisa etc) are typical Odia folk forms used since 15th century. Gopalakrishna has also written a song in Kalasa style. These typical indigenous folk forms juxtaposed with pure Sanskrit songs like Sri Radha Naksatramala and Vrishabhanuja Premanamavali not only signify Gopalakrishna's mastery over vocabulary (He read Amarakosa as a boy), but also his ability to reach the common readers, and listeners in the court circle. The people of Paralakhemundi were well acquainted with the Sanskrit tradition followed keenly in Telugu Literature.

He has written around thirty hymns captioned, Radhagovinda Keertana and Prarthana etc. These hymn songs are to be read as personal expressions. Poems captioned Sadhaka, Dehochita Lalasa" (Physical cravings of a perseverant) express about the compelling urges of the body as hinderances to achieve the Vaishnavite purity of perception, thought and feeling. Critics also consider such poems as lyrical monologues. The Vaishnavite author confesses candidly how physical desires block his way to total internalization. Beyond that the poems signify that poetry for Gopala was no longer an empty academic exercise playing with rhyme or image or myth expressed in embellished words. The greatest myth of Radha and Krishna turns out to be one's inner space. From a poetics of verbal tension, paradox, homonyms, puns and irony in the conventional riti sense, there was thus, a shift towards the apparent absence of tension. It was felt by now that there was no need to build up poetic tension by a deft and deliberate use of words as yamakas.

The eight poems captioned Svabhista Lalasa (Deep longings of the Self), two poems captioned Svanubhuti (Personal Experiences) and

Tri Lalasa (Cravings of the self) poems constitute a special corpus that signifies the indefiniteness or incompleteness of the poet's Vaishnavite inner journey. The sense of wonder, remorse, repentance and over all, the sense of mystery make them typical romantic poems (in Western sense; since Wordsworth (1770-1850) and Coleridge ((1772-1834) were his western contemporaries). A poem captioned Dainya Bodhika occupies a special position in the group since Gopalakrishna exteriorizes the feelings of inferiority and wretchedness (near equivalents of Dainyabodha) by intruding into Sri Radha's psyche. The poem suggests Gopal's preference for either open-ended forms or fusions that imply a rejection of rhetorical superabundance in Riti academics. The poetic persona as a learned device is replaced by the person of the poet. It sems, this scholar in Amarakosha and Yumara Vyakarana was no longer averse to talking about his Vaishnavite self, no longer content to be a mere catalysit like the epigrammatic Panchasakhas.

One witnesses in the 291 lyrics compiled in Gopalakrishna Padavali an incredibly rich and increasingly diverse body of literature on Vaishnavite experience, being the main field of enquiry in and of itself. Beginning with Sri Radha Nakshatramala, a prayer to Sri Radha, the compendium showcases eleven distinct varieties of poems calling for eleven sub-generic structures: kalasa, Koili, Poi, Chautisa hymns, Lyrical Monologues, dialogue with the self, dramatic lyrics extended personal expressions through the multi-structurality is an outcome of Gopalakrishna's multi-vocal versification.

It is to be kept in mind that Gopalakrishna was operating in a multicultural and multi-lingual background and his archetypal association is traceable in the culture of Jajpur. The basic problem with him was related to Odia identity in a milieu of Telugu, Bengali and Tamil literatures. Thus, his multivocality becomes a synthesis of approaches culled from folkloristics and Sanskrit Scholastisism. With Poi, Kalasa, Koili or Chautisa Gopalakrishna significantly reclaims the art-image as an imperative in forging a distinct Odia identity. Thus, the transformative power of the folk aesthetic structures is crucial to the techniques of Gopalkrishna's Versification.

Originally a Sanskrit scholar, and a master of Amarakosha and Yumara Vyakarana, Gopalakrishna's paradigm shift presents us with a return to the obsession that once had dominated Prataparudra Deva during the 15th Century. Yasoda's "Koili song" and "Doli gita" (Sung during the "Swing festival" in June) formulate the typical mode of folk aesthetics which later becomes a matrix, or a mediational site where familiar antinomies are resurrected and confronted, where borders are ruptured and reformed to negotiate intrapantheon identity and intercultural exchange. He emphasized the significance of reclaiming the poetic art image as an imperative in forging an Odia identity. Gopalakrishna's poetry illustrates how the performative aspect intrinsic to the collective experience of folk culture positions poetic art as community property that is mutually constructed by the poets, singers and participants/ Listeners. Gopalakrishna Padavali (not padyavali) presupposes Vaishnavite themes. His Guru, Lokanatha Goswamy belonged to the Gaudiya school of Sri Chaitanya and the cult imbedded eroticism in a sacralized form. But our historians and critics, for what reasons we do not know, have considered his poems as some loosely organized emotive lyrics (raganuga); perhaps' even chaotic poems held together, if at all by the robust literary personnel of the post-riti period. Our inability to find a structure in Gopalakrishna Padavali has resulted from a failure to find a centre of relevancy, an informing idea to which the parts of the Padavali may be related.

Gopalakrishna was in full command of his materials and his Padavali is constructed as the dramatic representation of a mystical experience through erotica. The term "dramatic representation" of a mystical experience indicates an important distinction. The poem is not necessarily a transcript of an actual mystical experience but rather a work of art in which such an experience, conceived in the imagination, is represented dramatically, with the author assuming the role of the Sutradhara. The mystical experience is represented dramatically in the sense that the poet portrays his preparation for and his entry into a state of mystical consciousness, his progressively significant and meaningful experience arranged in terms of events and "uktis" (Speech modes). Gopalakrishna has not attempted mythopoeic fiction as has been done by his contemporaries- Jadumani (in Prabandha Purnachandra) and Kavisurya (in Kishorachandrananda champu). But his Padavali could not escape the fictionalizing features. The poems of the Padavali compendium are positioned to give an impression of the Lila mode of dramatic performance. The scenario of the Lila is arranged in the following manner.

(a) The invocatory Sri Radha nakshatramala in Sanskrit (G.K. Padavali, P.21).34

(b) The introduction of he child srikrishna through the concern shown by Yashoda and his group causing great anxiety in Yashoda. The child Krishna didn't eat properly, had entered into the deep forest with a large herd of cows and the delay in his coming back home – such events treated with Yashoda's bleak apprehensions semioticize tender filial affection of an Odia mother: Braja Ku. Asichi (P.161), Uthilu Edebegi (P.162), Mo Krishna Chandrama Pari (P.163), Dukhidhana Chandranana (P.164)

(c) Navanuraga (P.42) articulates the poetic voices of Sri Radha. Her voice is also heard in the poems from P.42 to 62 we may include Purvanuraga and Vilapa poems till P.75). Radha asks Lalita, "who's that son of Braja Raja?" and Lalita, with a smile replies, "he, whose flute enthralled you the other day". Radha asks, "How does the fluteplayer look? What is his age? How tall is he? Has he tied a knot in wedlock? These questions are followed by auto-erotic speculations of Sri Radha in a cluster of poems.

(d) Union of Radha and Govinda

(e) Chandravali's intrusion into the scene and Srikrishna's lips raptured and injured by her kisses – Radha's jealousy intensifying toward separation.

(f) The interference of Radha's friends (sakhi)

(g) Re-Union signifying faith and love, singing of hymns and the emergence from the mystical state etc.

The basic nature of what Gopala is writing or he was struggling to perfect his work of art gradually transpires through the scenic structuration of the mythopoeic events. One may put the arrangement under the rubric of Rasalila.

"Lila's" are 16th century musicals that developed immediately after Jagannatha Dasa (1487-1550) translated Bhagavata into Oriya and started singing them out in solo voice in the Jagannatha temple. His Rasakrida may be analysed as lila, depicted in a highly potential, nonlinear arrangement of episodes.There were musical recitals of Gitagovinda since late 12th century and Purushottama Deva's Abhinava Gita govinda reinvigorated the Lila ritual through Devadasi tradition of dancers. However, when the Lila form was taken out of the temple precincts,it bifurcated into Krishnalila, Rasalila and Radhapremalila, Anandi Mishra's (1650- 1730) Rasagosthi Rupakam written in Khandapalli garh (Khandapada) provides one more extant category not found anywhere in India. "Rasakrida" or "gosthi rupakam" according to Srimad Bhagavatam is a blending of mime, song and dance in which Krishna multiplies himself into many and stands between every two women in a mandala(circular) dance". 35

'Lila', to brief here was based on the performative element imbedded in poetry, by the time Gopalakrishna was writing. But nowhere has he conformed to the norms of Lila performance through his ouevre. But in intensity, Gopalkrishna's lyrics are knockings against silence for an answering music. His language of poetry, varying from the colloquial Paralakhemundi word to the highly Sanskritised embelishments signify a language of gesture, not a language to be confused with rhyme or versification. We may take for example from any of those Yashoda poems, be it in "Koili" form or in the pattern of the swing festival song (Doli-gita), there is a scope for gestural enactment. "Koili Ki Buddhi Karibi Muhin"(What measures should I take, Oh, Cuckoo), or Sri Nanda-grihini Vana Patha Ku Chahin" (Sri Nanda's wife looks at the forest path) constitute the third voice of the poet in accordance with T.S. Eliots three voices in poetry" (the first voice is the voice of the poet talking to himself and the second voice is an address to an audience). The third or the impersonated voice for Yashoda, Sri Radha, Sri Krishna or Sakhi entails scopes for mimetic representation. To conceive of representation not in terms of mimesis but in terms of performance makes it necessary to dig into the structure of the Padavali text we have already pointed out how the lyrics in Gopalakrishna Padavali, in their multi vocality trigger off archaeology of the act of representation. This arises out of the doubling structure of fictionality.

Gopala Krishna's act of selection (of the theme or situation or the emotive sequences) also becomes an integral part to fictionality in the form of doubling. One may refer to Braja Sundar Pattnayak's (1728-1778). Chhapana Padia, Chandrasekhar Deva's (the King of Boudh who ruled between (1725 and 1760) Krishnalilamrita or Bhakta Charana's (1722-1813) Mathura Mangala for the selection of relevant ideas in Gopalakrishna. Keen research into Krishna literature would result in such intertextualities, but these should not be thought of in terms of blurring distinctions. On the countrary, the doubling process becomes even more complex, for the texts alluded to and segments of similar emotive poetry begin to unfold unforeseeably shifting relation ships. These shifting relationships include their own contexts, and contexts in relation to the new ones into which they have been transplanted. Two different types of discourses are ever present and their simultaneity triggers a mutual revealing and concerling of their respective contextual references.

Gaurahari Parichha (1797-1868)

Gaurahari Parichha, popularly known as the author of Prahallada Nataka was a junior contemporary of Gopalakrishna. He was the court poet of the king of Manjusha for a short spell and was a musician trained in classical vocal. Gaurahari was the author of Vastrapaharana Chautisa. Indoctrinated as a Gaudiya Vaishnava, Gaurahari wrote numerous small lyrics and Astakala Seva evidences his lyrical ability. Bhasa Sangita Vinoda embodies his lyrics written in Bengali, Hindi and Telugu languages. Gaurahari has also translated some cantos of Jayadeva's Gitagovinda. The minor contemporaries of Kabisurya, Jadumani and Gopal Krishna were many. The first half of the nineteenth century was a fort of Indian poetry with the practiners of the Sanskrit poetics. The list would be long:

Gobinda Rajguru (1861-1902)'s Vrindabana Chandra Champu and Abhinava Chaupadi Ratnakara) Damodar Pattnayak's Jivana Champu and efforts for compiling anthologies of his and other's choicest lyrics and the works of Banamali Dasa would be considered as some of the major efforts of this period. Viswaratha Khuntia (Vichitra Ramayana) Dasarathi Dasa's Kavya Vrajavihara Raghunatha Bhanja, Purushottama Misra's Ramachandrodaya Prabandha, Sangita Narayanam, Tala Samgraha), Damodara Singh (Utkanthamalika), Jaya Singh's (Gita Mahatmya, Kshetra Mahatmya), Krishna Charana Pattnayak (Translations of Ramayana, Bhagavata, Kalipurana and Vamana Purana), King Raghunath Singh (Ramayana Poems), Bharata Sena's (Sulochana Parinaya Poems), Ganapati Sahu (Radhakanta Janana, Markata janana), Chandramani Rath (Translation of Malavikagni Mitra, Ganeswara Kabichandra (Vaidharbi, Aja Vilapa) and many others may be enlisted as Gopala Krishna and Gaurahari's contemporaries. The dense cluster of poems and poets evidences how Jadumani, Kavisurya and Gopalkrishna had kept the literary milieu charged with translations and original works. The kings of the Southern Estates also patronised these poets. One may consider this period as the golden phase of Odia literary culture.

Gaura Charana Adhikary (1814-1890)

Gaura Charana was, perhaps, the last major poet of the Vaishnava Padavali literature. Born in Lahanga village near Atri (Khurda) on the Khurda-Nayagarh road, in Mukunda Mishra Adhikary's family. The poet was nurtured in a milieu of Odissan Vaishnavism, slightly different from what Sri Chaitanya preached exactly three hundred years ago. (Chaitanya had come to Puri in 1510). Jagannatha Dasa's Bhagavata in Odia was very popular by this time and every village had a Bhagavata Tungi or Bhagavata Club- house where the book was read out to the illiterate villagers. The villages in Odissa had their own Samkeertana Mandali and a troupe of singers marched through the village roads singing the Radha and Krishna prayers in Chorus to the rhythm of mardala and tiny cymbals.

Gaura Charana did not get any scope for studying vernacular language in any school, although the British records show thath 101 vernacular schools/ hardinges"had been opened in 1844. But the village folks were not interested to study in schools opened by the English government. The simple folks were living under British terrorism. They feared that the English men would convert their children into Christianity by force. The conservative villagers, thus retreated to their traditional Vaishnavism and clung to it avidly praying for a protection from the English system of education, which they thought might drag them into the vortex of profanity. On the other hand, Vaishnavism was not also considered a dignified pantheon since the caste boundaries were transgressed."Everything is lost when you join the pantheon of Vaishnavism"- they used to say. But it provided a collective life and courage to follow the traditional religion.

Gaurahari, whose original name before his empanelment was Padmacharana, studied Sanskrit at home, learnt Sanskrit rituals of worshipping and then studied Amarakosha, Sanskrit stuti and ashtakas (prayer songs) Lilavati Sutra(Vedic mathematics) and fundamentals of arthmatic. Mukunda Mishra Adhikary's financial status was not good and he had opened a primary school for teaching children. Dr. Sasiprabha Pattnayak, a Gaurachandra scholar reports that Gauracharana's poetic gifts began to manifest at a very early age, around twelve and then he was indoctrinated by Swamy Jagadananda Brahmachary of Sidha-Brahmachary Matha of Puri. Gauracharana was empowered thereafter to worship a wooden image of Sri Chaitanya in his home. 36

Gaura Charana is considered as a strong follower of Madhvacharya's philosophy as reported by Prof. Janaki Ballav Mahanty. Besides writing Chhandas, Chaupadi, Bhajanas, apophthegms and dialogic poems, Gauracharana has written the following literary works.

i) Lakshmi Narayana Kali (The quarrel between Lakshmi and Narayana)
ii) Gaura Krishan-Bhajana Sataka (99 Bhajanas)
iii) Srikrishna Lila (Constituted of 47 chaupadis, 1 poi-song and 317 Chhandas)
iv) Poems in Gaurachandra Padavali- part, Part-II.
v) Prabandha Pramodaya (14 long chhandas)
vi) Asta Kala Samkeertana (Samkeertan prayer Songs meant to be sung in chorus eight times a day: End of the night, Early morning, Pre-noon time, Noon, Post noon, dusk, evening and one for the eternity (these are the eight Chronotopic divisions of Vaishnavite Pantheon in Odissa)
vii) Astanayika Akhyana
viii) Kishorinka Pancha-Spriha (The five major desires of unmarried girls)
ix) Mukta latavali
x) Gobardhana utsava
xi) Nata Vrata Puja
xii) Advaita Mangala (A mangala-kavya in Bengali)
xiii) Gaura Rasa
xiv) Hamsa-Hamsuli Kali (A quarrel between a He-duck and a She-Duck)

Gaura Charana's Padavali literature can be classified into four taxonomical groups : i) Krishna conscious poems (ii) Poems based on Chaitanya Lila, (iii) Poems centering round the Cult of Jagannatha and (iv) Descriptive and environmental poems. Bichhanda Charana Pattnayak remarks that Gauracharana is the best of the Vaishnava poets of the post Riti era. 37 Although the statement appears hyperbolic, a little close perusal of his poems reveals that Gauracharana has culled ideas from different sources: The theme of Srikrishna Lila is taken from the 7th canto of Bhagavata, but Gobardhana Utsava, kaliya Dalana, Nata Vrata Puja are creatively elaborated. 'Muktalatavali' and 'Baghaboli' are pure imaginary creations. Out of the eight hundred songs compiled most of the lyrics appear to have been influenced by Gita

Govinda and Bidagdha Madhava, Prabandha Pramodaya, Astakala, Astanayika and Pancha Spriha (Five Prominent Desires) have been culled from Govinda Lilamrita. However, Gaura Charana's Vaishnavite lyrics were written in a period of active colonialism and religious conversions. The foreign priests were repeatedly attacking on the orthodox, conservative sectors of Hinduism.

Gauracharana had witnessed the sepoy mutiny, the reformistic zeal of the people and a general climate of religious resurgence in the country during which going back to one's own tradition and religion was considered modern. The Odia society in Khurda was undergoing a sea-charge from the shock and defeat and frustration to the trauma of inferiority feeling to a new-found Self-awareness and a self confidence. Radhanath Ray's use of new meter in writing Bengali and Odia poetry, the severe famine of 1866, publication of Utkala Deepika, the uprise of Brahmo religion, Debendranath Thakur's call for liquidating the caste system and the system of idol worship might not have affected Gauracharana, but the way he depicts the feelings of Radha, one feels a sense of reformative, modern anthropomorphic characterization, despite the language is loaded with Bengali inflections.

Gauracharana's representation of Vaishnavite vision almost turns into his personal representation with lots of modern changes incorporated into it. But the patron kings and their court poets did never cease to write Champus, Chaulisas and other numerical poems. But they were so much conscious about the structural designs that their poetry became mechanized products of a rhetorical grid.

The patrons and the poets aimed at self-expression but not in first person narratives. Since the themes remained almost constant, they strove to utter what often was thought, but most of the poems subtlety came from the psychology of Radha or Krishna, the oft repeated protagonists. Kavisurya and Gopala Krishna had immensely enlarged the formal boundaries of poetry and continued to keep up the jest for enjoying poetry in the colonial milieu.

Minor or major, the compositions of this initial period of British colonialism were experiments in expression. The 'Champu' and 'Chautisa' forms were generally followed, which meant that these poets belived in the "Craft theory of poetry". Jadumani, the carpenter, sculptor, painter, though was officially recognized as a poet of humour and wit, was perhaps emulated by a host of court poets and their patron kings (very often poets themselves) They were pretty close to the classical ideas of 'Uttama Kavya', that is adarasou, Sabdarthau, sagunau, alamkrita with sobhadayaka dharma, rasatmaka and ramaneeyartha pratipadaka. All of them were men of wisdom. They were meticulous about the "doshas" and then "gunas" of their compositions. They had to winnow words to separate the grain from the chaff and thus a blessed glory and a non-material, non-physical ananda was enshrined in their poetry. All of those poets believed that writing "uttama Kavya" is a means of attaining all the four Purusharthas of life: dharma (virtue), artha (wealth), Kama (fulfillment of desire) and moksha (liberation), SriAurobindo in his "The Future Poetry" equated the words of verses to "mantras". Gauracharana Adhikary is a product of this literary milieu, in which the prophets composed lyrics for causing a spiritual revival.

Dayananda Saraswati's foundation Arya Samaj (1878), the ideologic deconstruction of the concept of Hindu idolatry, the advent of Mahima dharma, political instability and all possible subversions on the socio-cultural front pushed Kavisurya, Gopala Krishna, GaurahariParichha and Gaura Charana Adhikary into the front line of cultural renaissance in which spiritual revivalism began to be considered as the most necessary and applicative literary modernism. Prabhakar Machwe in his Renaissance in Indian Literature therefore, comments: "The renaissance in India is janus-faced. It takes inspiration from the past, sifts the deadwood and plans to rebuild the future." (P.2)38

Besides, printed Odia scripts had developed and the English government had translated and printed the Holy Bible by 1814. The Odia alphabets used during the early nineteenth century (1814 version) can be discerned from the photograph of the first page of the translated and printed Bible.

Notes

1. M. Hiriyana, The Quest After Perfection, Kavyalaya Publishers, Mysore, 1952
2. Martin Heidegger, "Letter on Humanism", Basic Writings. Trans D.F. Krell, London, Routledge and Kegan Paul 1978, P.215.

3. Ibid
4. K.C.Panigrahi, History of Orissa, Kitab Mahal, Cuttack 1981, rpt. 1995 History of Ancient Odia Literature : 397
5. S.K.De Sanskrit Poetics, Vol-II, 2nd. Edn. Culcutta, 1960
6. Pabitra mohan NayakConfluence,Vol.1 Ed. P.M. Nayak and S. Mudali Sambalpur, 2000 Pp 73-74.
7. Sarat Chandra Rath "Kavya Ratnamanjari-o-Dhananjaya Bhanja"(Dhananjaya Bhanja and Ratnamanjari" Samiksha Sourava, Matrukrupa, Brit Colony, Bhubaneswar, 1990, Pp-45-53
8. Ibid
9. G.Vijaya Vardhana Outlines of Sanskrit Poetics, Chowkhamba Sanskrit Series, Varanasi, 1970
10. Sachidananda Mishra "Upendra Bhanjanka Rachanavalira Kala Nirupana", Sahitya Patra (Bhanja Literature Special) Ed. Natabara Satpathy and Teerthananda Mishra, Artaballava Snatakottara Pathachakra, Department of Odia, Ravenshaw College,Cuttack, 2003. Pp.1-15
11. W.W. Hunter Ganjam Manual, London
12. Pt. Nilakantha Das Odia Sahityara Krama Parinama P.639
13. Benimadhav Padhi, "Sahitya Samikshya Paddhati O Bhanja Kavya, Sandhana O Sameekshya, Tara Tarini Pustakalaya, Berhampur 1997, Pp. 50-60

14. G. Vijaya Vardhana	Outlines of Sanskrit Poetics, Chowkhamba Sanskrit Series, Varanasi, 1970 P.77
15. Farah Mendelsohn,	Rhetorics of Fantasy, Wesleyn Universty Press, 2008
16. Northrope Frye.	Anatomy of Criticism: Four Essays, Newyork, Atheneum, 1957 rpt. 1967
17. Santosh Kumar Tripathy	Vichitra Kavitva, Nalanda, Binod Behary, Cuttack, 2006
18. R.D.Laing	The Divided Self, Penguin Books Ltd. Harmondsworth, 1960. Rpt.1982.
19. Dinabandhu Hota	"Bauddha Darabari Sahitya", G a n d h a r a d i, Ed. Gauramohan Mishra, Basudev Patra, Nabakumar Mishra, Santanu K. Mahapatra, Bhavani Shankar Mahapatra and Yugal Samal, Yogindra Club, Baudh, 2009, Pp.132-138
20. Dr. Kanakalata Das,	"Odisara Dvitiya Buddha: Santh Kavi Arakhita Das, Chhanda.I-II. Oct'1997, Digapahandi, Pp.9-13. Arakhita's father Padmanabha Deva ruled in badakhemundi between 1774-1805)
21. Farah Mendelsohn,	Rhetorics of Fantasy, Wesleyn Universty Press, 2008. Mendelsohn has divided the genre of fantasy into 4 categories : (a) Portal/Quest fantasy (b) Immersive fantasy (c) Intrusion fantasy and (d) Liminal fantasy, in her book Rhetoric of Fantasy.

22. Krishna charana Behera,	Ed. Kavisurya Granthavali, Friends' Publishers, Cuttack 1998,rpt. 2004
23. Ibid.	
24 Dr. Sudha Mishra,	Sangita Sudha, quoted in B.K. Choudhury, Pravada Purusha Jadumani, Satyanarayana Book Store, Cuttack, 2005, P.271-272.
25. Ibid	
26.	This author is indebted to Dr. Bijoy Kumar Chaudhury's book Pravada Purusha Jadumani for having collected the details of Jadumani's life.
27. Chakradhara Mahapatra,	"Avataranika", Jadumani Granthavali, Pp 05-06.
28.	This author borrows the phrase from Gayatri Chakravorty Spivak's "Can the Subalterns speak?" in Marxism and The Interpretation of Culture, Ed. Carry Nelson and Lawrence Grossberg,Turia and Kant,1988,rpt. 2007.
29. W.W. Hunter,	The Anals of Rural Bengal, London, 1872, Vol.II, P.3.
30. Walter Ewer,	" Correspondence of the settlement of Khoordah in Poorie", Calcutta,1818, Reprinted O.H.R.J, Vol.III. No.4 (1- 4), 1995. XIII.
31. Ashis Nandy,	The Intimate Enemy : Loss and Recovery of self under colomialism, O.U.P. Delhi, 1983. p.x.
32. Gopal Krishna Pattnayak,	Gopalkrishna Padavali Ed. Orissa Sahitya Akademi and Sahitya Svetapadma,

33.
34. Gopalkrishna Pattnayak,

35. Ramesh Prasad Panigrahi,

36. Dr.Sasiprabha Pattanayaka,

37. Ibid.
38. Prabhakara Machwe,

Parlakhemundi, Orissa Sahitya Akademi, Bhubaneswar (in collaboration with EZCC, Kolkata) 2004.
See Gopalakrishna Padavali Pp.122-138.
Gopalakrishna Padavali, Ed. Orissa Sahitya Akademi and Sahitya Svetapadma, Paralakhemundi, (in collaboration with EZCC, Kolkata) The page marks are referred to this edition, since the poems are not either titled or numbered, the poems are alluded to by page numbers.
Perspectives on Odissi Theatre, "Orissa Sangit Natak Akademi, Bhubaneswar, 1998. p.3.
Odia Padavali Sahitya-0-Bhaktakabi Gaura Charana, Published by Pramoda Chandra Pattnayaka, 678, Laxmisagar, Bhubaneswar,1995. p.33

Renaissance in Indian Literature, United Writers, Calcutta, 1979. p.2.

■■■

www.ingramcontent.com/pod-product-compliance
Lightning Source LLC
Chambersburg PA
CBHW060548080526
44585CB00013B/488